Foundations of Economics

FOUNDATIONS OF ECONOMICS

ANDREW GILLESPIE

OXFORD

UNIVERSITY PRESS

2ND
EDITION

OXFORD

UNIVERSITY PRESS

Great Clarendon Street, Oxford OX2 6DP

Oxford University Press is a department of the University of Oxford.
It furthers the University's objective of excellence in research, scholarship,
and education by publishing worldwide in

Oxford New York

Auckland Cape Town Dar es Salaam Hong Kong Karachi
Kuala Lumpur Madrid Melbourne Mexico City Nairobi
New Delhi Shanghai Taipei Toronto

With offices in

Argentina Austria Brazil Chile Czech Republic France Greece
Guatemala Hungary Italy Japan Poland Portugal Singapore
South Korea Switzerland Thailand Turkey Ukraine Vietnam

Oxford is a registered trade mark of Oxford University Press
in the UK and in certain other countries

Published in the United States
by Oxford University Press Inc., New York

British Library Cataloguing in Publication Data

Data available

Library of Congress Cataloging in Publication Data

Data available

Typeset by Graphicraft Limited, Hong Kong
Printed in Italy
on acid-free paper by
L.E.G.O. S.p.A. – Lavis TN

ISBN 978-0-19-958654-7

3 5 7 9 10 8 6 4

This book is dedicated to
my family, especially my wife, Ali,
my two beautiful daughters,
Clemency and Romily,
and my fantastic son, Seth.

Outline contents

Detailed contents

PART 1 **Microeconomics**   1

Preface

This book is intended to provide an introduction to the principles of economics, and to help you to understand many issues that affect businesses and economies around the world: everything from why China has grown so fast, the causes and effects of the recent global recession, to the effects of the inflow of workers into the UK from Eastern Europe, to why some takeovers are prevented by the government. It will also help you to understand issues that affect your own daily life: Why are houses so expensive in the UK? What determines how much you have to pay to borrow from the bank? What are you likely to earn in your chosen career? By reading this book, you will develop the tools to analyse these issues from an economist's perspective, and, hopefully, you will soon find yourself talking and thinking like an economist as well! Going to university is an investment decision: is it worth it? Buying this book involves opportunity costs because you could have bought something else: is it worth the sacrifice? (I hope so!) Do the extra benefits from spending an extra hour on your assignment exceed the extra costs? As well as giving you an insight into economic issues, I also hope that this book will help you to analyse problems logically and to understand the economic consequences of any decision.

I am assuming no prior knowledge of economics at all. It does not matter if you have no background in economics at this stage. I aim to take you from knowing no economic theory to having a good solid foundation that gives you the knowledge and skills for further, specialized study in economics in higher education. With this background, you can study the subject, or parts of the subject, in much more detail, but will already have an overview of and insight into the key issues. I also aim to show you how relevant this subject is to everything going on around you and how valuable an understanding of economic theory can be. The examples in the book cover a range of markets from oil to cars, to chicken waste, and a range of countries from the UK to Cuba, to Venezuela, to India.

Do send me feedback on the book: let me know if you enjoy it and find it useful, as well as any ideas on how I can improve the next edition. You can email me at wattgill@aol.com

How to use this book

Gillespie's *Foundations of Economics* is enriched with a range of features designed to help support and reinforce your learning. This guided tour shows you how best to utilize your textbook and get the most out of your study.

LEARNING OBJECTIVES

By the end of this unit you should be able to:

✔ explain what is meant by effective demand;

✔ explain what is shown by a demand curve;

✔ understand the difference between a change in the quan demanded and a change in demand;

✔ explain the possible causes of a shift in a demand curve;

✔ appreciate the difference between marginal and total util

Learning objectives

Each chapter begins with a bulleted list of learning objectives outlining the main concepts and ideas you will encounter in this part of the text. These serve as helpful signposts for learning and revision.

Put into practice

Are the following statements true or false?

a. The PPF shows the amount that consumers want of each produ

b. Any combination of goods inside the PPF is productively efficien

c. Economic growth is shown by an outward movement of the PPF

d. Wants are limited, but resources are unlimited, which means th scarcity and choice.

Put into practice

The text regularly offers you the opportunity to test your understanding of a concept you have just learned by trying to use the theory in a practical way. This might take the form of answering a question, working through a problem, or working with graphs.

What do you think?

What do you think are the major determinants of the demand for each

• New cars.

• Textbooks.

• Diamond rings.

• Healthcare.

What do you think?

These questions give you the opportunity to stop and reflect on the material, either on your own or in a group.

Economics in context   Influences on demand

Demand can shift for all sorts of reasons, such as the weather, a major actions. There may be particular demand patterns in a market. In the to 50% of sales are made around the Christmas period. Demand is par in the toy market because of particular 'fad' products that take off eac television programmes or games, and often to the surprise of retailer Tamagochi, Furby, Teletubbies and Power Rangers are examples of po

 Question

Economics in context

Once you have understood the economic theory, it is important that you can see how it is applied to business and to everyday life. These topical illustrations also come with questions, to reinforce your understanding of the concept discussed.

Case studies

Each chapter is supplemented by a short case study designed to contextualize the material in the unit and to encourage you to apply your learning to more involved analyses of real situations.

> **Case Study**
>
> Although Apple has a relatively small share of the PC market, it has
> with its iPod. The iPod allows users to store large quantities of music
> The product was launched in 2001 and sold over 40 million in
> everyday life and has radically changed the way many people listen
> design capabilities and the style of the iPod soon made it a major fas
> the growth of downloaded music and led to a levelling off of sales o
> the initial model Apple has continued to innovate, launching new ve
> version called the Shuffle. The Shuffle randomly selects music loaded

Checklist

Each chapter ends with a checklist of the key topics, designed as a prompt for you to check that you have understood the important concepts. They also serve as a helpful revision tool.

> **Checklist**
>
> Now you have read this unit try to answer the following question
> ☐ Can you explain what is meant by effective demand?
> ☐ Can you explain what is shown by a demand curve?
> ☐ Do you understand the difference between a change in the
>   change in demand?
> ☐ Can you explain the possible causes of a shift in a demand
> ☐ Do you understand the difference between marginal and to

End of unit questions

Carefully devised review questions have been provided at the end of every unit. You can use these to check your understanding of the topics before moving on to the next unit, or for group discussion or revision.

> **End of unit questions**
>
> 1 Does a demand curve show what a consumer would like to
> 2 What is the difference between a movement along and a shi
> 3 Does an increase in income always shift the demand curve
> 4 Does the quantity demanded always fall if the price increase
> 5 To what extent do you think a supermarket can control the d

Key learning points

The author has outlined some important points for you to note at the end of every unit.

> **Key learning points**
>
> • Demand shows what customers are willing and able to pur
>   just what they want to buy.
> • A movement along a demand curve occurs when there is a
>   things being unchanged.
> • A shift in the demand curve occurs when more or less is der
> • A demand curve is usually downward sloping, but in some
>   good) it can be upward sloping.

Learn more

Some more advanced concepts are introduced or are further explored on the Online Resource Centre accompanying the book. This content is referenced at the end of relevant units.

> **Learn more**
>
> A demand curve can be derived using indifference curve analy
> change in price and income in terms of consumers' utility. To fin
> analysis and how a consumer maximises utility, visit our websit
> Visit our Online Resource Centre at www.oxfordtextbook
> questions and further information on topics covered in thi

About the online resource centre

The Online Resource Centre that accompanies this book provides students and lecturers with ready-to-use teaching and learning resources. These are free of charge and are designed to maximize the learning experience.

www.oxfordtextbooks.co.uk/orc/gillespie_econ2e/

For students

Visual Walkthroughs

Visual walkthroughs of key concepts, with screen grabs and an audio soundtrack are provided to help you to develop and consolidate your learning.

Author Blog

Read about topical news stories posted with author commentary by Andrew Gillespie and tagged by the relevant chapter of the book.

Oxford News Now

The Oxford News Now RSS news feed includes relevant articles from a variety of international sources, such as *Wall Street Journal Asia*.

Solutions to Questions

Solutions are provided to the 'put into practice' questions and are linked to the visual walkthroughs to help clearly illustrate key ideas.

Self-test questions

A suite of multiple-choice questions, with automatic feedback, is provided for each chapter in the book, to allow you to test your knowledge of the key themes in each unit.

Web links

A selection of annotated web links chosen by the author makes it easy to research those topics that are of particular interest to you. These links are checked regularly to ensure they remain up to date.

Unit support

The Online Resource Centre includes further stories, cases, and research for each chapter in the book. These will help you to reinforce your understanding of topics and to further apply the theory to the real world.

Advanced material

Some advanced topics are introduced or covered in more depth, to supplement the material in the book itself.

Flashcard glossaries

Key glossary terms are available in an interactive flashcard format, to allow you to check your understanding of the important concepts.

Business Strategy

An additional web-based chapter on business strategy is provided.

For lecturers

PowerPoint slides

A suite of adaptable PowerPoint slides has been included for use in lecture presentations. Arranged by unit theme, the slides may also be used as hand-outs in class.

Instructor's manual

Discussion and thinking points are included in a helpful guide for instructors. This also incorporates the answers to the 'Put into practice', 'Economics in context', and 'End of unit' questions set in the textbook.

Test bank

A ready-made electronic testing resource, which can be imported into your assessment software and customized to meet your teaching needs. Questions are provided for every chapter in the book.

Additional Questions

A series of topical questions relating to news stories mentioned in Andrew's blog can be used as a basis for your class discussion.

VLE cartridge

Importing the cartridge into your Virtual Learning Environment allows you to fully integrate your teaching materials with the book's online resources. By enabling you to import all the material at once it provides you with full control over resources and allows students access to course content in one designated place.

Acknowledgements

Many thanks to everyone at OUP for their support and help in putting this book together. For the first edition, thanks to Kirsty Reade, Fiona Loveday, Nicola Bateman, and Julie Harris. For the second edition, thanks to everyone again at OUP, especially Peter Hooper, Sarah Brett, Philippa Hendry, and Kevin Doherty.

About the book

This book is divided into the following two sections.

- **Microeconomics** This focuses on what happens in individual markets, and covers topics such as supply and demand, and market structures. When we analyse the price of oil, the salaries of merchant bankers, and the power of supermarkets, this is microeconomic analysis.
- **Macroeconomics** This focuses on the economy as a whole. Rather than examining one market, it considers the country as a whole. In macroeconomics, we will cover topics such as unemployment, growth in the economy, and international trade.

Whilst it is possible to read specific chapters in this book on their own, economics is a subject in which your understanding of a topic will often build on previous concepts and models that you have studied. To analyse a monopoly or a competitive market, for example, you need a good grasp of costs and revenues. To understand the way in which price adjusts to bring about equilibrium, you need to understand supply and demand. Even when it comes to macroeconomics, a lot of this relies on an understanding of microeconomic theory. Analysing the total demand in the economy and the total supply in the economy (macroeconomics) uses the same principles that are required to examine supply and demand in a particular market (microeconomics)—but on a much bigger scale.

The best way to read this book, therefore, is to start at the beginning and keep going until you reach the end! You will find that your understanding grows as you work your way through and that this enhances your ability to analyse new material when you come to it.

The structure of the chapters

At the beginning of each chapter, there is an overview of what the content of the chapter involves; there are also a number of learning objectives setting out what you should gain once you have read the chapter. The important issues raised by each chapter are summarized in the 'key learning points' at the end. You can see whether you have fully understood the chapter or not by using the 'checklist', and the 'review questions'. Further review tests on each chapter are available online at http://www.oxfordtextbooks.co.uk/orc/gillespie_econ2e/

If you would like to learn more about any of the topics in the chapters that you have been studying, then visit the Online Resource Centre that accompanies this book for further material.

Within each chapter, I have included a number of features to help you in your studies. These include the following.

- **Economics in context** This feature includes up-to-date stories that highlight how a particular economic concept relates to the 'real world'. You will find numerous interesting stories about different firms and economies throughout the book.

- **What do you think?** Every now and again it is worth sitting back and thinking about what you have read; if nothing else, this helps to make sure that you have absorbed the material and reflected on it. The 'What do you think?' feature raises particular issues related to the given topic that require you to think for yourself and to develop your own view. There is often no 'right' answer to economic issues, and the 'What do you think?' questions are intended to be thought-provoking and to highlight that many problems can be solved in different ways.

- **Put into practice** This feature asks you to apply your understanding—perhaps by calculating something or by illustrating a change using diagrams. It is designed to help you to check whether you could use the knowledge that you have just acquired.

Each chapter also features a case study toward the end, which covers a number of the topics that you have just studied; this is intended for you to think about or discuss with other students.

Overall, the book is designed to make the content relevant and accessible. I have tried to set out clearly what each chapter covers and to provide numerous opportunities for you to consolidate your understanding. There are also questions designed to help you to apply your knowledge to other economic issues and to develop your evaluative skills. This provides a modern introduction to economic theory that should develop your enthusiasm for the subject, and also give you the understanding and skills for further study.

Overview of the book

■ Microeconomics: Chapters 1–17

The book begins with a discussion of the basic economic problem; in Chapter 1, we look at what studying economics involves, and at some of the key concepts and issues.

In Chapter 2, we examine how resources are allocated within an economy—what determines who works where, what is produced, who earns what, and who gets what. One way of solving these economic problems is to leave it to market forces of supply and demand. In Chapters 3–6, we examine supply and demand conditions, and analyse how the price mechanism brings about equilibrium. Having established how the free market works, we then highlight some of the disadvantages of this approach in Chapters 7 and 8, and consider how the government might intervene to solve these.

Having examined the elements of a market, we then focus on market structure. We begin by developing an understanding of revenues and costs in Chapters 9 and 10. Once this has been covered, we analyse the different forms of market structure in detail, and the implications of these in terms of price and output decisions in Chapters 11–15.

In Chapter 16, we consider whether all firms do actually try to profit-maximize and examine the implications of other objectives. In Chapter 17, we examine the market for labour and consider how wages are determined for different jobs.

■ Macroeconomics: Units 18–30

In the macroeconomics section, we begin with an overview of the key issues in macro-economics in Chapter 18. We then analyse what causes equilibrium in the economy in Chapter 19 and whether national income is a good indicator of a country's standard of living in Chapter 20. In Chapter 21, we consider the determinants of economic growth, before looking at aggregate demand and aggregate supply in Chapter 22.

We examine the different elements of demand in the economy in turn in Chapters 23–25, when we analyse consumption, investment, and government spending. After this, we consider causes of, and possible cures for, unemployment in Chapter 26. We then examine the money market in Chapter 27, and analyse the impact of changes in money supply and interest rates on the economy. This then leads to a discussion of the causes of inflation, and whether there is a relationship between inflation and unemployment, in Chapter 28. Following this, we move on to the international environment, and examine issues such as free trade, exchange rates, the balance of payments, and the European Union. These are covered in Chapter 29. Lastly, in Chapter 30, we examine the import-ance of exchange rates in global economies.

Overall, this book should provide a good introduction to the key issues in economics and provide you with the tools necessary to analyse economics problems. I hope that you enjoy it.

Why study economics?

If you have ever wondered why the cost of a ticket to your favourite band's last concert was so expensive, why you are paid so little in your part-time job, why your petrol is taxed so heavily, or why it is more expensive to get into a nightclub at weekends than during the week, or if you have ever wondered what influences the rate at which you change your currency into another when you go on holiday, why some people seem to be so much richer than others, or why some firms make more profits than others, then studying economics will be of interest to you! In fact, whether you know it or not, you are already an important part of the economic system. You are a consumer of products: every day, you are out there buying and consuming goods and services, and influencing the demand for them. You may also have a job, and so help to generate goods and services. If you are working, you are also paying taxes that are used to finance the provision of other products. However, simply being part of an economy is one thing; studying it is another. By studying economics, you can develop an analytical approach that helps you to understand a wide range of issues from what determines the price of different products, to the causes, and consequences of unemployment, to the benefits of different forms of competition. By the end of this book, you should understand a whole range of economic issues, such as why some people earn more than others, why some economies grow faster than others, and why, if you set up in business, you might want to dominate a market.

The study of economics provides a number of models and frameworks that can be applied to a range of situations. I hope that, by the end of this book, you have the tools that you need to examine any number of economic issues, and to analyse the underlying causes and consequences of any changes that have occurred.

The impact of an ageing population, price increases by your local supermarket, the returns on your investment by choosing to go to university, and the costs to society of smoking are all issues that you can analyse as part of economics once you have the necessary tools.

And at the heart of economics is human behaviour: what influences it and what happens when it changes? What makes people choose one course of action rather than another? If we want to change behaviour, what is the best way of doing this? If we want people to be more environmentally friendly, is this best achieved by taxing environmentally unfriendly behaviour? Or by subsidizing 'good behaviour' or by legislating? Economics affects people's standard of living and how they live. The tax and benefits system will affect your incentive to work, your willingness to marry, to have children, to save money, and to have a pension. An understanding of economics therefore provides an insight into the factors that shape society and influence the success of your business or career.

Of course, you are not the only one wanting to understand the economy and the economic impact of policy decisions. Governments would also like to be able to influence the economy to achieve their objectives, such as faster economic growth and lower unemployment; most recently, there have been major debates on the best way to help governments to cope with major borrowings without causing another recession. Firms are interested in economic change because it will influence their ability to compete (for example, interest rates can affect their costs and demand for their products) and determine their future strategy (for example, what markets they should be targeting). Employees are interested in economic conditions because these affect their earnings. Consumers want to know what is likely to happen to the prices of the things that they buy. Many different groups in society will therefore be interested in what influences the economy and how economies might change in the future. This probably explains why economic stories receive such media attention and why the subject has been studied so intensely over the years by economists. I hope that, by the end of this book, you will have a greater insight into these issues and will want to explore them even further.

Microeconomics

What is economics?

In this chapter, we set out to explain the fundamental issues in economics. These centre on the ideas of scarcity and choice. At any moment, there are limited resources available in an economy and so choices have to be made about how to use them most efficiently. This chapter considers how these choices might be made, as well as introduces a number of key economic concepts.

LEARNING OBJECTIVES

By the end of this chapter, you should be able to:

✔ understand the basic economic problems of what is produced, how it is produced, and for whom it is produced;

✔ understand the different types of economy, such as the free market economy, the command (or planned) economy, and the mixed economy;

✔ explain the difference between positive and normative economics;

✔ explain the difference between microeconomics and macroeconomics;

✔ understand some of the key terms and concepts in economics that you will need in your analysis.

■ The basic economic problem

At the moment, you are likely to have many different things on your 'to do' list, such as write an essay, see friends, or go to a film. The problem is that you do not have enough time to do them all immediately, so you are going to have to make choices about which ones really matter and which need to be done first. You may decide to stay in and study;

by staying in and writing your essay, you may get a better degree, and this will benefit you in the long run. On the other hand, maybe you should go out and enjoy yourself now, even though the consequence of this may be that the essay is not handed in, your grades suffer, and you do not do as well as you hoped academically. Which course of action you choose depends on your priorities and your future plans; this will affect how you use your time. Whatever you do is likely to involve sacrificing another option. Going out a lot may mean sacrificing a better grade; staying in all of the time means sacrificing the fun of going out. Faced with the constraint of limited time, you have to make choices; choosing one option involves sacrificing another. Similarly, when you go shopping, there are many things that you might want to buy with your money, but with a limited income, you have to make a decision about what is best for you. You may want the iPad, iPhone, Xbox, and Glastonbury tickets, but these may not all be affordable in one go.

In fact, every day, you are having to choose between alternatives and this highlights the fundamental problem facing not only you as an individual, but also economies as a whole. At any moment in time, the amount of goods and services that an economy can produce is determined by the resources that it has available. These resources include the following.

- **Land** This includes physical land and sea, and the minerals associated with them, such as coal and diamonds. This resource is generally difficult to increase in an economy unless there is a new discovery of a resource such as oil.

- **Labour** This includes the number of people willing and able to work in an economy, and the skills that they have. The size of the workforce will vary if there is immigration into a country or if there is a change in the school-leaving age or retirement age.

- **Capital** This involves the quantity and quality of capital equipment in an economy, such as machinery, offices, and transport. If businesses invest in capital goods, this will increase the capital stock of a country over time.

- **Entrepreneurship** This refers to the ability of managers to think of new ideas, to manage people effectively, and to take risks. The political, legal, and economic environment in an economy can affect the willingness of people to innovate and the ease with which they can turn their ideas into reality successfully.

The quantity and quality of these resources will vary between countries: some countries have bigger populations than others or more natural resources. The resources will also change over time—for example, a higher birth rate or more investment into technology increases the resources available. However, at any given moment, the amount and quality of resources in any region are fixed. This places a limit on what can be produced. With a given number of people, machines, resources, and ideas, there will be a limit to the output that can be produced.

Economics in context   UK population

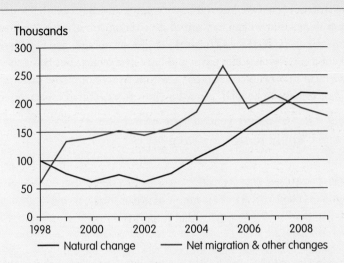

Figure 1.1 Components of population change, UK, mid-1998 to mid-2009.
Sources: Office for National Statistics, General Register Office for Scotland,
Northern Ireland Statistics & Research Agency.

The population of the UK was 61,792,000 in mid-2009. This was an increase of 394,000 (0.6 per cent) on the year before. Population growth has increased in the UK over recent decades. Changes in births, deaths, and the pattern of international migration into and out of the UK have all contributed to population change.

Figure 1.1 shows the contribution of natural change (the difference between births and deaths) and net migration (the difference between long-term migration into and out of the UK) on population growth. Natural change was the largest contributor to population growth until the year to mid-1999, and more recently in the years to mid-2008 and mid-2009. Between these periods, net migration was the main driver of population change. In the year to mid-2002, net migration accounted for 70 per cent of the total population change.

? Questions

What factors do you think influence:

• natural changes in the population?

• net migration into a country?

What impact do these changes have on the economy?

Whilst the amount that can be produced at any moment in an economy may be limited due to limited resources, what we want as consumers certainly is not. We want lots of everything! When we go shopping, for example, we are often tempted by many different things on the shelves even if we know that we cannot afford them all. Similarly, there are many different things that we might want to do with our time, but we cannot fit it all in. The problem is that our resources constrain us. As consumers, we face the problems of scarcity and choice: we would like to do and have everything, but because our resources are scarce, we must make choices. Similarly, within an economy, the scarcity of resources means that choices have to be made regarding how these limited resources are best used.

Economics in context   **Entrepreneurial culture**

The UK is said to have a less entrepreneurial culture than the USA. In the USA, it is not regarded as unusual if business people fail at some point: it is all part of the entrepreneurial learning curve. In the UK, failure is looked on less favourably. Starting up again once you have been made bankrupt has been very difficult in the past in the UK. However, recent changes of legislation have enabled entrepreneurs to get started again and to cancel their debts more quickly. Also, television programmes such as *Dragon's Den* and *The Apprentice* have helped to raise the profile of business, and may lead to more entrepreneurs in the future.

 Questions

Why does it matter whether an economy has an entrepreneurial culture?

How can a government encourage entrepreneurship?

This concept of scarcity and choice is critical to the study of economics. All of us—whether we are consumers, investors, firms, or policymakers—need to consider how best to use the resources that we have: Which job should we accept? How should we use our time? In which businesses should we invest? What should we buy? These are all decisions that need to be made because of scarcity.

In the case of an economy, the constraint provided by the resources available leads to three fundamental questions, as illustrated in Figure 1.2.

- **What is to be produced?** Given that an economy cannot produce everything, decisions have to be made about the right combination of goods and services, given its resources. For example, should an economy's resources be used for the production of flat-screen TVs, hospitals, schools, or MP3 players? Do you think that it is better for an economy to produce more cars, more music, or more hotels?

- **How to produce?** The fact that there are a limited number of people and limited amounts of land, capital, and entrepreneurship in an economy means that decisions have to be made about the best way of producing a given level of output. Given the various products that we want to produce, how should we allocate our employees between different sectors? Should we use the machinery and equipment that we have to produce the phones we want or should we use it to produce the shoes that we want?

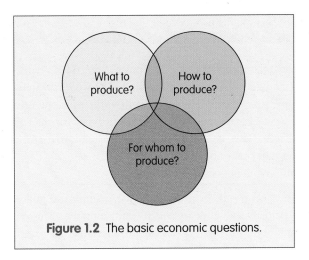

Figure 1.2 The basic economic questions.

- **For whom to produce?** As well as deciding *what* is being produced, an economy needs to decide *for whom* it is producing. Should items produced be distributed equally, so that everyone has the same access to goods and services, or should some people be allowed to have more than others? How should it be decided who gets what has been produced?

When solving these basic economic problems, we encounter the concept of opportunity cost. Opportunity cost measures what has been sacrificed in the next-best alternative—that is, it considers what is being sacrificed to achieve a particular combination of goods and services.

The concept of opportunity cost is an important one for all of us. When deciding to study at university, you naturally consider the money that you will lose in the short run by not taking a job immediately. By spending more time on one topic, you sacrifice time on other ones. By spending more time on your part-time job, you are spending less time studying. In terms of the economy as a whole, if we put more resources into one industry, then those resources are coming out of somewhere else: more resources going into the health service, for example, may mean fewer resources in the defence industry. Similarly, if someone decides to work in the computer industry, then he or she is not working in teaching: we get more computer programs and fewer lectures (which may or may not be a good thing for the economy as a whole). Economics is therefore based on choices, and this can be seen in government when political parties debate how best to use the resources of an economy and to what extent people should have the same access to products.

What do you think?

Imagine that you have finished your undergraduate degree and are considering studying for a master's.

What would be the opportunity cost of this decision?

What would determine whether studying for a master's would be the right decision for you or not?

▨ Solving the fundamental economic questions

Identifying the fundamental economic questions is one thing; working out the 'best' answers is another and generates much discussion. The way in which these questions of 'what?', 'how?', and 'for whom?' are solved will vary from one economy to another. One option is to have a government take full responsibility for the economy and for the allocation of resources. This is a very interventionist approach and would occur in a planned (or command) economy.

In a planned economy, the government decides:

- what goods and services should be produced—for example, the government may decide that defence is a priority and allocate a significant number of resources into this area; alternatively, it might decide that greater car production is the priority; equally, it may decide not to produce many sunglasses or cosmetics;

- the combination of resources, such as the quantity of machines and people employed in any particular industry, including who works where (jobs would be allocated to workers rather than individuals choosing for themselves what they want to do as a career); and

- the way in which goods and services are distributed—for example, everyone may be given access to free education and health care; prices, wages, and rents may be determined by the government.

In a planned economy, the government takes an overview of the economy and makes the key decisions rather than lets these be made by individual consumers, employees, and businesses. Economies in which the government has played a large role include those of North Korea, Cuba, and China.

A different approach is to leave the solutions to these questions to free market forces. This means that the government does not intervene, and leaves all decisions to individuals and private firms to work out for themselves. If there is a demand for a particular product and firms can produce it at a profit, then it will be produced, because businesses will want to supply rather than because the government has told them that they must do so. If you want to work in a particular industry, you can do so, and your decision to work there will be linked to the rewards available rather than whether you have been told to by the government. If using more machinery seems to generate a high return, then firms will invest in equipment rather than use labour, because this makes financial sense.

This free market approach has the advantage of not needing a central government to decide everything (which is extremely complex, and may be bureaucratic and inefficient); instead, decisions are made separately in many millions of individual markets by firms and their customers. Each firm pursues its own objectives and focuses purely on what it wants, as does each individual. There is no need for a central body to make decisions for everyone in the country. This means that a free market can avoid the dangers of a very cumbersome central planning system that needs to gather huge amounts of data and send out millions of directives. A free market approach should also mean that what is produced is definitely in demand (because if it is not demanded, then firms will not produce it), whereas if a government is in control, then it may order certain things to be produced only to find that they are not actually required and that no one wants to buy them. In this case, there would be waste.

In a free market, therefore, there is an incentive for firms to be competitive, and to develop new services and new ways of doing things. Being more efficient and meeting customer needs more precisely can boost profits, which firms or individuals can keep for themselves. The potential benefits from innovating mean that there is likely to be greater choice for customers. In the planned economy, any gains in one industry go back to the government to be used elsewhere, so there is not the same incentive to be efficient because the firm or individual does not personally gain.

However, the free market has many potential failings and imperfections. For example, some goods or services may not be provided because they are not profitable, even if some people might think that they are things that should be provided (for example, educational television programmes, the opera, museums, and libraries). On the other hand, some products, such as guns and drugs, may be openly available because they are profitable, even though society as a whole may think that they are undesirable. In the free market, products are available only if people can afford them; in the case of services such as health and education, this may be felt to be unacceptable. The pursuit of profit may also lead to unsafe products being produced, labour being exploited, consumers being badly informed, and businesses engaging in corruption to win orders. The failings of the free market therefore mean that some intervention by a government is inevitable. The real question is how much intervention there will be—that is, to what extent does a government take responsibility for allocating resources directly, and how much does it regulate the private provision of goods and services? The problems with the free market and the case for intervention are examined in Chapter 7.

Table 1.1 Comparison of the free market and a planned economy

Free market	Planned economy
Resources allocated by market forces of supply and demand	Resources allocated by government directive
Firms aim to maximize profits	Social objectives
Individuals make decisions to maximize their welfare	Decisions made by central authority; no incentive for individuals or firms to try to be more efficient or to innovate
Incentive to be efficient to make more profits	May be bureaucratic; there are huge amounts of information to gather and process, and millions of decisions to be made—all of which could lead to inefficiency
Competition can encourage innovation	May lack competition in markets

Economics in context — Immigration

The average income per person in the USA is around $46,000. In Mexico, it is $8,000. Perhaps it is not surprising, therefore, if millions of Mexicans have entered the USA illegally in an attempt to gain from the higher wages and higher standard of living. The total number of illegal immigrants in the USA is around 11 million.

? Questions

In what ways does this immigration demonstrate the workings of the free market?

Why might the US government want to prevent such immigration?

What do you think?

What goods and services do you think should be available in all economies even if they are not profitable? (That is, what products may a government need to provide?)

Can you think of goods and services that may be profitable to provide, but which you think should not be available in an economy? (That is, what goods and services might a government need to intervene to prevent?)

Do you think that the private provision of health care and education should be prevented or encouraged?

■ Mixed economies

In reality, no economy is completely free market or completely planned. All economies are a combination of the two (see Figure 1.3); this is known as a mixed economy. In a mixed economy, some goods and services are provided by the government, such as education and the police force. Other goods and services, such as mobile phones, laptops, and trainers, may be provided by private firms. However, whilst a mixed economy, in which the government steps in when the free market fails, may be the obvious solution, this still leaves open many questions, such as the following.

* To what extent should the government intervene?

* In what areas should it intervene? Should it provide transport, energy, and postal services? What about housing, dental care, broadband, and leisure facilities?

Free market economy: resources allocated by supply and demand ← Mixed economy: part free market and part planned → Command (planned) economy: resources allocated by the government

Figure 1.3 Different economic systems.

- How should the government intervene: does it need to provide products itself? Can it provide products in partnership with private firms? Should it let private firms provide some products, but regulate them, and if so, how?

What do you think?

In a free market, tobacco would probably be widely consumed because people would be willing and able to pay for it. However, we may think that this is wrong and the government should intervene in this market. Do you think that the government should:

a. ignore smoking on the grounds that it is not its role to intervene?

b. ban smoking?

c. tax tobacco more heavily?

d. spend more on anti-smoking promotional campaigns?

e. decide to focus on other issues?

Which of the above do you recommend and why?

Do you think that the government's policies should differ for different age groups (for example, for the under-18s)? Explain your answer.

Economics in context — Social change in Venezuela

In 2005, in Venezuela, the government under Hugo Chavez initiated a huge social programme. The aim was to reduce the country's major problems of poverty and economic inequality. The programme included the following:

- a literacy campaign;
- a discounted food and household goods shopping project, established in poor urban and rural areas where no supermarkets or general food stores existed before; and
- a basic preventative medicine programme, providing free health care and subsidized medicines to over 60 per cent of the population who previously had no medical services at all.

Other projects, such as the creation of a huge network of 4,600 businesses owned by the workers throughout the country, were aimed at creating jobs.

 Question

This programme introduced by Chavez was very interventionist. What do you think might be the problems of such a programme?

The trend in many economies for much of the last 30 years has been for governments to intervene less in their economies. In the UK in the 1990s, for example, many companies such as British Gas, British Steel, and British Airways were taken out of government control and sold to private firms. This process of selling government assets to private individuals and organizations is called privatization. In other sectors, the government has not sold off organizations, but has removed restrictions to allow more firms to compete: this is called deregulation. However, in some economies, notably in South America in recent years, there has been greater government intervention, because electors have felt that their societies would benefit if the government were to take greater responsibility for the provision of goods and services, and reduce the income gap between rich and poor. The global economic crisis in 2008 and 2009 has also made many governments look at whether an approach of privatization and deregulation has been effective. Leaving financial markets unregulated, for example, seemed to have led to speculative high-risk borrowing, which later threatened the banking system and created a strong argument for more intervention. On the other hand, increasing borrowing by many governments because they were receiving less income from tax when their economies were doing badly means that they had to consider reducing the number of areas in which they intervened.

What do you think?

Are we better off without government intervention?

Economics in context   Privatizing Japan Post

The ten-year privatization of Japan Post—the national postal delivery system, but also, through its banking and insurance facilities, Japan's largest financial institution and a huge employer—began in October 2007. This was a major change in the structure of the economy, marking much less intervention by the government, but in December 2009, the Democratic Party of Japan passed a law to freeze future sales of Japan Post shares, halting the privatization process begun by Liberal Democratic Party governments.

Questions

Why might the Liberal Democratic Party have wanted to privatize Japan Post?
Why might the Democratic Party of Japan have halted the privatization of Japan Post?

The decisions about the extent and method of government intervention are therefore continually being made and reviewed by governments, and their electorate. Almost every day, there are discussions over the appropriate balance between private and public sector, and the extent of government intervention. In the UK in 2009, the government took control of the majority of shares in the Royal Bank of Scotland to protect the banking system. In the USA in 2010, President Obama increased the government provision of health care despite much opposition. Think about a typical day and you will realize the number of areas in which there are debates over the role of government: Should the government provide more homes? Should it control rents? Should it run the transport system? Should it fund universities and students studying there? Should it control the rate of interest charged on borrowing? Should it control what people eat? Should it regulate whether we can gamble or not?

These questions all require a view about whether the free market is better at allocating resources and the extent to which a government is needed. Your role as a voter is to elect a government that has economic policies with which you agree. In part, this depends on whether you trust individuals and firms to make decisions for themselves without government control, or whether you think that the government needs to intervene to make the economy work effectively. If we leave businesses to themselves, will we get better products as they compete amongst themselves, or will we get false accounting, environmentally unfriendly production processes, and unsafe products?

These issues of government intervention, and the benefits and limitations of the free market economy, are examined in more detail in Chapter 7.

What do you think?

What goods and services does the government provide in your economy? How does this differ from another economy with which you are familiar?

Do you think that the government should intervene more in your economy? In what way(s)?

What do you think would happen if there were no government intervention in an economy?

■ Types of economics

The study of economics is vital to understand the society around you. When the election result in the UK seemed inconclusive in 2010, a Conservative and Liberal Democrat alliance was rapidly agreed because of fears of what would happen to the economy if a government were not quickly elected to start making vital decisions. When Bill Clinton was standing for election as US President in 1992 against George Bush, he reminded all of his team that winning an election was 'all about the economy, stupid'—that is, if you can convince electors that you will look after the economy, and their jobs and incomes, you will win the election.

This book will cover many of the essential issues in the study of economics, including an overview of different types of economics, such as those described below.

Positive and normative economics

- **Positive economics** examines the different relationships between economic variables and provides an analysis of these that can actually be tested. For example, we may think that an increase in demand for a product will increase its price, that more government spending will lead to faster growth in the economy, or that lower income taxes provide more incentive to work. These relationships can be tested over time to see whether they actually occur. Data can be collected and analysed to assess the validity of such claims, so this is positive economics.

- **Normative economics**, by comparison, focuses on value judgements about what you think should happen. For example, you might think that the government should spend more money on the health service compared with defence, that it ought to divert resources away from the education sector towards biotechnology, or that it should cut inheritance taxes even if it has to cut spending as a result. These are your opinions; they represent your view of what should be done or what is most important for the economy. You cannot test these ideas, because they are simply opinions of what matters and what needs to be done. Not surprisingly, normative economics is the area of economics in which most of the disagreements between policymakers occur! These differences are often at the heart of the manifestos of political parties. Everyone might agree that an increase in spending on health and education could improve the services in these sectors, but they may disagree enormously on which one of these is the priority or exactly how the money should be raised and used.

What do you think?

Normative economics is based on your views about economic issues.
Do you think that the government should regulate gambling or should it be left to the free market? Why?
Do you think that medical care should be free or should it be charged for?
Do you think that the government should tax cigarettes and alcohol more heavily?
Do you think that the level of income at which you start to pay income tax should be relatively high or low? Do you think that the rate of income tax should be increased?
Why do you think that the way in which governments deal with the issues above varies from country to country?

Microeconomics and macroeconomics

- **Microeconomics** focuses on the individual decisions of households and firms. It focuses on the demand and supply for goods and services within a particular market, such as the market for housing or labour. It helps to explain the price of a good, your decision whether to work in a particular industry, or the impact of an increase in the supply of a product. Microeconomics might analyse the determinants of the price of oil or a firm's shares, for example.

- **Macroeconomics** analyses the economy as a whole ('macro' means big, whereas 'micro' means small). For example, rather than focus on the price level in one market (microeconomics), macroeconomics considers the general price level in the economy; rather than examine one individual's decision whether to work, it considers the overall numbers employed in the economy. Macroeconomics therefore deals with topics such as inflation, unemployment, economic growth, and international trade, and usually analyses these from a government's perspective.

▓ Key terms and concepts in economics

In order to study economics effectively, you need to learn the language of the subject. The following are some of the key terms and concepts that you will need to help you on your journey.

Goods and services

- **Goods** are physical products, such as televisions and washing machines. They are tangible—that is, you can see them and touch them.
- **Services,** by comparison, are intangible—for example, education and banking are services.

In reality, most organizations provide a combination of goods and services. When you visit a restaurant, you buy a meal (tangible), but you also receive service and benefit from the experience of the overall environment. In this book, we use the term 'product' to include goods, services, and combinations of the two.

Consumer goods and capital goods

- **Consumer goods** are goods and services that are consumed by the final user—for example, magazines and sandwiches are bought by, or given to, the person who is going to consume them.
- **Capital goods** are goods that are bought to use in the production process—that is, they are bought to produce other goods and services. A production line is used to make products, such as cans of soup, which are then sold to customers to be consumed. A fleet of lorries is bought to distribute products. Lorries and production lines are, therefore, capital goods.

The decision by firms and governments over whether to spend money on consumer goods—which increases today's consumption—or on capital goods—which involves investment for the future at the expense of today's consumption—has important implications for the long-term growth of an economy. Would you buy shares in a business that invested all of its profits into new product development? Or would you prefer no investment in new products? Would you vote for a government that was investing heavily in long-term construction projects if it meant less provision in the short term of benefits to the elderly, ill, or unemployed?

Households also make these choices: do you spend your bonus on a holiday (consumption) or an extension to the house (investment)? Decisions about how much to save and how much to spend have important economic implications for your lifestyle today and in the future.

What do you think?

How important do you think it is to save money for your pension?

If the government were to have £100 billion to spend, do you think that it should use the funds to invest in education or should it be given away in the form of lower taxes?

Investment, savings, and consumption

The word 'investment' is often used in the media to mean money that is 'invested' into shares or banks. In economics, however, these are called savings. Savings represent the income of households that is not spent on consumption (that is, on buying goods and services): for example, savings include money put into a bank or into a pension fund. The term 'investment' in economics refers to the purchase of capital goods: for example, firms investing in new equipment that will be used to produce products in the future. Firms may invest in a new factory or information technology systems, for example.

Private and public sector

- The **private sector** is made up of organizations owned by individuals and firms. Companies such as Tesco plc and Barclays Bank plc are owned by private investors, as opposed to the government. Although the plc stands for a 'public limited company', these firms are in the private sector, because they are privately owned by the public. In the private sector, the owners can pursue their own interests; we usually assume that this is to maximize profits. Businesses will seek to produce products where they can make the most profits; if the rewards are not high enough, they will shift resources elsewhere in search of better returns.

- **Public sector** organizations are run by the government—for example, the National Health Service (NHS). These organizations may have social objectives as well as, or instead of, profit targets. The government may measure success in a much broader way than private businesses do: it may consider the effect on jobs, on happiness, on inequality, on the community, and the environment.

Your view of what businesses are there to do and whether pursuing profit is desirable (whether it leads to innovation or to too much power and unethical behaviour, for example) will influence your view of the 'right' mix of the private and public sector.

Economics in context   China

China's economy over the past 30 years has changed from a centrally planned system that was fairly closed to international trade to a freer market economy with a rapidly growing private sector. Reforms started in the late 1970s with the reduction of state-run agriculture, more independence for government organizations, less regulation of enterprises and markets, and more free market businesses. This reshaping of the economy and resulting efficiency gains have helped lead to a tenfold increase in gross domestic product (GDP) since 1978, making China the second-largest economy in the world after the USA.

? Questions

What is a centrally planned system and what benefits does this have?

Why do you think that China might have moved from a centrally planned system to a freer market economy?

How might this move affect:

- businesses?
- consumers?

What do you think?

Identify two organizations run by the government in your economy. Why do you think the government runs these? What are their objectives?

Do you think that all organizations should be owned by the government?

Economics in context | The US economy

The USA has the largest economy in the world, with an income per person of over $46,400. In this market-focused economy, private individuals and firms make most of the decisions rather than the government. US business firms enjoy greater flexibility than their counterparts in Western Europe and Japan in decisions to invest, to lay off surplus workers, and to develop new products. Following the global economic downturn, with investment bank failures, falling home prices, and tight credit, the US Congress established a $700 billion Troubled Asset Relief Program (TARP) to help stabilize the economy. In January 2009 the US Congress passed, and President Barack Obama signed, a bill providing an additional $787 billion to be used over ten years—two-thirds on additional spending and one-third on tax cuts—to create jobs and to help the economy recover.

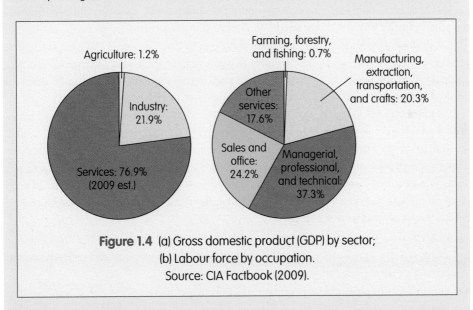

Figure 1.4 (a) Gross domestic product (GDP) by sector;
(b) Labour force by occupation.
Source: CIA Factbook (2009).

? Questions

What are the benefits of 'private individuals and firms making most of the decisions rather than the government'? What are the dangers, do you think?

What does the extract suggest about the degree of government intervention in the USA in recent years? Why has this changed?

Has the government intervened more or less in your own country in recent years? Why?

Economic models

An economy is made up of millions of households and firms, all of which are making many different decisions in many different markets. Not even the most powerful computer in the world could track all of the decisions and transactions happening in an economy every day. To understand the economy, therefore, economists build models, which make assumptions about how different aspects of the economy work. These are simplifications of reality, but provided that they help to analyse what a particular outcome will be, then they remain useful. We may predict, for example, that a market will move from A to B; in reality, it may move from A to C to B—but nevertheless the model has some validity because it predicts the end destination. Of course, models of the economy are continually reviewed, and new theories and approaches are being developed. This is because behaviours alter, the environment in which decisions are being made changes, and we gain new insights into what is determining decision making.

Obviously, economics may not always relate to the specific decisions of a particular individual or business firm; some people and some firms will always act differently from the majority. However, economics focuses on the overall market, sector, region, or country, and seeks to explain the general behaviour within these areas. We assume, for example, that consumers are rational. If a consumer is asked to choose between something that is very good or something that is average, we assume that he or she will choose the very good. Of course, one particular person may be perverse and may not choose this, but the vast majority will do as assumed! We also assume that firms try to profit-maximize. This is discussed in detail in Chapter 10 and is open to some debate. However, regardless of whether all firms seek to profit-maximize and even regardless of whether all succeed, if this is what the majority are trying to do, then the model has some value in terms of predicting the price and output outcome in a given market situation.

Economic modelling helps us to understand what has happened in a market or economy, and why; this is therefore helpful to analyse what has happened and to predict what will occur in the future, which is essential to managers and policymakers. Economic change affects billions of people in terms of what is produced, the standard of living in a society, the income distribution in an economy, economic growth, and the quality of their lives. Being able to predict the economic environment and to analyse how best to change behaviours is critical to governments.

Deciding at the margin

Two of the most important and powerful concepts in economics are those of marginal cost and marginal benefit. Whoever you are and whatever you do, you should consider the marginal (or extra) costs and benefits of your actions. If the extra cost of doing something is less than the extra benefit, then do not do it! By doing it, your overall welfare or happiness will fall. Equally, if the extra benefit from doing something is greater than the extra cost, then do it: if you do, you will gain. This concept of measuring things at the margin in order to work out what is best is important to remember and can be used when analysing any situation. If you do not like something, then this does not mean that you should stop it altogether, but you cut back to the point at which marginal cost equals marginal benefit.

Let us consider air travel: many people claim that this has terrible environmental effects. This is true—but it also brings many benefits: it helps to move supplies around for firms; it creates jobs; and it provides individuals with the opportunity to do business, and to travel and holiday abroad. An economist would argue that air travel should be undertaken up to the point at which the marginal cost equals the marginal benefit. If the marginal benefit of an activity exceeds its marginal costs, do more, because you will be better off; if its marginal benefit is less than its marginal cost, do less, because if you do it, you will be worse off. When marginal benefit equals marginal cost, your welfare cannot increase by consuming another unit and so you have maximized your welfare.

The marginal concept is examined in more detail in Chapter 10.

Real and nominal

- **Nominal** values in economics are those given at the current wages and prices. The amount of money that you receive in your wage packet is a nominal sum. It shows how much you have been given, but does not reveal what you can actually buy with it.

- A **real** figure takes account of inflation. If, for example, you receive a pay increase of 2 per cent, then in nominal terms, you are 2 per cent better off. However, if the prices of items that you buy have generally increased by 2 per cent, then in real terms, you are in the same position in which you were originally; there has been no real increase. If a firm has announced a 1 per cent increase in profits, but during the same period, the price of buying materials and resources has increased by 3 per cent, then in real terms, the firm has made less profit.

It is always important to think in terms of the 'real' (that is, the inflation-adjusted) effect, not only the nominal.

Case study National Institute for Health and Clinical Excellence (NICE)

The National Institute for Health and Clinical Excellence (NICE) recently decided that there is insufficient evidence to recommend the routine use by the NHS of two drugs to help to treat advanced bowel cancer. These drugs are called Avastin and Erbitux.

Pressure groups say that these drugs are the best option for treating seriously ill patients whose cancer has spread. They claim that these drugs can extend life expectancy by around five months in some cases, and that this has been proved in tests.

Bowel cancer kills almost 50 people per day in the UK and affects one in 18 people during their life-times. It is possible to treat it, but it really needs to be caught in the early stages.

The problem with prescribing such drugs is that they are both expensive. Treatment using Avastin costs on average £17,655 per patient and using Erbitux costs £11,739. The NHS has to consider how best to use its resources. It does not generate revenue, because it does not charge for its services and relies on the government for its funding. More funding for the NHS may mean less funding for other areas of government.

The deputy chief executive of NICE said that neither of the two drugs represents a good use of scarce NHS resources.

? Questions

- In what ways does the NICE decision about these two drugs highlight the economic problem of scarcity and choice?
- Do you think that NICE should have authorized the use of these drugs in the NHS? On what would your decision depend?
- Do you think that patients should be allowed to pay for these drugs themselves?

@ Web

To find out more about the work of NICE, visit http://www.nice.org.uk

Checklist

Now that you have read this chapter, try to answer the following questions.

- ☐ Do you understand the importance of scarcity and choice?
- ☐ Do you understand the basic economic problems of what is produced, how it is produced, and for whom it is produced?
- ☐ Can you distinguish between the free market economy, the planned (command) economy, and the mixed economy?
- ☐ Can you explain the difference between positive and normative economics?
- ☐ Can you explain the difference between microeconomics and macroeconomics?
- ☐ Do you understand the difference between capital and consumption goods?
- ☐ Do you understand what is meant by a real value as opposed to a nominal value?

Review questions

1 How do different types of economy try to solve the basic economic problem?
2 To what extent does the government intervene in your economy? Has this increased or decreased in recent years?
3 How do the concepts of scarcity and choice affect you in your day-to-day life?
4 How does the concept of opportunity cost relate to your decision to go to university?
5 What do you think are the fundamental products that a government should provide for its citizens?

Key learning points

- Resources in an economy are limited at any moment; consumer wants are unlimited.
- Economics considers the key economic questions of what is produced, how it is produced, and for whom it is it produced.
- The key economic questions can be answered by market forces of supply and demand (in a free market), by the government (in a planned economy), or by a combination of the two (in a mixed economy).
- Microeconomics focuses on what happens in a particular market.
- Macroeconomics focuses on the economy as a whole.
- Normative economics is based on opinions; positive economics focuses on facts.

 Visit our Online Resource Centre at http://www.oxfordtextbooks.co.uk/orc/gillespie_econ2e/ for test questions and further information on topics covered in this chapter.

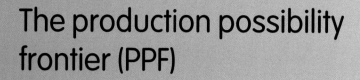

» 2

The production possibility frontier (PPF)

The starting point in our economic analysis is to consider what an economy can produce given its resources. As consumers, we may want many things, but there is a limit to what our economy can actually produce to meet these demands. These issues of scarcity and choice can be analysed using the production possibility frontier (PPF). In this chapter, we examine the factors that determine how much an economy can produce and the implications of different output decisions.

LEARNING OBJECTIVES

By the end of this chapter, you should be able to:

✔ understand what is meant by a production possibility frontier (PPF), also known as a production possibility curve (PPC);

✔ analyse the shape and the position of the PPF;

✔ understand the concept of productive efficiency;

✔ understand the concept of economic growth.

▪ Scarcity and choice

In Chapter 1, we saw how the study of economics was based around the issue of scarcity and choice. As consumers, our wants are unlimited, but there is a limit to what an economy can produce because of a scarcity of resources. What an economy is capable of producing can be shown on a production possibility frontier (PPF), also known as the production possibility curve (PPC).

The production possibility frontier (PPF)

The PPF shows the maximum output that can be produced in an economy at any given moment, given the resources available. If an economy is fully utilizing its resources, then it will be producing on the PPF.

To keep our analysis simple, we consider an economy that produces only two products: A and B (see Figure 2.1). Imagine that all of an economy's resources, such as land, labour, and capital, were used in industry A; then Q0 of A would be produced and no B would be made. Alternatively, if all resources were transferred to industry B, then Q5 of B would be produced and no A would be made. If resources were divided between the two industries, then a range of combinations of products is possible. For example, at point X, the economy produces Q1 of product A and Q2 of product B; alternatively, resources could be allocated differently between the two industries and it could produce at point Y, producing Q3 of A and Q4 of B. All of the points on the frontier, such as X and Y, are said to have productive efficiency (that is, to be productively efficient) because they are fully utilizing the economy's resources. This is attractive because it shows that resources are being used properly and not wasted. When an economy is productively efficient, it can only produce more of one product by producing less of another; resources have to be shifted from one product to another. The PPF therefore illustrates the concept of opportunity costs. As more units of product B are produced, this involves shifting resources into industry B and out of industry A: this will involve sacrificing some units of A in return for more B. The amount of A sacrificed for extra B is the opportunity cost. For example, the opportunity cost of producing the extra Q4 – Q2 units of B is Q1 – Q3 units of A.

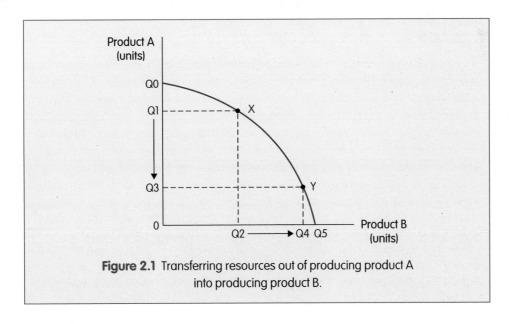

Figure 2.1 Transferring resources out of producing product A into producing product B.

Put into practice

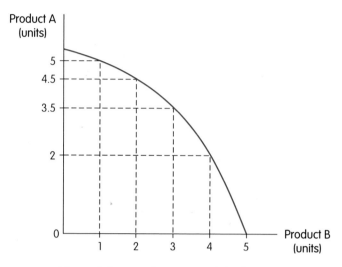

Figure 2.2 A production possibility frontier.

Using Figure 2.2, calculate the opportunity cost of the fifth unit of B in terms of the number of units of A sacrificed.

Economics in context   The importance of opportunity cost

The concept of opportunity cost is extremely important in economics and business. It represents the opportunities forgone. Whenever a manager makes a strategic decision, he or she is deciding to lead the business in one direction rather than another. Sometimes this works: for example, Nokia's decision to move out of all of its business areas apart from mobile phones was highly successful for many years. Other times, it is the wrong decision, such as Marks and Spencer's move into the USA, and Walmart's move into Germany. Any decision should be judged not only in terms of what it achieved, but also in terms of what else could have been done with those resources.

Imagine that a firm is earning a return on investment of 1 per cent. This means that the profits it earns are 1 per cent of the amount of long-term funds in the business. This is clearly better than 0 per cent, but is not better than the rate of interest available in most UK banks. Investors might rightly question how effectively the managers are using the resources available to them.

? Question

If you were to decide to invest money and buy shares in Microsoft, what would the opportunity cost be?

The Olympics

Whenever the opportunity comes to bid for major sporting events such as the World Cup and the Olympics, many countries rush to try to win them. The appeal is the mass media coverage, hundreds of thousands of tourists, and a focus for infrastructure investment. However, on financial grounds, almost every event ends up making losses. The costs are always underestimated as building projects overrun and the gains often disappoint in financial terms.

- The Athens Olympics was supposed to cost £1.5 billion, but ended up costing over ten times as much.
- The 2002 Japanese World Cup had little effect on the struggling Japanese economy.
- The London 2012 Olympics was estimated to cost £2.35 billion, but some estimates suggest that it will cost ten times that much.
- In the South African World Cup, $300 million costs were estimated for stadiums and infrastructure, but this turned out not to be enough even for one stadium!
- Some of the costly stadiums that were built for the Portuguese European Championships were simply knocked down after the event.

? Question

What is the opportunity cost to the UK of hosting the 2012 Olympics?

Reallocation of resources

The PPF shows all of the combinations of products that an economy can produce given its present resources. Any combination on the frontier is productively efficient, so to have more of one product produced, there will inevitably be a reduction in the amount of the other produced due to the reallocation of resources. The frontier shows the combinations of products that can be produced efficiently, but which is the right combination? What determines whether an economy should produce at X or Y? Do we want more of product A or more of product B, for example? How do we decide?

In a free market economy, decisions about what to produce are determined by market forces of supply and demand. If there were a high level of demand for product B rather than product A, then it would make this industry more attractive for producers. The greater demand for B would attract firms into this industry and out of A. The firms in industry B would then need more resources, such as labour and materials, to meet the higher demand. This increased demand for resources would increase the price paid for them, attracting resources into this industry and out of industry A. Market forces triggered by an increase in demand for the product would therefore lead to a reallocation of resources from one industry to another. On the PPF shown in Figure 2.3, this can be seen as a movement from X to Y. The demand for digital cameras, for example, has grown rapidly in recent years, whilst the demand for 'traditional' film has declined. As a result, firms such as Kodak have had to move resources out of traditional film and into digital, because that is where the rewards are. Likewise, individuals have had to learn the skills for digital production, because this is where the jobs are. Similarly, the music industry has

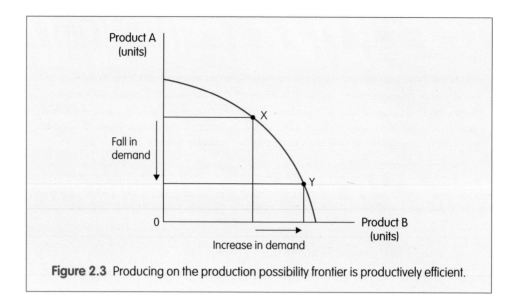

Figure 2.3 Producing on the production possibility frontier is productively efficient.

experienced a rapid growth in downloading at the expense of CDs. Companies such as EMI have had to move their resources into these newer areas.

In a planned economy, decisions about what to produce are determined by government instructions and directives. For example, the government may order that more factories and employees are used to produce product B rather than A. In this case, the reallocation from, say, X to Y is not determined by customers' demand, but by government orders.

This may happen if the government does not trust market forces to produce what it regards as the right combinations of products for society. For example, in a free market, con-sumers may want to consume products today, but may not be very good at thinking about their future—for example, we may not pay enough attention to environmental issues; the government may intervene to ensure that production takes account of these issues.

However, if the instructions given by the government do not match what people are actually demanding, then it can lead to too much of some goods being produced, whilst too few of other goods are available in relation to present demand. The government may decide that resources need to be diverted to defence or nuclear energy, for example, whereas consumers may want more iPods. This can lead to queues and rationing of some products for which demand is high. The lack of the profit incentive may also mean that resources are used inefficiently and that the economy operates within the PPF.

Put into practice

Are the following statements true or false?

a. The PPF shows the amount that consumers want of each product.

b. Any combination of goods inside the PPF is productively efficient.

c. Wants are limited, but resources are unlimited, which means that there is a problem of scarcity and choice.

Iceland

Iceland's Scandinavian-type social-market economy combines a capitalist structure and free market principles with an extensive welfare system. Prior to the 2008 crisis, Iceland had achieved high growth, low unemployment and a remarkably even distribution of income. The economy depends heavily on the fishing industry, which provides 40% of export earnings, more than 12% of GDP and employs 7% of the workforce. It remains sensitive to declining fish stocks as well as to fluctuations in world prices for its main exports: fish, and fish products, aluminum and ferrosilicon. Iceland's economy has been diversifying into manufacturing and service industries in the last decade, new developments in software production, biotechnology and tourism. Abundant geothermal and hydropower sources have attracted substantial foreign investment in the aluminum sector, and boosted economic growth, although the financial crisis has put several investment projects on hold. Much of Iceland's economic growth in recent years came as the result of a boom in domestic demand following the rapid expansion of the country's financial sector. Domestic banks expanded aggressively in foreign markets, and consumers and businesses borrowed heavily in foreign currencies, following the privatization of the banking sector in the early 2000s.

Source: CIA Factbook

 Questions

In what ways were resources being reallocated in the Icelandic economy?

What do think might have been driving these changes?

Student debt

A recent survey of UK students for university guide *Push* found that average yearly debt had increased by 5.4 per cent to £5,600 per year of study. This included everything from tuition fees to credit card and bank debts.

When you take into account the number of years of study on average, students are likely to incur £25,000 of debt. Given recent proposals to allow universities to charge more, this debt is likely to increase significantly in the future.

 Question

Given the opportunity cost of going to university, what would determine whether this was a worthwhile investment?

■ Productive inefficiency

If the economy is producing a combination of products on the PPF, then it is productively efficient. However, an economy may be operating within the frontier (for example, at the point V in Figure 2.4), in which case it is productively inefficient. This is because it could produce more of both products by using the existing resources effectively. Imagine that you are driving around a country and notice lots of factories that are closing down, high

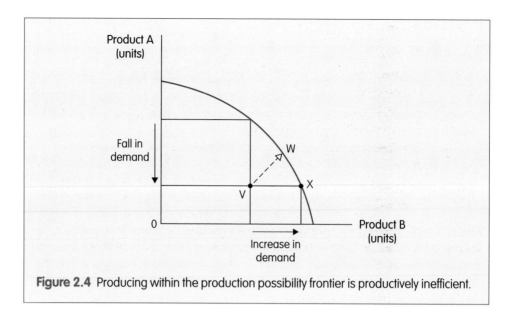

Figure 2.4 Producing within the production possibility frontier is productively inefficient.

levels of unemployment, and shops with very few customers in them; this economy will be productively inefficient. This can be illustrated using a PPF diagram: for example (see Figure 2.4), if an economy were to produce at point W and not V, then it would be making more of both A and B. No economy should be operating within the PPF, because it is wasting its resources. However, this can happen if resources do not reallocate effectively when conditions in an economy alter.

For example, demand for product B may increase, leading to firms wanting to move from A to B. Firms in industry A close down, and, in theory, they and their employees would switch to B. However, if managers and employees lack the necessary skills or experience, they may not be able to move easily. As a result, the economy may get stuck at V. Hopefully, over the long term, employees will be trained and will gain the skills required to take jobs. Firms will therefore be able to produce in industry B, enabling the economy to produce at a point such as X; however, in the short term at least, there is productive inefficiency. Alternatively, there could be a lack of demand in the economy, so that, although it can produce at W, customers can only afford the combination of products at V. Again, over time, demand will hopefully increase and the economy will end up on the frontier. Another reason for operating within the frontier may be the effect of poor management of the economy, meaning that production is inefficient and people's talents are not utilized fully.

■ Shifting the production possibility frontier outward

Once on the PPF, an economy can only produce more of both products by shifting the PPF outward—that is, by increasing the amount of both products that can be produced with the economy's resources. This is what happens over time when an economy grows. Economic growth enables more goods and services to become available to consumers.

An outward shift of the frontier might be due to:

- more training and better management of employees, enabling them to be more productive;

- greater investment in capital goods, such as machines and equipment—in the short run, this would mean that resources would have to be shifted from consumption goods toward capital goods, and in the long run, greater investment would enable the economy to produce more products for consumption;

- an increase in the population size, for example through greater net immigration or a rise in the birth rate;

- improvements in technology providing better ways of doing things, such as the improvements in communications technologies in recent years.

Most political parties put forward their policies to help an economy to grow in the future. Voters decide which policies they think are most likely to work. For more about economic growth, see Chapter 21.

What do you think?

How fast is your economy growing?
What actions would you take to make your economy grow faster if you were in government?

Put into practice

Imagine that technological developments enabled the production of product B to increase for any given amount of other resources, such as land, labour, and machinery. The technology has no impact on the production of A. Draw the new PPF that would occur following the technological development.

■ Consumption outside the production possibility frontier

The PPF shows what an economy can produce given its available resources. However, it is possible to consume outside the frontier through international trade. It may well be that another country can produce some items more efficiently than you can and that your economy is able to produce some products more efficiently than your partners overseas; through trade, both countries can benefit.

Imagine, for example, that an economy is producing at point W and then gives up ten units of product A (see Figure 2.5). Within its own country, it could produce only five units of B in return. If, however, it were able to find a country that is less efficient at producing A but better at producing B, then it would be able to sell these abroad at a profit. For example, it might be possible to sell its ten units of A for 20 units of B; this means that the economy could operate at Z.

The benefits of international trade are examined in detail in Chapter 29.

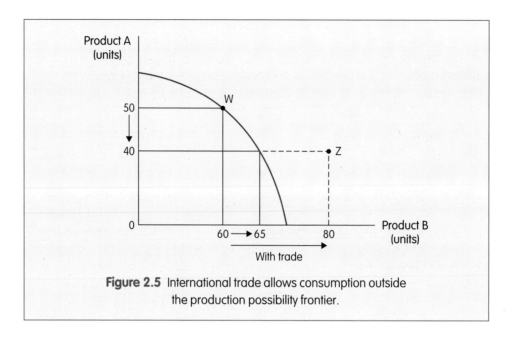

Figure 2.5 International trade allows consumption outside the production possibility frontier.

Put into practice

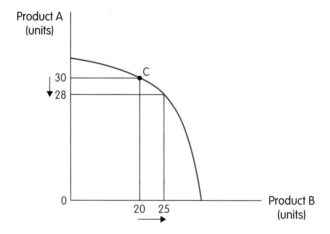

Figure 2.6 The benefits of international trade.

- Imagine that an economy is at point C in Figure 2.6. Within the domestic economy, what is the opportunity cost of five more units of B?
- Assume that two units of A can be traded abroad for 12 units of B. Then, starting at C, if an economy were to give up two units of A and trade overseas, how many units of B could it now have?

What do you think?

Which countries are the main trading partners of your own? What are the main exports?

Do you think that your economy is very dependent on trade? Is that a good or bad thing?

 Economics in context   India

India is developing into an open-market economy . . . Economic liberalization, including reduced controls on foreign trade and investment, began in the early 1990s, and has served to accelerate the country's growth, which has averaged more than 7% per year since 1997. India's diverse economy encompasses traditional village farming, modern agriculture, handicrafts, a wide range of modern industries and a multitude of services. Slightly more than half of the workforce is in agriculture, but services are the major source of economic growth, accounting for more than half of India's output, with only one-third of its labour force. India has capitalized on its large educated English-speaking population to become a major exporter of information technology services and software workers. An industrial slowdown early in 2008, followed by the global financial crisis, led annual income growth to slow to 6.5% in 2009, still the second-highest growth in the world among major economies.

Source: CIA Factbook

? Questions

India has grown rapidly in recent years and faster than most other countries. What might have accounted for such growth?

How would growth be shown on a PPF?

Do you think that a PPF could ever shift inwards? If so, why?

■ Present versus future decisions

The PPF is often used to illustrate the extent to which an economy is producing for the present or the future. Economies that focus on capital goods are investing for the long term: they are investing in machines and equipment that will allow the economy to produce more in the future. This will be shown over time by an outward shift of the PPF; when the machines are finished and being used, the economy can produce more. Economies that focus more on the here and now will produce more consumer goods; this is likely to lead to a smaller outward shift in the PPF over time, because the investment in the amount of machinery and technology is less.

What do you think?

Is it better for an economy to produce consumer goods—that is, focus on fulfilling people's demands today—or should it invest for the future?

The shape of the production possibility frontier

So far, we have drawn the PPF as concave to the origin. This is because of the assumptions that we make about what happens when resources to output are transferred from one industry to another. This depends on what is known as 'the returns to a factor'. If there are constant returns to a factor in industries A and B, then this means that every time resources are transferred from one industry to another, there is the same increase in output in B and the same decrease in output in industry A. This would lead to a PPF that is a straight line. For example, in the economy shown in Figure 2.7, every time a given number of resources are shifted from industry A to B, ten units of A are given up in return for 20 units of B.

In reality, resources are unlikely to be equally productive in both industries. Some equipment may be designed specifically for some types of production rather than others; some employees may not be able to transfer their skills easily from one sector to another. This may lead to 'diminishing returns to a factor'. This means that every time a given number of resources are transferred out of industry B into industry A, successively fewer units of A are produced (for example, see Figure 2.8). This means that the PPF is concave to the origin.

The concept of diminishing returns to a factor is examined in Chapter 9.

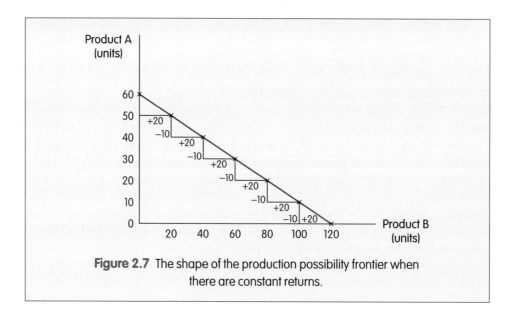

Figure 2.7 The shape of the production possibility frontier when there are constant returns.

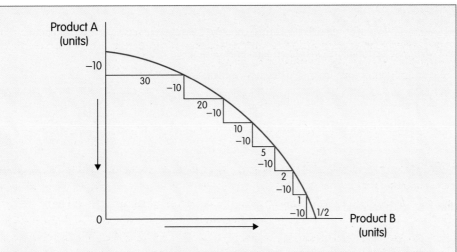

Figure 2.8 The shape of a production possibility frontier when there are diminishing returns. As resources are transferred into industry B, there are diminishing returns: successively less is produced each time.

Case study Immigration in the USA

The success of the USA over the centuries has been helped enormously by immigrants into the country. However, immigration is now a very controversial issue in the USA. Many of the immigrants working in the country at the moment are illegal, for example workers who have come over the border from Mexico. These immigrants want to be recognized and allowed to work in the USA officially, and on May Day 2006, over a million of them protested in rallies held in major cities across the country.

The USA accepts more legal immigrants as permanent residents than all other countries in the world combined. Over a million people were naturalized as US citizens in 2008. The leading emigrating countries to the USA were Mexico, India, and the Philippines. However, each year, up to a million illegal immigrants also enter the country, mostly from Latin American nations. There are now more than 11.5 million of them living in the USA. Over 2.5 million are based in California and over 1.4 million are in Texas.

The immigrants mainly work in particular industries. For example, around 22 per cent of all construction jobs in the USA are held by illegal workers. Other popular sectors are farming, cleaning, and preparing food. Typically, these are low-skilled, low-paid jobs. Overall, immigrants account for around 5 per cent of the workforce. Some argue that immigrants push down wages for everyone and take jobs away from Americans. Others argue that they provide a bigger workforce and help the economy. Defenders of immigration argue that the government receives tax receipts from immigrants and that the benefits paid to them are usually low—for example, most immigrants return home and do not retire in the USA, and so do not receive pensions.

? Questions

- How does immigration affect the PPF of an economy? Illustrate your answer using a diagram.
- In what ways can immigration help an economy?
- Do you think that economies should welcome immigration?
- Do you think that immigration should be controlled on economic grounds?

Checklist

Now that you have read this chapter, try to answer the following questions.

- ☐ Do you understand what is meant by a production possibility frontier (PPF)?
- ☐ Can you explain the shape and the position of the PPF?
- ☐ Do you understand the concept of productive efficiency?
- ☐ Do you understand what is meant by constant returns to a factor?
- ☐ Can you illustrate economic growth using a PPF?

Review questions

1 Can an economy produce outside the PPF? Can it consume outside?

2 Why might an economy be producing within the PPF?

3 What do you think is the best way in which to shift the PPF outward?

4 What do you think is the best point at which to be on the PPF?

5 In what way does the PPF illustrate the concept of opportunity cost?

Key learning points

- Given the present resources of an economy, there is a maximum combination of products that can be produced. This is shown by the PPF.
- The combination of goods and services produced may be determined, in theory, by the government or by market forces, or, in reality, by a combination of the two.
- If an economy is operating within the PPF, then it is productively inefficient.
- Economic growth can be seen by an outward shift of the PPF.
- By trading abroad, a country can consume outside its PPF.

Learn more

If you read Chapter 29, you can find out more about the principle of comparative advantage. This shows how economies can benefit from free trade and consume outside their PPF.

 Visit our Online Resource Centre at http://www.oxfordtextbooks.co.uk/orc/gillespie_econ2e/ for test questions and further information on topics covered in this chapter.

»3 Demand

In the previous chapter, we examined the maximum output of goods and services that an economy could produce given its resources. However, we did not analyse in detail what would determine which combination of products would be produced and consumed. What makes an economy produce more of some products and fewer of others? This depends on the nature of the economic system. In a free market, the allocation of resources is determined by supply and demand. The next three chapters consider the market forces of supply and demand that underpin the free market system, and the interaction between the two. We begin with demand.

LEARNING OBJECTIVES

By the end of this chapter, you should be able to:

✔ explain what is meant by effective demand;

✔ explain what is shown by a demand curve;

✔ understand the difference between a change in the quantity demanded and a change in demand;

✔ explain the possible causes of a shift in a demand curve;

✔ appreciate the difference between marginal and total utility.

■ Introduction

In a free market economy, the basic economic problems of what to produce, how to produce, and who gets what are solved by market forces.

- The demand and supply of goods and services determine what is produced and sold.
- The demand and supply of resources determine the combination of different resources being used—for example, how much labour and how much machinery are employed in a given industry, and how much people are paid.

- The amount that people earn, their wealth, and the relative prices of products determine who can afford to buy different goods and services.

Imagine that changes in technology lead to a greater demand for website designers and less demand for travel agents, because people can search for and book holidays directly online. This should lead to more web design companies setting up and more designers being recruited. Demand for this service, and therefore demand for resources in this industry, increase, highlighting how the markets for products and factors of production are linked. Meanwhile, there will be less demand for travel agency services and these businesses may have to make people redundant. Less demand for the product reduces demand for resources in this industry. The combination of products produced by the economy has moved, so that we are at a new point on the production possibility frontier (PPF). In the market for resources, rewards will go up for the web designers and down for the sales assistants, encouraging the reallocation of resources as the economy adjusts to change.

An economy is made up of millions of markets, and an understanding of supply and demand conditions is therefore crucial to economic analysis. All markets, whether for housing, oil, shares, labour, property, currencies, or even university places, are influenced by the market forces of supply and demand. We shall therefore begin with an analysis of demand in this chapter, then look at supply in Chapter 5, and finally put the two sides of a market together to examine the concept of equilibrium in Chapter 6.

■ The demand curve

The demand for a product is the quantity that customers are willing and able to buy at each and every price, all other things being unchanged. This is shown on a demand curve. A demand curve measures the quantity that customers are actually able to buy at each and every price, not only the quantity that they would like to buy. It therefore represents what is called 'effective demand', and depends on what they want and what they can afford. For example, at the price P1, the quantity Q1 is demanded (see Figure 3.1). At a lower price, P2, a greater quantity Q2 is demanded.

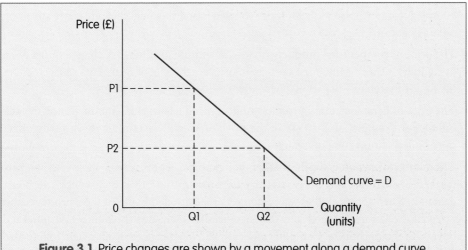

Figure 3.1 Price changes are shown by a movement along a demand curve.

Put into practice

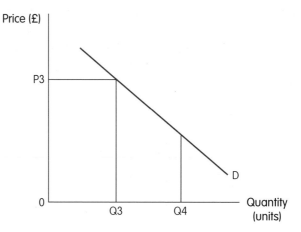

Figure 3.2 Price and quantity combinations.

Consider the demand curve in Figure 3.2.

- What quantity is demanded at price P3?
- What price is necessary for quantity Q4 to be demanded?

The level of demand for a product depends on factors such as the following.

- **The price level** As the price changes, this influences the relative value of the product compared with other goods and services, and the amount that customers want and are able to buy. Higher tuition fees may deter some students from going to university, for example. Lower prices may make a product more affordable and increase the quantity demanded.

- **The customers' incomes** This influences what customers can afford. If the economy is booming, for example, and people are earning more, this might lead to more spending on many goods.

- **The price of competitors' products (that is, substitute products)** A change in the price of Cadbury's Dairy Milk, for example, may affect the sale of Mars bars. A decrease in the price of satellite navigation devices may reduce demand for maps.

- **The price of complementary products (that is, products used in conjunction with each other)** For example, an increase in the price of Sony Playstation consoles may affect sales of Playstation computer games.

- **The number of customers in the market** For example, a product may be aimed at a new market segment (such as a new country or a new group of buyers), which can boost demand. When sports clothes manufacturers repositioned many of their products and targeted the leisurewear market, this significantly increased the number of potential buyers for their products. Computer games are now being developed to help to improve

the memory and to keep alert; this is to target the older buyer, because most buyers of computer games at the moment are relatively young.

- **Other factors** The factors affecting the demand for a particular product will, of course, vary. For example, the demand for textbooks will be influenced by the number of students; the demand for suncream will be influenced by the weather; the demand for nicotine patches may be affected by anti-smoking laws.

The shape of the demand curve

A demand curve is usually downward-sloping. This is because of the law of diminishing marginal utility. This law states that, as buyers consume additional units of a product, the extra satisfaction (or utility) that they gain from each unit will fall. The second cup of tea is not as satisfying as the first in a given time period; the tenth is not as satisfying as the ninth. If the extra satisfaction of a unit declines, then the amount that consumers are willing to pay to buy it will fall as well. For a higher quantity to be demanded, the price must therefore be lower, because the satisfaction from these additional units is less according to the law of diminishing marginal utility. We are assuming that consumers are rational and that, given a limited income, they allocate their spending between products to maximize their welfare. If by consuming more of a particular product the extra satisfaction falls, then you will only buy this if it becomes cheaper.

Marginal and total utility

- **Marginal utility** measures the extra utility (or satisfaction) from consuming an additional unit of a product.
- **Total utility** is the total satisfaction from the consumption of a product.

If, for example, the extra utility from consuming another unit of the product is six units of utility (called 'utils'), then the total utility will increase by 6 utils.

Notice in Table 3.1 that the law of diminishing marginal utility operates (see also Figure 3.3). This means that the total utility increases at a diminishing rate. When the marginal utility is 0, this means that there is no increase in total satisfaction from the consumption of that unit (in this case, the sixth unit); at this level of consumption, utility would be maximized. It is possible that you can overconsume some items (for example, eat or drink too much in a given time period), in which case the marginal utility might be negative (the seventh unit) and the total utility would then fall.

The difference between marginal and total utility is highlighted by the 'paradox of value'. In the case of water, there is a relatively large amount of water available and consumed in the world. This means that, although total utility is high, the extra utility is low and therefore people will not pay much for an additional unit of this, even though it is

Table 3.1 The relationship between marginal utility and total utility

Units	Marginal utility	Total utility
1	10	10
2	8	18
3	6	24
4	4	28
5	2	30
6	0	30
7	−2	28
8	−4	24

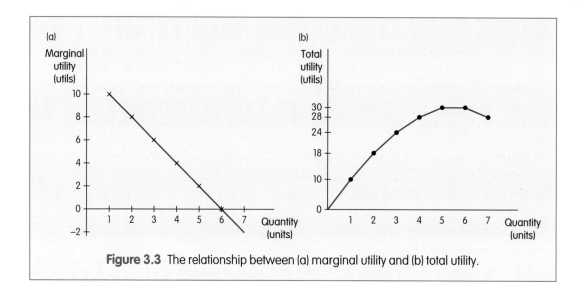

Figure 3.3 The relationship between (a) marginal utility and (b) total utility.

essential to survival. In the case of diamonds, consumption is much lower, meaning the marginal utility is high (although total utility is not, compared with water); people will pay a lot for another diamond even though it is not essential to survival.

■ A movement along the demand curve

If the price of a product falls, then there will be more units that have a higher extra utility than the price, and the quantity demanded will increase. The rational consumer will consume any unit shown on the demand curve where the extra utility is greater or equal to the price charged.

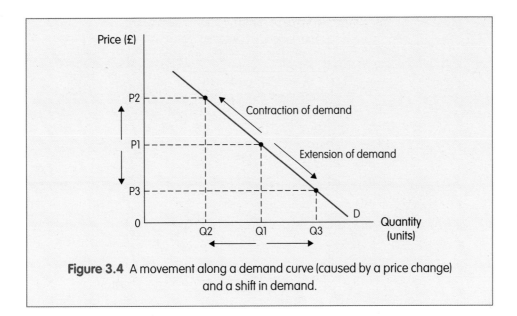

Figure 3.4 A movement along a demand curve (caused by a price change) and a shift in demand.

If the price increases, there are likely to be fewer units worth purchasing and the quantity demanded will fall. A change in the price of a product, such as P1 – P3 (see Figure 3.4), therefore leads to a change in the quantity demanded (Q1 – Q3). This is known as a movement along the demand curve.

An increase in the quantity demanded due to a price fall is called an extension of demand (Q1 – Q3). A decrease in the quantity demanded is called a contraction of demand (Q1 – Q2).

Income and substitution effects

Movements along the demand curve can also be explained in terms of income and substitution effects.

• The **substitution effect** occurs when consumers switch towards a relatively cheaper product. If the price of a product falls, consumers always switch towards it, because it is relatively cheaper than alternatives, and so the substitution effect increases the quantity demanded.

• The **income effect** occurs because, if a good is cheaper, consumers can purchase more with the same nominal income. Their money can buy more, which means that their real income increases. In the case of most goods, having more real income increases the quantity demanded.

This means that, with a fall in price, consumers substitute towards the relatively cheaper product; with more real income, they want to purchase more. These two effects increase the overall quantity demanded.

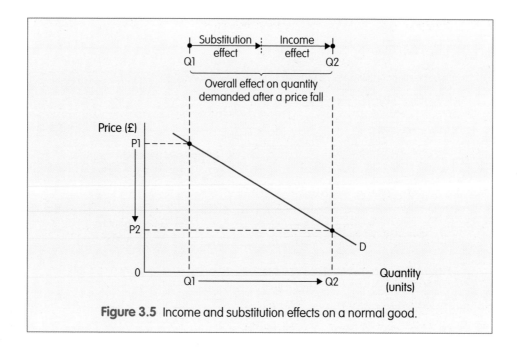

Figure 3.5 Income and substitution effects on a normal good.

Example

The equation for a straight-line demand curve can be given in the form:

$Q = a - bP$

For example:

$Q = 80 - 2P$

where

- Q is the quantity demanded; and
- P is the price in £s.

a. If the price is £5, the quantity demanded is:

$Q = 80 - (2 \times 5) = 80 - 10 = 70$ units

If the price increases to £10, the quantity demanded is:

$Q = 80 - (2 \times 10) = 80 - 20 = 60$ units

This shows that, given this equation, the higher the price, the lower the quantity demanded. This is shown as a movement along the demand curve, because the price has changed.

b. If the equation changes to $Q = 150 - 2P$, then the curve will have shifted, because more will be demanded at each and every price.
So, if the price is £5, the quantity demanded is:

$Q = 150 - (2 \times 5) = 150 - 10 = 140$ units

If the price increases to £10, the quantity demanded is:

$Q = 150 - (2 \times 10) = 150 - 20 = 130$ units

c. If $Q = 80 - 2P$ and the quantity demanded is 50 units, then:

$50 = 80 - 2P$

also expressed as

$2P = 80 - 50$
$2P = 30$
$P = \dfrac{30}{2} = £15$

This quantity is demanded at a price of £15.

Put into practice

If the equation for a demand curve is $Q = 50 - 4P$:

- what is the quantity demanded if the price is £5?
- what is the quantity demanded if the price is £10?
- what is the price at which the quantity demanded is 46 units?
- what is the price at which the quantity demanded is 42 units?

Upward-sloping demand curves

In exceptional cases, the demand curve for a product may be upward-sloping (see Figure 3.6). This may be due to one of the following two reasons.

- **The product is a Giffen good** This is a very basic product that is essential to survival in a poor economy, such as rice in a developing economy. When the price of this type of product rises, consumers find that they are spending so much on it (because it is essential to survival and one of the few things that they can afford to survive) that they have very little left over for anything else. Given the fact that consumers have so few funds left, they end up buying even more of the original product—that is, the quantity demanded increases when the price increases, because nothing else is now affordable.

- **The product is a Veblen good** Customers believe that the higher price of the product reflects a better quality or has a better image, and therefore want more even though it is more expensive. This type of product was described by Veblen (1899) who highlighted the desire by some customers for 'conspicuous consumption'—that is, they want to be seen to be buying more expensive items! For example, retailers sometimes find that a reduction in the price of a bottle of wine leads to a fall in sales, because buyers assume that the quality is worse or do not want to be seen buying cheap wine (or giving it to their guests).

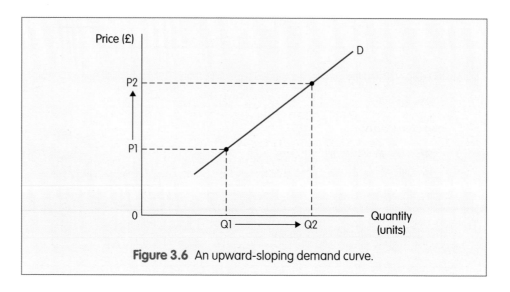

Figure 3.6 An upward-sloping demand curve.

Put into practice

If the equation for a demand curve is $Q = 20 + 2P$, why does this mean that the demand curve for this product is upward-sloping? Show your answer, using calculations.

In terms of income and substitution effects, what is happening with Giffen goods is that a fall in price means that:

• consumers want to substitute towards this product, so this increases the quantity demanded; and

• an increase in real income due to the lower price leads to a fall in quantity demanded as consumers switch to more luxurious goods.

The substitution and income effects therefore work against each other, and in the case of a Giffen good, the income effect outweighs the substitution effect and the overall quantity demanded falls with a price fall (see Figure 3.7). This means that the demand curve is upward-sloping.

▨ A shift in the demand curve

The demand curve for a product will shift if at each and every price customers are willing and able to buy more or less than they did before (see Figure 3.8). A movement

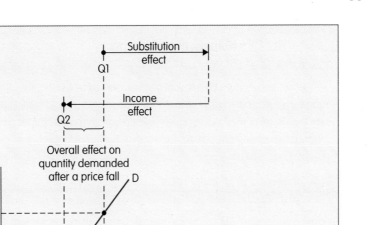

Figure 3.7 Income and substitution effects on a Giffen good.

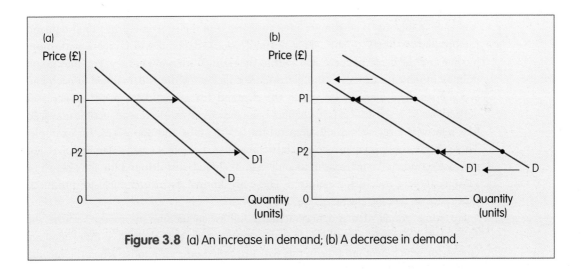

Figure 3.8 (a) An increase in demand; (b) A decrease in demand.

along a demand curve occurs when the price changes and all other things remain un-changed. A shift in demand occurs if these other factors do change. If consumers demand more, the curve will shift to the right. If they demand less, then it will shift to the left. When the demand curve shifts, this is known as a change in demand (as opposed to a change in the quantity demanded).

Influences on demand

In the toy market, over 50 per cent of sales are made around the Christmas period. Demand is particularly difficult to estimate in the toy market because of particular 'fad' products that take off each year, often linked to films, television programmes, or games, and often to the surprise of retailers. Pokemon, Thunderbirds, Tamagochi, Furby, Teletubbies, and Power Rangers are examples of past Christmas hits.

? Question

What particular problems are there likely to be for producers in the toy market?

What do you think?

What do you think will be the big hit in the toy market next Christmas? How would you try to estimate this?

The reasons for a shift in demand

The reasons for a shift in demand (that is, a change in demand) include the following.

- **A change in income** If customers have an increase in their incomes, then their demand for products is likely to shift. For 'normal' goods, demand will increase with more income and the demand curve will shift to the right. With more money, you may go on holiday more, eat out more, and go to more concerts. More is demanded at each and every price. The amount by which the demand for a particular product increases depends on how sensitive it is to changes in income. A given increase in income may lead to a relatively large increase in demand for health clubs and fine wines, for example. These goods are known as income-elastic products. For other goods, demand may not increase so much. An increase in income is unlikely to boost demand for shoe polish or toothpaste very much, for example. These are known as income-inelastic products. (For more on income elasticity, see Chapter 4.)

  For some goods, demand may actually fall when income increases, because the consumers switch to something that they prefer now that they have more income. Goods for which demand falls in this way are called inferior goods. When the income of developing economies grows, households usually switch from bicycles to motorbikes as a means of transport. The bicycles in this case are inferior and the motorbikes are normal products. However, the status of goods will vary for different people and over time. With even more income growth in developing economies, demand for motorbikes tends to fall as demand for cars increases. Motorbikes have now become inferior over time, as consumers now choose another, 'better', product.

NOTE This relationship between income and quantity demanded for inferior goods also affects the impact of a price change. If a price falls, consumers automatically switch towards this relatively cheaper product, which is the substitution effect. However, the lower price means that real income has increased and, in the case of an inferior good, this reduces the quantity demanded as consumers switch towards a more luxurious alternative. This means that the substitution effect and income effects following a price fall work in different directions; overall, the substitution effect outweighs the income effects and so the quantity demanded increases, but by less than in the case of a normal good.

What do you think?

Imagine that you win £1 million on the lottery. What products would you buy more of? What would you buy less of?

Economics in context — Demand for cars in China

The demand for cars in China has grown very rapidly in recent years. With around 5 million cars sold each year, China is already the third largest car market in the world after the USA (17 million cars sold per year) and Japan (around 9 million). At the same time, the Chinese government has spent heavily on the road network. By the end of 2004, the country had 21,000 miles of motorways, more than double the 2000 figure. In 1987, it had none! Only the USA now has more motorways than China. China's total road network is now the third longest in the world.

China is aiming to put the car industry at the heart of its economy. In bigger cities, consumers have gone straight from bicycles to cars, missing out motorbikes, because these were banned or the use of them was severely restricted. A big boost occurred when China joined the World Trade Organization (WTO) in 2001. This opened up its markets to trade, allowing foreign profits into the country, and car prices fell rapidly. Demand has also been boosted by cheap borrowing from state banks (in the past, banks did not lend to individuals) and by social change. Many state-owned factories have been sold off; these have then been closed or shifted to suburban areas. Employees now have to travel much further to work and therefore need a car.

? Questions

The above highlights how the Chinese government is intervening in the economy to influence decisions, but that there is a free market as well. Would you describe such an economy as free market, mixed, or planned?

If the government invests more into roads, what might the opportunity cost be?

What do you think are the main factors affecting demand for new cars? Do these differ from the main factors affecting demand for other products?

The demand for champagne

The UK is the largest customer for French champagne, with British consumers drinking over 30 million bottles per year. The demand for champagne is influenced by factors such as the following.

- **The number of celebrations happening** The demand was particularly high when there were celebrations for the Millennium. During any given year, sales are particularly high just before New Year.
- **Income** Higher levels of disposable income stimulate demand for many alcoholic drinks. Champagne is particularly sensitive to income changes.
- **Socio-economic trends** The demand for champagne is particularly high from the higher-income groups, so as they prosper, demand for champagne grows.

? Questions

Do you think that the demand for champagne is affected by different factors from the demand for other types of alcoholic drink? Why?

What do you think are the main factors affecting the overall demand for alcoholic drinks in a country? Do you think that demand is likely to grow or fall in your country in the future? Why?

- **A change in marketing policies** Managers of organizations will continually review their marketing strategies to try to boost the demand for their products. Changes to their marketing strategy may include new promotional campaigns or finding new distribution channels to make it easier for customers to buy the products. Effective marketing should shift the demand curve to the right.

The demand for cereal

The majority of cereals are sold through supermarkets. In the UK, over 90 per cent of sales are through stores such as Tesco and Sainsbury's. This gives the supermarkets a lot of power over the manufacturers. To increase demand, cereal manufacturers, such as Kelloggs and Cereal Partners, are always looking for new ways of getting their products to the market.

Recent efforts have included vending machines in schools and sports clubs. Also, in the USA, the fast-food chain Cereality has begun enabling customers to mix and match their cereals to tailor their own products.

Cereal companies have also stressed the health benefits of eating cereal in an attempt to boost demand. They highlight the vitamins in the cereal and the low level of calories. In the case of cereals, demand is influenced by both parents and children. The parents often make the final decision about what to buy, because they are paying for it; they are usually interested in the health issues.

The children influence this decision by making clear what they want; they are often influenced by gifts or promotional offers.

The demand for a product should not be taken as given: it will change over time. For example, in the UK, fewer people have breakfast than those living elsewhere, and people in the UK tend to eat on the move. Marketing managers have to respond to such changes. For example, many cereal manufacturers have moved into producing snack cereal bars or offering cereals in vending machines to be sold at work.

 Question

Cereals tend to be eaten mainly by children rather than people in their 20s and 30s. Why do you think this is and what could you do, if you were the marketing manager of a cereal manufacturer, to boost sales to these older age groups?

- **A change in the number of buyers** Over time, more people may move into an area or a country, creating more potential buyers. Alternatively, a change in customers' tastes may lead to more demand. In recent years, for example, there has been an increasing interest in healthy foods and fitness. This has increased demand for low-fat products and health clubs. At the same time, it has shifted demand for many fast-food restaurants to the left. Companies such as McDonald's have had to reconsider their range of products and marketing strategies.

- **A change in the price of substitute products** Customers have choices when it comes to deciding what to buy. You may be deciding whether to go for a meal out or the cinema, or choosing between decorating the kitchen and going on holiday. This means that all products have substitutes—that is, other products that customers may consider buying as an alternative. If these substitutes become more or less expensive, then this will affect demand for the original product. For example, if the price of football tickets goes up, you may decide to stop going to see the match every week and spend your money on Sky TV instead. The demand for Sky TV would shift to the right, because the price of football tickets increased. Easy, cheap access to reviews of restaurants, hotels, and cities online is leading to a fall in demand for guide books.

- **A change in the price of complements** Complementary products are those that you tend to buy together, for example, writing paper and envelopes, digital cameras and photographic printing paper, and flowers and greeting cards. Changes in the price of one of these items may affect sales of the other. If the cost of filter coffee increases significantly, it may decrease sales of filter coffee machines. If the price of airfares to Spain falls, the sales of suncream may increase as more people go abroad.

- **Weather** Changes in the climate can have a significant effect on the sales of some products. A hot summer boosts the demand for barbecues and lager. Amazingly, it also boosts sales of tanning lotion: office workers want to give the impression that they have been outside or on holiday and so buy fake tan. A wet winter increases the demand for umbrellas.

- **Events** Big events, such as sporting matches, can have a large impact on retail sales. In the build-up to an event such as the Olympics, retail sales are high as people stock up; sales are low during the competition, because people stay at home to watch it.

Economics in context   **England and hot weather**

England's defeat by Germany in the first knock-out stage of the last World Cup tournament in 2010 coincided with one of the hottest days of the year in the UK. Sales of televisions and food ahead of the World Cup in June were highlighted as a key reason for a strong increase in retail sales in May. However, analysts believe that the high temperatures at the weekend of the England match were more significant for sales of barbecue food than the football, which would have encouraged people to sit in front of the television 'with beer and a pizza'. It also helped clothes retailers to sell off their summer clothes ranges.

Garden centres and outdoor furniture retailers also benefit from hot weather. Meanwhile, cinema operator Cineworld said that it expected to regain filmgoers after the World Cup caused a slump in revenue growth.

In England's first match after the World Cup, following its disappointing performance in that competition, demand for tickets was so low that the price had to be cut by a third to try to fill the stadium.

 Questions

Major events can have a big effect on the demand for certain products. What businesses are likely to experience an increase in demand as a result of the 2012 Olympics?

What products are likely to experience an increase in demand during cold weather?

What factors do you think would determine whether a price cut of a third would fill the stadium?

- **A change in social patterns** Over time, the nature of society will change and this influences demand patterns for different products. In the UK, for example, the average age has been increasing over the last 50 years, the typical family size has been decreasing, there are more divorces, and there is a greater interest in healthy and organic foods. A noticeable development in the UK has been a change in the way in which we eat. Families are much less likely to sit down together and eat a family meal than they were 20 years ago; Sunday dinners are largely a thing of the past and we tend to eat now by 'grazing'—that is, by eating as we move about. This has helped firms such as Pret A Manger, which sells sandwiches, but negatively affected others such as Waterford and Wedgwood, which make traditional bone china crockery—something for which there is much less need these days, because formal meals are increasingly uncommon.

What do you think?

What do you think are the major determinants of the demand for each of the following?

a. New cars

b. Textbooks

c. Diamonds

d. Health care

e. Flat-screen TVs

f. Eggs

Put into practice

Using diagrams, show the effect on demand of the following.

- The effect on demand for a normal good if income decreases
- The effect on demand for an inferior good if income increases
- The effect on demand for a product of an increase in the price of a complementary product
- The effect on demand for a product of a decrease in the price of a substitute product

Put into practice

What is the only cause of a movement *along* a demand curve for good X?

a. A change in consumers' tastes

b. A change in consumers' income

c. A change in the price of the good

d. A change in the size of the population

Economics in context — More people living alone in the UK

By 2021, more than a third of the UK population will be living alone. Since 1975, Britain's population has risen by 5 per cent and the number of single-person households has risen by 31 per cent. The proportion of income spent by single-person households on alcohol, tobacco, and recreational drugs is noticeably higher than that of households with two or more people. The top supermarket products bought by people living alone are slimming aids; other products that they are more likely to buy are Marmite and herbal tea.

Supermarkets are now trying harder to target such individuals. Sainsbury's has doubled its range of 25 cl bottles, and has seen strong growth in the sale of its 2 l boxes of wine compared to its 3 l boxes. Its 'Taste the Difference' ready-meal range has also been extended to meals for one. Unilever, meanwhile, is making mini jars of Marmite and single servings of ready-made soups.

 Question

The above shows how the existence of more single-person households affects the demand for some products. In the UK, the population is also ageing. List five types of business that might benefit from this and five that might suffer.

Individual and market demand

An individual's demand curve shows the quantity that a consumer is willing and able to buy at each and every price, others things being unchanged. The market demand is the sum of all of the individual demand curves (see Figure 3.9). To derive the market demand, all of the individual demands are horizontally summated—that is, all of the individual demands are added up at each price.

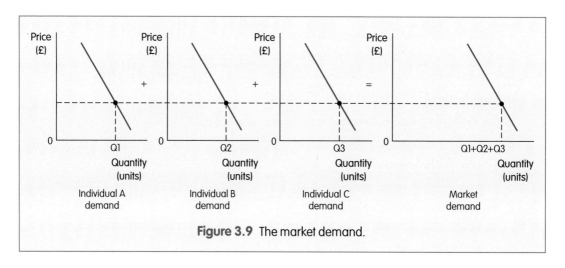

Figure 3.9 The market demand.

Case study Apple

In 2010, Apple had to delay the international launch of its iPad computer for a month, blaming 'surprisingly strong US demand' that was higher than the company's ability to produce them. More than 500,000 were delivered to retailers and customers in its first week on sale, but these soon sold out. The company had planned to launch the touch-screen device internationally at the end of April, after beginning sales in the USA on 3 April. But the strong demand meant that it could not hit that date.

The company said in a statement: 'We will announce international pricing and begin taking online pre-orders on Monday, May 10. We know that many international customers waiting to buy an iPad will be disappointed by this news, but we hope they will be pleased to learn the reason—the iPad is a runaway success in the US thus far.'

The news was a disappointment to thousands of people outside the USA who wanted to get the machines as soon as possible.

The iPad is a touch-screen computer with a 9.7-inch screen, which uses the same operating system as Apple's iPhone and iPod Touch. It comes in two basic models: one with WiFi wireless Internet connectivity, and another with both WiFi and 3G mobile connectivity.

Although Apple announced the iPad in January and gave US pricing at the time—starting from $499 for the cheapest model—it repeatedly declined to give any guidance about international prices. That may be to give it room for manoeuvre and to let it raise the price of non-US versions to control demand. The USA is by far the largest market for Apple products, generating about half its revenues.

Analysts have estimated that Apple could sell between 2.5 million and 6 million iPads this year, which would make it by far the largest seller of 'tablet' computers in the world. It is estimated that about 1.25 million non-Apple tablets will be sold in 2010.

❓ Questions

- What factors do you think influenced the demand for the iPad? How might these factors change over time?
- Do you think Apple was simply lucky with the iPad?
- What effect might the delayed launch have on sales of the iPad?
- The delay gave the company time to think about the international price of the product. What factors might determine how much the company could increase the price outside the USA?

Checklist

Now that you have read this chapter, try to answer the following questions.

☐ Can you explain what is meant by effective demand?

☐ Can you explain what is shown by a demand curve?

☐ Do you understand the difference between a change in the quantity demanded and a change in demand?

☐ Can you explain the possible causes of a shift in a demand curve?

☐ Do you understand the difference between marginal and total utility?

Review questions

1 Does a demand curve show what a consumer would like to buy at each and every price?

2 What is the difference between a movement along, and a shift in, a demand curve?

3   Does an increase in income always shift the demand curve to the right? Explain your answer.

4   Does the quantity demanded always fall if the price increases?

5   To what extent do you think a business can control the demand for its products?

Key learning points

- Demand shows what customers are willing and able to purchase at each and every price, not only what they want to buy.

- A movement along a demand curve occurs when there is a change in the price, all other things being unchanged.

- A shift in the demand curve occurs when more or less is demanded at each and every price.

- A demand curve is usually downward-sloping, but in some cases (such as a Veblen or Giffen good), it can be upward-sloping.

- The marginal utility shows the extra utility from consuming a unit; the total utility shows the total satisfaction that a consumer has from consuming a product.

- The marginal utility from consuming a product declines when additional units are consumed.

Reference

Veblen, T. (1899) *The Theory of the Leisure Class*, Macmillan, New York

Learn more

A demand curve can be derived using indifference curve analysis. This analyses the impact of a change in price and income in terms of consumers' utility. To find out more about indifference curve analysis and how a consumer maximizes utility, visit the Online Resource Centre.

 Visit our Online Resource Centre at http://www.oxfordtextbooks.co.uk/orc/gillespie_econ2e/ for test questions and further information on topics covered in this chapter.

The elasticity of demand

4

In the previous chapter, we examined the factors determining the level of demand for a product, and the differences between a shift in demand and a movement along a demand curve. In this chapter, we examine the extent to which changes in a number of variables can affect demand. For example, how much does demand change when the price or income changes and what determines the scale of these changes?

LEARNING OBJECTIVES

By the end of this chapter, you should be able to:

✔ explain the meaning of the price, income, and the cross-price elasticity of demand;

✔ outline the determinants of the price elasticity of demand for a product;

✔ explain the difference between a normal and an inferior good;

✔ understand the difference between a substitute and a complement;

✔ understand the significance of the concept of elasticity for a firm's planning;

✔ appreciate the limitations of the concept of elasticity of demand.

■ The elasticity of demand

The managers of a business will naturally be interested in what affects the demand for their products. If they can determine what affects their sales, they can then try to plan accordingly. For example, they can estimate the staff levels that they will need, the stocks that they have to hold, and their projected profits.

To estimate the likely demand for their products in the future, managers may use the concept of the elasticity of demand. This examines the sensitivity of demand to a number of other factors, such as price, income, and the prices of other products.

The general equation for the elasticity of demand is:

$$\text{Elasticity of demand} = \frac{\text{Percentage change in the quantity demanded}}{\text{Percentage change in a variable (such as price or income)}}$$

The following are the two keys to understanding the elasticity of demand.

- **The sign of the answer** If this is a negative answer, then it means that the change in the quantity demanded and the change in the variable move in opposite directions: for example, the answer would be negative if an increase in price were to decrease the quantity demanded or a fall in income were to increase the quantity demanded. A positive answer means that the variable and the quantity demanded move in the same direction—that is, both increase or both decrease: for example, the answer would be positive if an increase in income were to increase the quantity demanded of a product.

- **The size (or value) of the answer** The size of the answer shows how sensitive demand is to the variable. If the value of the answer (ignoring the sign—that is, ignoring whether it is positive or negative) is greater than one (> 1), then it means that the quantity demanded has changed more than the variable, and demand is said to be elastic. (Looking at the equation, if the answer is > 1, then the numerator has changed more than the denominator.) If the answer (ignoring the sign) is less than one (< 1), then this means that the change in the quantity demanded is less than the change in the variable. In this case, demand is said to be inelastic.

For example, if a change in price of 10 per cent were to lead to a change in quantity demand of 20 per cent, the size of the price elasticity would be:

$$\frac{20\%}{10\%} = 2 \text{ (that is, elastic)}$$

If a change in price of 10 per cent were to lead to a change in quantity demand of 5 per cent, the size of the price elasticity would be:

$$\frac{5\%}{10\%} = 0.5 \text{ (that is, inelastic)}$$

▩ The price elasticity of demand

The price elasticity of demand measures the change in the quantity demanded of a product relative to a change in price. Basically, this measures how sensitive demand is to price. If the prices at your favourite coffee shop were to go up, would you stop going there completely? Would you go less often? Would you drink less coffee when you are there? Naturally, the coffee shop manager would be interested in the impact of any price change on sales. Would the size of the impact on the quantity demanded be different if your bus

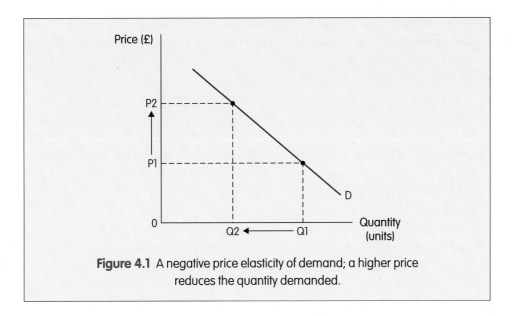

Figure 4.1 A negative price elasticity of demand; a higher price reduces the quantity demanded.

fare to get to work were to go up? Would you be likely to switch to another form of transport? What if the price of a haircut at your local hairdresser were to increase? How much would sales fall off there? The answers to all of these questions are linked to the concept of the price elasticity of demand.

The price elasticity of demand is calculated using the following equation:

$$\text{Price elasticity of demand} = \frac{\text{Percentage change in the quantity demanded}}{\text{Percentage change in the price of the product}}$$

In most cases, the price elasticity of demand is likely to be a negative number, because a price increase will reduce the quantity demanded (and vice versa)—that is, the answer is negative because the two variables move in opposite directions—assuming that the demand curve is downward-sloping (see Figure 4.1).

Once the sign (positive or negative) of the price elasticity of demand has been analysed, the next thing to consider is the size of the answer, which shows us how elastic or inelastic demand is in relation to price. For example, if the answer is 3 (ignoring whether it is positive or negative), this means that the percentage change in the quantity demanded is three times the percentage change in price. A 1 per cent change in price will lead to a 3 per cent change in the quantity demanded. This means that demand is sensitive to price.

If the value of the price elasticity is 0.5, this means that the quantity demanded changes 0.5 times as much as price (in percentages). This means that demand is not sensitive to price. A 1 per cent change in price will lead to a 0.5 per cent change in the quantity demanded. Whether the answer is positive or negative shows the direction of the relationship between price and quantity demanded, but does not show the strength of the relationship, because this depends on the value of the answer, not the sign.

Any answer (ignoring the sign) that is > 1 is known as a price-elastic product: the quantity demanded will change by more than the price (in percentages). If a product has a price

Table 4.1 The values of the price elasticity of demand

	Value (ignoring the sign)	Meaning
Price inelastic	< 1	The percentage change in the quantity demanded is less than the percentage change in price
Unitary elastic	1	The percentage change in the quantity demanded equals the percentage change in price
Price elastic	> 1	The percentage change in the quantity demanded is more than the percentage change in price

elasticity of demand of < 1 (ignoring the sign), this means that demand is price inelastic. The change in the quantity demanded is less than the change in price (in percentages). If a product has a price elasticity of demand equal to one (= 1), this is known as unitary price elasticity of demand. This means that the change in the quantity demanded is equal to the change in price (in percentages). These cases are summarized in Table 4.1.

If the price elasticity of demand is zero (0), this means that price changes have no effect on the quantity demanded. If the price elasticity of demand is infinity (∞), this means that a change in price will have an infinite effect on the quantity demanded.

Example

Suppose that the quantity demanded of a good rises from 200 to 300 units when the price falls from £10 to £6. This means that:

$$\text{Percentage change in the quantity demanded} = \left(\frac{+100}{200}\right) \times 100 = +50\%$$

$$\text{Percentage change in price} = \left(\frac{-4}{10}\right) \times 100 = -40\%$$

$$\text{Price elasticity of demand} = \frac{+50}{-40} = -1.25$$

The negative sign in the price elasticity of demand shows that the quantity demanded falls as price increases. The 1.25 shows that demand is price elastic. The quantity demanded changes by 1.25 times as much as price (50 per cent compared to 40 per cent).

NOTE To calculate a percentage change, we use the following expression:

$$\frac{\text{Change in value}}{\text{Original value}} \times 100$$

It should be noted that the price elasticity of demand can also be calculated using the following equation:

$$\text{Price elasticity of demand} = \frac{\text{Change in the quantity demanded}}{\text{Change in price}} \times \frac{\text{Original price}}{\text{Original quantity demanded}}$$

For the example above:

$$\text{Price elasticity of demand} = \frac{+100}{-4} \times \frac{10}{200} = -1.25$$

Example

a. Imagine that the price of a product falls from £10 to £9 and the quantity demanded rises from 400 units to 500 units. This means that the change in the quantity demanded is:

$$\left(\frac{100}{400}\right) \times 100 = 25\%$$

The change in price is:

$$\left(\frac{-1}{10}\right) \times 100 = -10\%$$

The price elasticity of demand is:

$$\left(\frac{25\%}{-10\%}\right) = -2.5$$

This means that demand is price elastic, because its value (ignoring the sign) is > 1. The change in the quantity demanded is 2.5 times the change in price.

b. Imagine that the price of a product falls from £20 to £10 and the quantity demanded rises from 400 units to 500 units. This means that the change in the quantity demanded is:

$$\left(\frac{100}{400}\right) \times 100 = 25\%$$

The change in price is:

$$\left(\frac{-10}{20}\right) \times 100 = -50\%$$

The price elasticity of demand is:

$$\left(\frac{25\%}{-50\%}\right) = -0.5$$

This means that the demand is price inelastic, because the value is < 1.

c. If the price elasticity of demand for a product is –2, then this shows that a change in price has twice the effect on quantity demanded in percentages (because the value is 2) and they act in opposite directions (because the answer is negative).

For example, a 5 per cent increase in price leads to a fall in quantity demanded calculated as:

$$2 \times 5\% = 10\%$$

A 5 per cent fall in price leads to a 10 per cent rise in the quantity demanded of the product.

d. Imagine that the price elasticity of demand is −3 and the price of the product is cut by 10 per cent. The original quantity demanded is 200 units. With the price cut, then, given that the price elasticity of demand is negative, this means that the quantity demanded will now increase. If the price is cut is 10 per cent, then the quantity demanded increases as follows:

$$3 \times 10\% = 30\%$$

$$30\% \times 200 \text{ units} = \left(\frac{30}{100}\right) \times 200 = 60 \text{ units}$$

So the new quantity demanded is:

$$200 \text{ units} + 60 \text{ units} = 260 \text{ units}$$

NOTE To calculate X per cent of a number Y, we use:

$$\left(\frac{X}{100}\right) \times Y$$

For example, 5 per cent of 200 units is:

$$\left(\frac{5}{100}\right) \times 200 = 10 \text{ units}$$

Put into practice

- If the price changes by 5 per cent and the quantity demanded changes by 2.5 per cent, what is the value of the price elasticity of demand?
- If the price increases from 10p to 12p, and the quantity demanded falls from 50 units to 45 units, what is the price elasticity of demand?
- If the price elasticity of demand is −0.5, what is the effect of a change in quantity demanded of:
  - a 10 per cent rise in price?
  - a 4 per cent fall in price?
- Four hundred units of a product are sold. If the price elasticity of demand is −2 and the price is cut by 5 per cent, what will the new quantity demanded be?

However, in some cases, the price elasticity of demand may be positive. This occurs when the demand curve is upward-sloping (perhaps because the product is a Giffen good or an example of conspicuous consumption—see Chapter 3). When the demand curve is upward-sloping, a higher price leads to a higher quantity demanded, meaning that both the denominator and numerator move in the same direction, leading to a positive answer (see Figure 4.2).

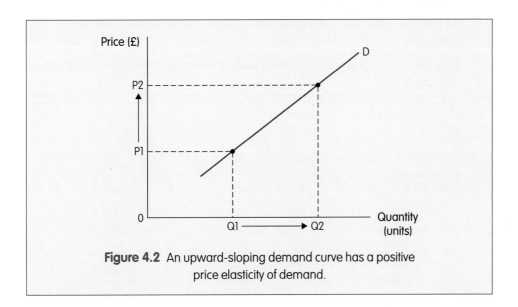

Figure 4.2 An upward-sloping demand curve has a positive price elasticity of demand.

Economics in context   High prices

Holiday companies know that parents are increasingly being prevented by head teachers from taking their children out of school and now fear being fined or taken to court if they decide to do it anyway. This means that there are particular weeks of the year during which families will have to go on holiday. Holiday companies respond to this by putting up prices—much to the annoyance of parents—because they know that, at these times, demand is not very sensitive to price: it is price inelastic.

Motorway cafes and restaurants often charge more for products than their city-centre rivals. This is because once you have decided to stop at a motorway cafe, the choice is limited, and most people cannot be bothered to leave and drive somewhere else to search for a cheaper alternative. Demand is therefore price inelastic.

Printer companies often charge relatively little to get you to buy a particular printer for your computer. After that, you have to buy specific ink cartridges and so demand for these is price inelastic, enabling the companies to make high profits on these. Similarly, what would you pay to restore your hard drive if your computer were to crash? Repairers know that demand for this service will be very price inelastic and charge accordingly.

❓ Question
Can you think of other situations in which demand is price inelastic, so that firms increase prices?

Put into practice

Calculate the price elasticity of demand for the following examples.

- The price increases from £10 to £12 and the quantity demanded falls from 400 units to 300 units.

- The price increases from £10 to £12 and the quantity demanded rises from 400 units to 500 units.

- The price decreases from £40 to £30 and the quantity demanded increases from 50 units to 55 units.

The price elasticity of demand will vary between products and can change over time for a given product as demand conditions change. For example, firms may take action to try to make demand more price inelastic.

What do you think?

Do you think that firms would prefer demand for their products to be price elastic or price inelastic? What action might firms take to influence the price elasticity of demand for their products?

Put into practice

The table shows a demand schedule for a product. Within what price range is the price elasticity of demand −2.5?

Price (£)	Quantity demanded
10	40
9	50
8	60
7	70
6	80

a. A price change from £10 to £9

b. A price change from £9 to £8

c. A price change from £8 to £7

d. A price change from £7 to £6

▪ Determinants of the price elasticity of demand

Whether the demand for a particular product is price elastic or price inelastic (that is, how sensitive demand is to price) depends on factors such as the following.

- **How differentiated the product is** If a product has a strong brand image or a unique selling proposition, then customers cannot easily find substitutes and so the impact of a price change on the quantity demanded of this product will be small relative to the price change. The demand will be price inelastic. Visiting the Eiffel Tower in Paris, for example, may be a unique experience and so demand to go up it may not be very sensitive to price.

- **The time period involved** If a firm puts its price up, then customers may find it difficult to find an alternative in the short term. Customers may be used to buying a particular brand, going to a particular restaurant, or using a particular accountant, and so demand for these goods and services is price inelastic at any given moment. With more time, customers may be able to find other providers that are similar, but cheaper, and so demand becomes more price elastic. A price increase by your insurer, or gas or electricity provider, may have a limited impact in the short run because you are locked into a contract or do not have the time to look for alternative providers, but over time, you are likely to search for a cheaper option.

- **Whether the firm has built a relationship with its customers** Some organizations aim to develop loyalty from their customers (for example, supermarket loyalty programmes or frequent flyer rewards); these will make the customer less sensitive to price changes, because they feel loyal to the business. Internet companies such as Amazon build relationships by tracking your favourite types of books and films, and recommending other options that you might like, in order to build loyalty.

- **The breadth of product category being considered** Demand for petrol as a whole is likely to be price inelastic: car drivers cannot easily do without it. However, demand for any one garage's petrol is likely to be more price elastic than for petrol as a whole; this is because drivers can switch to a competitor's garage if there is a noticeable price difference. Similarly, the demand for Marlboro cigarettes is more price elastic than the demand for all cigarettes, the demand for Levis is more price elastic than the demand for jeans, and the demand for Nescafé is more price elastic than demand for instant coffee, because people can switch more easily from the brand than from the product. The wider the category examined, therefore, the more price inelastic demand will be.

- **Who is paying** If you have to pay a bill yourself, you are likely to be fairly sensitive to the price. If, however, someone else is paying (for example, your parents or your company), then you are likely to be less sensitive to price. You may not be so concerned about price increases or search so hard to compare prices, because it is not your money. Demand would therefore be more price inelastic. You can see this when travelling: first-class and business seats are much more expensive, because firms are paying rather than the individuals themselves. How many of those passengers would have travelled economy class if they had been paying themselves?

- **The awareness and availability of substitutes** If customers know that there are many similar substitute products available, then they will be more likely to switch between them if there are noticeable differences in price. The demand will be more price elastic. The growth of the Internet has made it easier to compare prices (not least because there are websites that search for the best deal for you) and this has made demand for many products more price elastic.

- **The percentage of income spent on the product** If you spend a considerable amount of money on an item, then you may be more likely to shop around for the best buy. You may be more aware of the price of a new car or a holiday, for example, than of the price of a pint of milk. Demand for products that account for a high percentage of your income are therefore likely to be more price elastic than those that involve a small percentage of income, because you will compare and look around more for such a big purchase.

- **The nature of the product** If a product is habit-forming or addictive, such as cigarettes, demand is likely to be price inelastic. The impact of a price increase will be relatively small. Similarly, demand for necessities such as bread, coffee, tea, electricity, and gas is price inelastic. If, however, it is a 'shopping good', for which people tend to look around and compare prices between stores (for example, washing machines, dish-washers, and beds), then demand is likely to be more price elastic.

Put into practice

Which of the following statements is true and which are false?

a. Demand for a product is likely to be more price inelastic if there are only a few substitutes.

b. Demand for a product is likely to be more price inelastic if a large percentage of income is spent on it.

c. Demand for a product is likely to be more price inelastic if someone else is paying for it.

d. Demand for a product is likely to be more price inelastic in the short term compared to the long term.

What do you think?

Do you think that people are likely to be more sensitive to prices when the economy is in decline or booming? Explain your answer.

Under what circumstances might a firm want demand for its products to be price elastic?

Put into practice

What do you expect the effect on the price elasticity of demand for a product to be in the following situations?

- A competitor enters the market with a similar product.

- A firm invests in a successful advertising campaign for the product.
- The product is tehnologically advanced and has **patent** protection, meaning that it cannot be copied by others for several years.

Put into practice

Are the following statements true or false?

a. The price elasticity of demand on a downward-sloping demand curve is negative.

b. If the price elasticity of demand is −2, this means that demand is price inelastic.

c. If a 5 per cent change in price changes the quantity demanded by 20 per cent, then demand is price elastic.

d. If the price elasticity of demand is −0.5, then a 20 per cent increase in price reduces the quantity demanded by 10 per cent.

The price elasticity of demand along the demand curve

The price elasticity of demand for a product changes along its demand curve (see Figure 4.3). At the top of the demand curve, the demand is price elastic (see Figure 4.4): a price change leads to a bigger percentage change in the quantity demanded. At the bottom of the demand curve, the demand is price inelastic. In the middle of the demand curve

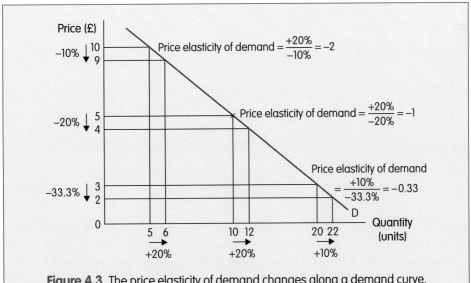

Figure 4.3 The price elasticity of demand changes along a demand curve.

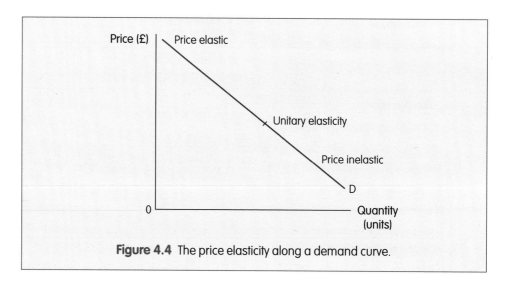

Figure 4.4 The price elasticity along a demand curve.

(exactly halfway along the curve between the origin and where it cuts the quantity axis), the price elasticity of demand is unitary.

When we talk of a price-inelastic demand or a price-elastic demand curve, this is because we are focusing on a particular section of a demand curve. Demand may be insensitive to price within a given price band, for example, but if the price continues to increase, then the demand will, at some point, become price elastic (see Figure 4.5).

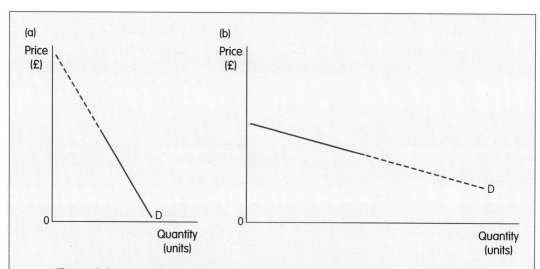

Figure 4.5 Price-inelastic demand: (a) The demand curve is price inelastic for the part of the curve indicated by the solid line, but is price elastic at higher prices; (b) The demand curve is price elastic for the part of the curve indicated by the solid line, but is price inelastic at lower prices.

▣ The price elasticity of demand and total revenue

The total revenue is the earnings generated from selling a product. It represents the value of sales and does not consider costs. The value of the total revenue depends on the quantity sold and the price per unit, as follows (see Figure 4.6):

Total revenue = Price per unit × Quantity sold

For example, if the price of a product is £10 and the quantity sold is 20 units, then the total revenue earned is:

£10 × 20 = £200

If the demand for a product is price inelastic, then an increase in price will lead to an increase in revenue. Although there will be a fall in the quantity demanded, the higher price per item sold will more than compensate for the loss in the number of products sold. If demand is price inelastic, then a fall in price will lead to a fall in revenue. This is because the quantity demanded will increase, but not enough to compensate for the fall in price per item. If demand is price elastic, then an increase in price will lead to a fall in revenue. The fall in sales outweighs the increase in price per item. However, a fall in price will lead to an increase in revenue; this is because the increase in sales is so great that it outweighs the fall in price per unit.

These statements are summarized in Table 4.2.

If demand has a price elasticity of one (1), then the total revenue will not change when the price changes (see Figure 4.7). The effect of the change in sales exactly offsets the change in revenue from the change in the price per unit.

The estimation of the price elasticity of demand is therefore very important for firms when determining a pricing strategy. Managers will often want to increase the revenue that they generate from sales. To do this, managers should:

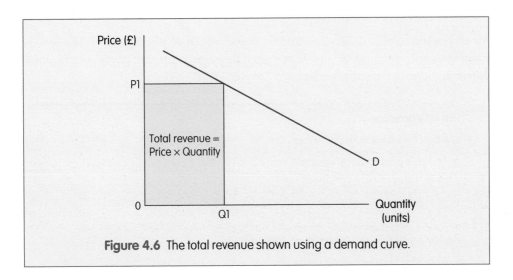

Figure 4.6 The total revenue shown using a demand curve.

Table 4.2 The impact of a price fall on revenue, depending on the price elasticity of demand

	Value (ignoring the sign)	Impact on revenue of a price fall
Price elastic	>1	Revenue increases
Unitary elastic	1	Revenue stays the same
Price inelastic	<1	Revenue decreases

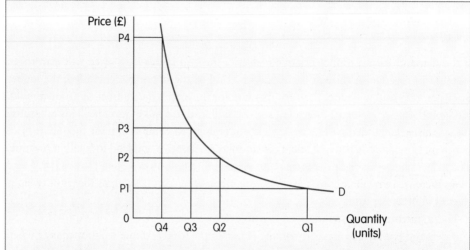

Figure 4.7 A unitary elastic demand curve. A change in price does not change the revenue (and therefore the areas P1Q1, P2Q2, P3Q3, and P4Q4 are all equal).

- lower price if demand is price elastic; or
- increase price if demand is price inelastic.

An understanding of price elasticity and the impact of this on pricing policies can be seen when firms price discriminate; this occurs when they charge different groups of customers different prices for the same product (see Chapter 15).

Put into practice

Consider the following two situations.

a. The price of a product is increased from £10 to £11. The quantity demanded falls from 50 units to 30 units.

b. The price of a product is increased from £10 to £11. The quantity demanded falls from 50 units to 49 units.

Answer the following questions for each situation.

- What is the price elasticity of demand?

- What is the original total revenue before the price change?
- What is the new total revenue after the price change?
- Delete as appropriate in the following:

  The conclusion is that when demand is price elastic, total revenue will [increase/decrease] following a price increase.

Put into practice

The following table shows estimates of price elasticities of demand for various goods and services.

Goods	Estimated elasticity of demand
Inelastic	
Salt	0.10
Matches	0.10
Toothpicks	0.10
Airline travel, short run	0.10
Coffee	0.25
Tobacco products, short run	0.45
Legal services, short run	0.40
Taxi, short run	0.60
Automobiles, long run	0.20
Approximately unitary elastic	
Movies	0.90
Housing, owner-occupied, long run	1.20
Private education	1.10
Elastic	
Restaurant meals	2.30
Foreign travel, long run	4.00
Airline travel, long run	2.40
Fresh green peas	2.80
Automobiles, short run	1.20–1.50
Chevrolet automobiles	4.00
Fresh tomatoes	4.60

Sources: Bohi (1981); Cheng, and Capps Jr (1988); Gwartney, and Stroup (1997); Houthakker, and Taylor (1970); US Department of Agriculture.

a. Based on the estimates above, which is more price elastic?
- Demand for matches or demand for fresh tomatoes.
- Demand for cars in general or demand for Chevrolet cars.

Explain why you think this is.

b. Would an increase in price increase or decrease the total spending on:
- restaurant meals?
- taxis?

Explain why you think this is.

Put into practice

Are the following statements true or false?

a. If demand is price elastic, a price fall increases revenue.

b. If demand is price inelastic, a price increase decreases revenue.

c. If demand has unit price elasticity, then a price change has no effect on revenue.

d. Demand has a constant value along a demand curve.

The income elasticity of demand

Imagine that you get a promotion at work and, as a result, your income increases by 10 per cent. What will you do with the money? Of what products will you buy more? Which products that you purchase already will experience the greatest increase in demand? Will you actually buy fewer of some products? The effect of a change in income on demand is measured by the income elasticity of demand. The income elasticity of demand measures the sensitivity of demand to a change in income. It is calculated using the following equation:

$$\text{Income elasticity of demand} = \frac{\text{Percentage change in the quantity demanded}}{\text{Percentage change in income}}$$

The following are the two keys to understanding the income elasticity of demand.

- **The sign of the answer** If the income elasticity of demand is positive, then this means that an increase in income leads to an increase in demand (and a fall in income leads to a fall in demand)—that is, income and the quantity demanded move in the same direction. Products with a positive income elasticity of demand are known as 'normal goods'.

  If the income elasticity of demand is negative, then this means that an increase in income leads to a fall in demand (and a fall in income leads to an increase in demand)—that is, income and the quantity demanded move in opposite directions. These products are known as 'inferior goods'. With more income, for example, people may switch from own-brand items to more luxurious brands.

- **The size of the answer** If the value of the income elasticity of demand (regardless of the sign) is > 1, then the product is known as a luxury product: demand is very sensitive to income. For example, a value of +3 means that the percentage increase in demand is three times as much as the percentage increase in income. A 1 per cent increase in income will lead to a 3 per cent increase in the quantity demanded. These may be luxury products such as health clubs, sports cars, and cruise holidays.

  If the income elasticity of demand is < 1, then the product is known as a necessity: demand is not particularly sensitive to income. For example, if the income elasticity of demand is +0.5, then this means that the percentage change in demand is 0.5 times as much as the percentage change in income. These may be necessity items such as soaps and shampoos.

The different forms of income elasticity can be illustrated on an Engel curve (see Figure 4.8).

Understanding the income elasticity of demand is important to firms because it shows what the effect of income changes might be on demand. If, for example, an economy is expected to grow faster in the future, then the income elasticity should give an insight into what might happen to sales. Sales of luxury normal goods should increase relatively significantly; sales of inferior products should fall. The effect of a change in income on sales would then influence a number of decisions within the business, such as planning staffing levels, cash flow, and profit forecasts.

The income elasticity of demand determines the extent to which the demand curve shifts when income increases; this shows the size of the income elasticity of demand.

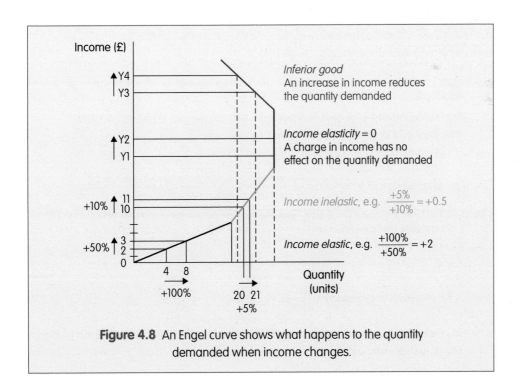

Figure 4.8 An Engel curve shows what happens to the quantity demanded when income changes.

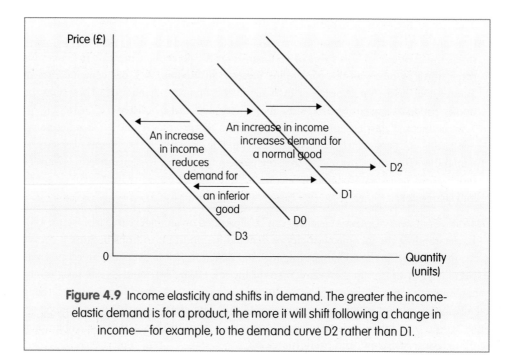

Figure 4.9 Income elasticity and shifts in demand. The greater the income-elastic demand is for a product, the more it will shift following a change in income—for example, to the demand curve D2 rather than D1.

The direction of the shift (that is, outward or inward) shows whether the good is normal or inferior (see Figure 4.9). A luxury normal good would shift a relatively significant distance to the right if income were to increase (e.g. D0 to D2); with an inferior good, the demand would shift inwards (e.g. D0 to D3).

Example

The average income in an area increases from £40,000 per year to £44,000 per year. Membership of local health clubs increases by 20 per cent.

The income elasticity of demand is defined as follows:

$$\text{Income elasticity of demand} = \frac{\text{Percentage change in the quantity demanded}}{\text{Percentage change in income}}$$

$$\text{Percentage change in income} = \left(\frac{4{,}000}{40{,}000}\right) \times 100 = 10\%$$

So:

$$\text{Income elasticity of demand} = \frac{+20\%}{+10\%} = +2$$

The demand is positive, which means that it is a normal product, and has a value of > 1, which means that it is income elastic.

Put into practice

- The average income in an area increases from £40,000 per year to £60,000 per year. Sales of carpets increase by 10 per cent. Calculate the income elasticity of demand for this product. Is demand for it income elastic or inelastic?
- What would it mean if the income elasticity of demand for a product were to be zero?

What do you think?

How might an understanding of income elasticity of demand affect a retailer of consumer electrical goods?

The cross-price elasticity of demand

So far, we have examined the sensitivity of demand to a change in price and a change in income. However, demand will also be affected by changes in the price of other products. When you are choosing a new laptop or washing machine, you naturally look at the prices of a range of models. When you are buying a car, you will also consider the other costs associated with running it, such as fuel, insurance, and tax. Changes in the price of other products (both substitutes and complements) will therefore affect demand for any given product. This effect is measured by the cross-price elasticity of demand.

The cross-price elasticity of demand measures the sensitivity of demand of one product to changes in the prices of other goods and services. It is calculated using the following equation:

$$\text{Cross-price elasticity of demand} = \frac{\text{Percentage change in demand for product A}}{\text{Percentage change in the price of product B}}$$

If the cross-price elasticity of demand is positive, this means that demand for one product increases when the price of another product increases (or one falls when the other falls). These products are substitutes—for example, two brands of coffee. An increase in the price of one brand causes customers to switch to another one.

The size of the answer shows how close the two products are as substitutes: the bigger the answer, the more closely related they are. For example, if the cross-price elasticity of demand is +2, this means that the increase in the quantity demanded of product A is twice the percentage increase in the price of product B. The easier it is for customers to switch between the two and the more similar they think the products are, the greater will be the value of the cross-price elasticity.

If the cross-price elasticity of demand is negative, this means that the products are complements—that is, an increase in the price of one product leads to a fall in the quantity demanded of the other. If the price of Sony Playstation consoles increases, for example, this is likely to reduce the quantity demanded of Playstations and the demand for PS computer games as well. Playstation consoles and PS computer games are therefore complements.

If the cross-price elasticity of demand is −3, for example, this means that a given percentage increase in the price of product B will lead to a fall in demand for product A that is three times bigger (in percentages).

The cross-price elasticity of demand is important because it shows the relationship between price changes of other products and the likely impact on your demand. In most markets, managers keep a close eye on competitors' pricing strategies; they will be particularly interested in those with a high cross-price elasticity of demand.

What do you think?

What do you think a cross-price elasticity of demand of zero would mean?
What if the value of the cross-price elasticity of demand were infinity?

What do you think?

We have analysed the impact of a change in price, in income, and the price of other firms on a demand curve using elasticity. There are many other factors affecting demand that could be analysed using the concept of elasticity of demand, such as changes in advertising expenditure. Can you think of any more?

Table 4.3 provides a summary of our discussions of price, income, and cross-price elasticities of demand.

Table 4.3   Summary table for price, income, and cross-price elasticities of demand

Type of elasticity of demand	Sign	Size	Type of product
Price	−	>1	Price elastic; downward-sloping demand curve
Price	−	<1	Price inelastic; downward-sloping demand curve
Price	+	Any value	Veblen good or Giffen good; upward-sloping demand curve
Income	+	>1	Luxury
Income	+	<1	Necessity
Income	−	Any value	Inferior
Cross-price	−	The higher the value, the stronger the relationship	Complements
Cross-price	+	The higher the value, the stronger the relationship	Substitutes

Practical limitations of the concept of elasticity of demand

In theory, the various measures of the elasticity of demand help managers to understand the impact of changes in different variables on their sales. This is important to their planning: for example, when estimating their production and financial requirements, or required staffing and stock levels. However, whilst a knowledge of the price, income, and cross-price elasticities of demand can certainly be useful, in reality using them can be difficult for the following reasons.

- Each of the equations for the elasticity of demand measures the relationship between one specific factor and demand: for example, the price elasticity of demand analyses the impact of a change in price on the quantity demanded. In reality, many factors may be changing at the same time, such as the spending on advertising, competitors' promotional strategies, and customers' incomes, as well as the firm's price. It may therefore be difficult to know what specifically has caused any change in the quantity demanded. A fall in price may be accompanied by an increase in quantity demanded, but this may not be the cause— it could have been due to other factors that also changed at the same time, such as the weather. A value of the price elasticity of demand that is calculated assuming the change in quantity demanded was all due to the price change may be very misleading.

- To know the elasticity of demand, managers must either look back at what happened in the past when, for example, prices or incomes were changed (but the conditions are likely to have altered since then), or estimate for themselves what the values are now (in which case, they may be wrong because it is an estimate). The value of elasticity is, therefore, not actually known at any moment; rather, it is merely estimated—perhaps based on past data. This means that managers should be careful about basing decisions on their estimates of the elasticity, because the values will be changing all of the time as demand conditions change.

Economics in context   Different types of elasticity of demand

The concept of elasticity is very flexible and can be extended to any variable. It is, after all, simply trying to quantify any correlation between a variable and the quantity demanded, which firms can then use in their planning. In some sectors, the weather may have a big impact on the quantity demanded: for example, cold weather leads to fewer people going shopping, whilst it increases the number of people going into hospital. Retail and health-care managers would be interested in the weather elasticity of demand. Umbrella manufacturers may be interested in the rainfall elasticity of demand. Managers will naturally look for the key variables that affect demand for their specific products and calculate their own forms of elasticity of demand. The advertising elasticity of demand, for example, is commonly used because it shows the relationship between advertising expenditure and the quantity demanded. This could be a very important relationship for marketing

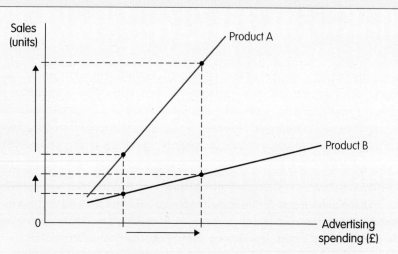

Figure 4.10 The correlation between advertising spending and sales. Product A is more sensitive to changes in advertising spending (that is, demand is more advertising elastic). A given change in advertising spending has less impact on demand for product B.

managers to understand when deciding how to allocate their marketing budget. The greater the advertising elasticity of demand, the greater the effect of any percentage change in advertising spending (see Figure 4.10).

? Questions

What might be important influences on the demand for each of the following?

- Barbecue sets
- Skis
- Solar panels
- Cosmetics
- University places
- Dentists

Put into practice

Which of the following statements are true and which are false?

a. The cross-price elasticity of demand for substitutes is positive.

b. The income elasticity of demand for an inferior good is negative.

c. A Giffen good has a positive price elasticity of demand.

d. A normal good has a negative price elasticity and a positive income elasticity of demand.

Case study Liverpool Football Club

In 2010, Liverpool Football Club increased the price of its season tickets by 7 per cent. The Club defended the price increase, saying that there is 'no difference in real terms' because of a rise in inflation and VAT. A season ticket seat at Liverpool booked online cost £680, with the main stand priced at £732. 'Our prices remain extraordinarily competitive, particularly compared with other clubs in the top half of the table,' argued a Liverpool spokesman.

Liverpool is £351 million in debt, and was put up for sale by the owners Tom Hicks and George Gillett earlier in the year. The ownership of Hicks and Gillett had led to a lot of discontent for many fans, who were unhappy with the way in which the club was being run. There have been regular protests and public disputes led by those who think that the Club has become too much of a business.

The Liverpool season ticket price rise announcement came on the day that a group of Liverpool fans suggested a **takeover** bid.

Manchester United season ticket holders were paying up to £931 to watch their club.

❓ Questions

- What do you think determines the demand for Liverpool season tickets?
- Liverpool has increased the price of season tickets. Do you think that demand will be price elastic or inelastic? Explain your answer.
- What will be the effect on revenue of the price increase in Liverpool's season ticket? Illustrate your answer with a diagram.
- What could a club like Liverpool do to make demand fror the tickets more price inelastic?
- What non-financial reasons might there be in favour of not increasing the price of season tickets at Liverpool? Do you think that the owners should listen to these arguments?

Checklist

Now that you have read this chapter, try to answer the following questions.

- ☐ Can you explain the meaning of the price, income, and the cross-price elasticity of demand?
- ☐ Can you outline the determinants of the price elasticity of demand for a product?
- ☐ Do you understand the difference between a normal and an inferior good?
- ☐ Do you understand the difference between a substitute and a complement?
- ☐ Do you understand the significance of the concept of elasticity for a firm's planning?
- ☐ Do you appreciate the limitations of the concept of elasticity of demand?

Review questions

1 If the price elasticity of demand equals zero then what does this mean?
2 How can a firm try to make demand for its products more price inelastic?

3   Is it better for a firm wanting to increase prices to have a price elastic or a price inelastic demand?

4   If a firm has a high income elasticity of demand for its products how might this affect its marketing?

5   How might an understanding of the cross-price elasticity of demand be useful to business?

Key learning points

- The concept of elasticity measures how sensitive demand is to a change in a variable.

- The sign of the answer highlights whether changes in quantity demanded and the variable move in the same direction or in opposite directions.

- The size of the answer shows the strength of the relationship between the variable and quantity demanded.

- There are many types of elasticity measuring how different variables such as price, income, and the prices of other products affect the quantity demanded.

- An understanding of the elasticity of demand will help a firm in its planning, for example of stock levels, pricing, and staffing.

References

Bohi, D.R. (1981) *Analyzing Demand Behavior*, Johns Hopkins University Press, Baltimore, MD

Cheng, H.-T., and Capps, Jr, O. (1988) 'Demand analysis of fresh, and frozen finfish, and shellfish in the US', *American Journal of Agricultural Economics*, 70(3): 533–42

Gwartney, J.D., and Stroup, R.L. (1997) *Economics: Private, and Public Choice*, 8th edn, Dryden Press, Fort Worth, TX

Houthakker, H.S., and Taylor, L.D. (1970) *Consumer Demand in the US, 1929–1970*, Harvard University Press, Cambridge, MA

Learn more

The concept of elasticity can also be applied to supply. To find out more about the price elasticity of supply, see Chapter 5.

 Visit our Online Resource Centre at http://www.oxfordtextbooks.co.uk/orc/gillespie_econ2e/ for test questions and further information on topics covered in this chapter.

Supply

The previous chapter examined the factors that influence the demand for products, showing what consumers are willing and able to buy. This chapter examines the factors that influence the supply of a product—that is, what suppliers are willing and able to produce at different prices. We will then combine the market forces of supply and demand to find the equilibrium price and output in a market in Chapter 6.

LEARNING OBJECTIVES

By the end of this chapter, you should be able to:

✔ explain what is shown by a supply curve;

✔ understand the difference between a change in the quantity supplied and a change in supply;

✔ explain the causes of a shift in a supply curve;

✔ understand the concept of the price elasticity of supply.

■ Introduction to supply

The demand curve shows what consumers are willing and able to purchase at each and every price, all others things being unchanged. This is one part of a market. The other part is the supply curve. The supply of a product is the amount that producers are willing and able to produce at each and every price, all others things being unchanged. For example, it might show how many houses a construction firm might want to build at different selling prices, or how many live performances a band might want to make at different appearance fees. The amount supplied will depend on factors such as the price, costs, the number of producers, and the resources available.

The supply curve is usually upward-sloping. A higher price is needed for firms to be willing and able to produce more, all other things being unchanged; as the price increases, it becomes more feasible and appealing to produce more units. This assumes that to produce more, the extra costs will increase, which means that a higher price is needed by producers to be able to produce.

■ Movement along the supply curve

Businesses usually need a higher price to cover the extra costs of producing extra units: for example, to extract more oil may require more complex technology, to open more stores may require more land, and you may need to pay a higher price to acquire this and you may need to pay staff overtime. This means that the supply curve is usually upward-sloping.

An increase in price (P1 – P2) will usually lead to an increase in the quantity supplied (Q1 – Q2). This is known as an extension of supply (see Figure 5.1). A fall in the quantity supplied is called a contraction of supply (see Figure 5.2). A change in the price of a

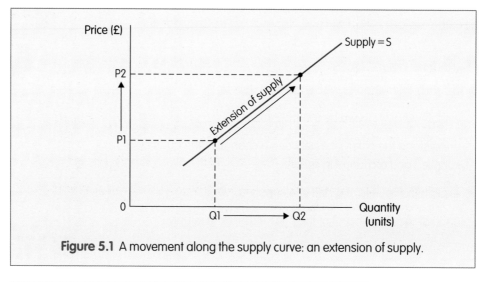

Figure 5.1 A movement along the supply curve: an extension of supply.

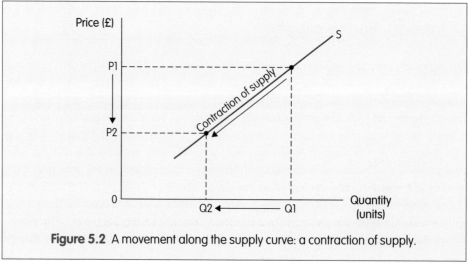

Figure 5.2 A movement along the supply curve: a contraction of supply.

product will therefore cause a change in the quantity supplied; this is shown as a movement along the supply curve. The shape of the supply curve is linked to the extra costs of producing a unit; the derivation of the supply curve is examined in more detail in Chapter 9.

Put into practice

Price (£)

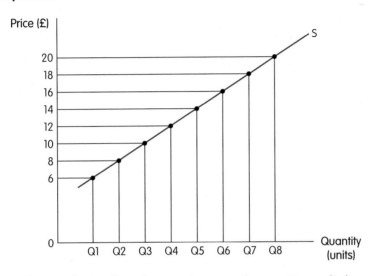

Figure 5.3 The effect of a price change on the quantity supplied.

Consider the supply curve shown in Figure 5.3. What happens to the quantity supplied if the price increases from £6 to £20?

Example

The equation for an upward-sloping, straight-line supply curve can take the form of:

$Q = 20 + 2P$

For example, if the price is £10, the quantity supplied is:

$Q = 20 + (2 \times 10) = 20 + 20 = 40$ units

If the price is £15, the quantity supplied is:

$Q = 20 + (2 \times 15) = 20 + 30 = 50$ units

Put into practice

- If the supply curve is given by the equation $Q = 5 + 3P$, what is the quantity supplied when the price is £10?
- If the supply curve is given by the equation $Q = 5 + 3P$, what is the quantity supplied when the price is £20?

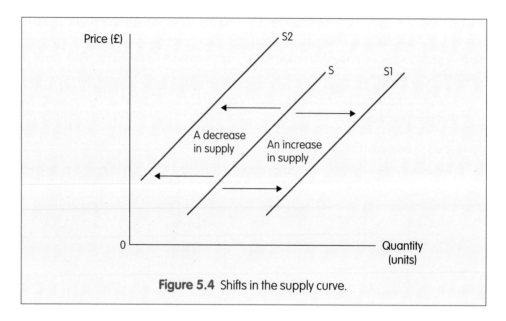

Figure 5.4 Shifts in the supply curve.

Shifts in supply

A shift in supply means that the supply curve shifts to the right or left (see Figure 5.4). More (or fewer) products are supplied at each and every price. A change in price leads to a movement along the supply curve and assumes all other factors are unchanged; a shift in supply occurs when these other factors do change. An increase in supply is shown by a shift of the supply curve to the right: more is supplied at each and every price. A decrease in supply shifts the supply curve to the left: less is supplied at each and every price.

The reasons for a shift in the supply curve

The reasons for a shift in the supply curve include the following.

- **A change in the number of producers** If there is an increase in the number of producers in an industry, then this should lead to an increase in supply. More can be produced at each and every price, because there are more suppliers. Producers may be attracted into an industry because they are attracted by the prospect of high returns.
- **A change in technology** New technology should enable firms to produce more at any price, thus shifting the supply curve to the right. Technological change might also enable more firms to enter the market. For example, online trading means that new banks, estate agents, or travel agents do not need to establish the same network of high-street outlets that they had to have in the past. Entry into these types of market is therefore easier than it used to be.
- **A change in costs** An increase in wages or the price of raw materials will mean that firms cannot supply as much at a given price because of higher costs. For any given level

of output, they will need a higher price. The supply curve will therefore shift to the left. In recent years, increases in the price of oil have significantly increased the energy costs of many firms; this has shifted the supply curves in some industries inwards.

- **A change in indirect taxes** If a tax, such as value added tax (VAT), is placed on the sale of goods, then this will increase the selling price of any given output. This type of tax increases the producers' costs and means that they will need a higher price for any given level of output. This will have the effect of shifting the supply curve inwards. (This is analysed in more detail in Chapter 6.)

- **A change in weather conditions** This can be particularly important in agricultural markets, which are very vulnerable to changes in the natural environment. Poor weather can lead to supply shocks shifting supply to the left. Given the time period involved in growing crops, supply cannot quickly be increased again, which means that markets are affected significantly.

Economics in context   Sugar

In 2009, poor weather conditions hit crops in the world's two biggest sugar-producing nations, which sent the price of sugar soaring on international markets, because it was so scarce. In 2010, however, output from Brazil and India has been high, thanks to good weather.

Brazil's Sugar Cane Association said: 'We always depend on weather conditions at the moment of the harvest.'

❓ Question

What problems do you think sugar producers face as a result of being so dependent on the weather?

Put into practice

Using diagrams, illustrate the impact of the following on a supply curve.

- A decrease in price
- A reduction in the number of producers
- A decrease in the costs of raw materials

Example

If there is a change in supply conditions, the equation might change from:

$Q = 20 + 2P$

to:

$Q = 40 + 2P$

This would mean that more would be supplied at each and every price.

If the price is £10, the quantity supplied is:

$Q = 40 + (2 \times 10) = 40 + 20 = 60$ units (whereas before it was 40 units)

If the price is £15, the quantity supplied is:

$Q = 40 + (2 \times 15) = 40 + 30 = 70$ units (whereas before it was 50 units)

The supply curve has shifted outwards.

Put into practice

If the equation for the supply curve changes from $Q = 20 + 2P$ to $Q = 5 + 2P$, what has happened to the supply curve?

Put into practice

Which of the following could explain a shift in the supply curve for a product to the right?

a. A decrease in the cost of raw materials

b. An increase in the cost of raw materials

c. An increase in the wages paid to the workers

d. A reduction on the number of firms producing

Economics in context   The supply of steel

Over the last 50 years, the supply of steel has been increasing rapidly. In 1950, around 200 million tonnes of steel were produced worldwide. By 2005, output was over 1,100 million tonnes. China is now the world's biggest steel maker, producing one third of the global total. The next biggest producer is Japan, then the USA, Russia, and South Korea. Production has increased due to new producers and new technology. Increases in demand have led to more incentive to produce the product, which has increased the number of firms in the industry.

This relates back to our earlier analysis in Chapter 2 about the production possibility frontier (PPF). As steel becomes more attractive to produce due to increased demand, firms reallocate resources, moving out of other industries and into steel production.

? Questions

What do you think determines the demand for steel?

If more steel is demanded at each and every price, how is this shown on a demand curve diagram?

If more steel is now supplied at each and every price, how is this shown on a supply curve diagram?

With more firms producing steel and more demand, what do you think is likely to happen to the price of steel? On what might it depend?

What do you think?

What do you think are likely to be the main determinants of the amount supplied of the following?

- Personal computers
- Wine
- Wheat
- Diamonds
- Schools

Economics in context Oil

In 2005, Hurricane Katrina caused huge levels of damage to households and businesses in the New Orleans area of the USA. The region had many major oil production and refining facilities, and was responsible for one-quarter of US oil and gas production. Over 90 per cent of these energy production facilities were closed due to the damage caused by the hurricane. World oil prices were already high due to increased demand, but the impact of Katrina significantly reduced supply. As a result, US motorists, who were already paying $3 per gallon for petrol, had to pay $4—a major increase on the price of $1.86 in the year before.

? Questions

Why do you think the fall in supply of petrol led to an increase in the price?

An increase in oil prices increases energy costs for producers. Illustrate the effect of this on a supply curve for manufactured goods.

What do you think?

Can you think of three products of which it might be difficult to increase supply quickly? Why is it so difficult?

■ Industry supply

The industry supply curve is derived from the horizontal summation of all of the firms' supply curves (see Figure 5.5). At each and every price, the quantity that all of the firms are willing and able to supply are added together. An increase in the number of producers should therefore increase the total industry supply; this occurs when firms enter the industry. This may be because the government removes restrictions on the number and type of firms that can compete in a market, or because higher rewards provide an incentive to enter. In declining industries, firms will leave in search of higher rewards elsewhere and this will shift the industry supply to the left.

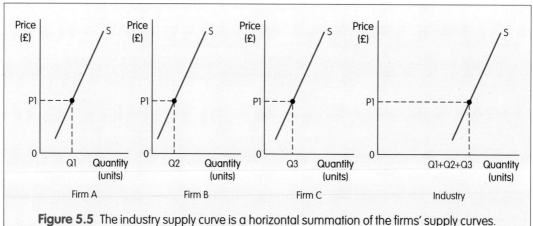

Figure 5.5 The industry supply curve is a horizontal summation of the firms' supply curves.

Economics in context

Growth in agricultural production in the BRIC economies

The emerging economies of Brazil, Russia, India, and China (known as the BRIC economies) are likely to enjoy a boom in their agricultural sectors over the next decade as production falters in Western Europe. Agricultural output in the BRIC nations will grow three times as fast as in the major developed countries, a recent report said.

These developing countries will provide the main source of growth for world agricultural production, consumption, and trade.

According to the report, overall world net production of commodities is forecast to grow by 22 per cent, but production among the 30 most developed economies is estimated to grow by just 10 per cent. This growth rate is almost three times slower than the growth rate of the BRIC countries, which is forecast to expand by 27 per cent. Brazil is forecast to see by far the fastest growth in agriculture, with an expansion of more than 40 per cent through to 2019. China and India are expected to see growth of 26 per cent and 21 per cent, respectively, to 2019. Projections for Russia and Ukraine are 26 per cent and 29 per cent.

Looking beyond the next decade, the report forecasts global food production to expand by 70 per cent by 2050.

❓ Questions

What factors do you think are causing such growth in global food production?

Why do you think production might be growing so quickly in BRIC economies compared to more developed economies?

Joint supply

In some cases, products may be supplied together. If we kill more cows in order to eat their meat, then we will also have more leather hides produced. Although demand conditions for leather may not have altered, the supply of leather will shift to the right, changing the equilibrium price and output in this market.

The price elasticity of supply

The slope of a supply curve will depend on how sensitive it is to changes in price. Can supply be easily changed in relation to a price increase or decrease, or not? The relationship between changes in price and the quantity supplied is analysed by the price elasticity of supply. The price elasticity of supply measures the extent to which the quantity supplied in a market varies with a change in price. It is calculated using the following equation:

$$\text{Price elasticity of supply} = \frac{\text{Percentage change in the quantity supplied}}{\text{Percentage change in price}}$$

The following are the two key elements to understanding the price elasticity of supply.

- **The sign of the answer** The sign of the answer will usually be positive, meaning that an increase in price increases the quantity supplied (and a fall in price reduces the quantity supplied)—that is, the price and the change in quantity supplied move in the same direction, assuming that the supply curve is upward-sloping.

- **The size (or value) of the answer** The size of the answer measures the strength of the relationship between the price and the quantity supplied. If the answer is greater than one (> 1), then this means that the percentage change in the quantity supplied is greater than the percentage change in price: supply is price elastic. For example, if the price elasticity of supply is +3, it means that a 1 per cent increase in price increases the quantity supplied by 3 per cent. If the price that people were willing and able to pay for a soft drink were to go up by 10 per cent, and producers could increase production by 30 per cent, supply would be price elastic.

If the answer is less than one (< 1), then this means that the percentage change in the quantity supplied is less than the change in price: supply is price inelastic. For example, if the price elasticity of supply is +0.5, it means that a 1 per cent increase in price increases the quantity supplied by 0.5 per cent. If the price that the government is willing to pay to build nuclear power stations were to increase by 10 per cent, then the number available could not increase overnight. It would take several years to build any more nuclear power stations and so the supply is not very sensitive to price in the short term: it is price inelastic. Similarly, supply in agriculture in the short run is usually price inelastic: you cannot quickly grow more crops.

Economics in context   Flexible production

Many businesses are now focusing on making their production more flexible. They are investing in the latest technology to enable them to respond rapidly to changes in orders—adopting a 'just in time' approach to production, whereby they produce when the order arrives rather than in advance of the order. They are also:

- providing broad job descriptions to enable managers to move staff around the business to different sections as and when help is required;
- spending more money on training staff so that they are multi-skilled and can undertake a range of tasks—this means that they can be moved to where they are needed;
- using flexible suppliers who can quickly increase output if required; and
- employing more people on temporary contracts so that managers can increase or decrease the number of staff as needed.

? Question

By being more flexible to demand, manufacturers are trying to avoid producing, and hoping that demand materializes. What are the benefits of producing in response to demand rather than in advance of demand?

What do you think?

What problems might firms have when trying to make production more flexible?

The value of the price elasticity of supply

The value of the price elasticity of supply for a product will depend on the following.

- **The number of firms in the industry** The more producers there are in an industry, the more likely it is that the level of output in the industry will change easily with price changes—that is, supply is likely to be more price elastic.
- **The time period** Over a longer period of time, resources can be shifted more easily from one sector to another; this will increase or decrease supply to a greater extent than in the short term, when at least one factor of production is fixed. In the immediate run, it may be impossible to change the quantity supplied at all, because resources are committed to their present use. This means that the supply curve may be totally inelastic and the price elasticity of supply would have a value of zero. Over time, with more resources and more businesses in the industry, the effect of a price increase will be greater, making supply more price elastic.

The price elasticity of supply is illustrated in Figure 5.6.

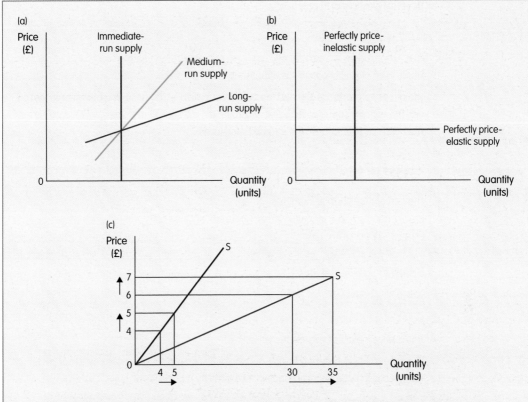

Figure 5.6 (a) Supply conditions change over time; (b) A perfectly price-elastic supply curve (a change in the price leads to an infinite change in the quantity supplied; the price elasticity of supply equals infinity) and a perfectly price-inelastic supply curve (a change in the price has no impact on the quantity supplied; the price elasticity of supply equals zero). (c) Supply curves that have a price elasticity equal to one are straight lines from the origin.

Example

a. The price of a product is £10 and the quantity supplied is 200 units. The price increases to £12 and the quantity supplied increases to 300 units.
   The percentage change in the quantity supplied is:

   $$\left(\frac{100}{200}\right) \times 100 = +50\%$$

   The percentage change in price is:

   $$\left(\frac{2}{10}\right) \times 100 = +20\%$$

The price elasticity of supply is:

$$\frac{+50}{+20} = +2.5$$

This is price elastic because the value is > 1.

b. The price of a product is £10 and the quantity supplied is 200 units. The price increases to £12 and the quantity supplied increases to 220 units.
The percentage change in the quantity supplied is:

$$\left(\frac{20}{200}\right) \times 100 = +10\%$$

The percentage change in price is:

$$\left(\frac{2}{10}\right) \times 100 = +20\%$$

The price elasticity of supply is:

$$\frac{+10}{+20} = +0.5$$

This is price inelastic because the value is < 1.

c. The price elasticity of supply is +0.8 and the price of a product increases by 10 per cent. This means that the quantity supplied increases by:

$$0.8 \times 10\% = 8\%$$

d. The price elasticity of supply is +0.2. The price increases from £10 to £12. The quantity supplied was 500 units.
The change in price is:

$$\left(\frac{2}{10}\right) \times 100 = 20\%$$

The change in quantity supplied will be:

$$0.2 \times 20\% = 4\%$$

The quantity supplied is:

$$\left(\frac{4}{100}\right) \times 500 = 20 \text{ units}$$

So the new quantity supplied is:

$$500 \text{ units} + 20 \text{ units} = 520 \text{ units}$$

Put into practice

a. The price of a product increases from £5 to £8. The quantity supplied increases from 200 units to 400 units.
    - What is the price elasticity of supply?
    - Is supply price elastic or inelastic?

b. The price of a product increases from £5 to £8. The quantity supplied increases from 200 units to 210 units.
    - What is the price elasticity of supply?
    - Is supply price elastic or inelastic?

c. The price elasticity of supply is +0.1 and the price of a product increases by 10 per cent. How much does the quantity supplied increase?

d. The price elasticity of supply is +0.4. The price increases from £10 to £15. The quantity supplied was 200 units. What will be the new quantity supplied after the price increase?

What do you think?

Can you think of products that would have a price-elastic supply? What about ones with a price-inelastic supply?

Case study Water shortages

In recent years, water shortages in the southeast of England became so severe that the government's Environment Agency proposed that five new reservoirs needed to be built over the next 25 years. Reservoirs that would normally be over 90 per cent full in February were less than 40 per cent full after more than a year of drought conditions. Rainfall for the southeast had been less than 25 per cent of its usual level during that time.

According to a water company spokesperson, the public were still behaving as if water was unlimited and cheap, and needed to appreciate that, in fact, it was not available in unlimited quantities. This was particularly a problem in the southeast. In mid-Kent, for example, consumers were using around 160–170 litres each per day—around 15 litres per head per day more than in the northeast.

Given the shortages, water companies tried to get customers to cut down their use of water. Hosepipe bans were brought in, and then restrictions imposed on car washes and the watering of sports pitches. Bills were also increased: on average, bills in England and Wales increased by 7.5 per cent. The water companies were also keen for customers to have water meters installed. Instead of being charged a flat fee, customers would be charged according to how much they used.

However, some analysts and pressure groups, such as the Campaign to Protect Rural England, attacked the water companies for failing to deal with the rising demand and with the effect of climate change.

The companies have also been heavily criticized for the amount of water lost through leaks. South East Water produced an extra 35 million litres per day through stopping leaks, but a large amount of water was still being wasted due to old pipes.

Problems with water shortages are forecast to get worse, with the building of hundreds of thousands of homes in the southeast. New houses will be fitted with water meters.

? Questions

- What are the main factors influencing the supply of water to households in the UK?
- How can demand for water be reduced if supply is limited?
- Do you think that water meters are a better way of charging for water than a flat fee?
- Do you think that the government should provide water in the UK rather than private companies?

Checklist

Now that you have read this chapter, try to answer the following questions.

- ☐ Can you explain what is shown by a supply curve?
- ☐ Do you understand the difference between a change in the quantity supplied and a change in supply?
- ☐ Can you explain the causes of a shift in a supply curve?
- ☐ Can you explain the meaning of the price elasticity of supply?
- ☐ Can you explain why the price elasticity of supply might change over time?

Review questions

1 Does a supply curve show how much producers would like to supply at each and every price?
2 Why is a change in the quantity supplied different from a change in supply?
3 What might shift the supply curve for a product to the left?
4 Why might the price elasticity of supply for a product be price inelastic?
5 What might shift the supply curve of a product to the right?

Key learning points

- The supply curve is usually upward-sloping.
- The supply curve is derived from the extra costs of production.
- A movement along the supply curve occurs when there is a change in price, all other factors unchanged.
- A shift in the supply curve occurs when there is a change in the quantity supplied at each and every price.
- An increase in supply means that more can be supplied at each and every price.
- A decrease in supply means that less is supplied at each and every price.
- The supply curve shows the decisions of producers; the demand curve shows the decisions of customers.

Learn more

A supply curve is actually derived from a marginal cost curve. To find out why, see Chapter 11.

 Visit our Online Resource Centre at http://www.oxfordtextbooks.co.uk/orc/gillespie_econ2e/ for test questions and further information on topics covered in this chapter.

» 6

Market equilibrium

The previous two chapters have examined the market forces of supply and demand. Supply shows what producers are willing and able to produce at each and every price, and demand shows what consumers are willing and able to buy at each and every price. In this chapter, we consider how these forces interact and how equilibrium is reached in a market via changes in the price.

LEARNING OBJECTIVES

By the end of this chapter, you should be able to:

✔ explain the meaning of equilibrium in a market;

✔ explain how the price adjusts in a market to bring about equilibrium;

✔ understand the impact on the equilibrium price and quantity of a shift in a supply or demand curve;

✔ understand the effect of indirect taxes and subsidies on the equilibrium price and output;

✔ understand the factors that determine the incidence of an indirect tax or subsidy on consumers and producers.

▓ Markets

A market occurs when buyers and sellers interact to exchange goods and services. This can be a physical market, such as a local farmers' market, in which local producers sell their goods, or a virtual market, such as eBay, in which the buyers and sellers never physically meet each other. The market may be primarily a local one with regional buyers and sellers, such as a taxi business, a national one, such as the market in the UK for health care, or a global one, such as the world market for oil.

Equilibrium

Equilibrium occurs in a market when, at the given price, the quantity supplied equals the quantity demanded and there is no incentive for this position to change. In a free market, the equilibrium output is reached by changes in the price. The decisions of producers and customers are made independently of each other; the price mechanism acts to bring these decisions together, and to equate the quantity supplied and demanded.

How equilibrium is reached in theory in a market is highlighted in Figure 6.1. At P1 in this figure, the price is above the equilibrium level. At this price, the quantity supplied (Q1) is higher than the quantity demanded (Q3). There is excess supply (also known as a surplus) equal to Q1 – Q3. Given the relatively higher price, the amount that producers want to produce is greater than the quantity demanded by customers. This puts down-ward pressure on the price. To get rid of their stock and boost sales, firms will reduce prices. As the price falls, the quantity that firms are willing and able to sell falls, whilst the quantity demanded increases. This process continues until equilibrium is reached at P2. The price mechanism adjusts to equate supply and demand.

At P3 in Figure 6.2, the price is below the equilibrium level. At this price, the quantity demanded (Q3) is above the quantity supplied (Q1). This means that there is a shortage in the market (also known as 'excess demand') equal to Q3 – Q1. This will put upward pressure on the price. As the price increases, firms will be more willing to supply, whilst the quantity demanded will fall. This process continues until the equilibrium price is reached at P2, and again there is no further incentive to change.

In this free market, the price mechanism changes to affect the decisions of producers and consumers. Price acts in the following ways.

- **As a signal and incentive** If the price rises, for example, this acts as a signal to other producers that this is an industry that they might want to enter to earn high profits.

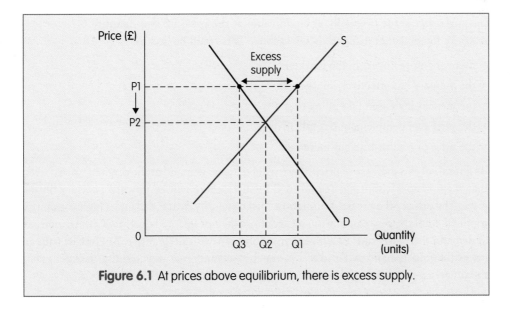

Figure 6.1 At prices above equilibrium, there is excess supply.

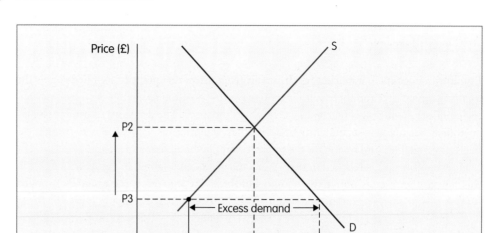

Figure 6.2 At prices below equilibrium, there is excess demand.

The high price acts as an incentive for firms to enter into this industry because of the potential rewards. This can be seen when a new business idea proves to be successful: within months, the idea is likely to be copied as others enter the industry.

- **As a rationing device** If the price increases, it reduces the quantity demanded until it equals the quantity supplied. This can be seen at an auction, where the price keeps rising until only one person can afford the product for sale.

■ The effects on the equilibrium price and quantity of a change in demand

Imagine a market is originally at equilibrium at the price P2 and quantity Q2 (see Figure 6.3). Imagine that demand then increases. This could be because:

- there are more buyers in the market;
- the industry has effectively marketed its products;
- income has increased (assuming that it is a normal good);
- the price of a complement has fallen; or
- the price of a substitute has increased.

As a result of this increase in price, there will be excess demand at the original price. Given that there is now a shortage (equal to Q1 – Q2), there will be upward pressure on the price. The price will increase, leading to a lower quantity demanded and a higher quantity supplied, until the new equilibrium is reached at the price P3 and quantity Q3. An increase in demand therefore leads to a higher equilibrium price and quantity. By comparison, an inward shift in demand will lead to a lower equilibrium price and quantity, assuming that the supply curve is upward-sloping.

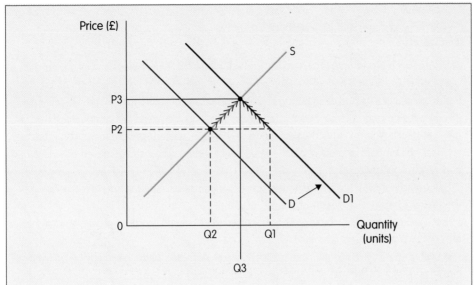

Figure 6.3 An outward shift in demand leads to a higher equilibrium price and output.

A shift in demand for cocoa

In July 2010, Anthony Ward bought 241,000 tonnes of cocoa beans. He now owns enough cocoa beans to manufacture 5.3 billion quarter-pound chocolate bars. The former Chairman of the European Cocoa Association has accumulated up to 15 per cent of the word's cocoa stocks in the last ten years.

The cocoa beans from his latest trade will be kept in warehouses in the Netherlands, Hamburg, London, Liverpool, or Humberside, and are the equivalent of the entire supply of the commodity in Europe.

Cocoa prices rose by 0.7 per cent as a result of the trade to £2,732 per metric tonne—the highest price for cocoa in Europe since 1977. It follows a series of weak harvests in Ghana and the Ivory Coast, the main areas in which the crop is grown.

In 2002, Mr Ward made £40 million in two months after making a similar deal. He bought 204,000 tonnes of cocoa when West Africa was experiencing poor harvests and political instability in the equatorial area. The price of cocoa then increased from £1,400 a tonne to £1,600 a tonne. Cocoa prices have more than doubled since 2007, following increased demand particularly from China and India, forcing chocolate makers to raise prices and, in some cases, to change recipes to use less cocoa.

? Question

Analyse the effect of Antony Ward's purchase, using supply and demand analysis. Think carefully about the elasticities of demand and supply.

Economics in context — A shift in demand for oil

At 7.45 a.m. on 30 June 2009, the senior trader for PVM Oil Futures was contacted by a clerk questioning why he had bought 7 million barrels of crude in the middle of the night. At first, the trader claimed that he had been buying on behalf of a client, but this could not be substantiated. It soon became clear that Mr Perkins had single-handedly increased the world price of oil to an eight-month high during a 'drunken blackout'. Prices increased by more than $1.50 a barrel in under half an hour at around 2 a.m.—the type of sharp swing usually caused by events of geopolitical significance.

By the time that PVM realized the trades were not authorized and began to try to rectify the positions taken, it had incurred losses of over $9,760,000.

In the early hours of the morning, the trader placed $520 million in orders, gradually edging up the price by bidding higher each time.

He has since told investigators that he has 'limited recollection' of the entire episode, claiming that he had placed the trades during a drink-induced stupor.

 Question

Illustrate the effect of the trader's actions in the oil market, using supply and demand curves.

Put into practice

Identify three reasons why demand for chocolate might shift inwards.

Economics in context — The price of art

Picasso's *Nude, Green Leaves, and Bust* sold for $106 million (£70 million) at Christie's in New York in 2010, setting a new world record for a work of art sold at auction.

The large piece of work depicting Picasso's mistress Marie-Thérèse Walter was the highlight of a world-class collection assembled by the late Los Angeles art patrons Frances and Sidney Brody.

More than half a dozen people bid on the 1932 canvas, which the Brodys acquired in the 1950s from Picasso's dealers, with the winning bid taken by a Christie's executive via telephone.

 Questions

What do you think determines the demand for a particular artist's work?

In terms of supply and demand analysis, why do you think the price of some artist's work is so high compared to the price of a tin of paint?

Economics in context

The price of copper

Global metal prices have fluctuated greatly in recent years, and are now rising rapidly. Copper in particular has increased in price, leading to stories in the press of a major increase in the amount of copper pipes and wire being stolen all over the world. Much of the increase in recent years has been driven by the growth of the Chinese economy. Although the global recession did affect demand adversely, leading to a slump at the end of 2008, the recovery of most major economies since 2009 has boosted demand again.

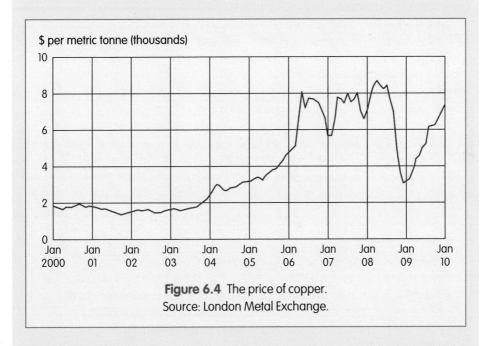

Figure 6.4 The price of copper.
Source: London Metal Exchange.

? Question

Illustrate, using supply and demand analysis, the possible causes of the changes in the price of copper as illustrated above.

A shift in demand leads to a new equlibirum price and quantity in the market. The size of the effect on price and quantity depends on:

- how much the demand curve shifts; and
- the relative price elasticities of supply and demand. The more price inelastic supply is, for example, the more that price will change relative to output. If, however, supply is relatively price elastic, then the effect will mainly be on output rather than price.

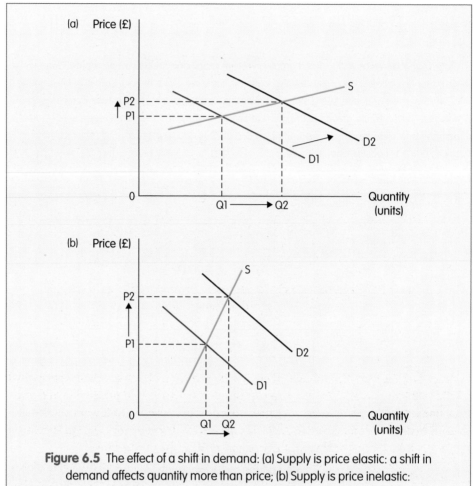

Figure 6.5 The effect of a shift in demand: (a) Supply is price elastic: a shift in demand affects quantity more than price; (b) Supply is price inelastic: a shift in demand affects price more than quantity.

The effects on the equilibrium price and quantity of a change in supply

A market is originally at equilibrium at the price P2 and quantity Q2 (see Figure 6.6). Imagine that supply now increases. This could be because:

• there are more producers in the industry;

• technology has improved; or

• the costs of production have fallen.

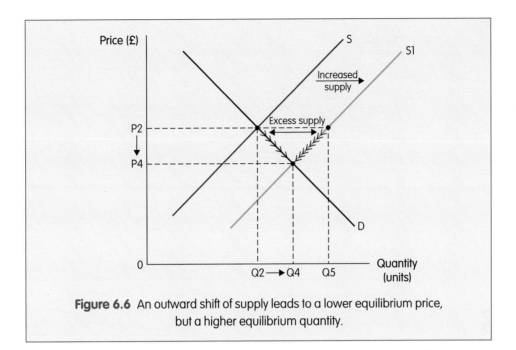

Figure 6.6 An outward shift of supply leads to a lower equilibrium price, but a higher equilibrium quantity.

As a result of this increase in supply, there will be excess supply at the original price equal to Q5 – Q2. Given that there is a surplus, there will be downward pressure on the price. The price will decrease, leading to a higher quantity demanded and a lower quantity supplied, until the new equilibrium is reached at the price P4 and quantity Q4. An increase in supply has led to a lower equilibrium price and a higher quantity supplied.

By comparison, a fall in supply will lead to an increase in the equilibrium price and a reduction in the equilibrium quantity, assuming that the demand curve is downward-sloping.

Put into practice

Using supply and demand diagrams, illustrate the effect of each of the following.

- An increase in income for a normal good

- An increase in material costs

- A decrease in the price of a complementary good

- An increase in the number of firms producing in the industry

---

The effect of a change in supply on the equilibrium price and quantity depends on the extent of the shift and the price elasticity of demand. If demand is price inelastic, then the effect is mainly on price rather than quantity. If demand is price elastic, then the effect is more on the quantity than the price.

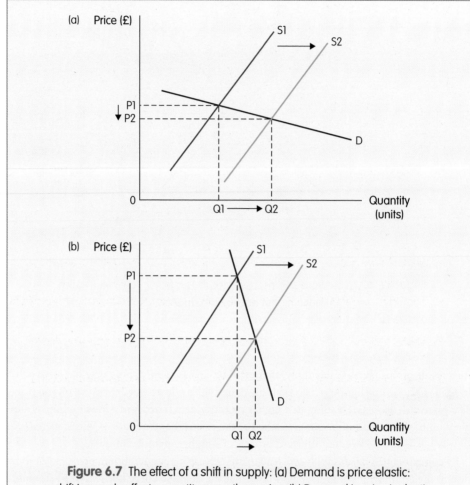

Figure 6.7 The effect of a shift in supply: (a) Demand is price elastic: a shift in supply affects quantity more than price; (b) Demand is price inelastic: a shift in supply affects price more than quantity.

Put into practice

- An increase in the price of complementary products
- An increase in costs
- An increase in income (if it is a normal good)
- An increase in the number of producers

a. Which of the events above could cause the equilibrium price of a product to change from X to W in Figure 6.8?

b. Which of the events above could cause the equilibrium price of a product to change from X to T in Figure 6.8?

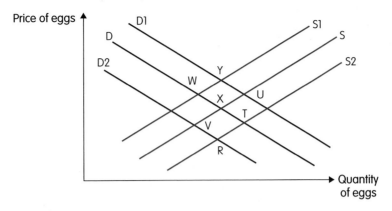

Figure 6.8 Different equilibrium points.

c. Which of the events above could cause the equilibrium price of a product to change from X to V in Figure 6.8?

d. Which of the events above could cause the equilibrium price of a product to change from X to U in Figure 6.8?

e. Which combination of the events above could cause the equilibrium price of a product to change from X to Y in Figure 6.8?

f. Which combination of the events above could cause the equilibrium price of a product to change from X to R in Figure 6.8?

Example

Imagine the equation for a straight-line demand curve is given by:

$$Q = 50 - 2P$$

The equation for the suppy curve is:

$$Q = 20 + 3P$$

Equilibrium occurs when demand equals supply—that is:

$$50 - 2P = 20 + 3P$$

rearranged as:

$$50 - 20 = 3P + 2P$$
$$30 = 5P$$
$$P = \frac{30}{5} = 6$$

So equilibrium occurs when the price is £6 and the quantity, if we use the supply equation, will be:

$$20 + (3 \times 6) = 20 + 18 = 38 \text{ units}$$

Demand now increases and becomes:

$Q = 80 - 2P$

Equilibrium now occurs when:

$80 - 2P = 20 + 3P$

rearranged

$$80 - 20 = 3P + 2P$$
$$60 = 5P$$
$$P = \frac{60}{5} = £12$$

The equilibrium price is £12.
Putting this value back into the demand equation:

$Q = 80 - (2 \times 12) = 80 - 24 = 56$

Equilibrium occurs at price £12 and output 56 units. An increase in demand has led to a higher equilibrium price and output.

Put into practice

Demand is $Q = 40 - P$

Supply is $Q = 6 + P$

- What are the equilibrium price and quantity?
- What would the new equilibrium price and quantity be if demand were to fall to $Q = 10 - 2P$?

Put into practice

Which of the following statements are true and which are false?

A fall in price in a market could be:

a. because of a movement along the demand curve.

b. because of an increase in supply.

c. because of a fall in the quantity supplied.

d. because of an increase in the price of a substitute.

▪ How can supply and demand analysis help us?

An understanding of supply and demand can help us to analyse many market situations, and to understand why the prices and quantity available in any given market are increasing or decreasing. An understanding of supply and demand will give you an insight into all kinds of markets, from diamonds to housing, from shares to oranges. The following are some examples.

- The UK economy was shrinking in 2008. This reduced demand for many normal goods and led to a switch to inferior products, such as discount brands.

- In recent years, trade between Europe and China has become much more open. This has led to a significant increase in the number of products that are produced in China now being sold in countries such as the UK. This has shifted the supply curve in a number of markets in Europe, such as clothes and footwear, to the right and led to a reduction in the worldwide price of these items.

- Developments in technology in consumer electronics markets have enabled cheaper production. This has shifted supply to the right over time and reduced the price of these products.

- If the grades required to gain a place on a particular course at university are getting higher each year, then this suggests that demand for the course is rising and/or that the supply of places is decreasing. The grades requirement acts as a price of entry.

Economics in context — Commodity prices

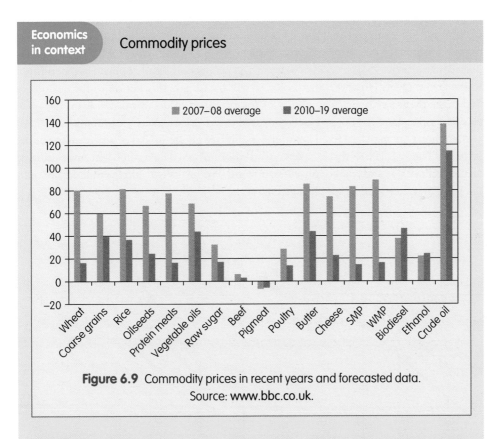

Figure 6.9 Commodity prices in recent years and forecasted data.
Source: www.bbc.co.uk.

International commodity prices are anticipated to be higher in the next decade compared to the decade before the price spike of 2007–08, which occurred due a sharp fall in supply. The forecasted increase is based on the resumption of economic growth above all in developing countries, increased demand due to rising biofuel production, and anticipated higher costs of energy-related inputs.

Average wheat and coarse grain prices are projected to be nearly 15–40 per cent higher in real terms relative to 1997–2006, while for vegetable oils, real prices are expected to be more than 40 per cent higher.

? Question

Use supply and demand analysis to explain the higher commodity prices expected in the future.

Supply and demand analysis can also be used to analyse the impact of the introduction of indirect taxes or subsidies, and the effects of these on consumers and producers.

▨ The introduction of an indirect tax

In some markets, the government may intervene, and this can affect supply and demand conditions. For example, to raise income or reduce consumption, a government may impose an indirect tax. An indirect tax, such as value added tax (VAT), is one that is placed on the provider of a good or service. The producer is legally obliged to pay this tax to the government. However, the producer will try to pass this tax on to the customers and make them pay for it. The ability of the producer to do this depends on the price elasticity of demand for the product compared to the price elasticity of supply.

An indirect tax may be a fixed amount per unit (see Figure 6.10a) or a percentage of the price (see Figure 6.10b)—this is called an 'ad valorem' tax. The result of the imposition of an indirect tax is to shift the supply curve upward. Producers will add the indirect tax onto the price that they need to supply a given output.

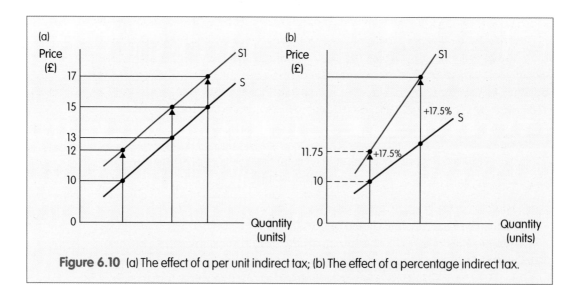

Figure 6.10 (a) The effect of a per unit indirect tax; (b) The effect of a percentage indirect tax.

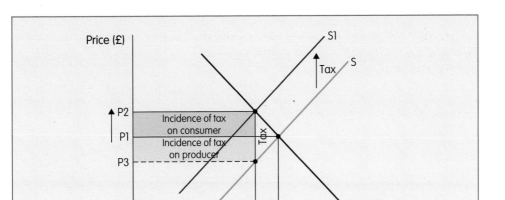

Figure 6.11 The incidence of an indirect tax on consumers and producers.

The effect of the imposition of an indirect tax on equilibrium is to increase the price in the market and reduce the quantity sold. In Figure 6.11, the effect of introducing an indirect tax is to increase the equilibrium price from P1 to P2, and to reduce the equilibrium quantity supplied from Q1 to Q2. An indirect tax therefore shifts the supply curve, and leads to fewer units being bought and sold at a higher price.

However, although the price has increased, this is not usually by the full amount of the tax imposed. The producer can shift some of the tax onto the buyer, but not all of it. In Figure 6.11, the price has risen from P1 to P2, but the tax per unit is P2 – P3. The amount of the incidence of taxation on the producer and the consumer depends on the relative price elasticity of demand and supply. If demand is more price inelastic than supply, then the consumer will pay more of the tax than the producer (see Figure 6.12a). If supply is more price inelastic than demand, then the producer will pay more of the tax than the consumer (see Figure 6.12b). The amount of tax will only be fully passed on to the customer if demand is completely price inelastic or supply is perfectly price elastic.

What do you think?

What indirect taxes exist in your country and what rates are they?
Do you think that these tax rates are too high or too low?
Do you think that they are fair?
What rates would you impose?

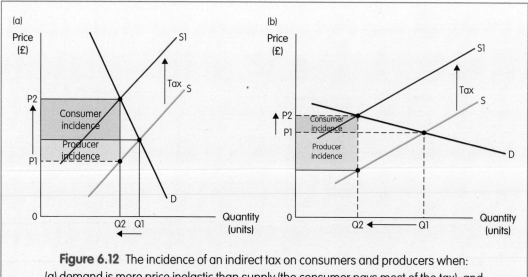

Figure 6.12 The incidence of an indirect tax on consumers and producers when: (a) demand is more price inelastic than supply (the consumer pays most of the tax); and (b) supply is more price inelastic than demand (the producer pays most of the tax).

The introduction of subsidies

In some cases, the government may want to encourage production of products (for more on this, see Chapter 8). To encourage production, the government could subsidize production. Subsidies may be paid by a government to producers of particular products to reduce their costs of production. This may be to support a developing industry, to create jobs, or to protect domestic firms against foreign competition. A subsidy will mean that producers can produce any given output at a lower market price (see Figure 6.13a). This leads to a downward shift of the supply curve and thus to a new equilibrium at which more is supplied at a lower price in the market. The extent to which the price falls depends on the price elasticity of supply and demand. The more price inelastic demand is relative to supply, the more the subsidy is passed on to suppliers (see Figure 6.13b and 6.13c).

What do you think?

What do you think might be the problems of the government subsidizing producers?

Interrelated markets

So far, we have analysed the effect of changes in supply and demand conditions in a market on the equilibrium price and output. However, markets rarely exist in isolation;

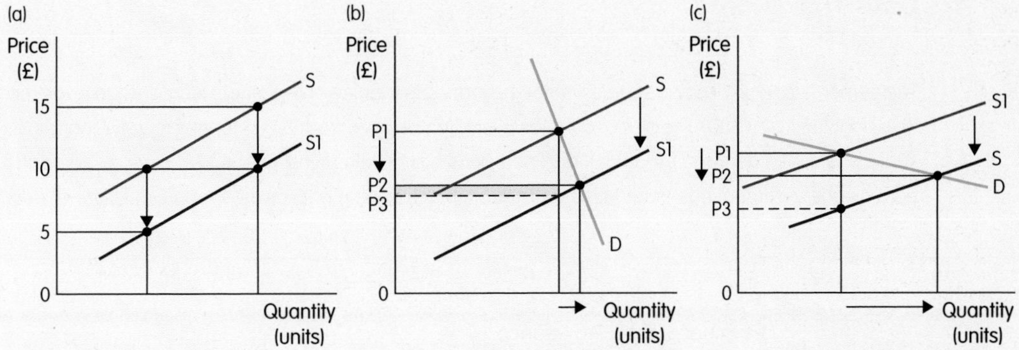

Figure 6.13 (a) The effect of a subsidy to producers on a supply curve; a subsidy means that each quantity can be supplied at a lower price; (b) The effect of a subsidy on producers and consumers when demand is more price inelastic than supply; the majority of the subsidy is passed on to the consumer (P1 – P2 out of P1 – P3). (c) The effect of a subsidy on producers and consumers when supply is more price inelastic than demand; the majority of the subsidy is kept by the producer (P2 – P3 out of P1 – P3).

in fact, an economy is a collection of millions of different markets. Many markets are therefore interrelated, meaning that changes in one market will impact on others, as in the following examples.

- Society as a whole has become more health-conscious in the UK in recent years. This has reduced demand for some products, such as high-fat foods, but at the same time has shifted demand to the right for healthier low-fat foods.

- Markets for resources such as land and labour are dependent on the demand for the final product—they are derived demands. An increase in the popularity of computer games, for example, increases demand for computer programmers; a decrease in the demand for UK coal reduces the demand for UK coal miners.

- In recent years, there has been increased demand for biofuels to use in cars. This has meant that the supply of various crops, such as sugar, has been used for this purpose, which has reduced the amount available for other uses. The increased demand for bio-fuel has increased price and made the crops scarcer in other markets.

The effect of a change in one market can therefore be traced through into the impact on other markets. A change in supply or demand conditions may well benefit some but adversely affect others, for example.

Put into practice

Can you think of examples of how changes in supply or demand may benefit some groups (for example, some firms or households), while others may be worse off?

Case study Gold

The demand for gold has two sources: some buyers want it for jewellery; others want it as an investment. Between 2000 and 2007 the global gold-jewellery demand slid from 3,205 tonnes to 2,417 tonnes; as a share of the total demand for gold, it declined from nearly 80% to just over 60%. However demand for gold as an investment has gone up. Annual 'identifiable investment', as the World Gold Council puts it,

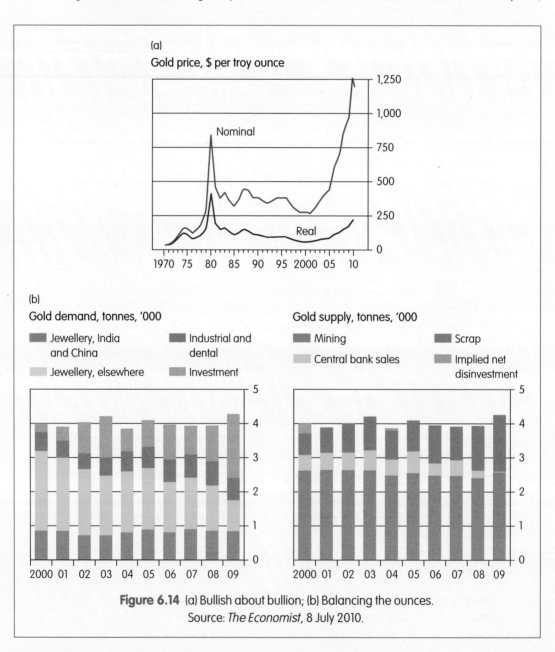

Figure 6.14 (a) Bullish about bullion; (b) Balancing the ounces.
Source: *The Economist*, 8 July 2010.

was 611 tonnes in 2004–07, a little more than twice the average for the four previous years. That just about offset the fall in jewellery demand.

Since then, however, investment demand has accelerated and jewellery demand has collapsed. 2009 was the first year in which investment demand exceeded jewellery demand. Purchases of gold for jewellery dropped to 2,193 tonnes in 2008, and then to 1,758 tonnes in 2009. Meanwhile, the signs of surging investment have been everywhere. This has more than made up for the slump in the jewellery trade: total demand in 2009 was the highest since at least 2000.

On the supply side the main source of new gold—what is dug out of the world's goldmines—has been flat or declining. Mine production peaked in 2001 at 2,646 tonnes, and has been a little less than that ever since. A combination of rising production and exploration costs, dwindling output from long-established mines in North America and South Africa, and political and economic instability in other parts of Africa means that mine supplies cannot be ramped up at will.

Another potential source of supply is sitting in the vaults of central banks. In June, national central banks, the ECB [European Central Bank], and the IMF [International Monetary Fund] held more than 30,000 tonnes in all. On average, they sold 520 tonnes a year between 2000 and 2007. Last year the flow of central bank gold almost dried up, even as the price soared. Only 41 tonnes made it to market.

The third main source of supply is scrap: jewellery sold to dealers for the value of the metal. While the price was rising steadily in the first few years of the century, scrap sales did not respond: in 2003, when the price averaged $300, sales amounted to 986 tonnes; in 2007, when the price was $700, the amount was 4 tonnes smaller. But as the price has climbed steeply since, record quantities have been sold for scrap—1,674 tonnes last year.

The sellers include middle-class Indian housewives, who habitually put their savings into gold jewellery. Last year Indians sold 115 tonnes from their private collections, a third more than in 2008. In Turkey, where 217 tonnes were sold back to jewellers, the deputy head of the Istanbul Gold Exchange says that 'a widespread belief that gold is overpriced' is leading some to sell 'anything they have'. Some sellers may also be feeling the pinch. Last year scrap sales leapt by nearly a third in America, where companies that allow people to mail jewellery in have helped drive up supply. 'Cash For Gold paid me $829 for gold jewellery I never even wear!' screams one firm's website.

Where the gold price heads in the future depends on the answers to three questions. First, for how long will investors keep piling into gold? Second, if and when they quit the market, will the demand for jewellery revive enough to support the price near recent levels? Third, how will supply respond if the price stays high?

The answer to the first question lies largely in the state of the world economy. Western investors' new interest in gold has coincided with the rich world's deepest period of economic turmoil since the 1930s. Harold James, a historian at Princeton University, argues in his latest book, *The Creation and Destruction of Value*, that crises lead to a fundamental uncertainty about what things are worth. In a world of unpredictable currencies, riven by fears of massive inflation, and with enormous doubts about the true value of many other financial instruments, gold becomes an attractive option.

Yet at some point the world will become a less nervous place. When interest rates eventually rise, the opportunity cost of holding gold will go up, taking off the shine. When the overall economic climate improves so that uncertainty about the prospects of companies is no longer so pervasive, that will provide another reason for some investors to retreat from gold. These things suggest that the swelling in investment demand in 2009 and the first half of 2010 cannot last indefinitely.

At that point, the second and third questions will become pertinent: will demand for jewellery be strong enough at today's prices to compensate for the falling away of interest from investors in the West and how will supply respond? The gold industry would hope for vigorous jewellery demand in its traditional markets, mainly India and China. Indian demand, especially, has long been reliable.

Nevertheless, the experience of the past year suggests that accounts of India's eternal attachment to gold are somewhat overplayed. Although Indians have continued to buy at high prices, they have done so in ever smaller quantities: purchases last year, at 480 tonnes, were more than 200 tonnes lower than in 2008. India and China would have to more than triple their annual purchases just to soak up the world's newly mined gold.

All this suggests that the traditional markets for gold cannot be expected to pick up the slack if rich-world investors' appetite should pall. And if prices remain high, more of the world's existing stock will augment supply. In theory, there is a lot more that could be sold for scrap. Gold's boosters are fond of pointing both to the roughly 4,000 tonnes traded every year, and emphasizing that 'all the gold that's ever been mined is still around'. Some reckon the world's total stock of gold to be about 160,000 tonnes. Only a fall in the price can hope to restore balance to the market, by boosting demand and restricting scrap supplies.

As the world economy returns to business as usual, the gold market may also return to some semblance of normality. Only when the price retreats will the housewives of Delhi go back to being net buyers. Over the years, as they get richer, their demand may increase. Or they may find other kinds of financial instruments increasingly attractive as the Indian financial market deepens.

As long as the world economy remains uncertain, and investors fear inflation and sovereign default, gold will keep its allure. Eventually, however, the price will weaken: it is even possible that the recent slide to below $1,200 marks the turn. And investors may look back on the bull run of 2009–10—or 2009–11— with the sort of wonder that humanity has too often reserved for the yellow metal itself.

❓ Questions

- Analyse two factors that influence the demand for gold. How have these factors changed in recent years?
- Analyse two factors that influence the supply of gold.
- Explain why gold prices have been relatively high in recent years, using supply and demand analysis.
- Analyse the factors determining the likely price of gold in the future.

Checklist

Now that you have read this chapter, try to answer the following questions.

- ☐ Can you explain the meaning of equilibrium in a market?
- ☐ Can you explain how the price adjusts in a market to bring about equilibrium?
- ☐ Do you understand the impact of a shift in a supply or demand curve on the equilibrium price and quantity?
- ☐ Do you understand the effect of indirect taxes and subsidies on the equilibrium price and output?
- ☐ Do you understand the factors that determine the incidence of an indirect tax or a subsidy on consumers and producers?

Review questions

1 What might cause the equilibrium price in a market to increase?

2 What might cause the equilibrium quantity in a market to increase?

3 If the supply in a market increases, what will happen to the equilibrium price?

4 How does a market return to equilibrium after an increase in demand?

5 House prices vary tremendously between regions of the UK. Explain why this might be the case by using supply and demand analysis.

Key learning points

- When a market is in equilibrium, there is no incentive to change.
- A change in supply and demand conditions will lead to a new equilibrium price and output.
- Supply and demand analysis helps to explain price and quantity changes in a wide range of markets.
- The effect on the equilibrium price relative to the equilibrium quantity of a change in supply or demand depends on the price elasticity of supply and demand.

Learn more

To see how changes in supply and demand affect market equilibrium, visit the Online Resource Centre.

 Visit our Online Resource Centre at http://www.oxfordtextbooks.co.uk/orc/gillespie_econ2e/ for test questions and further information on topics covered in this chapter.

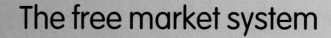

The free market system

In the preceding chapters, we have examined the workings of the free market, and the influences of supply and demand. In this chapter, we analyse the advantages and the disadvantages of the free market system as a means of allocating resources within the economy.

LEARNING OBJECTIVES

By the end of this chapter, you should be able to:

✔ explain the advantages of the free market system;

✔ understand the meaning of consumer, producer, and community surplus;

✔ analyse market failures and imperfections in the free market system;

✔ understand the difference between merit and public goods;

✔ understand the meaning of external costs and benefits;

✔ understand why a government might intervene in a free market.

■ The free market

In a free market, decisions about what to produce are determined by supply and demand in product markets. The demand for the product will then influence demand for resources. The price paid for these resources and the quantity used will be determined by supply and demand in the markets for these factors of production. The free market system assumes that consumers are attempting to maximize their utility and that producers are aiming to maximize their profits.

■ Advantages of the free market system

The question facing all societies is the extent to which private individuals and businesses should make the economic decisions, as opposed to the government. To what extent should the basic economic questions of what to produce, how to produce, and for whom to produce be left simply to market forces? Or should a centralized government try to coordinate production and consumption in its country? There are many arguments in favour of the market approach, at least in theory; one of these is the view that the free market can lead to the best allocation of resources from society's perspective and maximize social welfare. If this is true, then the government should not intervene in a market economy.

Maximizing social welfare

In a free market system, the price mechanism will adjust to equalize supply and demand. At this point, the welfare of society will be maximized. This is due to the following reasons.

- The demand curve is derived from the consumers' extra utility (or satisfaction) from consuming a unit—known as the marginal utility (MU) or benefit (MB) (see Chapter 3). For the moment, let us assume that the benefits to consumers of consuming a unit reflect the extra benefit to society as a whole. This means that the demand curve is derived from the social marginal benefit (SMB).

- The supply curve is derived from the extra costs of producing a unit (see Chapter 11). Let us assume that this shows the extra cost to society of producing a unit—that is, the social marginal cost (SMC).

At equilibrium, the quantity supplied equals the quantity demanded. This means that the extra benefit to society of the last unit produced and sold equals the extra cost to society of that unit—that is:

Social marginal benefit (SMB) = Social marginal cost (SMC)

Therefore the welfare of society will not be increased or decreased by producing another unit, which means that it must be maximized. This is shown in Figure 7.1.

In Figure 7.1, on all of the units up to Q1 the extra social benefit is greater than the extra social cost of providing it:

SMB > SMC

Therefore society as a whole will gain from these units being produced and consumed, because the benefits exceed the costs and so welfare increases.

For the units after Q1, the extra social benefits are less than the extra social costs:

SMB < SMC

This means that society would lose out if these units were produced and the total welfare would fall.

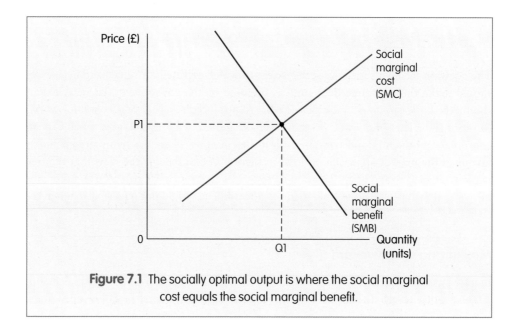

Figure 7.1 The socially optimal output is where the social marginal cost equals the social marginal benefit.

At Q1, the extra social benefit of consuming the unit equals the extra social costs of producing it:

SMB = SMC

The welfare to society is therefore maximized by producing at this level of output. This is the output level that occurs at equilibrium in the free market at Q1—that is, in the free market, the equilibrium output maximizes society's welfare.

Community surplus

Another way of analysing the way in which the free market can bring about an optimal allocation of resources is to consider the areas of consumer surplus and producer surplus.

- **Consumer surplus** measures the difference between what a consumer is willing and able to pay for a product, and what he or she actually pays. It represents utility for the customer for which he or she has not paid.

   Given the law of diminishing marginal utility, the extra satisfaction of each extra unit of a product that is consumed will fall. This means that the amount that consumers are willing to pay for a unit will fall as extra units are demanded. The price paid would fall for the extra unit and all of the ones before; this creates consumer surplus (see Figure 7.2).

   For example, a consumer may be willing to pay £10 for the first unit of a product. If two units are demanded, then the consumer may think that the second one is only worth £9, and so pays £9 for each of them. This means that, on the first unit, there is £1 of utility that is not paid for; this is consumer surplus. Similarly, if the third unit

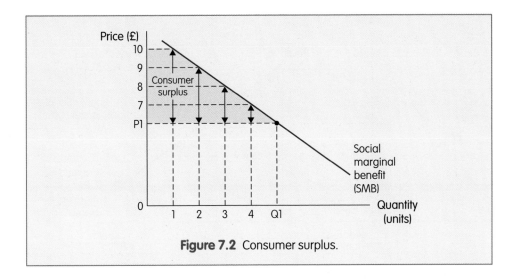

Figure 7.2 Consumer surplus.

has a utility worth £8 and the consumer buys three units at £8 each, then there is a consumer surplus of £2 on the first unit and £1 on the second unit—that is, £3 of utility that is not paid for in total.

- **Producer surplus** measures the difference between the price that producers are willing and able to sell at and the price that they actually receive. To sell more units, a firm will want a higher price to cover the higher additional costs. Assuming this higher price is paid on all of the units produced, this creates a producer surplus.

  For example, imagine that a firm is willing to sell one unit at £5, but would need £7 to sell a second unit; if it sells two units at £7 each, then a surplus of £2 is created on the first one. In Figure 7.3, the producer surplus equals the shaded area.

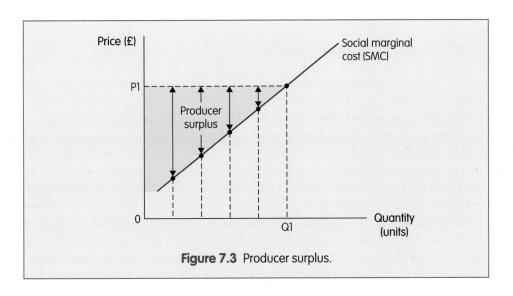

Figure 7.3 Producer surplus.

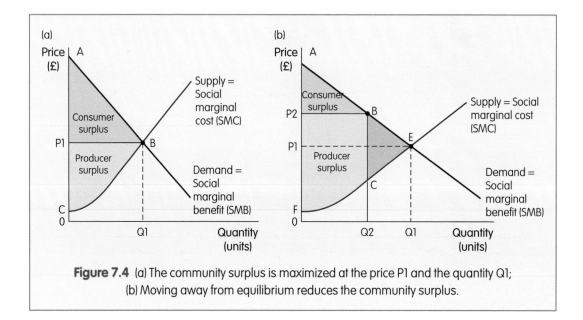

Figure 7.4 (a) The community surplus is maximized at the price P1 and the quantity Q1; (b) Moving away from equilibrium reduces the community surplus.

- **Community surplus** is made up of producer surplus and consumer surplus. This combines the extra utility to consumers for which they do not pay, and the rewards to producers over and above the price that they need to supply these units. Community surplus represents welfare to consumers and producers that has not been paid for, and can be written as:

    Community surplus = Consumer surplus + Producer surplus

In Figure 7.4a, in a free market equilibrium at the price P1 and the quantity Q1, the community surplus is equal to the area ABC. This area is the maximum that it can be, so welfare is maximized in this situation in the free market. No combination of price and quantity would generate as much community surplus as the free market result of the price P1 and the quantity Q1. This another way of demonstrating that, in theory, the free market leads to the optimal allocation of resources.

Imagine, for example, that the market price was forced up to P2 (see Figure 7.4b). The quantity demanded and therefore sold would be Q2. The consumer surplus would be equal to the area P2AB and the producer surplus would be equal to the area P2BCF. Overall, the community surplus would be the area ABCF—less than it was at equilibrium by the area BEC.

In theory, then, the free market could lead the economy to an optimal position in equilibrium, maximizing community surplus. In reality, however, there are numerous market failures and imperfections that prevent this optimal allocation being generated. This is why there is a case for government intervention. The issues, then, are how much intervention is justified and what is the best way of intervening.

The disadvantages of the market system: Market failures and imperfections

The socially optimal output exists when society is producing and consuming at the level at which

Social marginal benefit (SMB) = Social marginal cost (SMC)

At this output, society's welfare cannot be increased further.

A market failure exists if the market is selling an output where the marginal cost to society of making a product does not equal the marginal benefit to society of consuming that good or service.

If a market settles at an output where the social marginal benefit is greater than the social marginal cost (SMB > SMC) (for example, at Q3 in Figure 7.5), then society would benefit from an additional unit being produced. Social welfare would be increased if more units were produced. If, on the other hand, the social marginal benefit of a unit is less than the social marginal cost (SMB < SMC) (for example, at Q4 in Figure 7.5), then producing this unit reduces the total social welfare and this unit should not be produced or consumed.

The causes of market failures and imperfections in the free market include the following.

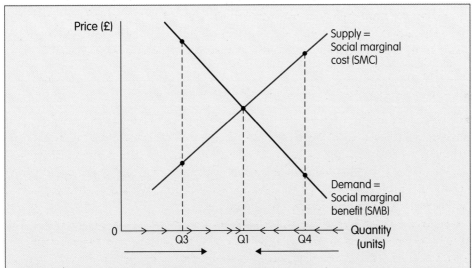

Figure 7.5 The socially optimal output is at the quantity Q1. Here, the social marginal cost equals the social marginal benefit; the welfare of society cannot be increased—it is maximized. At the quantity Q3, the social marginal benefit is greater than the social marginal cost; the welfare of society would be increased if more was produced. At the quantity Q4 the social marginal benefit is less than the social marginal cost; the welfare of society would be increased if less was produced.

Monopoly power

So far, we have assumed that market forces are allowed to operate, and that these will lead to an equilibrium price of P1 and an output of Q1. However, in some markets, one or more firms may come to dominate and exert monopoly power. A pure monopoly occurs when one firm has 100 per cent control of a market. In this situation, a monopolist is able to determine how much output it sells and at what price.

A monopolist is a price-setter. For example, it may decide to restrict output and push up the price, selling the quantity Q2 at price P2 (see Figure 7.6). This has the effect of increasing producer surplus from P1AB to P2CDB, which means that producers gain even more than the costs of producing these units. However, the effect of this monopoly action is also to reduce consumer surplus from EAP1 to ECP2. This means that, with monopoly power, producers gain at the expense of consumers (which, of course, is why they do it). There is also a reduction in the overall community surplus, which has fallen from EAB to ECDB. This means that there is a welfare loss (also called a deadweight social burden triangle) equal to CAD.

On all of the units between Q2 and Q1 that are not produced by the monopolist, the extra benefit to society is greater than the extra cost of producing them. Society as a whole would therefore benefit from producing these units. However, the monopolist would not benefit, because it would have to lower prices to sell these extra units; this is why it chose to restrict output in the first place.

Monopoly power is therefore likely to lead to a lower output and higher price than would be achieved in a competitive market. The effect of monopoly is to reduce the overall welfare of society. This is examined in more detail in Chapter 12.

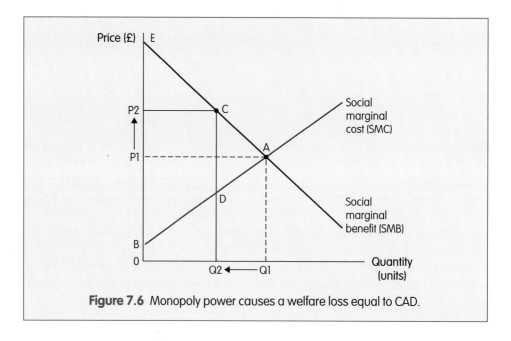

Figure 7.6 Monopoly power causes a welfare loss equal to CAD.

What do you think?

If monopolies can cause problems in an economy, should the government stop firms from getting bigger?

Put into practice

If a market is producing where the social marginal benefit of a unit is greater than the social marginal cost, should it produce more or fewer units? Explain your answer.

Externalities

In a free market, the amount that customers demand and are willing to pay for products naturally depends on the benefits that they personally receive. Individuals pursue their own interests and aim to maximize their utility. However, the benefit (or utility) that an individual customer derives from consuming a unit is not necessarily the same as the benefit that society as a whole derives from a product. This can mean that the allocation of resources in the free market is not the allocation that society as a whole would want, because of the differences between private and social benefits.

For example, when you are considering whether or not to have a flu vaccination, you will think of the personal benefit of not catching flu in the future; you will not think about the benefits to others if you were vaccinated. However, if you do not catch flu, then you are not going to pass it on to others, so this will have a benefit for other people as well as yourself. The social benefits of vaccination are therefore greater than the private benefits. This is known as a positive consumption externality: the social benefits are equal to the private benefits plus the external benefits to society. In this case, the demand curve from society's point of view is higher than it would be from a private perspective; this is because the social marginal benefits of each unit are greater than the private marginal benefits.

In a free market, the equilibrium price and output outcomes would be P1 and Q1, respectively (see Figure 7.7). However, given the additional social benefits of these units, the most socially desirable outcome is the price P2 and the quantity Q2. This means there are underproduction and underconsumption of the product (in this case, vaccinations) in the free market. On every unit between Q1 and Q2, the extra benefit to society is greater than the extra cost to society. So society would benefit if more units were provided. This means that the shaded region in Figure 7.7 represents a potential welfare gain if there were intervention to move the market to the socially optimal price and output.

Another situation in which the free market system may fail is if the extra cost of producing is higher for society as a whole than the extra cost of producing for private producers. This is known as a negative production externality. Left to themselves, firms will only take account of the costs for which they have to pay, such as labour, land, and

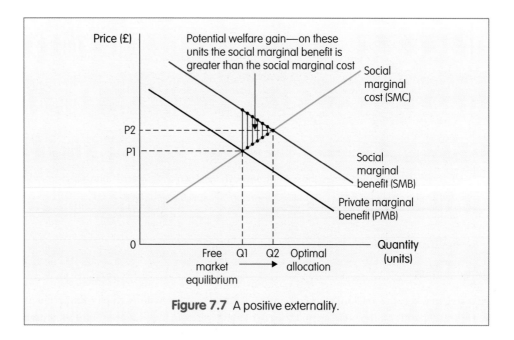

Figure 7.7 A positive externality.

machines. These are private costs. They will not take account of other costs that affect society as a whole—for example:

- their factory may be noisy and this may upset local residents;
- the production process may be generating pollution; and
- when employees come to work in the morning they may cause traffic jams and congestion.

This means that the firm's activities are generating external costs; these are costs imposed on society as a whole of which a firm would not take account in a free market. The social costs to society are equal to the private costs *plus* the external costs:

Social costs = Private costs + External costs

If the social costs are higher than the private costs, then a negative externality exists. In this case, the supply curve in the free market does not fully reflect the extra costs of producing each unit because the external costs are not included. If they are included, then the supply curve would move upwards. A higher price is needed for each unit to cover the additional external costs.

What do you think?

Pollution is an external cost. Left to themselves, firms and private drivers would not take account of the costs of pollution. Do you think that, if you were in government, the right thing to do would be to aim to reduce pollution to zero?

At the moment, in the UK, all private drivers pay the same road tax. Should we tax drivers according to how many miles that they drive?

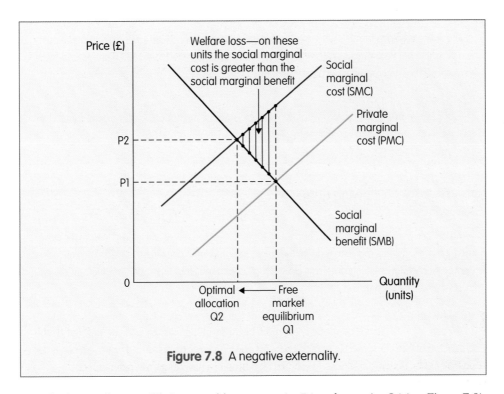

Figure 7.8 A negative externality.

In the free market, equilibrium would occur at price P1 and quantity Q1 (see Figure 7.8). However, taking account of the full social costs of production, the socially desirable outcome would be at price P2 and quantity Q2. In the free market, there are overproduction and overconsumption. This is because the firm does not appreciate the full costs of providing the product. This leads to a welfare loss. On the units Q1 to Q2, the extra social cost of these units is greater than the extra benefit. This means that the welfare of society is being reduced by producing these units. A more socially optimal allocation of resources would be at the price P2 and the quantity Q2.

NOTE Just because a negative external cost exists, it does not mean that we should stop production of the product altogether: this is because producing the product does provide benefits as well. What is needed is intervention to achieve the optimal allocation of resources, which would not happen in the free market. This happens at the output at which the social marginal benefit equals the social marginal cost.

Economics in context   Chickens

A huge amount of toxic waste is created by poultry farms in Arkansas; this runs into streams and pollutes the water for the Illinois watershed that supplies 22 public water companies in eastern Oklahoma. For years, Oklahoman officials have complained about this and, a few years ago, they took Arkansas to court. The phosphorus from poultry is equivalent to that generated by 10.7 million people (more than the populations of Arkansas, Kansas, and Oklahoma combined).

The waste is sold to farmers who use it as fertilizer and it then finds its way into the water. Poultry is a $2 billion per year business. The poultry industry has threatened to leave Arkansas and move to Mexico if the requirements become too tough.

 Question

One solution to this toxic problem would be to tax the Arkansas farmers for the external costs that they generate. How would you estimate this?

Economics in context   Chewing gum

In the UK, chewing gum costs local councils well over £4 million per year to clean up from the pavements. It actually costs more to clean up the chewing gum than it does to produce it! The producers and consumers of chewing gum are generating an external cost to society that we have to pay through taxes to clean up.

 Question

Taxes are already placed on many consumers because of the external costs generated by the products that they consume. For example, drivers pay high taxes on petrol and air travellers pay tax on their flights. Do you think that a tax should be placed on chewing gum consumers?

Merit goods

- A **merit good** is one that society believes is more beneficial than private individuals do. For example, individuals may not appreciate at the time how important and beneficial education or health care is to them. In one sense, a merit good is like a positive externality; however, they occur specifically because the government may know more than we do what is good for us (as opposed to positive consumption externalities, the external benefits of which we may know, but about which we may not care). Merit goods would be underconsumed in the free market because we underestimate their benefits. For example, the government might sponsor the arts, opera, museums, and art galleries on the basis that these are good for society as a whole.

- **Demerit goods** are products that we might want to consume without appreciating the harm that they are doing to us—for example, cigarettes. Once again, they arise because the government may know more than we do, or may know what is in our best interests, and may therefore discourage or prevent consumption of them. We may thank the government later on when we appreciate how bad these products were!

What do you think?

What products would you classify as merit goods?

What do you think are demerit goods?

Do you think that society's views of what are and what are not merit goods might change over time?

What do you think?

The total legal global gambling market in 2009 was worth around $335 billion. In 2006, the US Congress passed the Unlawful Internet Gaming Enforcement Act, which made it illegal for financial institutions to transfer funds between gamblers and online gambling sites. Do you think that governments should intervene to ban online gambling?

Public goods

A public good is a product that is non-diminishable and non-excludable. This means that, once it is provided, it does not matter how many people consume it—it will still be available to everyone. The addition of extra users does not reduce the amount that others can consume. For example, a lighthouse is a public good. Once it is built, all ships can benefit from it—it does not matter how many ships are passing by, they can all gain from the light being shown. This means that the provision of this service is non-diminishable. With private goods, there is a limited amount available at any moment. More consumption by one person reduces the amount left for others: for example, if you buy a pair of Nike trainers in a shop, then you have reduced the number of pairs available at that particular moment for others to buy—you are competing with others to buy this product.

Public goods are also 'non-excludable' because it is difficult to stop people (or ships!) from benefiting from them. Any ship passing by a lighthouse will gain from it. Similarly, if you install a street light or make an area safer by having regular police patrols, then everyone can gain and it is difficult to restrict the service to those who pay. The development of open-access wireless networks has created a public good in recent years. However, many people protect their networks to prevent anyone being able to access them.

The problem with public goods is that, in a free market, firms will be unwilling to provide them because they cannot restrict consumption to those who pay for them. Households will be unwilling to pay for something from which others will be able to benefit. Many will try to benefit from someone else providing it. This creates the 'free rider' problem: people will wait in the hope that someone else will pay for the service, so that they can be a free rider and benefit from it as well without actually paying for it. In this case, the government has to step in to provide such products.

Instability

Another problem in the free market is that prices can fluctuate significantly. The fact that the price adjusts to ensure that supply equals demand can lead to major and sudden swings in price as supply and demand conditions change. A fall in supply can lead to a higher equilibrium price and a lower quantity; a fall in demand can lead to a fall in the equilibrium price and sales. This instability can make it difficult for firms and consumers to plan. Price instability can be seen in many sectors, such as the markets for currency, shares, and oil. If the government thinks that instability is undesirable (for example, unstable agricultural prices may deter farmers from continuing production, and problems in planning because of price instability may reduce investment and growth in an

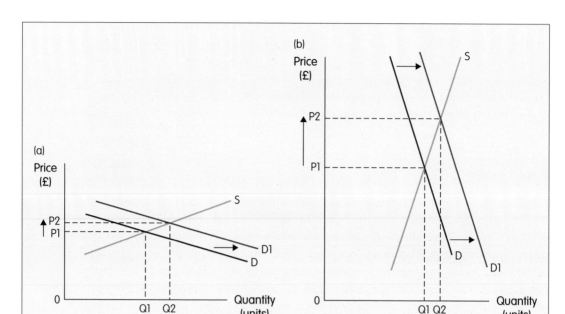

Figure 7.9 A shift in demand when: (a) demand and supply are price elastic (a shift in either curve affects output more than price); and (b) demand and supply are price inelastic (a shift in either curve affects price more than output).

economy), then it may intervene to bring about more stable prices. Price instability is a particular issue if supply and demand are price inelastic, because any given shift in the curves has relatively more impact on price than quantity (see Figure 7.9).

Put into practice

- What should happen to the equilibrium price and quantity if the supply curve shifts to the right?
- What if demand shifts to the left?

Income inequality

A free market is likely to lead to income inequality. Some firms and individuals may earn very high incomes if they have products or skills that are in demand; other people's skills may be less in demand and, as a result, they may have lower incomes—for example, a cleaner compared with a premier league football player. In terms of an economic outcome, this may be efficient, and the labour market may be working perfectly well; however, voters may decide that it is unfair and not a desirable outcome. If this is the case, society may want a government to do something about the income distribution:

for example, a government may provide some products freely to everyone so that they can all benefit from them. It may also use taxes and subsidies to redistribute income in the economy. Income inequality is examined in more detail in Chapter 20.

What do you think?

Do you think that the government should intervene to reduce the amount of income inequality in an economy? If so, how much intervention do you think is desirable?

What do you think would be a fair tax rate on people's earnings?

Do you think that people should be allowed to inherit money and property?

Missing information

Problems may occur in the free market due to a lack of information. Buyers may not know what is available or what alternatives they have. Many cinemas and restaurants will be half-empty some of the time and have queues outside them on other occasions. In theory, the price mechanism adjusts to make supply equal to demand. In the case of a cinema, then, given that there is a limited number of seats, when there is a high level of interest in a film, the price should increase to ration demand. On other occasions, if demand for a film is going to be low, then the price should fall to attract more customers. However, cinema managers do not know in advance what demand will be for any particular showing. Therefore they set an average price. Sometimes, this will be too high for the actual level of demand, leading to excess supply and empty seats in the cinema. At other times, it will be too low for the actual level of demand, leading to excess demand and queues outside. For major sporting events, you will usually find ticket touts trying to sell you tickets at a much higher price than that for which they were originally sold. This is because the initial price that was set for these events was too low. Therefore there was excess demand. Ticket touts get hold of the tickets at the original price and sell them on to others who really want them for a much higher price. In this case, the ticket touts are helping the market mechanism to work because the original price was not the equilibrium one.

Other information problems include the following.

- **Asymmetric information** This was examined by George Akerlof in his analysis of the second-hand car market in which he analysed the problem of 'lemons'. A 'lemon' is the name given to a poor-quality second-hand car. Akerlof showed that buyers of second-hand cars are never sure if they will be buying a lemon or not, and so are only willing to offer average prices for what might actually be better-than-average second-hand cars. This then means that people with better-than-average second-hand cars decide not to sell them; therefore the average price becomes too high for what is actually on the market and the price falls. This could potentially lead to the collapse of the market entirely.

- **Adverse selection** This occurs when individuals have inside information and use this to decide whether to accept or reject an offer. Imagine, for example, a medical insurance company that bases its premiums on the typical mortality rate for the country as a whole. Amongst the population there are those who smoke, drink excessively, and do not exercise. These people would regard this premium as very cheap. On the other hand, the very healthy individuals would regard it as very expensive. Unfortunately, the insurance company cannot easily tell who is unhealthy and who is not. The result is that the healthy people will not buy the insurance because it is too expensive, but the unhealthy will, because it is cheap for them. To try to overcome this problem, insurance companies try to gather evidence (for example, medical testing) to prove that the person to be insured is healthy.

What do you think?

Ticket touts are selling tickets for major sports and music events on online auction sites with a typical profit of 59 per cent, according to recent research. Prices are being inflated after touts buy tickets for events that they have no plans to attend. Touts also target fans outside gigs and matches, and charge a huge mark-up.

The average mark-up on online black market tickets has fallen from 64 per cent in 2009 and 71 per cent in 2008, owing to a better supply of tickets on the Internet.

Some key events still attract large price tags. Examples from the survey include:

- a pair of Paul McCartney tickets sold for £450—some 235 per cent over face value;
- two tickets for the V Festival sold for £430—the pair had a face value of £162.50; and
- a £35 international rugby ticket sold for £85.

Do you think that ticket touting should be illegal?

Economics in context — Goldman Sachs

In 2010, US bank Goldman Sachs agreed to pay $550 million (£356 million) to settle civil fraud charges of misleading investors. The charges concerned Goldman's marketing of mortgage investments. The US finance regulator, the Securities and Exchange Commission (SEC), said that it was the biggest fine for a bank in its history. The SEC said that Goldman had acknowledged that marketing material contained 'incomplete information'. In a statement, Goldman did not admit legal wrongdoing, but said that the move was 'the right outcome for our firm, our shareholders, and our clients'.

 Question

In what way does the Goldman Sachs example highlight a potential failure of the free market?

Another information problem in the free market is known as moral hazard. Take the case of an insurance company trying to decide on how much to charge people for health care. Someone who has been insured faces a moral hazard, because he or she is likely to be less concerned about his or her health now he or she is insured, and this may bring about more claims. Similarly, a car driver may drive less carefully if he or she is insured because the damage will be covered.

Economics in context   Moral hazard

In 2008, the UK government had to intervene to support the Royal Bank of Scotland and Lloyds Bank to prevent a financial crisis. Some analysts felt that this created a moral hazard issue. This moral hazard arose because, through rapid growth, some banks became so big and so vital to the economy and the financial system that, because they knew that government would ultimately save them, they had less incentive to protect themselves against incurring excessive risk. This problem has posed a major threat to financial stability in the UK, has caused and prolonged the downturn of the economy, and has exposed taxpayers in the UK to more risk. Similarly, there have been worries about subsidizing industries such as the car industry when it is struggling. If a business knows that it will be subsidized, then will it stop trying as hard to be efficient?

❓ Question

How might the government avoid the moral hazard issue outlined above?

Case study Wheat prices

Wheat prices hit a 22-month high in 2010 after a major drought and ensuing wildfires in Russia devastated crops. In August 2010, the price broke through the $7-a-bushel level in US trade for the first time since September 2008, before falling back to $6.93. There were concerns that this rise would increase the prices of flour-related products, such as bread and biscuits.

The head of wheat procurement at Premier Foods, which makes Hovis bread, told the *Financial Times* that the industry would be 'unable to ignore a 50 per cent rise in wheat prices'.

Russia is the world's fourth-largest wheat exporter after the USA, the European Union (EU), and Canada. Along with other former Soviet Republics such as Kazakhstan, it accounted for about 25 per cent of the world's wheat exports in 2009.

The drought and fires would have an effect on food prices and hit the consumer, as well as food company profits. Not only would products directly affected by wheat, such as bread, be affected, but, given that animals are fed on wheat or wheat derivatives, this supply shock was also likely to affect meat and poultry prices.

However, Russia has high levels of grain in reserves and these may be able to compensate for at least some of the fall in supply. Even so, the likely output from Russia was likely to be between 70 million and 75 million tonnes compared with 97 million tonnes in 2009.

The likely rise immediately affected speculators, who started to buy wheat, expecting greater increases in the future.

❓ Questions

- Using supply and demand analysis, show the effect of the drought and fires in Russia on the wheat market. Think about the price elasticity of demand and supply, and explain your choices.

- Using supply and demand analysis, show the effect of an increase in the price of wheat on the meat and poultry markets.
- Analyse the possible effects of an increase in the price of wheat on the economy.
- If Russia releases reserves of wheat onto the market, how would this be shown on a supply and demand diagram?

Checklist

Now that you have read this chapter, try to answer the following questions.

- ☐ Can you explain the advantages of the free market system?
- ☐ Do you understand the meaning of consumer, producer, and community surplus?
- ☐ Do you understand the difference between merit and public goods?
- ☐ Do you understand the meaning of external costs and benefits?
- ☐ Are you able to analyse market failures and imperfections in the free market system?

Review questions

1 Is a public good any product that is provided by the government?
2 Why might monopolies be undesirable?
3 Should the government ban all smoking because it has negative external costs?
4 Should the UK government subsidize opera? What about football?
5 What problems can imperfect information cause in a free market?

Key learning points

- In a perfect world, the free market would lead to an optimal allocation of resources. It would maximize community surplus and society would be producing an output at which the social marginal benefit equals the social marginal cost.
- There are many imperfections in the free market that move it away from the optimal allocation of resources. This is why government intervention may be necessary.
- Market failures and imperfections include public goods, externalities, monopolies, instability, merit goods, and information problems.

Learn more

Monopoly power is a major imperfection in the free market system. For a more detailed analysis of the impact of a monopoly on a market, see Chapter 12.

 Visit our Online Resource Centre at http://www.oxfordtextbooks.co.uk/orc/gillespie_econ2e/ for test questions and further information on topics covered in this chapter.

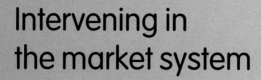

Intervening in the market system

In the previous chapter, we examined some of the potential advantages of the free market system as a way of allocating resources within an economy. However, we also highlighted several limitations and problems of the free market system. In this chapter, we consider how a government might intervene in a free market to help to overcome such problems.

LEARNING OBJECTIVES

By the end of this chapter, you should be able to:

✔ explain how governments intervene in the free market;

✔ understand the impact of maximum and minimum prices;

✔ understand the workings of a buffer stock scheme;

✔ explain the reasons for nationalization and privatization;

✔ explain the problems of privatization.

■ Intervention in markets

In a perfect free market system, the market forces of supply and demand would lead to the optimal allocation of resources where the social marginal benefit equals the social marginal cost, and community surplus is maximized (see Chapter 7). However, as we saw in the previous chapter, a number of market failures and imperfections exist that may justify government intervention.

The ways in which the government may intervene in a market include the following.

• **The direct provision of goods and services** For example, society may believe that education, police protection, natonal defence, and health care should be freely available to all of its citizens, and therefore the government may provide these. A key political, as well as economic, decision is the extent to which governments should directly provide goods and services.

- **Legislation and regulation** A government may pass laws to control certain types of behaviour. For example, if it feels that wages are too low in a free market, then it may introduce a minimum wage that employers have to pay. It may also organize stabilization schemes to prevent price instability in markets such as agriculture. Laws affect a number of areas of business behaviour, such as employment, competition, health and safety, and consumer protection.

Economics in context **Bank regulation**

During the global banking crisis of 2008, several major banks closed down (such as Lehman Brothers in the USA) following their excessively risky lending. As a result, governments around the world wanted to prevent such a disaster from happening again. Attempts to assess the potential risks included stress tests introduced by the Committee of European Banking Supervisors (CEBS); this was to see what the banks' financial position would be if there were to be further economic problems. A total of 91 banks from across Europe underwent 'stress tests' to analyse their ability to survive future economic shocks. Seven of the 91 European banks investigated failed the health checks. They included five Spanish banks: Diada; Espiga; Banca Civica; Unnim; and Cajasur. The other two were Germany's Hypo Real Estate and Greece's ATE bank. The seven banks needed a total of €3.5 billion (£3 billion) of new capital to meet the standards required, according to the CEBS.

Questions

Why might the banks have made excessively risky loans?

Do you think that the government should take control of the banking system?

Should governments provide the banks at risk with the billions of pounds required?

- **Subsidies and taxes** These can be used as 'carrot' and 'stick' policies to encourage certain types of behaviour and to deter other activities. This will change the allocation of resources away from the free market position toward a more socially optimal outcome. For example, undesirable behaviour may be taxed to discourage it; desirable behaviour may be subsidized to encourage it.

- **Providing information to promote particular forms of behaviour** For example, the government may invest in publicity information to encourage individuals to undertake training, to relocate to get a job, to recycle, or to conserve energy.

What do you think?

In what ways do you think consumers need protecting from firms?

The UK water industry has been privatized, enabling private businesses to sell the supply of water to households and firms. However, the industry is dominated by relatively few providers and this is an essential service, and therefore the government closely regulates this market. Ofwat is the UK regulator of the water industry. Ofwat defines its role as:

> Our job is to make sure that your water company provides you with a good quality service at a fair price.
>   We do this by:

- keeping bills for consumers as low as possible
- monitoring, and comparing the services the companies provide
- scrutinizing the companies' costs, and investment
- encouraging competition where this benefits consumers

If a company falls short of what we or customers expect we take the action necessary to protect consumers' interests, which may include legal steps such as enforcement action, and fines.

❓ Questions

What do you think might happen if the water companies were not regulated by the government? How might the performance of the water companies be different under private ownership compared with being government owned?

▩ Examples of government intervention in the market system

The following are examples of government intervention in the market system.

Regulating monopoly and competitive behaviour

Competition policy aims to prevent anti-competitive behaviour. For example, it is possible that if a few firms dominate a market, then they will charge relatively high prices and provide a poor service to customers. There may be less investment in research and development (R&D), leading to less innovation and a fall in quality. Producer surplus rises, consumer surplus falls, and there is a welfare loss (see Chapter 7, or for more detailed analysis, Chapter 12). Given that buyers do not have many alternatives, they may have to accept such behaviour. To prevent this, the government may decide to intervene.

Other forms of anti-competitive behaviour include:

- firms fixing prices as part of a cartel;
- firms engaging in price wars (or predatory pricing) to undercut the competition and gain control over a market; and
- firms controlling supply and preventing other firms from gaining access to the market.

The following is a description of competition policy according to the UK government's Department for Business Innovation and Skills:

> Competitive markets provide the best means of ensuring the economy's resources are put to their best use by encouraging enterprise, and efficiency, and widening choice. Where markets work well they provide a strong incentive for good performance—encouraging firms to improve productivity, to reduce prices, and to innovate whilst rewarding consumers with lower prices, higher quality, and wider choice . . . But markets can and do fail. Competition policy is therefore used to ensure the efficient workings of markets, and to avoid market failure, most notably the abuses of market power.

What do you think?

Do you think that greater competition in markets is a good thing?
Can monopoly power ever be justified or desirable?

In the UK, competition policy is regulated by the following organizations.

- **Office of Fair Trading (OFT)** The OFT exists to make markets work better. It deals with anti-competitive practices through enforcement and communication.

- **Competition Commission** The Commission conducts inquiries into mergers, markets, and the regulation of regulated markets if an issue is referred to it by, for example, the OFT or the relevant secretary of state. The Commission can investigate if a merger or takeover leads to a market share of over 25 per cent. It has the ability to force such firms to sell parts of their business or reduce their prices. It can also prevent one firm from buying another (a takeover) or firms joining together (a merger) if it feels that it would lead to too much market power, and to behaviour that would act against the public interest.

- **Restrictive Practices Court** The Court examines agreements between firms supplying goods and services in the UK, such as collusive pricing. These agreements are presumed to be unfair unless they meet one of eight possible 'gateways' or justifications: for example, that they are needed to prevent high levels of unemployment in an area.

UK competition legislation includes the Competition Act 1998 and the Enterprise Act 2002. The UK is also subject to Articles 85 and 86 of the Treaty of Rome—that is, the treaty establishing the European Economic Community (EEC), subsequently the European Union (EU)—which cover restrictive practices and monopolies.

UK firms are also subject to EU legislation on competition. Article 85 states that restrictive practices (for example, when firms collude) must be stated and these are usually prohibited. Article 86 bans the abuse of a 'dominant position' by a firm.

Economics in context — Competition Commission

The Competition Commission (CC) is one of the independent public bodies which help ensure healthy competition between companies in the UK for the benefit of companies, customers, and the economy.

We investigate, and address issues of concern in three areas:

- In mergers—when larger companies will gain more than 25% market share, and where a merger appears likely to lead to a substantial lessening of competition in one or more markets in the UK.

- In markets—when it appears that competition may be being prevented, distorted or restricted in a particular market.

- In regulated sectors where aspects of the regulatory system may not be operating effectively or to address certain categories of dispute between regulators, and regulated companies.

Our inquiries are always initiated following a concern referred to us by another authority: usually the Office of Fair Trading.

Source: Competition Commission

 Questions

What do you think are the potential dangers of companies having more than 25 per cent market share? Can you think of businesses that do have more than 25 per cent market share? How do you think they have achieved this dominance? Do you think that this dominance of a market is likely to be good or bad for customers in their markets?

Economics in context — Collusion

In 2003, the OFT launched an investigation into possible collusion between tobacco manufacturers, Imperial Tobacco and Gallaher, and 11 retailers to fix prices (which is a restrictive practice). As a result of its investigations, the OFT decided to impose fines of £225 million.

The OFT has concluded that each manufacturer had a series of individual arrangements with each retailer whereby the retail price of a tobacco brand was linked to that of a competing manufacturer's brand. These arrangements restricted the ability of these retailers to determine their selling prices independently, and breached the Competition Act 1998.

The OFT said that the companies were guilty of 'price linking', or 'price matching'. It said that Imperial and Gallaher had come to an arrangement with each retailer that if one or other manufacturer were to increase or decrease prices, the retailer would alter the price of the competitor brand in line, up or down accordingly—a practice known in competition law circles as 'vertical price collusion'.

Source: Competition Commission

 Questions

Why might companies engage in price fixing?

Why should the government intervene in the case of price fixing?

Are there situations in which you think price fixing should be allowed?

Taxing negative externalities

Negative production externalities occur when the social cost of an activity is greater than the private cost of providing it. Given that private firms do not take account of the external effects of their actions, they will overproduce these products in a free market. To remedy this, the government may place indirect taxes on the products concerned. This will increase their private costs and, hopefully, raise them to the level of the social costs. This is known as 'internalizing external costs'. Indirect taxes on products such as cigarettes, petrol, and alcohol are to ensure that producers take account of external costs. However, this may be easier to do in theory than in practice; this is because it is often difficult to quantify external costs precisely, and therefore the government may not know exactly what level of taxes to place on selected products to achieve the optimal allocation of goods and services.

What do you think?

What other products can you think of that generate a negative externality when they are produced or consumed?

Using new plastic bags every time you go to the supermarket creates more waste. Should the supermarkets charge you for each bag that they give you or should they subsidize you if you bring your own bag? Is one of these policies likely to be more effective than the other?

Economics in context   Externalities

According to a recent RAC report, UK traffic levels could increase by 33 per cent within 15 years thanks to population growth and a growing economy. At the same time, limited government budgets mean that more roads are unlikely.

As a result, the RAC argues that charging motorists for each mile that they travel is 'inevitable' if a future traffic gridlock is to be avoided.

The government says that it has no plans to charge drivers on existing roads, but has said that it may consider charging on new routes, using the M6 toll road in the Midlands as an example. The RAC report found that 58 per cent of drivers agreed that a per-mile, pay-as-you-go system would make them think about how much they drive.

However, to gain public support, a system of charging motorists per mile would probably have to be backed by a cut in fuel duty and abolition of vehicle tax. Local road-pricing schemes already exist in the UK. Congestion charging was introduced in Durham in 2002 and in London the following year, while other areas have considered similar schemes. However, the previous Labour government's drive to encourage such schemes was effectively abandoned after people in Greater Manchester voted four to one against its introduction.

 Questions

Outline the case for a road-pricing scheme.

Why do you think motorists might object to such a scheme?

Waste charges

Households are now being awarded points for the amount of their waste that they recycle, which can be redeemed at shops, restaurants, and leisure centres, or donated to schools. The pilot schemes in Windsor and Maidenhead had increased recycling by 35 per cent, and supporters argue that an incentive-based approach is more effective than taxes or fines in reducing the amount of rubbish sent to landfill sites.

Incentivizing people is said to be the quickest way to increase recycling levels, which a government spokesperson said would be badly needed if the UK were to meet its target of becoming 'one of the green economies of Europe'.

'It does not put the costs up,' he added. 'Actually, what it does is it increases the recycling rate and puts money into the local economy.'

Almost 37 per cent of home rubbish was recycled in England in 2008–09—a massive increase since 2000–01, when only 11.2 per cent was recycled.

What is collected varies too: all English councils take glass, cans, and paper, and most gather plastic bottles, but only a fifth accept all plastics.

Over a hundred local authorities now collect food waste—a figure that is likely to increase as pressure grows to keep biodegradable waste out of landfill, where it creates methane gas.

 Questions

In what ways are recycling schemes offsetting a market failure?

What factors do you think will influence the success of the schemes outlined above?

Do you think that there are better ways of achieving more recycling?

Tobacco

In China attitudes to tobacco are very different from the UK. The Ministry of Health has published an annual tobacco control report, and there have been campaigns to increase the tobacco tax and warnings added to packaging. However, tobacco control faces great opposition. Tobacco control is not mentioned at all as a priority in the health reform plan, and the budget for tobacco-related problems only accounts for 0.5% of the total budget for disease control and prevention.

The State Tobacco Monopoly Administration controls the China National Tobacco Corp, which is a state-owned monopoly and the largest single manufacturer of tobacco products in the world. The administration is responsible for policy and enforcing regulations, such as those governing warnings on packaging. It issued regulations on cigarette package labelling that took effect in January 2009. These warnings on packaging fall well short of the requirements. According to the legally binding Article 11 of the WHO FTCT [World Health Organization Framework Convention on Tobacco Control] endorsed by China, warning signs should cover 50% of the display area; Chinese regulations require only 30% and the warnings are in tiny characters. The WHO FCTC requires health warnings to describe the harm tobacco can cause, but Chinese warnings merely state: 'Smoking harms your health,' and 'Quitting smoking early helps reduce the risk' . . . Meanwhile, the tobacco companies target young people. For instance, a primary school rebuilt after the Sichuan earthquake with funds from a tobacco company is named 'Sichuan Tobacco Hope Primary School'. On the school walls it says: 'Talents are brewed by intelligence; tobacco helps you grow up and become accomplished.'

Smoking rates among Chinese men have been consistently high in recent history, comparable to those in Poland, the Republic of Korea, and the Russian Federation a few decades ago.

Source: WHO (2010)

 Question

Why do you think that the government's attitude to tobacco in China is different from that of the UK government?

What do you think?

Is legislation or tax the best way of changing people's behaviour to make them become more environmentally friendly?

Creating a market in pollution

In a free market, firms do not take account of the pollution that they generate. To make firms take account of these external costs, a government can impose a tax on firms to increase the private costs to the same level as the social costs, as has been suggested above. Alternatively, the government can regulate production by passing laws governing the levels of pollution that are allowed. For example, in the UK, the Clean Air Acts limit the amount of pollution that can be generated. A third option is to create a market for pollution so that firms decide for themselves how much they are willing to pollute. For example, firms are given permits allowing them to generate a certain amount of pollution. They are then allowed to trade these permits. This means that if one firm wants to increase its output, then it can bid for the permit of another firm that does not need to use all of its allowance. If the price is right, then the permit will be sold from one firm to another. Rather than a government deciding who should be allowed to produce and pollute, it sets an overall level of pollution and then the free market decides who pollutes within this.

The Coase theorem

According to Coase (1960), the reason why externalities create a problem is because of a lack of well-defined property rights. In the case of noise pollution, for example, the following are not defined in law.

- **Whether we all have a right to silence** If the right to silence were universally accepted, then, in a free market, the people making the noise would have to pay the rest of us to be allowed to continue. The noisemakers would offer different prices for different amounts of noise and negotiate with the rest of the community to find the equilibrium level.

- **Whether we do not have a right to silence** If the right to make a noise were universally accepted, then, in a free market, the people who want silence would have to pay the noisemakers to reduce their noise. The people wanting quiet would offer different prices to reduce the level of noise. A price and level of noise would be found that suited both parties.

According to the Coase theorem, if we could clearly establish the rights of individuals, then markets could be established to set a price for such things as pollution.

Economics in context **BP**

In 2010, President Barack Obama appointed Kenneth Feinberg to administer the $20 billion (£13.5 billion) fund that BP set up to compensate victims of the company's Gulf of Mexico oil spill. The oil spill caused disruption along the US Gulf Coast, affecting fishing and tourism, and fouling some beaches and marshes.

Individuals and businesses affected by the spill can file a claim for compensation for lost wages or profits, personal injuries, or even death, Mr Feinberg has said.

The main precedent is the compensation fund administered by Mr Feinberg for victims of the 9/11 attacks. The fund was created by an Act of Congress shortly after the attacks.

By the time the fund was wrapped up in 2005, $7 billion had been awarded to 97 per cent of the more than 7,000 claims. The average award to relatives of those who died was $2 million; for those injured, it was $390,000.

? Questions
What problems might there be in allocating compensation following the BP oil spill?
Do you think that this oil spill means that all deep-sea drilling, such as that in the Gulf of Mexico, should now end?

Subsidizing positive externalities

Positive externalities occur when the social marginal benefit is greater than the private marginal benefit. In a free market, products with a positive externality are under-consumed because consumers do not realize how good they are. In this case, the government would subsidize them to encourage consumption. By making them cheaper and more affordable, this can increase the equilibrium quantity.

Minimum and maximum prices

Minimum prices

A government may intervene in a market to ensure that the price does not fall below a minimum level. For example, in the labour market, the government may believe that the

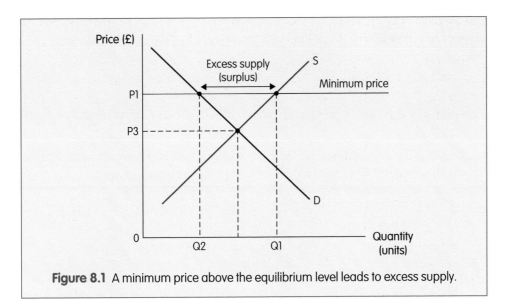

Figure 8.1 A minimum price above the equilibrium level leads to excess supply.

equilibrium wage in some industries is unacceptably low and is unfair (rather than inefficient). The government might therefore introduce a minimum wage to ensure that all employees must earn at least a given amount of money. In other markets, such as agriculture, a government may also want intervene to protect producers' earnings by preventing prices from falling too low.

If a minimum price is set above equilibrium, then the result is that the quantity supplied will exceed the quantity demanded (see Figure 8.1). At price P1, the amount that suppliers are willing and able to sell exceeds the amount that buyers are willing and able to buy—that is, there is excess supply. This leads to a surplus equal to Q1 – Q2. In a free market, the price would fall to bring back equilibrium at price P3.

Put into practice

Using supply and demand diagrams, illustrate the possible effect on overall earnings of introducing a minimum wage.

What might influence the overall effect on employees' total earnings?

Maximum prices

If a government believes that the equilibrium market price would be too high (for example, the rent being charged for accommodation), then it may intervene to place a maximum level in the market. If this maximum price is below the equilibrium—for example, the price P0 in Figure 8.2—then the impact of this is to create a shortage: the quantity demanded will be greater than the quantity supplied at the given price. There is a shortage equal to Q2 – Q1.

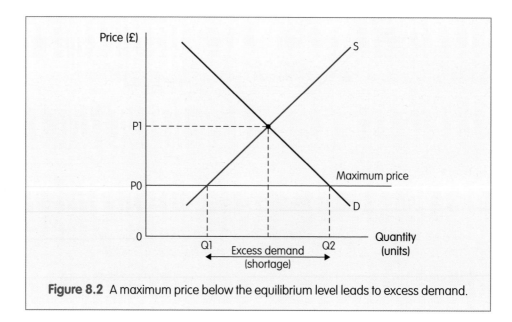

Figure 8.2 A maximum price below the equilibrium level leads to excess demand.

Those who benefit from the limit on the price pay less than they would in a free market. However, the market as a whole has less supplied to it (for example, fewer people would rent out their houses). In a free market, the price would rise to P1 and the quantity supplied would be Q1.

Put into practice

Using a supply and demand diagram, illustrate the effect of a maximum price above the equilibrium price and quantity sold.

Economics in context Price fixing

Kenyan members of parliament (MPs) recently passed a Bill to give powers to the finance minister to set maximum prices for basic goods such as maize and fuel following price increases after last year's drought. It is a move away from the free market approach that Kenya has followed for the last 20 years.

When a severe drought drove up the price of basic commodities such as flour, sugar, and fuel across the country last year, the government came under intense pressure to limit the price rises and introduced price controls in response.

 Question

What do you think might be the effects of the price control scheme in Kenya?

Economics
in context

Pricing controls

The UK supermarket chain Tesco recently announced that it wanted to see limits on the sale of cheap alcohol and would not sell alcohol at a price below what it costs. Research by the company found that excessive drinking and the antisocial behaviour that it causes are one of the public's most serious concerns. The British Liver Trust backed Tesco's decision. The coalition government has said that it will ban the sale of alcohol below cost price.

The health secretary welcomed Tesco's decision to support the ban: 'There is a vast social and financial cost attached to irresponsible drinking. We need to tackle not only issues of supply, but also the behavioural drivers that lead to irresponsible behaviour.'

However, it is not clear how a ban on selling alcohol below cost price could be enforced, because retailers would be reluctant to reveal commercially sensitive details of deals with suppliers.

Some, such as the British Medical Association, argue instead for a minimum price.

❓ Questions

Using supply and demand analysis, show the effect of introducing a minimum price for alchohol above the present equilibrium price.

What effect will this have on the quantity of alcohol consumed?

What other policies might a government introduce to deal with this problem?

Introducing price stabilization schemes

Changes in supply and demand conditions in the free market can lead to major changes in the price level. This can be seen in agricultural markets, in which supply can shift significantly due to changes in weather conditions. The consequent price and income instability may discourage farmers from staying in the industry. If the government wants to maintain agriculture as a sector within the economy (perhaps to protect a way of life or, for strategic reasons, to maintain domestic control over some food supplies), then it may use price stabilization schemes.

To stabilize prices, the government can use a buffer stock scheme (see Figure 8.3). If there is excess supply (perhaps due to a good harvest or developments in farming technology), then the price will fall in the free market due to a surplus being created. To stop this from happening, the government can buy up the excess, so that supply equals demand at the original price. This surplus can then be stored for future years.

When there is a fall in supply (perhaps due to a poor harvest), the government can sell the stock that it has built up in the good years (assuming that there have been good years). By selling its stock, the government can increase the supply of the product in the market back to its old level and thereby keep price at its original level.

Such intervention does, of course, incur costs, because the government must pay to organize the stockpiling in the good years. This involves warehousing, security, and possible depreciation costs. Also, if there are continually 'good years', this means that the government will buy up more each year, creating even bigger stockpiles.

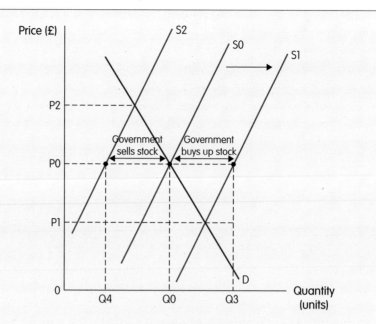

Figure 8.3 A buffer stock scheme. In a free market, the price would fluctuate between P0, P1, and P2 with changes in supply. In a buffer stock scheme, the government maintains the price at P0. In a good year (that is, with an increase in supply), the government buys up the quantity Q3 – Q0; this is the buffer stock. In a bad year (i.e. when supply falls) the government sells the quantity Q4 – Q0 to increase supply and to keep the price at P0.

What do you think?

Do you think that the government should intervene in agricultural markets by using price stabilization schemes?

Problems of government intervention in the market system

The following are problems that occur during government intervention.

- **Valuation problems** When trying to take account of external costs and benefits, the government will have to try to place a value on things such as the beauty of the countryside, the impact on wildlife activity, the quality of life, the risk to health and personal safety, and the impact of an activity on the environment and future generations. It is obviously difficult to place a monetary value on such items.

- **Bureaucracy** Large organizations such as governments often struggle to respond quickly and efficiently to change. Decisions may involve many different groups and take time. Imagine a government trying to control lots of different markets: by the time a decision is taken and implemented, it may no longer be appropriate or correct.

- **Lack of incentive** The more the government intervenes, the less incentive there is for private firms to innovate and become more efficient. For example, inefficient firms that benefit from subsidies may continue to be inefficient rather than face the harsh realities of competition.

Economics in context From wine to fuel

A few years ago, nearly a billion bottles of wine were ordered by the EU to be turned into fuel and disinfectant. The EU spent €131 million to distil 430 million bottles of French wine and 371 million bottles of Italian wine into fuel. Nearly a quarter of Spanish wine was also being used for industrial purposes. The European agriculture commissioner said: 'Crisis distillation is becoming a depressingly regular feature . . . Europe is producing too much wine for which there is no market.' Proposals from the EU were likely to put 400,000 hectares under the plough. Farmers would then be paid not for producing wine, but for keeping up environmental standards. One problem was that there were too many small wine makers. In France, there was one worker per hectare of vineyards; in Australia, there was one worker for every 50 hectares.

? Questions
In the free market, how would equilibrium be reached in this market?
Why do you think that the EU bought up the excess supply?

Nationalization

Rather than trying to influence market forces of supply and demand through policies such as tax and benefits, a government may decide to take over the provision of some products from private businesses; this is known as nationalization. Nationalized industries are organizations the ownership of which has been transferred from the private sector to the public sector—that is, the government buys the shares of a private company and takes it into state control.

The following are possible arguments in favour of nationalization.

- **Natural monopolies** These occur when the cost advantages of expanding are very high. For example, if there are massive initial costs to set up a gas or electricity network, these fixed costs can be spread over more units as output increases. In this situation, one firm is likely to expand and dominate the industry to benefit from lower unit costs. Other firms entering the market would find it difficult to compete if they were to enter at low levels of output, because their unit costs would be much higher. This means that this industry is likely to be a monopoly. The government may need to nationalize to ensure that this natural monopoly does not abuse its market power.

It is felt in a number of countries that competition in the utilities (such as gas, electricity, and water) would lead to a wasteful duplication of resources, and that these are better run by the state. Do we need two sets of water or gas pipes, electricity pylons, or roads, for example?

- **Social objectives** Private firms will consider private benefits and costs when making output and investment decisions. The government may believe that there are significant external benefits and costs to consider; therefore a government may want to intervene in this industry to focus on issues such as safety, and ensuring the service is available and affordable for every household.

Economics in context **Nationalization**

By 2010, Venezuela's biggest beer producer, the food and drink giant Polar, still managed to be in private hands despite President Hugo Chavez's programme of nationalization. Polar has been one company that Chavez has wanted to nationalize, but has not succeeded in gaining parliament's permission to do so yet.

Recently, Chavez accused the company of pushing up food prices by hoarding products to cause artificial shortages. The authorities seized 114 tonnes of food that they said had been illegally stored in Polar warehouses. 'I'm not afraid to nationalize Polar,' said Mr Chavez. 'Let's see who lasts longer—you, with your Polar and your riches, or me, with my people and the dignity of a revolutionary soldier.'

Harina PAN maize flour, Chiffon margarine, Efe ice creams, and Toddy chocolate milk are just some of the brands produced by Polar.

If Mr Chavez does fulfil his threat to nationalize Polar, he will be extending his control over Venezuela's food production even further. The government says that it has a duty to secure food supplies and to prevent what it sees as 'economic sabotage' by private companies. Mr Chavez believes that a bigger economic role for the state is the only way to ensure the effectiveness of his price controls.

The food industry body Cavidea says that the government now controls 42 per cent of maize flour, 40 per cent of rice, 25 per cent of cooking oil, 52 per cent of sugar, and 25 per cent of milk. About 75 per cent of Venezuelan coffee production is also state-run.

However, there are questions about the government's effectiveness in guaranteeing food supplies after the discovery of thousands of tonnes of decomposing food that had been imported by state retailer Pdval, but never actually distributed. Conindustria, the employers' organization, points out that most of the companies nationalized by the government have seen no improvements in productivity.

The coffee industry highlights some of the problems of state control. At the start of the 20th century, Venezuela was the world's second-biggest coffee exporter, but it is now importing significant amounts for the first time in its history.

Coffee producers say price controls imposed by Mr Chavez meant that the price they were getting for their crop did not cover production costs.

Producers found that they could get twice as much for their crop in neighbouring Colombia, which provided an incentive to smuggle out as much as they could.

At the same time, price controls took away the incentive to invest in the industry, so new trees were not planted in response to the shortage.

❓ Questions

Why might Chavez want to nationalize Polar?

How might the performance of Polar be affected if it were under government control?

▨ Privatization

Although nationalization is occurring in some countries and the effects of unstable economic conditions in recent years have led to greater intervention by many governments, the general trend in the 20 years before this was for the government to intervene less directly in the provision of goods and services. This led to many privatizations. Privatization occurs when resources are transferred from the public sector to the private sector.

Forms of privatization may include the following.

- **Denationalization** This occurs when assets that were owned by the government are transferred into private ownership—for example, when a state-owned business is sold to private investors.

- **Contracting out** This involves introducing private contactors to provide some services, such as food in schools, and the transportation of prisoners to and from court.

- **Selling public sector assets** For example, between 1980 and 1983, nearly 600,000 council houses and flats were sold to private individuals in the UK.

- **Selling government shares in private sector businesses**

- **Deregulation** This introduces competition into markets that were previously restricted (that is, opens markets to greater competition).

- **Private finance initiative (PFI)** This occurs when projects are jointly funded by the private and public sectors—for example, the expansion of the London Underground.

Economics in context — Examples of UK privatizations

The following are examples of privatizations in the UK.

- 1984—Enterprise Oil; Jaguar; British Telecom
- 1986—British Gas
- 1987—British Airways; British Airports Authority; BP
- 1988—British Steel
- 1989—ten water companies
- 1990—12 regional electricity companies
- 1996—HM Stationery Office (HMSO)

? Question

What would you consider before buying a share in a privatized business?

▪ Reasons to privatize

The government may privatize an industry for the following reasons.

- **To raise revenue** By selling shares in organizations that were previously state-owned, the government will earn money. This can then be used to finance investment projects or to enable the government to reduce the taxes that it charges. The government can also gain from contracting out by reducing its costs.

- **To free organizations from government control** When firms are government-run, the danger is that they will be run for political means. For example, when elections are approaching, nationalized (state-run) industries may deliberately keep people employed even if it is uneconomic to do so, because the government does not want to lose votes. Privatized businesses may be forced to become more efficient and more innovative to survive; if they cannot compete, they may close.

- **To provide more incentives** If organizations are state-owned, then managers may lack the incentive to run them more efficiently. Given that the profits belong to the state, an increase in profits may simply mean that more funds go to central government rather than are invested back into this particular business or reward those who made them. In private sector organizations, there may be more incentive to provide a better service or be more efficient because this creates more profits that are kept by the owners. Managers may be more interested in understanding and meeting customer needs.

- **To create more competition** When transferring resources into the private sector, the government will often open up that market for other firms to compete in, which should provide more choice for consumers. Greater competition should encourage more innovation and more efficiency, leading to better products at lower prices. Greater efficiency can stimulate further economic growth.

- **To provide firms with more access to finance** Once firms are privatized, they are able to sell shares to investors to raise finance. When they are nationalized, they rely on the government for funding and, given that the government has many demands on its funds, they may not get the long-term investment that they need to be competitive. With access to private finance, they may be able to raise more money for investment.

- **To enable firms to have access to private finance** The government has many different demands on its funds. This may lead to underinvestment in some sectors. By privatizing, firms can sell shares to raise the finance needed for investment and modernization.

- **To create more share owners in the economy and raise the general level of awareness in the economy regarding investment** This may then lead to more investment in other firms, helping firms to finance expansion.

Economics in context **Privatization**

In an effort to deal with an increasing budget deficit (that is, a situation in which spending exceeded income), the Russian government announced a plan to sell shares in state-owned companies. Russia's finance and economic development ministries have agreed on a number of companies that will be sold. However, this has raised some concerns after the sell-off of state assets in the 1990s, which created a group of very powerful business people. Russia's largest oil company Rosneft, and big banks Sberbank and VTB, have been mentioned as potential assets for sale. The aim is to raise about 1 trillion roubles ($33 billion; £21 billion) over three years.

Source: Rozhnov (2010)

? Question

Analyse the potential consequences of the privatization of more state-owned companies in Russia.

What do you think?

Do you think that privately owned motorways in the UK would be a good thing?

Problems of privatization

The following are problems associated with privatization.

- Privatization may create private monopolies that abuse their power (in which case, privatized organizations may need to be regulated by the government).

- Privatized firms are likely to pursue private objectives rather than social objectives. This may mean that the needs of society are not met as effectively as they were when the industry was nationalized; the socially optimal price and output decisions may not be achieved.

- Some people criticize privatization on the basis that it is selling the nation's assets back to the nation—that is, in some ways, it is selling what we already own.
- If the public sector industries were making profits, then by privatizing them, the government will lose this income.
- The industry may be a natural monopoly. This means that the economies of scale are so great that one firm is bound to expand and dominate to benefit from the cost advantages. By splitting up this industry into smaller firms, the unit costs of smaller firms will be higher and this may lead to higher prices.

Economics in context   ## Railtrack in administration

In 2001, Railtrack, the company that was in charge of the UK's railway infrastructure (for example, tracks and bridges), was put into administration when the government refused to put more money into the business. The company needed £700 million to continue. The company had been successful in its first few years following the privatization of the railways in 1996, but problems started in 1999. Firstly, there was the Ladbroke Grove rail crash in which 31 people died; this led to recommendations that billions of pounds should be invested in better safety systems. Then, in October 2000, there was the Hatfield crash in which four people died, caused by a broken rail. Once again, more investment was needed and there were major disruptions to the rail system as work was carried out. Railtrack simply could not afford the investment required.

Following the administration, Railtrack's core railway business was handed over to Network Rail, a not-for-profit company controlled by train operators, rail unions, and passenger groups. Network Rail is 'dedicated to the interests of rail users'. Unlike Railtrack, profits are invested into the business instead of being given to shareholders as dividends. Management incentives are tied to performance targets, such as safety and punctuality, rather than profits. Railtrack had been criticized for focusing too much on profits instead of safety.

 Question

How can a government make sure that a privatized business still acts responsibly?

 Web

For information on Network Rail, visit http://www.networkrail.co.uk

Regulatory capture

Regulatory capture occurs when the regulating body identifies so much with the industry that it is regulating that it protects its interests rather than monitors the industry. Those involved in the regulated industry will devote a great deal of time, effort, and resources to protecting their own interests, and may well influence the regulator to see these from their own perspective.

Case study Carbon emissions

Within the EU, there is a carbon emissions trading scheme. Under this scheme, governments set quotas for the level of carbon dioxide emissions that are produced by 9,400 large factories and power stations. Countries are given an overall allocation of permits and these are then allocated to firms within the country. The permits can be traded with other countries and other firms. By reducing its own pollution, a country or firm can sell the remainder of its permits to another business and earn profits by doing this. The other country or business, meanwhile, can pollute more, but its costs will increase. Emissions of carbon dioxide are thought to be a major factor in global warming. By controlling the overall level of emissions, governments hope to limit the impact on the environment.

However, according to an EU report, it seems that too many permits were issued. The result was a 2.5 per cent surplus, with 44.2 million tonnes more carbon dioxide permits being issued than were actually needed. With an excess supply of permits, the price of carbon credits fell by around 60 per cent. Even so, the UK claimed that its own targets were too tight when they were first set.

The idea of carbon trading began to take off after the Kyoto Protocol was signed. Under this treaty—which came into effect in February 2005—industrialized countries have to reduce their total greenhouse gas emissions by an average of 5.2 per cent (compared with 1990 levels) between 2008 and 2012. The World Bank estimated that the value of carbon traded in 2005 was about $10 billion. However, there are problems. Simply creating a market, for example, does not reduce carbon emissions; this depends on the amount allowed. Also, it depends what is being reduced and its effect on environmental issues. Finally, it depends on who is taking part in the scheme. The USA is the world's largest carbon dioxide polluter, but did not agree to Kyoto. Meanwhile, China, one of the fastest-growing economies in the world, does not have to reduce its emissions. Furthermore, the scheme extends only to some industries; some sectors, such as transport, homes, and the public sector, are exempted.

On the domestic front, there are proposals for personal carbon allowances. Individuals would be given a carbon allowance; this would be monitored and individuals could sell on any surplus or buy extra credits. It would cover people's direct use of energy through their electricity, gas, petrol, and air travel, which make up around 44 per cent of the economy's emissions. Cards would store carbon points, and when people bought energy, points would be deducted from the card.

❓ Questions

- What factors determine the price of carbon permits?
- What factors would firms consider before buying more carbon permits?
- Do you think that the personal carbon allowance scheme will work? Is it better than taxing consumption?

Checklist

Now that you have read this chapter, try to answer the following questions.

- ☐ Can you explain how governments intervene in the free market?
- ☐ Do you understand the impact of maximum and minimum prices?
- ☐ Do you understand the workings of a buffer stock scheme?
- ☐ Can you explain the reasons for nationalization?
- ☐ Can you explain the reasons for privatization?
- ☐ Can you explain the problems of privatization?

Review questions

1 If a monopoly develops, what is the likely impact on the price charged and the quantity available compared with the free market?

2 Travelling by air has a major negative environmental impact. Do you think that air travel should be stopped completely?

3 What action would a government that is operating a buffer stock scheme take if there were a surplus of a product?

4 Do you think that privatizing an industry is a good idea?

5 Why might a government want to nationalize an industry?

Key learning points

- In theory, a free market may provide an optimal allocation of resources; in reality, there are many market failures and imperfections

- A government can intervene in a number of ways to try to remedy market failures and imperfections, such as through legislation, price fixing, indirect taxes, subsidies, and direct provision.

- A buffer stock scheme can be used to stabilize good prices.

- Nationalization occurs when a government takes firms under its control.

- Privatization occurs when assets and contracts are transferred to the private sector.

- Privatization can lead to greater efficiency and innovation, but may need regulation to ensure that customers are not exploited.

References

Coase, R. (1960) 'The problem of social cost', *Journal of Law, and Economics*, 3(Oct): 1–44

Rozhnov, K. (2010) 'Russian privatization plans spark fears', 4 August, available online at
http://www.bbc.co.uk/news/business-10850855

 Visit our Online Resource Centre at http://www.oxfordtextbooks.co.uk/orc/gillespie_econ2e/
for test questions and further information on topics covered in this chapter.

Costs: Short run and long run

In this chapter, we examine the determinants of a firm's costs, and consider the differences between short-run and long-run costs. This will be vital to understanding and calculating the profits of a business, which will be examined in the next chapter.

LEARNING OBJECTIVES

By the end of this chapter, you should be able to:

✔ distinguish between short-run and long-run costs;

✔ explain the law of diminishing returns;

✔ understand the difference between marginal, average, and total product;

✔ understand the difference between marginal, average, and total cost;

✔ understand the significance of economies and diseconomies of scale;

✔ understand the difference between internal and external economies of scale;

✔ understand the meaning and significance of the minimum efficient scale.

■ The importance of costs

To be able to decide on the appropriate price and output required to maximize profits, managers need a detailed understanding of the level of costs at different levels of output and how costs might change over time. They will be interested in factors such as the total cost of producing, the cost per unit (average cost), and the extra costs of producing another product (marginal cost). This unit examines the factors that determine the nature of costs in both the short run and the long run. Managers will aim to achieve the lowest possible cost per unit for any given level of output and this involves getting the correct combination of resources. Their ability to do this varies from the short run to the long run. In the short run, there will be more constraints than in the long run.

The pressure on firms to be efficient has generally increased with greater worldwide competition, and the ability of consumers to search more easily and compare prices via the Internet. This makes it even more important for firms to look for the best way of producing. The costs structure in an industry is also important because it influences the number of firms that can survive within it. If costs are very high to start up or at low levels of output, for example, then it is likely that established firms or large producers will face limited competition.

Economics in context **Vietnam**

The Vietnamese economy is booming, with the economy growing at around 7 per cent a year. Traditionally, the country's income has come from agricultural exports and low-cost industries, such as shoes and garments. But products such as these are global commodities: basic items that generate very low profit margins. Therefore, in recent years, the government has been trying to attract higher-value industries to Vietnam. This has led to the creation of industrial complexes of modern purpose-built offices for companies such as Canon and Foxconn.

Average wages in Vietnam are lower than those of its neighbours Thailand and China. Vietnamese factory workers typically earn just two-thirds of what workers in China bring home. Companies such as Foxconn, which assembles consumer electronic products for big brand companies such as Apple and Sony, already operate on very low profit margins. They rely on producing huge volumes of goods. Given recent wage increases of 15–20 per cent in some parts of China, Vietnam looks increasingly very attractive.

? Question
What factors other than labour costs might companies consider before locating in Vietnam?

Short-run costs

The short run in economics is the period of time during which there is at least one factor of production fixed. In the short run, at least one of the resources cannot be changed—for example, a firm cannot recruit the staff that it wants, cannot acquire new equipment, or cannot find new premises. This means that, in the short run, a firm is constrained and cannot necessarily find its optimal mix of resources. As a result, there are fixed costs in the short run. For example, you may have rented premises and be committed to a contract for a period of months or years, or you may be repaying a loan on equipment for a five-year period.

Short-run total costs are therefore made up of fixed costs and variable costs.

• **Fixed costs (FC)** These are costs that a firm has to pay, but which are not dependent on the level of output. For example, the interest on a loan is related to the size of the loan and the interest rate, not the level of output. Even if output is zero, a firm must pay its fixed costs. High levels of fixed costs represent a high level of risk for a business because the business still has to pay these costs even if sales fall.

- **Variable costs (VC)** These are costs that are directly related to the level of output, such as the costs of materials and components used in the production process. As output increases, variable costs will increase as well.

How long the short run lasts will vary from industry to industry. If it is easy to sell and buy land and equipment, for example, the short run may be months, or a year or so. If, however, expansion involves a major investment—for example, in a new airport terminal—then it may take five to ten years to expand capacity.

> **What do you think?**
>
> In what ways do you think firms might be able to shorten the short run?

The law of diminishing returns

In the short run, a firm's ability to produce will be constrained by its fixed factors of production. For example, a business may be constrained by its equipment or office space. Although it will be able to change these factors over time (for example, invest in new equipment or buy new office space), in the short term it cannot do so. Therefore, to increase production, it can change some its factors of production (for example, managers could ask employees to work overtime or the business might recruit more employees), but not others; expansion involves adding variable factors of production to fixed factors to increase output. As a result, the business will experience the law of diminishing returns. Under the law of diminishing returns, the extra output produced as more units of a variable factor are added to fixed factors will decrease. This means that the total output increases at a decreasing rate.

The extra output produced by the variable factor is known as the marginal product. If labour is the variable factor, then we measure the marginal product of labour (MPL). If capital is the variable factor, then we measure the marginal product of capital (MPK—K is used to represent capital).

The marginal product (MP) can be calculated using the following equation:

$$\text{Marginal product} = \frac{\text{Change in the total output}}{\text{Change in the variable factor of production}}$$

Imagine increasing output by adding additional people to an office environment with a given amount of equipment. There will simply not be enough computers or telephones for them all to use if you keep adding staff; they will begin to get in each other's way. The first person you employ could be very useful and productive; the sixth or seventh employee may add little to the overall output of the office if you cannot increase the fixed factors, such as office equipment.

The law of diminishing returns is illustrated in Figure 9.1.

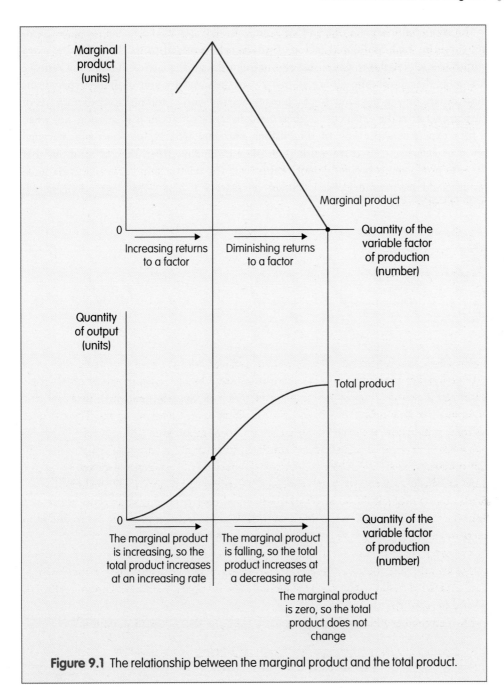

Figure 9.1 The relationship between the marginal product and the total product.

Short-run marginal costs

The marginal cost curve shows the extra cost of producing a unit. The marginal cost is calculated as follows:

$$\text{Marginal cost} = \frac{\text{Change in the total cost}}{\text{Change in output}}$$

The short-run marginal cost (SRMC) curve is inversely linked to the marginal product curve. As each additional factor of production is added to the business, the extra output of each employee diminishes in accordance with the law of diminishing returns. Assuming that the employees are all being paid the same amount of money, this means that you are paying the same for each extra worker who is adding fewer extra units of output; therefore the extra cost of these units in terms of labour is increasing. So, when a firm experiences the law of diminishing marginal returns, its short-run marginal costs are increasing. If extra workers are less productive, then the extra output that they are producing is becoming more expensive. The relationship between the marginal product and the marginal cost is shown in Figure 9.2. The SRMC curve is usually a 'tick' shape.

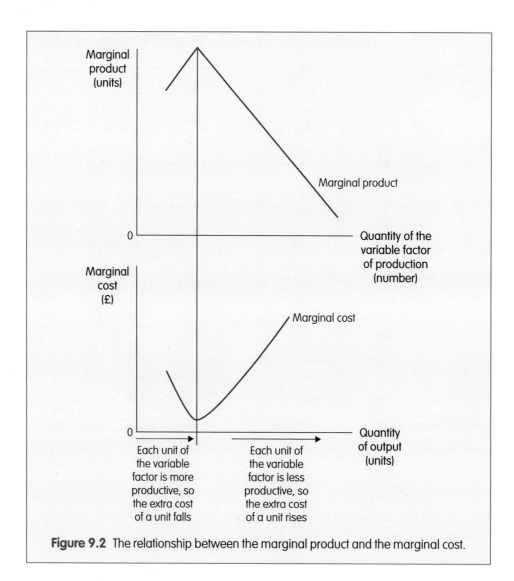

Figure 9.2 The relationship between the marginal product and the marginal cost.

What do you think?

If the wage rate were to be increased to attract more employees, what would this do to the marginal cost curve?

Marginal product and average product of labour

The average product of labour is the output per employee (often called labour productivity).

If the marginal product of labour is greater than the average product, this means that the extra employee is more productive than the employees were, on average, before. This will pull up the average—that is, if the marginal product is greater than the average product, then the average product will increase. Imagine employees produce ten units each on average and then an additional employee is hired, producing 20 units: the average rises.

If the marginal product of labour is less than the average product, this means that the extra employee is less productive than employees were, on average, before. This will pull down the average—that is, if the marginal product is less than the average product, then the average product will fall. If employees are producing ten units each and then an additional employee is hired producing two units, the average falls.

This means that the marginal product will cross the average product at its maximum point (see Figure 9.3).

Put into practice

a. Employees are hired at a wage of £200 each per week. You have four employees producing a total of 400 units.
- What is the total cost of production?
- What is the average output per employee?

Table 9.1 The relationship between the marginal product, the average product, and the total product (output)

Number of employees	Total output (units)	Average product of labour = Total output / Number of employees (units)	Marginal product of labour = Change in total output / Change in number of employees (units)
1	10	10	–
2	30	15	20
3	60	20	30
4	76	19	16
5	80	16	4

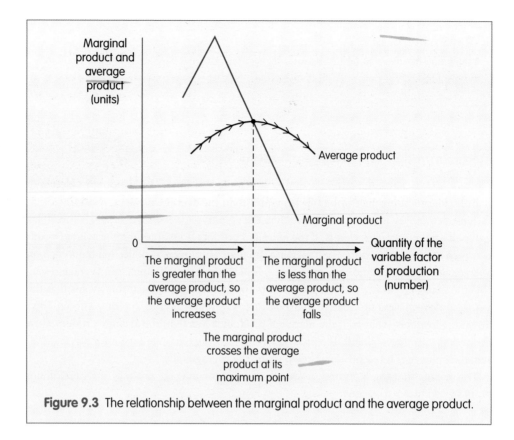

Figure 9.3 The relationship between the marginal product and the average product.

b. You hire a fifth employee and output rises to 450 units.
- What is the total cost of production?
- What is the marginal product of the fifth worker?
- What is the average output per employee now?
- What is the average cost per unit now?

Short-run average costs

The short-run average cost (SRAC) curve shows the lowest cost per unit for any level of output given the fixed factor(s) of production. The SRAC curve is generally U-shaped. It is made up of the average fixed costs and the average variable costs. Using the equation:

Total cost = Fixed cost + Variable cost

we divide by the output level to obtain:

$$\frac{\text{Total cost (TC)}}{\text{Output (Q)}} = \frac{\text{Fixed cost (FC)}}{\text{Output (Q)}} + \frac{\text{Variable cost (VC)}}{\text{Output (Q)}}$$

which means that:

Average cost (AC) = Average fixed cost (AFC) = Average variable cost (AVC)

The average fixed cost curve will fall continuously as the fixed costs are spread over more units. The average variable cost curve is usually U-shaped and is the inverse of the average product curve.

Assume that the variable factor is labour and the wage rate is constant. When, on average, labour is less productive, then the average cost of a unit in terms of labour will rise. When, on average, labour is more productive, then the variable cost per unit in terms of labour will fall. (This is similar to the inverse relationship between marginal product and marginal cost.) The relationship between productivity and costs is shown in Figure 9.4.

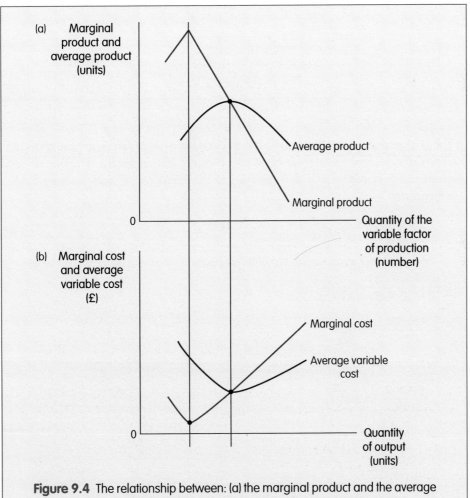

Figure 9.4 The relationship between: (a) the marginal product and the average product; and (b) the marginal cost and the average variable cost.

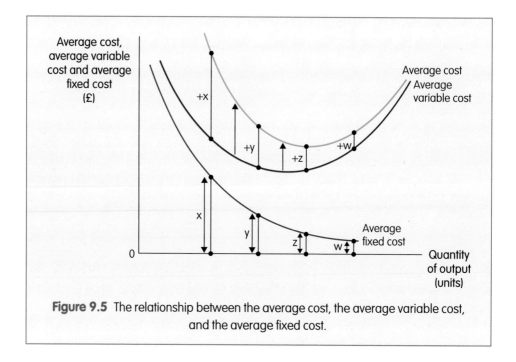

Figure 9.5 The relationship between the average cost, the average variable cost, and the average fixed cost.

The average cost and average variable cost curves converge (that is, get closer) as output increases, because the average fixed cost becomes less significant. The overall costs are increasingly dominated by variable costs as the fixed cost per unit becomes smaller (see Figure 9.5).

Example

The fixed costs of a business are £50,000. This means that the fixed cost per unit will be as follows.
At 1,000 units:

$$\frac{£50,000}{1,000} = £50 \text{ a unit}$$

At 10,000 units:

$$\frac{£50,000}{10,000} = £5 \text{ a unit}$$

At 50,000 units:

$$\frac{£50,000}{50,000} = £1 \text{ a unit}$$

The fixed cost per unit falls as output increases
If the variable cost per unit is £5—

At 1,000 units, AFC is £50 and AVC is £5, so:

$$AC = £50 + £5 = £55$$
$$\text{Total costs} = £55 \times 1,000 = £55,000$$

At 10,000 units, AFC is £5 and AVC is £5, so:

$$AC = £5 + £5 = £10$$
$$\text{Total cost} = £10 \times 10,000 = £100,000$$

At 50,000 units, AFC is £1 and AVC is £5, so:

$$AC = £1 + £5 = £6$$
$$\text{Total costs} = £6 \times 50,000 = £300,000$$

Put into practice

- The fixed costs of a business are £10,000. What is the average fixed cost if output is either one unit, ten units, 100 units, or 1,000 units? What is happening to the average fixed cost as output increases?
- Suppose that the variable cost per unit is £2. Calculate both the total cost and the average cost for one unit, ten units, 100 units, and 1,000 units.

The relationship between marginal cost (MC) and average cost (AC)

If the marginal cost is greater than the average cost, then this will pull the average cost up. For example, if a firm produces three units at an average cost of £10 and then it produces a fourth unit for £50, then this will pull the average cost up (see Table 9.2).

Conversely, if the extra cost of a unit is less than the average cost, it will pull down the average cost. For example, if a firm produces three units at an average cost of £10 and then it produces a fourth unit for £6, then this will bring the average cost down. The total cost of three units is:

$$3 \times £10 = £30$$

So the total cost of four units is:

$$£30 + £6 = £36$$

Table 9.2 Output and costs

Output (units)	Total cost (£)	Marginal cost (£)	Average cost (£)
3	30	–	10
4	80	50	20
5	150	70	30

This means that the average cost is:

$$\frac{£36}{4} = £9 \text{ a unit}$$

Put into practice

Fill in the two blank cells in the table below.

Output (units)	Total cost (£)	Marginal cost (£)	Average cost (£)
3	30	–	10
4	36	6	9
5	40		

This relationship between marginals and averages means that the marginal cost will cross the average cost at its minimum point. This is shown in Figure 9.6.

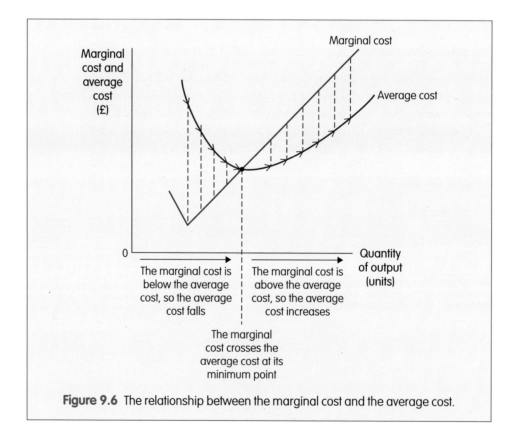

Figure 9.6 The relationship between the marginal cost and the average cost.

Put into practice

- The average cost of ten units is £6. What is the total cost?
- The marginal cost of the 11th unit is £17. What is the total cost now? What is the average cost? What does this show in terms of the relationships between marginal costs and average costs?
- The marginal cost of the 12th unit is £7. What is the total cost now? What is the average cost? What does this show in terms of the relationships between marginal costs and average costs?

A summary of the key terms of covered so far is shown in Table 9.3.

Put into practice

Which of the following statements are true and which are false?

a. The short-run average cost and short-run average variable cost converge as output increases.

b. Costs are zero when output is zero.

c. If marginal costs are positive, total costs are increasing.

d. If average costs are £25, average fixed costs are £15, and output is 20 units, then variable costs are £200.

Table 9.3 Summary table of key terms

Item	Description
Marginal product (MP)	Extra output from employing an extra factor of production $= \dfrac{\text{Change in the total output}}{\text{Change in the variable factor of production}}$
Average product (AP)	$= \dfrac{\text{Total output}}{\text{Number of factors of production}}$
Total cost (TC)	$= \text{Fixed cost} + \text{Variable cost}$
Marginal cost (MC)	$= \dfrac{\text{Change in the total cost}}{\text{Change in output}}$
Average variable cost (AVC)	Variable cost per unit $= \dfrac{\text{Variable cost}}{\text{Output}}$
Average fixed cost (AFC)	$= \dfrac{\text{Fixed cost}}{\text{Output}}$
Average cost (AC); also known as average total cost (ATC)	$= \dfrac{\text{Total cost}}{\text{Output}}$ $= \text{Average fixed cost} + \text{Average variable cost}$

Long-run cost curves

Long-run average costs

The long-run average cost (LRAC) curve shows the lowest possible cost per unit for any level of output when all factors of production are variable.

In the long run, managers are able to change all of their resources to find the optimal combinations. If, as a result of changing its combination of resources, the firm is able to reduce its unit costs when it produces more, then this means that the firm is experiencing internal economies of scale.

Imagine that a firm has a fixed amount of machinery K1 (see Figure 9.7). The lowest cost per unit for any level of output given this level of machinery is shown by the short-run average cost curve SRAC1. This will be the optimal amount of capital for a particular level of output—in this case, Q1. With K1, the unit cost at Q1 is the lowest it can possibly be; even in the long run, this is the amount of capital that would be chosen. However, for any other level of output, K1 would not be the optimal amount of capital. To produce Q2, for example, K2 may be the optimal amount of capital. In the short run, the firm is committed to K1 capital and so the lowest unit costs achievable are shown at 'x'.

In the long run, however, the firm is able to change the level of equipment and can find the optimal level of machinery K2. This means that it can move onto a new short-run average cost curve SRAC2 and that unit costs fall to 'y'. In the long run, it can produce more cheaply. The unit costs have fallen as the firm has increased the scale of production. This means that the firm is benefiting from internal economies of scale.

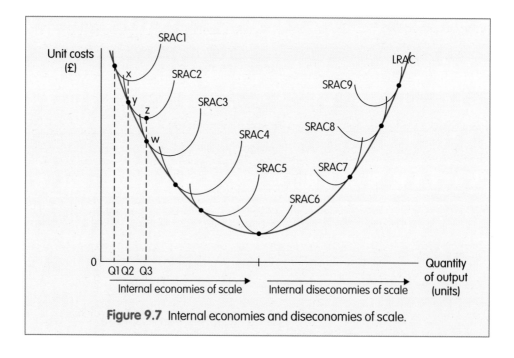

Figure 9.7 Internal economies and diseconomies of scale.

Similar observations can be made if the firm expands further to Q3. In the short run, it is now constrained by the level of equipment K2. The lowest unit costs possible in the short run with this level of equipment are 'z'. In the long run, the amount of capital can be changed, and, as a result, the firm moves onto a new SRAC curve and unit costs fall to 'w'.

Types of internal economy of scale

The reasons for internal economies of scale include 'plant economies'. These specifically refer to lower unit costs as a result of a larger size of factory and include the following.

- **Technical economies** With larger production levels, it may be possible to adopt production techniques that are more efficient on a large scale within the plant, such as mass production. At large volumes, such techniques lead to lower unit costs. These techniques require heavy investment that can be spread over high volumes to reduce the unit cost.

- **Indivisibilities** Some machines are indivisible—that is, they can be used on a certain scale, but cannot be split up or divided—so to produce on a small scale is relatively expensive. Imagine that you buy an excavator; this may be cost-effective if used on a regular basis, but not if used only once a month.

- **Volume** If you double the height, width, and depth of a container (such as a lorry, warehouse or transport vessel), then the volume that it contains will increase more than proportionately compared to the surface area. For example, a box that has six sides of $1\text{ m} \times 1\text{ m}$ has six sides each with an area of 1 m^2—that is, 6 m^2 overall (see Figure 9.8). The volume is:

$$1\text{ m} \times 1\text{ m} \times 1\text{ m} = 1\text{ m}^3$$

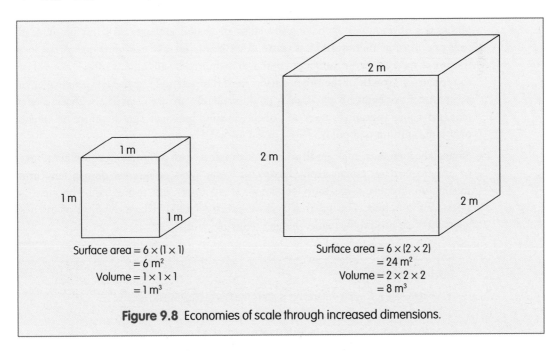

Figure 9.8 Economies of scale through increased dimensions.

If the measurements are doubled, then the area is now 24 m²—that is, six sides each with an area 4 m² (see Figure 9.8)—and the volume is:

$$2 \text{ m} \times 2 \text{ m} \times 2 \text{ m} = 8 \text{ m}^3$$

So a four-times increase in surface area has led to an eight-times increase in volume. This will reduce the average storage or transportation costs per unit. By spending four times as much to build a container, you can carry eight times as much, so the transport costs per unit will be lower.

- **Specialization and division of labour** As firms produce on a larger scale, the production process can be divided into a series of clearly and narrowly defined jobs. This means that employees do not need extensive training. By undertaking tasks again and again, they may become more productive, making production more efficient.

Other economies are known as 'firm' or 'enterprise' economies. These include the following.

- **Purchasing economies** When a firm operates on a larger scale, it will need to purchase more, such as components, materials, and advertising space. Being larger puts the firm in a better bargaining position with suppliers, and should mean that it is possible to negotiate better payment terms and lower prices for these resources, thereby reducing unit costs. One of the reasons for the success of the US retailer Walmart is its sheer size; this enables it to buy products from suppliers at much better prices than many competitors and to pass these cost savings on to consumers. This makes it difficult for smaller firms to survive. Similarly, discount retailers such as Aldi and Lidl focus on a limited range of products, which they then buy in bulk to enable them to buy relatively cheaply.

- **Managerial economies** As an organization expands, it may be able to employ specialist managers to undertake various functions, such as marketing, human resources, and the purchasing of resources. By having specialists dedicated to these tasks, this should lead to better decision making and less waste. Another managerial economy occurs because the rate of increase in the number of managers required by an organization is not as fast as the rate of growth of the organization itself. For example, if there is a manager of a department of eight people, then it could probably grow to, say, 12 without a new manager being appointed; the costs of the existing manager can therefore be spread over more staff up to a point.

- **Financial economies** A larger firm with more assets, such as land and equipment, may be able to borrow money from a bank at lower rates of interest than a new firm starting up, because it has more collateral. It is a lower risk to the banks because its assets can be seized. This greater level of security should reduce the level of interest payments that need to be made, thereby reducing costs.

Put into practice

a. Which of the following statements is true? The law of diminishing returns:
- applies in the long run.
- shows that utility falls as more units of a product are consumed.

- states that, after a point, each additional unit of a variable input produces less than the previous unit.
- shows that revenue falls as the price is reduced to sell more units.

b. In the short run, as output is increased, more variable inputs are added to a given amount of fixed inputs. After some point, we expect:
- no change in average fixed costs.
- average variable cost to stop falling and to begin rising.
- average total cost to stop rising and begin falling.
- marginal cost to decline throughout all ranges of output.

c. Which one of the following is *not* an explanation for the presence of economies of scale?
- As a firm gets larger, it becomes more specialized in production.
- As a firm gets larger, management becomes too bureaucratic.
- As a firm gets larger, it can use better and more efficient capital equipment.
- As a firm gets larger, it can spread its fixed factors of production over more units of output.

d. Which one of the following is incorrect?
- $AVC = AC - AFC$
- $AFC = AC + AVC$
- $AC = AVC + AFC$
- $AFC = AC - AVC$

e. Economies of scale are associated with _____ average total costs.
- rising
- falling
- constant
- growing

Internal diseconomies of scale

If a firm grows too large, then it may find that the average costs begin to rise. This is because of internal diseconomies of scale. These include the following.

- **Motivation issues** When a business is too large, employees may no longer feel part of the organization as a whole. They may lack a sense of connection to the overall business. Low motivation can lead to mistakes being made, low levels of attendance, and low productivity; all of these tend to increase unit costs. Firms will try to overcome these problems in a variety of ways, such as introducing mission statements to provide a sense of direction for employees. A mission statement sets out the purpose and values of the business.

Unilever's mission update

Unilever is an international manufacturer of leading brands in foods, home care, and personal care. Its mission statement is as follows.

> Our purpose in Unilever is to meet the everyday needs of people everywhere—to anticipate the aspirations of our consumers, and customers, and to respond creatively, and competitively with branded products, and services, which raise the quality of life.

How useful do you think having a mission statement such as the one above would be?

• **Management problems** Managing a larger business is a more complex process than running a small business. For example, you are likely to be controlling a wide range of products, communicating between many different sites or outlets, and coordinating many different departments. This can be very difficult, and may lead to inefficiency, mistakes being made, and higher unit costs. Firms may try to overcome these problems with budgets, regular meetings, and review sessions called appraisals.

What do you think?

To what extent do you think growth brings more problems than benefits?

Newspapers

The newspaper industry is one that has been pursuing economies of scale, with big companies buying up regional newspapers. This enables them to share resources such as local news gathering, printing, and advertising sales. For example, Newsquest, a Gannett company, has 315 market-leading local daily and weekly newspapers. Similarly, local radio stations have been merging or taking each other over to form bigger companies that can share resources, such as national news items, national weather, media space buying, and recording studios.

 Question

If economies of scale exist in the newspaper industry, does this mean the end of local independent newspapers?

Economics in context **Economies of scale**

Walmart is the biggest company in the world based on revenues. In 2009, it had a sales revenue of over $408 billion.

 Questions

Analyse the possible economies of scale that this retailer might experience.

Many of the biggest companies in the world, such as BP, Exxon, and Royal Dutch Shell, are energy businesses. Explain how their size might be related to economies of scale.

Returns to scale

Increasing, decreasing, and constant returns to scale are described as follows.

- **Increasing returns to scale** occur when an increase in *all* of the factors of production leads to a more proportionate increase in output. For example, if doubling the amount of labour, land, and capital leads to a tripling of output, then this is known as increasing returns to scale. This leads to a fall in the average costs and is another example of internal economies of scale.

- **Decreasing returns to scale** occur when an increase in *all* of the factors of production leads to a less-than-proportionate increase in output. For example, if tripling the amount of labour, land, and capital leads to a doubling of output, then this is known as decreasing returns to scale. This leads to an increase in average costs and is an example of internal diseconomies of scale.

- **Constant returns to scale** occur when an increase in *all* of the factors of production leads to a proportionate increase in output. For example, if doubling the amount of labour, land, and capital leads to a doubling of output, then this is known as constant returns to scale. Average costs stay constant.

Economics in context **More about newspapers**

Each issue of a newspaper or a magazine is in some respects a new product in that the content will vary from issue to issue, albeit within a consistent 'product image' that publishers will seek to maintain—this means that demand can vary from issue to issue depending on the content, and publishers may be better able to gauge these likely fluctuations in demand than retailers, particularly if there is little notice that the 'big story' or feature will be included. The fixed costs involved in production and printing are substantial, and the marginal costs are relatively low, and producing editorial content involves significant fixed costs and zero marginal costs—this means that it is relatively cost effective for publishers to print more copies than they expect to sell to allow for variability in sales at individual outlets, and to use availability as a form of promotion.

Source: Office Fair Trading

Minimum efficient scale

The long-run average cost may have a variety of shapes depending on the industry and the revelant cost conditions.

The minimum efficient scale (MES) is the first level of output at which the long-run average costs of a firm are minimized—that is, at which internal economies of scale are no longer being experienced. This is illustrated in Figure 9.9. The MES may be significant in determining the structure of an industry. If, for example, the MES is relatively high compared to demand in the industry, then this suggests that only a few firms could operate efficiently (at the lowest unit cost) within it—that is, the industry may be more likely to be an oligopoly (see Chapter 13).

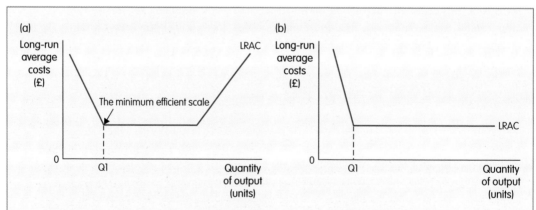

Figure 9.9 (a) The minimum efficient scale; (b) An L-shaped long-run average cost curve (may occur if diseconomies of scale do not exist).

If, however, the MES occurs at very low levels of output compared to the total demand in the industry, then this suggests that many firms could operate efficiently. This suggests that the market may be much more competitive, with more smaller firms operating in it at the same time and providing more choice for customers.

However, the precise impact of the MES on the market structure also depends on the cost disadvantage of operating below this level of output—that is, it depends on what happens if a firm enters and produces below the MES (for example, at one-third of the MES). If the consequences of this are that this firm would have much higher unit costs, then it will clearly struggle to compete with the bigger firms; for example, it would be likely to suffer in a price war. In this situation, it is unlikely that inefficient firms will survive, because the cost disadvantage is so great. In this case, the MES is a very good indicator of how many firms are likely to be in the industry.

However, if the unit costs of operating below the MES are not significant, then it may be possible for many firms to be operating inefficiently. This is because they are not operating at any major disadvantage. In this case, the MES may not be a good indicator of market structure, because there may be many inefficient firms also operating alongside the efficient ones.

The potential impact of the MES on the market structure is illustrated in Figure 9.10.

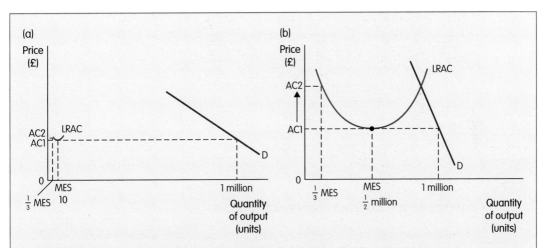

Figure 9.10 The relationship between the minimum efficient scale (MES) and market structure: (a) The MES is low relative to the market demand and the cost disadvantage of operating below the MES is also low. This means that this market is likely to be very competitive, with many firms competing. (b) The MES is high relative to the market demand, and the cost disadvantage of not operating at the MES is also high. This industry is likely to be dominated by a few firms, probably two given that the MES is half of the market demand.

Economics in context

Concentration ratios of top five UK businesses as a percentage of total output in 2004

Market	Concentration ratio (%)
Sugar	99
Confectionery	81
Tobacco products	99
Soft drinks and mineral waters	75

Source: ONS.

? Question

The concentration ratios above measure the market share of the largest five companies in the market. How might these concentration ratios be linked to the concept of the MES?

Economics in context

Cost efficiencies

In 2010, Sir Philip Green, the owner of clothing retailer Arcadia Group, was asked by the UK government to examine expenditure from the past three years to try to identify potential savings. One idea was to centralize buying to cut costs.

Sir Philip Green owns more than 2,000 shops in the UK, including BHS, Topshop, Burton, Dorothy Perkins, Evans, and Miss Selfridge. He has a personal fortune of over £4 billion.

? Question

Do you think bringing someone from business to review government costs is a good idea?

Internal versus external economies of scale

Internal economies of scale refer to cost advantages that a firm experiences when it grows—that is, the average cost per unit falls in the long run as the scale of production expands.

External economies of scale occur when changes outside the firm reduce the unit cost of operating at all output levels.

This may be because there are government subsidies in the area that reduce the costs. Governments sometimes target areas that they want to develop and so provide incentives to firms wanting to set up or grow there. Also, other firms in the same industry may have located there, encouraging the development of a local supplier network that reduces transport costs. The close proximity of several firms in the same industry may lead to a pool of labour with relevant skills that can make recruitment and training cheaper. These

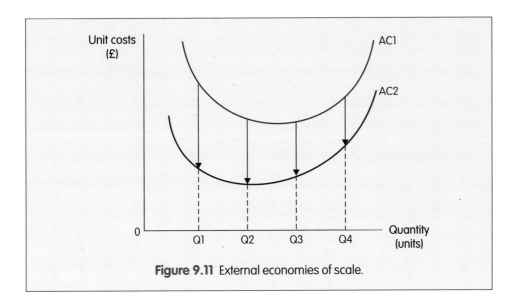

Figure 9.11 External economies of scale.

cost benefits of location near other firms are called 'economies of agglomeration'. For example, in the UK, Northampton has traditionally attracted shoe firms; in the USA, Silicon Valley has attracted computer businesses; northern Italy has attracted clothing companies.

External economies of scale are illustrated in Figure 9.11.

The significance of economies of scale

The drive for economies of scale is a very important one as firms seek to reduce their unit costs and increase their efficiency. This enables them to offer lower prices to consumers and/or benefit from higher profit margins. This is also how they can compete against other firms worldwide. With more free trade worldwide, local producers are now facing much greater competition and need to be as efficient as they can. You will often see economies of scale given as the reason behind a takeover or merger as firms join together to benefit from shared resources and reduce the unit costs. Industries such as banking, music, insurance, car production, and pharmaceuticals have seen major restructuring as firms join to gain economies of scale and be more competitive.

Economics in context   Economies of scale

A few years ago, Vodafone, the world's biggest mobile phone operator, had to examine its corporate strategy. With a new boss in place, it was time to take stock of where the business was going. The share price had started to underperform relative to other big firms in the UK and there was concern that the business was undervalued. Part of the problem seemed to be the many acquisitions that the company had made, expanding rapidly overseas in markets such as Japan, the USA, and Turkey. Over the years, Vodafone had built an unrivalled global scale. The company always insisted that its size provides huge economies of scale when buying equipment such as handsets, network equipment, and software. However, this is not always true, in that the technology in the USA and Japan is very different from that in its other markets. Japan, for example, is several years ahead in terms of handset technology; to reverse falling sales, Vodafone had to introduce Japanese-specific handsets. Also, regardless of the benefits of scale, an emerging problem was a decline in average revenue per user, especially when its rival O2's revenue per user was rising. This might suggest that greater customer focus is at least as important as scale.

? Question

Analyse the possible problems that Vodafone might have encountered while growing rapidly and globally.

Case study Jetstar alliance

In 2010, Qantas airlines claimed that a strategic alliance between its budget airline subsidiary Jetstar and rival AirAsia would significantly reduce costs.

The deal would include working together to gain better deals on the next generation of aircraft, sharing aircraft parts and ground handling services, and joint purchasing of engineering and maintenance supplies.

Qantas's chief executive said the initial arrangements might be the first step towards closer ties between Jetstar and Asia's largest budget airline.

The prospect of an even closer alliance probably poses the largest threat to Tiger Airways (part of Singapore Airlines), which continues to experience large losses.

Cost savings from the Qantas AirAsia deal could reach $300 million within two years, split approximately equally between the two firms.

However, some analysts question the scale of the savings: for example, they doubt the effect of the combined airline when negotiating with manufacturers such as Boeing and Airbus.

The president of the Australian and International Pilots Association said that staff feared that the deal would lead to Qantas and Jetstar sending jobs offshore in an effort to slash labour costs.

Qantas share prices fell 1 cent to $2.95 when the deal was announced.

? Questions

- Analyse the potential costs savings as a result of the Qantas AirAsia deal.

- Discuss the possible effects if the anticipated cost savings do occur.

- Why might the anticipated cost savings not occur?

Checklist

Now that you have read this chapter, try to answer the following questions.

☐ Do you understand the difference between marginal, average, and total product?

☐ Do you understand the difference between marginal, average, and total cost?

☐ Do you understand the significance of economies and diseconomies of scale?

☐ Do you understand the difference between internal and external economies of scale?

☐ Do you understand the meaning and significance of the minimum efficient scale?

Review questions

1 If the marginal cost of producing another item is positive and increasing, what is happening to the total costs?

2 If the marginal costs of producing a unit are below the average costs, then what will happen to the average costs?

3 What is the relationship between short-run average costs and long-run average costs?

4 Is a competitive market more likely if the minimum efficient scale is high or low relative to the level of demand in the industry? Why?

5 Does expansion inevitably reduce unit costs?

Key learning points

- There is a difference between the short run and the long run: in the long run, all of the factors of production are variable; in the short run, at least one factor of production is fixed.

- It is important to distinguish between the marginal product (or costs) and the average product (or costs).

- The law of diminishing returns states that, as additional units of the variable factor are added to a fixed factor of production, the marginal product of the variable factor falls.

- In the long run, a firm may benefit from internal economies of scale if it increases the scale of its production, but if its size increases too much, then it may experience diseconomies of scale.

Learn more

Firms will want to identify the minimum cost combination of resources for any level of output. This can be analysed in more detail using what is called 'isoquant analysis'. To learn more about this, visit the Online Resource Centre.

 Visit our Online Resource Centre at http://www.oxfordtextbooks.co.uk/orc/gillespie_econ2e/ for test questions and further information on topics covered in this chapter.

Revenues, costs, and profits

A great deal of economic analysis is based on the assumption that firms want to maximize their profits. Profits occur when a firm's revenue is greater than its costs. In this chapter, we examine the determinants of a firm's revenue and its costs, and analyse the price and output decisions that will maximize profits. We also examine how low the price level must fall before firms will shut down in the short run and in the long run. An understanding of all of these issues will help us to predict how firms will behave in a particular market situation, and analyse the price and outcome results in perfect competition.

LEARNING OBJECTIVES

By the end of this chapter, you should be able to:

- ✔ explain the difference between revenues and costs;

- ✔ outline the difference between marginal and total revenue;

- ✔ explain the difference between marginal and total costs;

- ✔ explain the difference between normal and abnormal profits;

- ✔ appreciate the difference between profits and profitability;

- ✔ explain the output level at which firms profit-maximize;

- ✔ understand the decision regarding whether or not to produce in the short run and the long run.

▨ Introduction

An important element of economic analysis involves examining the structure of a market and the behaviour of firms within it. Doing this requires an understanding of revenues, costs, and profits. This chapter examines these topics in detail.

▨ Total revenue

The total revenue (TR) of a firm measures the value of its sales. If a car dealership sells ten cars at £30,000 each, then its total revenue is £300,000. The total revenue of a business equals the price of the products multiplied by the number sold:

Total revenue (TR) = Price of a unit (P) × Quantity sold (Q)

The total revenue is also called 'sales', 'sales revenue', and 'turnover'. The total revenue may not be the same as the cash received at that particular moment because a sale may be on credit, but it represents what the sale is actually worth. The cash may be paid later and controlling cash flow effectively is an important business activity.

On a demand curve, the total revenue is illustrated by the area under the curve for any price and quantity combination (see Figure 10.1).

What do you think?

Why do you think that many firms sell their products on credit rather than insisting on cash being paid?

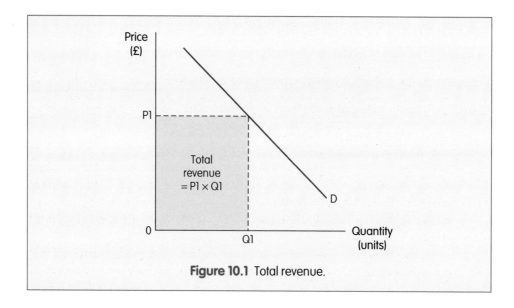

Figure 10.1 Total revenue.

▪ Marginal revenue

The marginal revenue (MR) is the difference in the total revenue when an additional unit is sold:

$$\text{Marginal revenue} = \frac{\text{Change in total revenue}}{\text{Change in the number of units sold}}$$

Assuming that the firm faces a downward-sloping demand curve, to sell another unit it may have to reduce the price not only on the last unit, but also on all of the ones before. For example, imagine that one unit is sold for £10, but to sell another, the price of both must be reduced to £9. This means that:

(One unit) Price per unit = £10; Total revenue = £10

(Two units) Price per unit = £9; Total revenue = £9 × 2 = £18

The marginal revenue for selling the second unit is £8. Although the second unit sells for £9, the price of the first one has been reduced by £1, so the gain in revenue is:

£9 – £1 = £8

Thus we have:

Marginal revenue = Price of the last unit – Reductions in price on the units before

Now, imagine that to sell a third unit, the price is reduced to £8. This means that:

(Two units) Price per unit = £9; Total revenue = £18

(Three units) Price per unit = £8; Total revenue = £24

The marginal revenue for selling the third unit is £6.

This is because the price of the last unit is £8, whilst the price of the previous two units has been reduced by £1 each. So the marginal revenue is:

£8 – £2 = £6

As the number of units being sold increases, then, to sell another one, the price must be reduced on an increasing number of previous units. This means that the difference between the marginal revenue and the price becomes ever greater as more units are sold. The marginal revenue curve therefore diverges from the demand curve.

At some point, the price cut will not change the total revenue. This means that the extra revenue (the marginal revenue) is zero. The effect of higher sales on revenue is exactly cancelled out by the lower price per unit. This occurs when the price elasticity of demand is equal to one (= 1—see Chapter 4). This is at the midpoint of the demand curve. The relationship between the price, the marginal revenue, and the total revenue is highlighted in Table 10.2.

When a relatively large number of units are being sold, the total revenue can fall following a price reduction. This is because of the price cut on so many previous units that is required to sell one more. If the total revenue falls, then this means that the marginal

Table 10.1 The relationship between the marginal revenue and the total revenue

Quantity (units)	Price (£)	Total revenue = Price × Quantity sold (£)	Marginal revenue = Extra revenue from selling an additional unit (£)
1	10	10	–
2	9	18	8
3	8	24	6
4	7	28	4
5	6	30	2
6	5	30	0
7	4	28	−2
8	3	24	−4

Table 10.2 The effect of marginal revenue on total revenue

Marginal revenue	Effect on total revenue
Positive, but falling	Increasing at a slower rate
Zero	Unchanged
Negative	Falling

revenue is negative. It also means that the price elasticity of demand is price inelastic (see Chapter 4).

The relationship between demand, the marginal revenue, and the total revenue is shown in Figure 10.2.

Put into practice

a. Ten units are sold at £15 each. To sell an 11th unit, the price must be reduced to £12.
   • Calculate the old and new total revenue.
   • Calculate the marginal revenue of the 11th unit.

b. To sell a 12th unit, the price must be lowered to £10 for all units.
   • Calculate the marginal revenue of the 12th unit.

Marginal revenue and total revenue

The marginal revenue shows the change in the total revenue. If the marginal revenue is positive following a cut in price and the sale of an extra unit, then this means the total

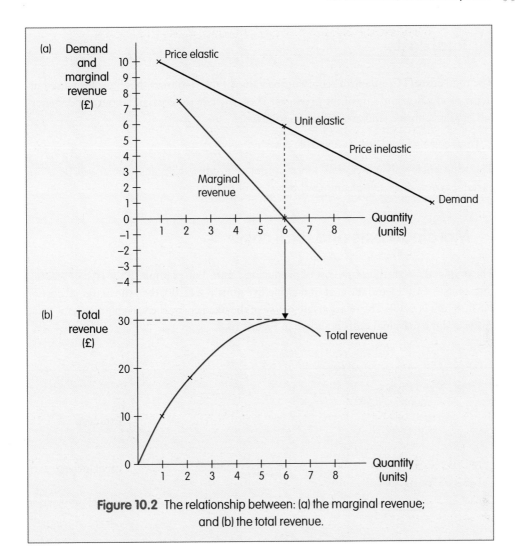

Figure 10.2 The relationship between: (a) the marginal revenue; and (b) the total revenue.

revenue increases: demand is price elastic. If the marginal revenue is zero when another unit is sold, then the total revenue does not change: demand is unit-price elastic. If the marginal revenue is negative when another unit is sold, then the total revenue falls; this means that demand is price inelastic.

Put into practice

The total revenue from selling 20 units is £300. Imagine that the marginal revenue from selling the 21st unit is either £30, £100, £0 or −£50.

What is the total revenue from 21 units for each of these four situations?

Total costs

The total costs (TC) of a firm represent the value of the resources that have been used up in the production and sale of the products. These include the costs of labour, land, materials, and machinery, and are written as follows:

Total costs = Fixed costs + Variable costs

The total costs will increase as more output is produced because there will be more variable costs—for example, more materials will be used up.

Marginal costs and total costs

The marginal cost is the extra cost of producing a unit. For example, if the cost of making four units is £1,000 and the cost of making five units is £1,200, then the marginal cost of the fifth unit is £200. The relationship between the fixed costs, the variable costs, the total costs, and the marginal costs is shown in Figure 10.3.

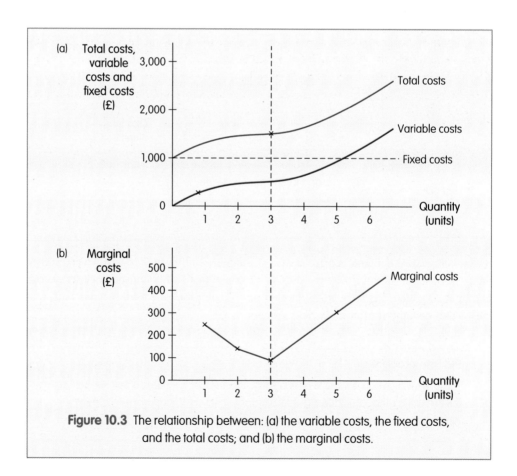

Figure 10.3 The relationship between: (a) the variable costs, the fixed costs, and the total costs; and (b) the marginal costs.

The relationship between the different types of cost is also highlighted in Table 10.3.

Table 10.3 The relationship between the total costs, the marginal costs, and the average costs

Output (units)	Fixed costs (£)	Variable costs (£)	Total costs = Fixed costs + Variable costs (£)	Marginal costs = Change in total costs / Change in output (£)	Average cost (£) = Total costs / Output
0	1,000	0	1,000	–	–
1	1,000	250	1,250	250	1,250
2	1,000	400	1,400	150	700
3	1,000	500	1,500	100	500
4	1,000	800	1,800	300	450
5	1,000	1,200	2,200	400	440
6	1,000	1,700	2,700	500	450

If the marginal cost is positive, then this means that the total costs must have increased. For example, a marginal cost of £300 means that the total costs have gone up by £300 when another unit is made. If the marginal cost is £400, then the total costs will rise by this amount. If the marginal cost is £0, then this means that the total costs do not change when an extra unit is produced. The marginal cost therefore shows the rate of change of the total costs. The relationship between the marginal costs and the total costs is shown in Figure 10.4.

Put into practice

Complete the following table.

Output (units)	Fixed costs (£)	Variable costs (£)	Total costs = Fixed costs + Variable costs (£)	Marginal costs = Change in total costs / Change in output (£)	Average cost (£) = Total costs / Output
0	___	?	10,000	–	–
1	___	1,000	___	___	___
2	___	?	13,000	___	___
3	___	4,000	___	___	___
4	___	?	___	3,000	___
5	___	?	___	___	5,000
6	___	8,000	___	___	___

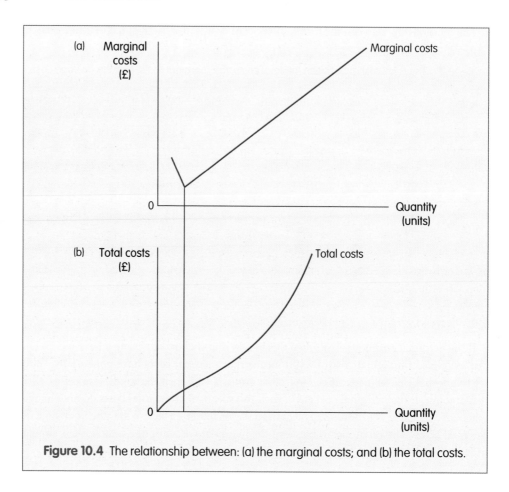

Figure 10.4 The relationship between: (a) the marginal costs; and (b) the total costs.

Table 10.4 The effect of marginal cost on total cost

Marginal cost	Effect on total cost
Positive, but falling	Increasing at a slower rate
Positive, but rising	Increasing at a faster rate

▨ Profit and loss

The profit of a firm measures the difference between the value of what has been sold and the value of what has been used up to provide these goods—that is:

Profit = Total revenue – Total costs

If the total costs are greater than the total revenue, then a loss is made.

■ The difference between accounting profit and economists' profits: Normal and abnormal profit

When an accountant thinks of costs, he or she measures the costs of items used up to produce and sell the products; these include labour, materials, components, land, and equipment. An economist, however, will add opportunity costs to this list. This means that an economist will estimate how much a firm's inputs could have earned if used in another industry and include this as a cost of being in business in a particular market. As a result, in economics, when a firm is only covering its costs, it is earning a sum of money that it could earn elsewhere with these resources. Therefore there is no incentive to move these resources into other industries. In accounting terms, a profit will be declared to investors, but to an economist, this simply means that the firm has earned the amount of money required to keep resources where they are; if less than this were earned, then resources would be shifted into other sectors of the economy. When revenue equals costs (including opportunity cost), an economist calls this normal profit; if all of the firms in an industry were earning normal profit, then there is no incentive to move resources into or out of this industry.

If a firm earns more than the costs included by an economist, then this is called abnormal profit, or supernormal profit. This means that the resources are generating rewards that are higher than those needed to keep them in this particular industry. This will act as a signal for resources to shift into this sector to try to benefit from such high returns. Abnormal profit will attract other firms into this sector.

If the revenue does not cover economists' costs, then a loss is made; resources should be moved out of this sector and into a more profitable one. The resources are not earning enough to justify keeping them in their present use. In accounting terms, the firm could still be declaring a profit, but to an economist, if this does not justify the resources being in this industry, then it is a loss.

Economics in context   Losses

In 2010, the Vatican announced its third consecutive financial loss, with a €4.1 million (£3.4 million; $5.2 million) deficit in the previous financial year. It saw revenues of €250.2 million against expenses of €254.3 million. But annual donations from churches worldwide—known as Peter's Pence—were up by about 9 per cent at $82.52 million.

Most of the Vatican's outlay was to cover the activities of Pope Benedict XVI and services such as Vatican Radio, which is broadcast on five continents in 40 different languages. The Vatican said that it also faced costly improvements to its telecommunication system, while restoring cultural treasures and ensuring security added to the bill. The Vatican began publishing annual financial reports in 1981 when Pope John Paul II set out to challenge perceptions that the Vatican was rich.

In 2008, the Vatican lost €900,000, but in 2007 had seen a €9.1 million deficit.

❓ Question

What do you think the Vatican could do to make a profit?

▩ Profits versus profitability

The profit made by a firm is measured as an absolute amount, such as £X million. However, this does not show an analyst what funds were invested to generate such a return. A £3 million profit earned in a year may be a high sum for a small business, but is not so impressive for a very large organization such as Tesco plc. We may therefore want to measure profit in relation to the amount of long-term funds invested in the business. This is known as the return on capital employed (ROCE).

The ROCE is a very common measure of a firm's financial performance and can be written as follows:

$$\text{Return on capital employed} = \frac{\text{Profit}}{\text{Capital employed}} \times 100\%$$

Managers and investors will usually seek to generate the highest possible ROCE. This will mean that they are using their resources to generate a relatively high level of profit.

Economics in context	World's biggest companies 2009		
Rank	Company	Revenues ($m)	Profits ($m)
1	Walmart Stores	408,214	14,335
2	Royal Dutch Shell	285,129	12,518
3	Exxon Mobil	284,650	19,280
4	BP	246,138	16,578
5	Toyota Motor	204,106	2,256
6	Japan Post Holdings	202,196	4,849
7	Sinopec	187,518	5,756
8	State Grid	184,496	−343
9	AXA	175,257	5,012
10	China National Petroleum	165,496	10,272

Source: Fortune.

❓ Questions

Why is there a difference between the revenues of a company and its profits?

Calculate the profit margins (that is, the profit as a percentage of sales) for the top five companies above. Why do you think they differ?

Profit-maximization: The marginal condition

To maximize their profits, firms must sell the number of units for which there is the largest positive difference between the total revenue and the total costs. To identify this level of sales, economists often use the marginal condition, also known as the profit-maximizing condition. This means that they look for the highest level of sales at which the marginal revenue from selling an extra unit equals the marginal cost of producing and selling another unit.

If the marginal revenue from selling a product is greater than the marginal cost of producing it, then the extra unit will make a profit and total profits will go up. The extra revenue is greater than the extra costs, and so profits increase by producing and selling it. The firm should therefore produce all of the units for which the marginal revenue is greater than the marginal costs because, by doing so, profits will rise.

The profit-maximizing firm should stop producing when the marginal revenue equals the marginal costs. At this point, no extra profit can be made, which means that profits must be maximized. They cannot be increased further. A firm will therefore profit-maximize if the marginal revenue equals the marginal costs.

If the marginal revenue is less than the marginal costs, then a loss will be made on the extra unit. These units should not be produced.

So the profit-maximizing output occurs when:

Marginal revenue (MR) = Marginal costs (MC)

The profit-maximizing output in terms of the total revenue and the total costs, and the marginal revenue and the marginal costs, are shown in Figure 10.5.

Put into practice

- If the extra revenue from selling an item is greater than the extra cost, would a profit-maximizing firm produce and sell it, or not?

- If the extra cost of an item is greater than the extra revenue, does this mean that the firm is necessarily making a loss?

Table 10.5   The profit-maximizing output decision

MR and MC	Output decision
Marginal revenue > Marginal cost	Produce more because there is extra profit to be made
Marginal revenue = Marginal cost	Profit-maximizing because there is no extra profit to be made
Marginal revenue < Marginal cost	Produce less

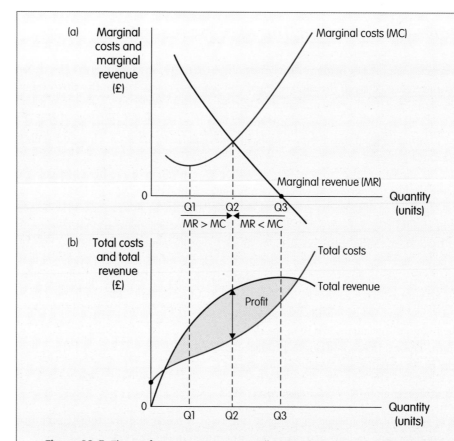

Figure 10.5 The profit-maximizing output, illustrated in terms of: (a) the marginal revenue and the marginal costs; and (b) the total revenue and the total costs. The marginal costs fall up to Q1 and therefore the total costs rise at a decreasing rate. After Q1, the marginal costs increase, so the total costs increase at an increasing rate. At Q3, the marginal revenue is zero, so the total revenue does not increase. After Q3, the marginal revenue is negative, so the total revenue falls. Up to Q2, the marginal revenue is greater than the marginal costs, so by selling more the profits will increase. At Q2, the marginal revenue equals the marginal costs, so no extra profit can be generated; this means that profit is maximized. At output levels beyond Q2, the marginal revenue is less than the marginal costs, so the firm makes a loss on these extra units; profit would increase by cutting output back to Q2. The profit-maximizing output is Q2; this is also shown by the largest positive difference between the total revenue and the total costs.

What do you think?

Why do you think it is important for firms to make a profit?

Why might there be pressure on managers to maximize profits?

How else might you measure the success of a business apart from profits?

■ The decision of whether to produce or not

Producing in the short run

Given that there are fixed factors of production, in the short run this means that a firm must pay fixed costs even if output is zero. This means that the firm will lose an amount equal to the fixed costs even if it does not produce or sell anything. The decision of whether it is financially viable to produce will therefore depend on the variable costs (the costs incurred by producing, such as materials and components), because the fixed costs must be paid anyway. The fixed costs are 'sunk costs' and should not affect a decision about whether to continue to produce in the short run.

If the revenue earned from making and selling the units can at least cover the variable costs, then this means that it is financially worth producing them. Anything earned over and above the variable costs is called a 'contribution'; it contributes towards the fixed costs. For example, if the revenue is £200 and the variable costs are £180, then there is a £20 contribution towards the fixed costs. Figure 10.6 shows a contribution being made to fixed costs. This does not mean that the firm necessarily makes a profit (this depends on the relative size of the contribution to the fixed costs), but the loss will be less than it would be by not producing. (Remember that fixed costs must be paid anyway.)

For example, imagine that the fixed costs are £100. If the firm does not produce, then it makes a loss of £100. If it does produce and gains a £20 contribution towards the fixed costs, its losses are only £80. This means that it is better to produce than not to produce. The firm should therefore continue in production even though it makes a loss, because the revenue at least covers the variable costs. When the revenue only equals the variable costs, the loss will be the same whether producing or not producing. This is known as the shut-down point. If the revenue is less than the variable costs, then the firm should not produce. For example, if the revenue is £150, the variable costs are £180, and the fixed costs are £100, then, by producing, the firm will make a loss of £130. Not only are fixed costs being paid, but there is also another £30 of variable costs that cannot be covered by the revenue. In this situation, the firm would reduce its loss by not producing.

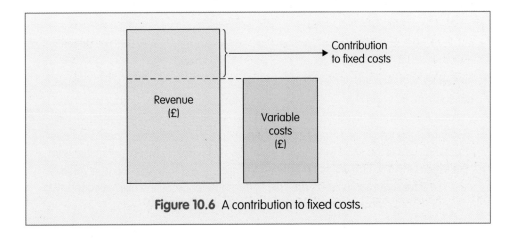

Figure 10.6 A contribution to fixed costs.

So, in the short term, a firm should only produce provided that its revenue at least covers its variable costs.

This analysis can also be undertaken on a 'per unit' level. If the price per unit more than covers the variable costs per unit, then the sale generates a contribution per unit that can be put towards the fixed costs and so production should continue. If the price per unit cannot cover the variable cost per unit, then not only do fixed costs have to be paid, but also variable costs cannot be covered either, so the firm should shut down.

Thus, in the short run, we have the following two possibilities.

- **A firm should produce if the price is greater than or equal to the average variable costs** This means that a contribution is being made on each unit towards the fixed costs and so production should continue. Even if a loss is made, then it is less than the loss that would be made if the firm were to shut down and still had to pay the fixed costs.

- **A firm should not produce if the price is less than the average variable costs** This means that the firm cannot pay its variable costs and has fixed costs to pay as well. The firm should shut down. The shutdown point is illustrated in Figure 10.7.

The long run

In the long run, a firm will not continue producing at a loss. It is not constrained by resources and so is not committed to fixed costs. The firm will produce only if it breaks

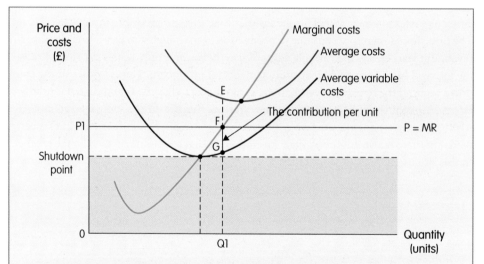

Figure 10.7 The shutdown price. At Q1, the average fixed cost (which is the difference between the average cost and the average variable cost) is EG. By producing, a loss is made. The loss per unit is shown by EF (where the price is below the average cost). However, this loss is less than if the firm did not produce, because it would still pay the fixed costs in the short run. By producing, the firm contributes FG per unit toward the fixed costs. The firm will not produce if the price is less than the average variable cost. We have assumed all units are sold at the same price, so the extra revenue (MR) equals the price. Firms produce where MR = MC.

even—that is, if all of its costs can be covered—and at least a normal profit is made. This means that the total revenue must at least cover total costs.

Looking at this on a 'per unit' level, this means that the price per unit needs to be at least equal to the average cost per unit. If the price were less than the average cost, then this means that a loss would be made on each unit and so the firm would not produce.

The break-even point is illustrated in Figure 10.8. Again we have assumed that every unit is sold at the same price, so the extra revenue (MR) equals the price. Firms produce where MR = MC to profit-maximize.

Table 10.6 defines some of the key terms used in this section.

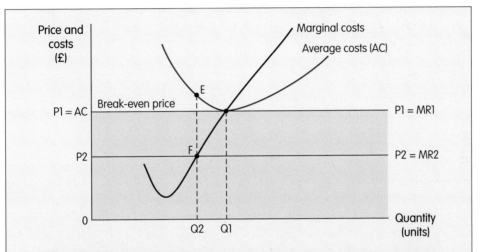

Figure 10.8 A supply curve and the break-even price. The firm will not produce below the price that equals the minimum of the average costs curve, because then a loss would be made. For example, at P2, the loss per unit is EF (the price is less than the average costs). In the long run, the firm will not produce if the price is below P1 as a loss is made.

Table 10.6   Summary table of key terms

Term	Description
Total cost	= Fixed cost + Variable cost
Marginal cost	Extra cost of an additional unit $= \dfrac{\text{Change in total cost}}{\text{Change in output}}$
Total revenue	Revenue earned from sales = Price × Quantity sold
Marginal revenue	Extra revenue from selling an extra unit $= \dfrac{\text{Change in total revenue}}{\text{Change in the number of units sold}}$
Profit	= Total revenue − Total cost

Case study Walmart

Fiscal year ended 31 January	2010	2009	2008	2007	2006
Sales	$405.0 bn	$401.1 bn	$373.8 bn	$344.8 bn	$308.9 bn
Net sales increase	1.0%	7.3%	8.4%	11.6%	9.8%
Operating profit	$24.0 bn	$22.8 bn	$22.0 bn	$20.5 bn	$18.7 bn
Dividend per share	$1.09	$0.95	$0.88	$0.67	$0.60

Source: Walmart Corporate Factsheet, March 2010.

About Us

Walmart serves customers and members more than 200 million times per week at more than 8,446 retail units, in 15 countries. With fiscal year 2010 sales of $405 billion, Walmart employs more than 2.1 million associates worldwide.

Our Purpose

Saving people money to help them live better was the goal that Sam Walton envisioned when he opened the doors to the first Walmart more than 40 years ago. Today, this mission is more important than ever to our customers and members around the world. We work hard every day in all our markets to deliver on this promise. We operate with the same level of integrity and respect that Mr. Sam put in place. It is because of these values and culture that Walmart continues to make a difference in the lives of our customers, members, and associates.

Walmart employs more than 2.1 million associates worldwide, including more than 1.4 million in the US. Walmart is not only one of the largest private employers in the US, but the largest in Mexico and one of the largest in Canada as well.

Potential associates know that Walmart provides good jobs with competitive pay and benefits. For example, our average, full-time hourly wage for Walmart stores is $11.75, and is even higher in urban areas. Additionally, associates can receive performance-based bonuses.

Walmart insures more than 1.2 million associates and family members, making us among the nation's largest providers of private sector health insurance.

Unlike the employees of many of our retail competitors, Walmart associates—both full- and part-time—can become eligible for health benefits.

❓ Questions

- Why is the profit declared by Walmart not the same as economic profit?
- Explain the types of costs that Walmart might have.
- Calculate the profit margin (that is, the profit as a percentage of sales) for the years shown above.
- Comment on the financial performance of Walmart.

- What is the average revenue in 2010:
  a. per customer?
  b. per outlet?
- 'Saving people money to help them live better.' How does Walmart try to achieve this objective?
- Do you think that the benefits provided for colleagues at Walmart are an unnecessary cost?

Checklist

Now that you have read this chapter, try to answer the following questions.

☐ Can you explain the difference between revenues and costs?

☐ Can you outline the difference between marginal and total revenue?

☐ Can you explain the difference between marginal and total costs?

☐ Can you explain the difference between normal and abnormal profits?

☐ Do you understand the difference between profits and profitability?

☐ Can you explain the output level at which firms profit-maximize?

☐ Can you identify the price at which firms will stop producing in the short run? In the long run? Can you explain why?

Review questions

1 If the output of a firm were zero units, would its total costs equal its variable costs?

2 Do you think that labour is a fixed or a variable cost?

3 If the marginal cost is positive but falling, what is happening to the total costs?

4 If a firm is profit-maximizing, why is it impossible for the marginal revenue to be greater than the marginal cost?

5 What is the difference between abnormal and normal profits?

Key learning points

- Profit is the difference between total revenue and total cost.
- There is a difference between an economist's view of profit and an accountant's view of profit.
- Profit is maximized at an output for which the marginal revenue equals the marginal cost.

- Normal profit occurs when the total revenue equals the total cost.

- Abnormal profit occurs when the total revenue is greater than the total cost.

- A loss occurs if revenue is less than total costs.

- In the short run, a firm will produce only if the price is equal to, or greater than, the average variable cost.

- In the long run, a firm will produce only if the price is equal to, or greater than, the average cost.

Learn more

The relationship between short-run and long-run costs can be analysed in more detail using isoquant analysis. To learn more about this, visit the Online Resource Centre.

 Visit our Online Resource Centre at http://www.oxfordtextbooks.co.uk/orc/gillespie_econ2e/ for test questions and further information on topics covered in this chapter.

Perfect competition

An important part of economic analysis is to consider how firms behave in different types of market and the impact of this on consumers. Perfect competition is one form of market structure. In this chapter, we examine the features of a perfectly competitive market, and the consequences of this form of market structure in terms of price, output, and efficiency. In the following chapters, we then examine other market structures and compare them with perfect competition.

LEARNING OBJECTIVES

By the end of this chapter, you should be able to:

✔ understand the key features of a perfectly competitive market;

✔ analyse the price and output decisions in the short run and the long run in a perfectly competitive market;

✔ explain why the supply curve is the marginal cost curve in perfectly competitive markets.

■ Why study market structure?

Not all markets are the same. Some are dominated by a few firms; some have many competitors in them. In this chapter and the following three, we examine different types of market to consider how the structure affects firms and consumers within them. This is an important aspect of economic analysis because it helps us to decide whether one form of market structure is better than another; this has implications for government policy. Microsoft dominates the PC market at the moment; Intel dominates the microprocessor market; and Wrigley's the market for chewing gum: is this desirable or should governments intervene to limit the firms' power and encourage more competition? By comparison, the market for fruit and vegetables is usually divided between hundreds of thousands of farmers: should the government intervene to encourage the growth of a few big farmers or not? Is it better to have one business responsible for delivering the mail or many? Is it dangerous or desirable to have a few firms dominating the sale of food, petrol, banking services, and insurance in the UK, or should the government leave them to it?

In the following chapters, we consider these issues, as well as think about why markets differ in the first place. There are many providers of kennels, there are thousands and thousands of pubs in the UK (although the number is declining), and there are lots of hair-dressers, plumbers, and taxi firms. There are far fewer energy companies, airlines, private medical care firms, and electrical goods retailers. In the following chapters, we examine why this might be and the effects of these differences.

We begin by analysing a market structure known as perfect competition.

Introduction to perfect competition

A perfectly competitive market is one in which:

- there are large numbers of buyers and sellers;
- products are homogeneous (that is, exactly the same);
- there is perfect knowledge (so buyers know what all firms are charging and firms know what profits are being made in the industry); and
- there is freedom of entry into, and exit from, the market, so that firms can easily move into and out of the market.

In reality, all of these conditions are unlikely to be met; the closest are likely to be commodity markets, such as wheat, which have millions of small farmers operating in a global market with a world price for their products. Even though it may be extreme, by analysing the model of perfect competition, it is possible to decide whether society should attempt to move towards this market situation or not.

Perfectly competitive firms as price takers

In a perfectly competitive market, there are many firms. One firm's output decisions cannot influence the overall market supply to any noticeable extent. If one firm changes its output level, then this has such a small effect on the industry supply that the market price does not alter.

Each firm is therefore a 'price taker'—that is, it is so small that its actions cannot influence the market price. The firm can sell as much as it wants without bringing down the market price. This means that every unit can be sold at the market price. For example, every unit can be sold at £10, so the extra revenue generated from a sale is the same as its price. This means that:

Marginal revenue (MR) = Price

This is illustrated in Figure 11.1.

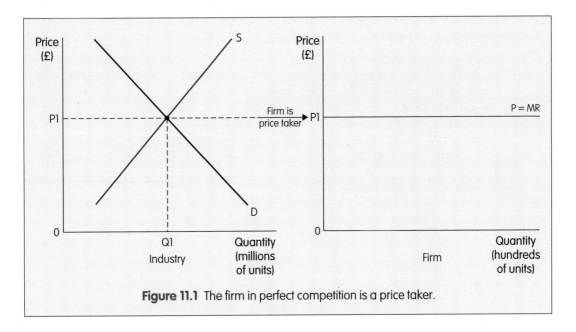

Figure 11.1 The firm in perfect competition is a price taker.

■ Short-run equilibrium in perfect competition

- A profit-maximizing firm in perfect competition will produce at the highest output where the marginal revenue equals the marginal cost. This is the marginal condition.
- The amount of profit being made will depend on the average revenue (price) compared to the average costs. This is the average condition.

In the short run, firms in perfect competition are able to make abnormal profits (when the price is greater than the average cost) or losses (when the price is less than the average cost). However, this situation will not continue in the long run.

If firms are making abnormal profits, then this acts as a signal for other firms to enter the market to benefit from this. The entry of more firms will lead to more being supplied and this will shift the industry supply curve to the right; this will reduce the market price. (Although one firm cannot shift the industry supply on its own, the entry of many firms will shift the curve to the right.) This process will continue until only normal profits are being made (the price equals the average cost), as shown in Figure 11.2. When normal profits are being made, there is no incentive for more firms to enter or leave the industry.

If firms are making losses, then this means that businesses will leave the industry. This shifts the industry supply curve to the left and increases the market price. This will continue until only normal profits are being made, as shown in Figure 11.3. At this point, there is no further incentive for firms to enter or leave the industry.

What do you think?

Why are the assumptions of perfect information, freedom of entry and exit, and a homogeneous product important to reach the long-run equilibrium of normal profits in perfect competition?

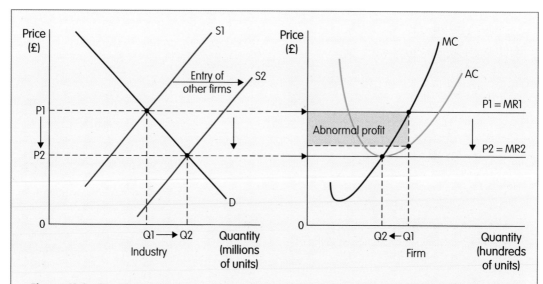

Figure 11.2 The adjustment process from short-run abnormal profits to long-run equilibrium in a perfectly competitive market. The firm is initially making abnormal profits when the price is P1. This attracts other firms into the industry, thereby shifting the industry supply curve to the right. With more firms in the industry, the price falls until normal profits are made at P2.

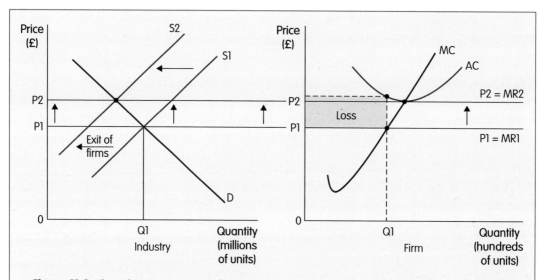

Figure 11.3 The adjustment process from short-run losses to long-run equilibrium in a perfectly competitive market. The firm originally makes a loss at the price P1 because this price is less than the average cost per unit. This leads to an exit of firms from the industry. The industry supply curve shifts to the left. This increases the price until only normal profits are made (P = AC). At this point there is no further incentive to leave the industry.

Put into practice

Which of the following defines:

a. normal profits?

b. break-even point?

c. shutdown point?

d. abnormal profit?

- Price equals average fixed cost.
- Price equals average variable cost.
- Price equals average total cost.
- Price equals average revenue.
- Price is greater than average cost.
- Price is greater than average variable cost.

■ Long-run equilibrium in perfect competition

The long-run equilibrium in perfect competition is shown in Figure 11.4. In the long run, in perfect competition, firms can only make normal profits. Assuming that they are profit-maximizers, they will produce when the marginal revenue equals the marginal costs (MR = MC) (see Chapter 10).

Given that the firm is a price taker, the marginal revenue will equal the price (P = MR). This means that firms will produce when the price, the marginal revenue, and the

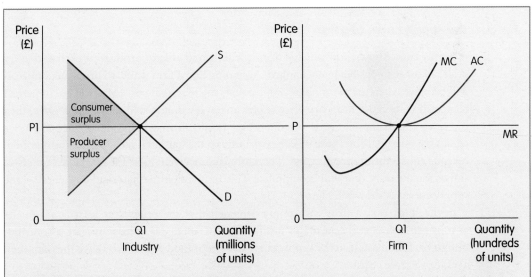

Figure 11.4 Long-run equilibrium in a perfectly competitive industry. In long-run equilibrium, we have P = MR = MC = AC.

marginal cost are all equal. As a result, firms will be allocatively efficient. Allocative efficiency occurs when the extra benefit to society (as shown by the price that consumers are willing to pay) equals the extra costs—that is, the price equals the marginal cost. In the long-run equilibrium of perfect competition, firms are producing all of the units for which the price (which represents the extra benefit or utility to the consumer) is greater than the extra cost of producing it, up to the point at which the extra benefit equals the extra cost. At this point, the community surplus is maximized (see Chapter 7).

In the long run, firms in perfect competition are also productively efficient. Productive efficiency occurs when firms are producing at the minimum of the average cost curve; they have the lowest unit cost possible and therefore they are not wasting resources.

To summarize, in the long run, in perfect competition:

- firms earn normal profits;
- the industry is allocatively efficient (the price that represents the marginal benefit of a unit to a consumer equals the marginal cost); and
- the industry is productively efficient (firms are producing at the minimum of the average cost curve).

Put into practice

Imagine that a perfectly competitive market is in long-run equilibrium. Show the impact of a fall in demand in the short run and the long run on both the industry and a firm.

■ Deriving the supply curve in perfect competition

The supply curve of a firm

A supply curve shows how much a firm is willing and able to produce at each and every price, all other things being unchanged. Assuming that a firm wants to profit-maximize, it will produce when the marginal revenue equals the marginal cost (MR = MC). In perfect competition, because firms are price takers and every unit is sold at the same price, then the price equals the marginal revenue. As a result, firms will produce when the price equals the marginal costs (because the price equals the marginal revenue and the marginal revenue equals the marginal costs). Therefore, at any given price, the marginal cost curve shows the quantity that will be supplied. This means that the marginal cost curve is the supply curve, as shown in Figure 11.5.

In the short run, a firm will supply provided that the price is at least equal to the average variable cost (because this means that the revenue is at least making a contribution to the fixed costs), so the supply curve is the marginal cost curve above the minimum average variable cost.

In the long run, a firm will supply only if the price covers the average costs (otherwise a loss would be made), so the supply curve is the marginal cost curve above the average cost curve.

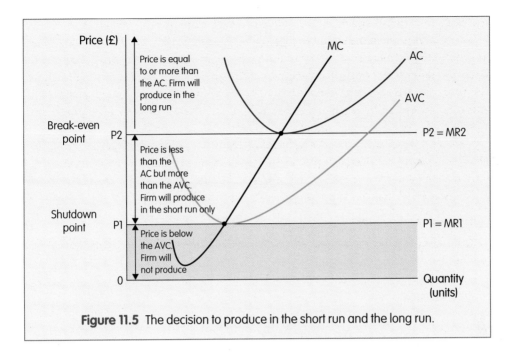

Figure 11.5 The decision to produce in the short run and the long run.

The short-run and long-run industry supply curve

The short-run supply curve in perfect competition is derived from the marginal cost curve. In the short run, an increase in demand leads to a movement along the supply curve from equilibrium at 'a' to 'b' (Figure 11.6). This increase in price will lead to higher profits and lead to entry of other firms into the industry. The short-run supply shifts to the right. If the price falls back to its existing level, this would mean that firms are making normal profits at the same level of average costs as before (see Figure 11.6a). If, however, entry into the industry bids up the price of inputs, such as employee wages, this means that normal profits would be earned only with a higher price and the long-run supply curve would be upward-sloping (see Figure 11.6b).

If the expansion of the industry leads to lower average costs—perhaps because of the build-up of specialist support services—a normal profit will be made at a lower price in the long run. This means that the long-run supply curve is downward-sloping (see Figure 11.6c).

Put into practice

a. In perfect competition, which of the following statements is true?
- Each firm in the market has some, but not complete, control over the price of its product.
- Firms are completely free to enter or leave the market.
- There are many producers producing similar, but not identical, products.
- Firms in the market advertise in order to shift the demand curve for their product.

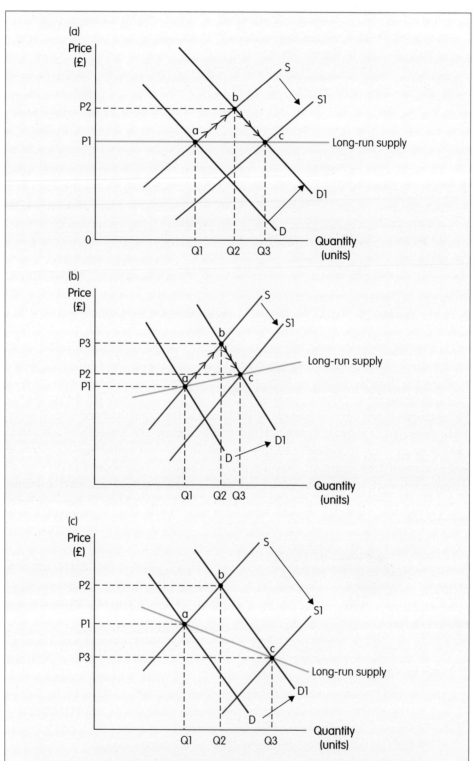

Figure 11.6 (a) A horizontal long-run supply curve; (b) An upward-sloping long-run supply curve; (c) A downward-sloping long-run supply curve.

b. The demand curve for the perfectly competitive firm is determined by:
- the firm's marginal cost of producing an extra unit of output.
- the price that is established by the firm.
- the market demand for, and supply of, the good.
- the average total cost of producing a particular level of output.

■ Summary

Perfect competition may or may not exist in reality as a market structure, but it provides a benchmark against which to judge other forms of market. It highlights the benefits of competition, and this may well influence government policy regarding helping start-up firms and limiting the power of firms to dominate an industry.

Case study Global cocoa production

Global cocoa production is over 3 million tonnes per year. The production of cocoa is undertaken by thousands of small producers in countries such as Ghana, the Ivory Coast, and Cameroon. Although there are a few big farmers, almost 90 per cent of production is by small producers with farms of less than 5 hectares.

These producers produce similar crops and have no power to control prices on the international markets. The world price is determined by the industry supply and the level of demand from the huge multinationals, such as Cadbury and Mars. The small firms are often said to be exploited by the larger confectionery companies. Fairtrade organizations attempt to rectify this by guaranteeing a reasonable price for their crops. The underlying principle of Fairtrade is that the product must have been traded in such a way that:

- the primary producer gets a fair deal;
- the primary producer receives a proportion of the price in advance to enable it to pay for its inputs; and
- the Fairtrade company enters into a long-term relationship with the supplier.

The Fairtrade Labelling Organizations International standard for cocoa outlines the calculation of Fairtrade cocoa prices. The prices are calculated on the basis of world market prices plus Fairtrade premiums.

❓ Questions
- What factors do you think determine the supply of cocoa?
- What factors do you think determine the demand for cocoa?
- Do you think that the price of cocoa is relatively stable or unstable? Why?

- In what ways is the market for cocoa like perfect competition? In what ways is it different?
- Do you think that the Fairtrade scheme is desirable? Why is it needed?

 Web

For more information on Fairtrade, visit http://www.fairtrade.org.uk

Checklist

Now that you have read this chapter, try to answer the following questions.

☐ Do you understand the key features of a perfectly competitive market?

☐ Can you explain the price and output decisions in the short run and the long run in a perfectly competitive market?

☐ Can you explain why the supply curve is the marginal cost curve in perfectly competitive markets?

Review questions

1 Why are firms in perfect competition price takers?

2 Can firms in perfect competition make abnormal profits?

3 Why is the absence of barriers to entry an important assumption in perfect competition?

4 Why is the fact that firms offer homogeneous products an important assumption in perfect competition?

5 How is the supply curve in perfect competition derived?

Key learning points

- A firm in perfect competition is a price taker.
- Firms profit-maximize where Price (P) = Marginal revenue (MR) = Marginal cost (MC).
- In the short run, in perfect competition, firms can make abnormal profits or losses.
- In the long run, due to the entry and exit of firms, only normal profits are made.
- In the long run, in perfect competition, firms are allocatively and productively efficient.

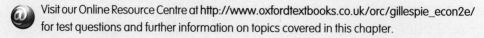 Visit our Online Resource Centre at http://www.oxfordtextbooks.co.uk/orc/gillespie_econ2e/ for test questions and further information on topics covered in this chapter.

Monopoly

Monopoly is a very different form of market structure from perfect competition. This chapter outlines the nature of a monopoly, and examines the price, output, and efficiency outcomes in this type of market. Governments are often concerned about the effects of monopoly power; in this chapter, we outline the arguments for and against monopoly power.

LEARNING OBJECTIVES

By the end of this chapter, you should be able to:

✔ explain the key features of a monopoly;

✔ explain the price and output decisions in a monopoly;

✔ discuss the efficiency of a monopoly;

✔ explain the theory of contestable markets.

■ Introduction to monopoly

A monopoly occurs when a firm dominates a market. This means that the firm determines the price in the market rather than accepts the industry price. It is a 'price maker' rather than a 'price taker'.

A 'pure' monopoly occurs when one firm has a market share of 100 per cent: for example, in nationalized industries, the government might allow only one state-owned firm to provide a particular service, such as health care or electricity. More generally, a monopoly exists when a firm exerts a major influence over a market. Under UK competition law, a monopoly occurs when a firm has a market share of 25 per cent or more—that is, its sales are over 25 per cent of the total sales in a market.

Demand and marginal revenue for a monopolist

A monopolist faces a downward-sloping demand curve. To sell more units, it must lower the price. This involves lowering the price on the additional unit and on all of the units before. As a result, the marginal revenue diverges from the demand curve (see Chapter 10).

Price and output decisions in a monopoly

A monopolist is assumed to be a profit-maximizer. This means that it produces at the highest output when the marginal revenue equals the marginal cost (see Chapter 10). In Figure 12.1, this occurs at the price P2 and the quantity Q2.

At this price and quantity combination, the firm will make an abnormal profit—that is, the price is greater than the average cost at that output. This means that the firm is earning more with its resources in this industry than it could earn with them elsewhere. This abnormal profit will attract other firms into this industry from other sectors. They will

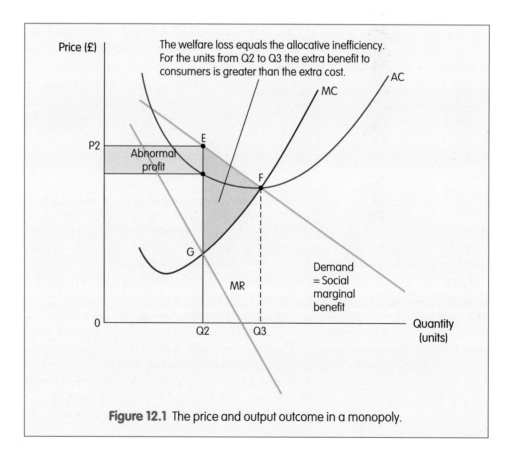

Figure 12.1 The price and output outcome in a monopoly.

want to shift resources into this industry to share the abnormal profits. However, unlike firms in a perfectly competitive industry, a monopolist can continue to make abnormal profits in the long run because it can prevent other firms from entering the market to erode its profits. This is because barriers to entry exist. (For more information on barriers to entry, see Chapter 15.)

Unlike the firms in the long-run equilibrium position in a perfectly competitive market, a monopoly is allocatively and productively inefficient.

It is allocatively inefficient because the price paid by consumers for the last unit produced is greater than the marginal cost of providing it. Customers are paying more for the last unit of the product than the extra cost of producing it. Society would like more units to be produced and sold.

For the units from Q2 to Q3, the extra benefit of these units to society (as shown by the price that the consumer is willing to pay) exceeds the extra cost of providing them. Therefore, if these units were to be produced, then society's welfare would increase. The monopoly price and quantity outcome has led to a welfare loss. The triangle EFG in Figure 12.1 is a welfare loss area (also called a deadweight social burden triangle) that exists because the firm is allocatively inefficient. The monopolist does not produce these units because to sell them requires a reduction in price on all previous units, which means that marginal revenue would be below the marginal costs and profits would fall.

A monopolist is also likely to be productively inefficient because the firm may not be producing at the minimum average cost. To benefit from the lowest possible average costs, the firm would have to sell more and produce at Q3. This would involve reducing the price because the demand curve is downward-sloping and the firm's profits would fall (because the marginal revenue is less than the marginal cost on these additional Q3 – Q2 units). Although the monopolist is maximizing its profits, it is not usually producing at the most efficient output level. The unit costs are minimized at Q3, but because the price would have to be lowered so much, the overall profits would fall.

Put into practice

Imagine that demand for a monopolist's products increases. Show the effect of this on the price, quantity, and profits of the firm, using a diagram.

■ Monopoly compared to perfect competition

Perfect competition and monopoly are two market structures at the opposite ends of the competitive spectrum. However, a comparison of the two structures may influence our view of which structure is more desirable, and therefore our view of how they should be treated by the government and the types of competition policy that the government should adopt.

In both types of market, we assume that the firms are profit-maximizers. Apart from this, there are many differences, as shown in Table 12.1.

Table 12.1 A comparison of a firm operating in a perfectly competitive industry and a monopoly

	Perfect competition	Monopoly
Price taker	Yes	No
Barriers to entry	No	Yes
Long-run abnormal profits	No	Yes
Differentiated product	No	Yes
Allocatively efficient	Yes	No
Productively efficient	Yes	No

Put into practice

Can you remember the following?

a. The profit-maximizing condition

b. The condition for allocative efficiency

c. The condition for productive efficiency

d. The difference between normal and abnormal profits

■ Should we prevent monopolies?

There is much debate regarding monopolies. Some commentators argue that they need to be regulated and controlled for the following reasons.

- They can abuse their market power to restrict their output and to force up prices for the customer relative to a perfectly competitive situation. Given that there are limited substitutes available, the customer may be forced to pay more than he or she would in a competitive market.

- The lack of competition in a market may reduce the pressure on firms to innovate and be efficient. This may lead to a cutback in research and development spending, and less new product development.

- According to Leibenstein (1966), a monopoly situation leads to 'X inefficiency'; with less competitive pressure on firms due to barriers to entry, costs will drift upwards, and this wastes resources. This means that costs in a monopoly may be higher than in a competitive market and so monopolies are bound to be inefficient.

If monopolies do behave in the ways described above, then a government may want to prevent them from occurring. If they already exist, it may want to regulate them.

In the UK, the Competition Commission has the powers to:

- prevent takeovers or mergers that would lead to a monopoly position if it can show that this would act against the public interest; and

- investigate any firm with more than 25 per cent market share and force it to sell off parts of its business or reduce its prices.

@ **Web**

For more information on the Competition Commission and its cases, visit http://www.competition-commission.org.uk

---

What do you think?

If a government were to tax monopoly profits, it would not affect the profit-maximizing price and output; these would still be the best financial outcomes for the monopolist although the monopolist would obviously keep less of the profits. Do you think that it would be a good idea therefore to tax monopoly profits heavily?

However, in the UK, monopolies are not automatically assumed to be undesirable. The following are some arguments in favour of monopolies.

- As a monopoly firm dominates the industry, it may be bigger than any individual business in a more competitive industry. This means that it is more likely to benefit from internal economies of scale. Its unit costs may be lower than they would be for firms in a competitive market. This could lead to lower prices and higher output than in a competitive market situation.

- The ability to make monopoly profits provides dominant firms with the funds that they need to invest in more research and development. As a result, they can afford to take risks, and to invest in more long-term research and development projects than firms in a competitive industry. This may lead to greater efficiency and more choice for customers.

- A firm may have achieved its monopoly position because it is so innovative and/or so efficient. In this case, splitting it up would work against the public interest. Most governments allow firms to protect inventions with patents. These are intended to reward innovation, and to encourage other firms to develop new products and new ways of doing things. The patent system highlights that governments think that monopoly power can be justified in certain circumstances.

- Any abnormal profits that are made will either be invested in the business or paid out to shareholders in the form of dividends. These shareholders will often be individuals or financial institutions, such as insurance companies and pension funds. This means that the abnormal profits of monopolies may be redistributing money from customers to investors. The money is not disappearing from society altogether; rather, it is simply moving from one group to another.

- The fact that monopolies can make high levels of profits is an incentive for other firms to be innovative and to establish a monopoly position. This is known as the Schumpeter effect (named after Joseph Schumpeter). Monopoly profits may therefore encourage innovation as other firms try to gain control of a market for themselves. Schumpeter (1942) described this as 'the perennial gale of creative destruction'. Barriers to entry may exist at some point, but new firms will find ways of overcoming these to gain from the abnormal profits—that is, by creating new markets to replace the old ones. Monopoly profits therefore act as a beacon to encourage the development of new products and new ways of doing things, and this stimulates economic growth.

What do you think?

According to Schumpeter (1942): 'The fundamental impulse that sets, and keeps, the capitalist engine in motion comes from the new consumers, goods, the new methods of production or transportation, the new markets, the new forms of industrial organization that capitalist enterprise creates.'

What major developments in markets, technology, transportation, or methods of production have occurred in your lifetime?

- In some cases, the existence of a monopoly may rectify another market failure. For example, in a freely competitive market, firms may create negative externalities, such as pollution, and overproduce relative to the socially optimal position (see Chapter 7). A monopoly, by comparison, may cut back on output, which in this case might move the economy nearer to the socially desirable level of output. Given that the First-best World (in which there are no market failures and imperfections occur) does not exist and therefore we are operating in the Second-best World (in which they do exist), a monopoly may actually be desirable in some circumstances to offset some other failures.

- Monopolies might prevent wasteful duplication. For example, if there are several gas, telecommunications, electricity, or railway companies, then they might simply be investing in unnecessary infrastructure that duplicates the resources of other firms.

What do you think?

Should monopolies be allowed? What do you think is the best way of regulating them?

Intel is the world's largest producer of computer processors. Do you think that governments should allow Intel to be this big?

Economics in context   The monopoly railway in Peru

In 2010, the railway link to Machu Picchu, the ruined Inca citadel that is the biggest tourist attraction in Peru, reopened after floods had previously shut down the transport link.

The railway is a natural monopoly: the only other way of reaching the ruins is a four-day hike along the Inca Trail. When the government privatized it in 1999, it gave the rights to PeruRail for 30 years. PeruRail invested in new trains, but nevertheless has benefited enormously from its monopoly position. It carries 1.1 million passengers a year, with fares starting at $96. Last year, it made a profit of $12.8 million from PeruRail and its four hotels in Peru. One is a formerly state-owned hotel that overlooks the ruins at Machu Picchu, where rooms now start at $825 a night.

Peru's competition watchdog recently accused PeruRail and two related firms of a 'predatory strategy' involving litigation to force rivals out of business, and recommended that they be fined $10.8 million.

 Questions

Analyse the possible effects on customers of a business such as PeruRail having a monopoly. How could the government regulate this monopoly? Should it?

Economics in context   Anti-monopoly law in China

Towards the end of 2009, after 14 years of debate, the Chinese government finally introduced an anti-monopoly law. This was an interesting development in a country that has many state-run monopolies. In the following months, observers were interested in how the law would be applied and whether it would really lead to more competition. One answer came in 2010, when the largest takeover of a Chinese business by a foreign company was rejected.

This was a $2.4 billion offer by Coca-Cola for China Huiyuan, the country's largest juice company. The offer price was three times Huiyuan's valuation at the time. Huiyuan is a private company and juice had previously been free of government control, so theoretically it should have been available for purchase. Its rejection might have reflected a response to recent criticisms by the US administration of the Chinese government. Alternatively, it was a barrier to foreign companies trying to compete in China. Ironically, this comes at a time when the government is bringing about greater concentration in many industries such as steel, cars, and airlines; none of these mergers or takeovers has been prevented under the new monopoly law.

 Question

Why do you think the Chinese government has a different approach to monopolies from that of the UK government?

▨ Contestable markets

Traditional economic theory examines monopolies in terms of the existing market share of the dominant firm in an industry—that is, it focuses on whether a firm already has a market share of over 25 per cent. However, the theory of contestable markets considers the likelihood that other firms will enter the market in the future. This recognizes that a firm that has, say, 25 per cent of a market with no threat of others entering is in a very different position from a firm that has 25 per cent of a market with a high threat of others joining. In the former situation, the established firm is indeed in a strong position and there is the possibility of sustained long-term abnormal profits. In the latter situation, short-term abnormal profits are likely to attract more firms into the industry and this will compete away the abnormal profits over time. To avoid this happening, the established firm may deliberately avoid profit-maximizing in the first place.

In a perfectly contestable market, the costs of entry and exit are zero, so any abnormal profits could quickly be eradicated by others coming in and competing them away. The threat of this happening will mean that the existing firm will:

- keep prices down so that only normal profits are made; and
- have to be as efficient as possible so that entrants do not come in and undercut it.

The theory of contestable markets highlights the dynamic nature of monopolies and the importance of barriers to entry in terms of influencing monopoly behaviour.

Case study Microsoft and the European Commission

In 2004, Microsoft, the software giant, was fined €497 million by the European Commission under its anti-competitive legislation. This followed a five-year investigation into the way in which Microsoft behaved. Following the investigation, the company had to make elements of its programming more openly available to allow others to produce software that was compatible. At the time, Microsoft had about 90 per cent of the market for PC operating systems. It held cash of around $50 billion. Microsoft was accused of bundling its own programmes together and making it difficult for other software manufacturers to be compatible with its Windows system. Microsoft had to offer its operating system without its own media player already installed and it had to make its codes available.

Rival software firms, such as Sun Microsystems, claimed that the punishment would lead to lower prices, greater competition, and greater variety for consumers. Microsoft, however, claimed that the decision would actually harm customers. Others felt that Microsoft was being penalized simply for competing aggressively and that it might lead to less innovation in the market. This was the highest fine that the European Commission had imposed at that point. Previously, the record had been €462 million, which had been imposed on the pharmaceutical group Roche after a scandal involving price fixing in the vitamin pills market.

According to the European commissioner: 'Dominant companies have a special responsibility to ensure that the way they do business doesn't prevent competition . . . and does not harm consumers, and innovation.'

In October 2007, Microsoft agreed to comply with the Commission's 2004 ruling that it broke European Union competition laws.

The US firm's move came after it lost an appeal against the verdict. Microsoft pledged in October to give third-party program developers access to information that will allow them to make systems inter-operable with Windows. It also said that it would substantially cut the fees that it charges for such data.

In 2008, the European Commission launched two more anti-competition investigations against Microsoft. The first looked at whether Microsoft unfairly tied its Explorer Internet browser to its Windows operating system; the second looked at the interoperability of Microsoft software with rivals' products.

❓ Questions

- Why was Microsoft fined by the European Commission?
- Do you think that the European Commission was right to fine Microsoft?
- Do you think that dominant firms have special responsibilities?
- If a business dominates a market, do you think that this should automatically be prevented?

Checklist

Now that you have read this chapter, try to answer the following questions.

- ☐ Can you explain the key features of a monopoly?
- ☐ Can you explain the price and output decisions in a monopoly?
- ☐ Can you discuss the efficiency of a monopoly?
- ☐ Do you understand the significance of barriers to entry in markets?
- ☐ Can you explain the theory of contestable markets?

Review questions

1 At what level of output does a profit-maximizing monopolist produce?

2 Can monopolies make abnormal profits in the long run?

3 What is meant by 'creative destruction'?

4 Why does the marginal revenue curve in a monopoly lie below, and diverge from, the demand curve?

5 Are monopolies good or bad for the economy?

Key learning points

- A monopoly is a dominant firm in an industry.
- In a monopoly, it is possible to earn abnormal profits, even in the long run, due to barriers to entry.
- A monopolist faces a downward-sloping demand curve; the marginal revenue curve is below the demand curve and diverges from the demand curve.
- In the long run, monopolies may be allocatively and productively inefficient.
- When analysing a monopoly market, it may be important to consider the possibility of entry in the future as well as the existing levels of competition.
- The theory of contestable markets considers the likelihood of entry by other firms as well as the number of rivals in the market at present.

References

Leibenstein, H. (1966) 'Allocative efficiency, and X-efficiency', *The American Economic Review*, 56(3): 392–415

Schumpeter, J.A. (1942) *Capitalism, Socialism, and Democracy*, Harper and Row, New York

 Visit our Online Resource Centre at http://www.oxfordtextbooks.co.uk/orc/gillespie_econ2e/ for test questions and further information on topics covered in this chapter.

Oligopoly

So far, we have examined the market structures of perfect competition and monopoly. Another type of market is oligopoly. This has elements of monopoly power, but also involves some degree of competition. An oligopoly is a relatively common form of market structure, and therefore an important one to study and understand. In particular, governments are interested in the impact of an oligopoly on price and output, and whether there is a need for intervention.

LEARNING OBJECTIVES

By the end of this chapter, you should be able to:

✔ explain the meaning of oligopoly;

✔ understand the significance of interdependence in an oligopoly;

✔ outline different models of behaviour in an oligopoly;

✔ explain the meaning of cartel.

■ Introduction

An oligopoly occurs when a few firms dominate a market. This is a common occurrence in many markets; in the UK, for example, the car industry, the petrol market, the airline industry, the banking sector, and the supermarket sector are all oligopolies. In these industries, the largest few firms have a large market share. Economists often measure the four-firm or five-firm concentration ratio; this shows the combined market share of the largest four or five firms.

Oligopolies are particularly interesting markets to analyse because the firms involved are interdependent. The actions of one business will clearly affect the others. As a result of this interdependence, oligopolistic firms have to decide on how they want to behave in relation to others in a market. In a monopoly, one firm dominates and so it does not have to consider what others might do; in perfect competition, there are so many other firms

Competitive	←		→	Uncompetitive
Perfect competition	Monopolistic competition	**Oligopoly**	Monopoly	
Many firms producing identical products	Many firms producing differentiated products	**A few firms dominating a market**	A single firm dominating a market	

Figure 13.1 Different forms of market structure.

that it is impossible to take into account how they might all react. Only in an oligopoly is the number of firms competing so few that decisions have to be made regarding how to work with them. For example, before cutting the price of its major brands, Cadbury will consider how Nestlé and Mars might react. The relationship between oligopoly and other forms of market structure is shown in Figure 13.1.

What do you think?

The table below illustrates the market share of the UK's leading food retailers in 2007.

Grocery retailer	% share in 2007
Tesco	27.6
Asda	14.1
Sainsbury's	13.8
Morrisons	9.9
Safeway	0.0
Somerfield chain	3.9
M&S	3.8
Co-operative Group Ltd.	3.8
Waitrose	3.3
Iceland	1.5
Aldi	1.5
Lidl	1.5
Netto	1.3
Kwik Save	0.6
Others	14.9
Total	100.0

Source: Competition Commission.

- What was the combined market share of the top five grocery retailers in the UK in 2007?
- The main supermarkets have a large share of the grocery market in the UK. Do you think that this matters? Why?
- The market share of the main supermarkets in the UK has been increasing. What significance do you think this has for suppliers and customers?
- How might the UK government intervene to reduce the supermarkets' market share?
- Try to find the latest data; has Tesco's share increased or decreased recently? Why might this be?

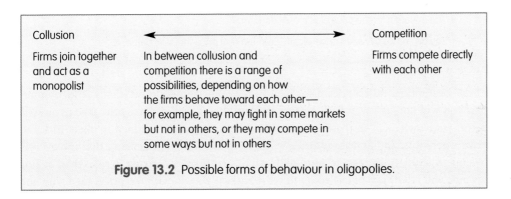

Figure 13.2 Possible forms of behaviour in oligopolies.

One strategy that the major firms in an oligopoly might adopt is for all those involved to join together and act as if they were a monopoly. When this happens, it is called a cartel; the firms collude to set the price and agree how much each one is going to produce (this is called a quota). Alternatively, the firms may decide to compete against each other, in which case this is likely to drive prices down (in what is known as a price war). In between these two extremes of cartel and price war, there are many different possible outcomes, depending on how firms decide to act. The range of options open to firms in oligopoly is shown in Figure 13.2. The importance of the interdependence of firms has led to the development of game theory, in which the strategic planning of one firm depends on its assumptions about the behaviour of others.

The study of oligopolies is extremely important because so many markets have this structure; as a result, governments, regulators, member firms, and would-be entrants are interested in knowing what determines the behaviour of the firms involved, and the possible consequences of the different strategies that they adopt.

■ The kinked demand curve model

The kinked demand curve model of oligopoly developed by Hall and Hitch (1939), and by Sweezy (1939), is based on the following two key assumptions.

- If the firm being considered increases its price, then the other firms in the market will not follow. This means that the fall in the quantity demanded is likely to be relatively high because customers will switch to other firms; demand is therefore price elastic.
- If the firm being considered decreases its price, then the other firms will follow this price cut (because they do not want to lose sales). This means that the increase in the quantity demanded will be smaller than the price change (in percentages); demand will therefore be price inelastic.

Put into practice

Can you remember the following?

- The equation for the price elasticity of demand
- The difference between price-elastic demand and price-inelastic demand

---

These assumptions take a pessimistic view of how others might react (that is, they assume that you will not get away with a price cut, and that if you increase price, then you will be on your own). Given these assumptions, the firm being examined is likely to leave price where it is. An increase in price will lead to such a fall in demand that the overall revenue will fall. A decrease in price will lead to such a small increase in sales that, again, revenue will fall. If revenue is going to fall whatever you do with the price, then why not leave it where it is?

The kinked demand curve

The demand curve D2 in Figure 13.3 is price inelastic; it assumes that a price change will have relatively little effect on the quantity demanded because any price change by one firm will be followed by the others, and so there will be little difference between them. By comparison, the demand curve D1 is price elastic; it assumes that a price change will have a relatively large effect on the quantity demanded because any price change by one firm will not be followed by the others.

Starting from P1Q1 in the kinked demand curve model, it is assumed that a price increase will not be followed—so D1 is relevant—but a price decrease will be followed—D2 is relevant. This gives the kinked demand curve indicated by the thicker line in Figure 13.3.

The marginal revenue linked to this kinked demand curve is also indicated by a thicker line. You will notice a gap in this curve; marginal costs can move between F and G, and the profit-maximizing output (where the marginal revenue equals the marginal costs) is still at the price P1 and the quantity Q1. This shows that costs can change without affecting the profit-maximizing price and quantity in this model of oligopoly.

The kinked demand curve that is derived from the two demand curves in Figure 13.3 is shown in Figure 13.4.

The kinked demand curve model provides an explanation of why prices in oligopolistic markets are often 'sticky'—that is, they do not change very much. Price competition is not

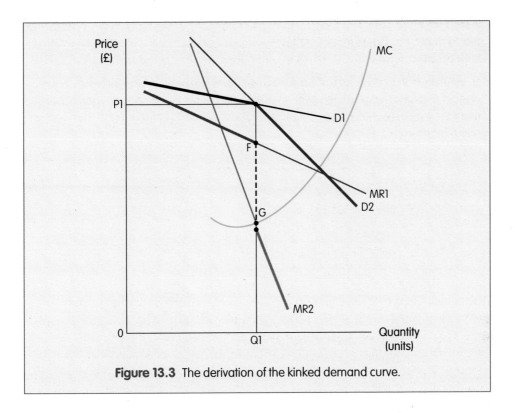

Figure 13.3 The derivation of the kinked demand curve.

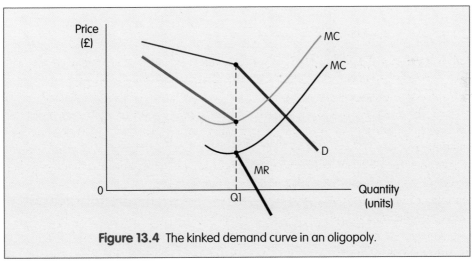

Figure 13.4 The kinked demand curve in an oligopoly.

common in many markets because it is relatively easy for a firm to copy another firm's price cut. Many firms prefer to try to differentiate their products—for example, by building a brand or developing some unique selling point—and using this as a means of competing rather than the price. It is much more difficult for competitors to imitate a brand image than it is for them to follow a price cut.

Economics in context — Breakfast cereals

In some oligopoly markets, such as breakfast cereal, there may be many different brands, but the majority are owned by some major firms. The table below shows the top-selling breakfast cereals in the UK, by estimated brand shares, in 2009.

Brand (manufacturer)	2009 £m	%
Weetabix (Weetabix Food Co)	113.0	8
Special K (Kellogg's)	110.0	7
Crunchy Nut Cornflakes (Kellogg's)	74.3	5
Corn Flakes (Kellogg's)	66.9	5
Coco Pops (Kellogg's)	56.5	4
Cheerios (Nestlé)	52.0	4
Rice Krispies (Kellogg's)	46.1	3
Oatso Simple (PepsiCo)	40.9	3
Shreddies (Nestlé)	36.1	2
Frosties (Kellogg's)	34.2	2
All-Bran Flakes (Kellogg's)	33.5	2
Alpen (Weetabix Food Co)	25.4	2
Sugar Puffs (HM Foods)	25.3	2
Dorset Cereals (Dorset Cereals)	24.5	2
Shredded Wheat (Nestlé)	24.5	2
Fruit 'n' Fibre (Kellogg's)	23.8	2
Kellogg's Variety (Kellogg's)	19.3	1
Crunchy Nut Clusters (Kellogg's)	18.6	1
Weetos (Weetabix Food Co)	17.8	1
Country Crisp (Jordans)	16.4	1
Shredded Wheat Bitesize (Nestlé)	14.9	1
Own label	339.0	23
Others	273.8	18
Total	1,487	100

Source: Mintel.

- In this market, the dominant manufacturers have capitalized on their high brand awareness, have built on the trust associated with their brand to launch brand extensions, and have supported these new launches with marketing activity.

- As a proportion of sales value, advertising on breakfast cereals accounted for just over 7 per cent of sales. This is relatively high compared to other breakfast food categories, such as bread and morning goods (0.6 per cent).

- Despite the dominance of a few large manufacturers in the breakfast cereal category, it is a very competitive market, and brands have invested in significant advertising activity to defend their position against own-label products and to retain loyalty with their core consumers.

? Question

Why do you think the big producers have so many different brands in this market?

Economics in context   **Advertising expenditure in the UK**

The advertising industry employs nearly 250,000 people. Advertising expenditure in the UK in 2009 was £14.5 billion.

? Questions

What do you think determines the level of advertising spending in the UK in a given year?
What do you think determines the relative spending in different categories of advertising?
What do you think the impact of high levels of spending on advertising is likely to be on each of the following?

- The level of demand

- The price elasticity of demand

- The cross-price elasticity of demand

How would you measure the impact of an increase in such spending on the level of demand?

■ Cartels

A cartel occurs when the firms in an oligopoly work together to agree on the price and output that are set in a market. This agreement may be explicit (that is, they may formally agree) or implicit (that is, both sides may agree without anything actually being said or written down). The aim of a cartel is to maximize the profits of its members by restricting the amount available and pushing up price. Cartels may decide on who sells to whom, and what the terms and conditions are, as well as price and output levels. Cartels occur between countries as well as firms. For example, the Organization of the Petroleum Exporting Countries (OPEC) is a cartel of petroleum-exporting countries and has a huge influence on the price of oil.

Economics in context Memory chips

The EU competition authorities recently fined ten producers of memory chips a total of €331 million for operating a cartel. One of the ten, Micron, will not pay a fine because it was a whistle-blower (that is, it confessed and told the authorities about the cartel). The others, in turn, have had their fines reduced by 10 per cent for cooperating with the authorities.

The cartel was in operation between 1 July 1998 and 15 June 2002. It involved a network of contacts and sharing of secret information, through which the member firms coordinated the price levels and quotations for dynamic random access memory chips (DRAMs), which were sold to major PC or server original equipment manufacturers (OEMs).

 Question

Can you think of any circumstances under which a cartel might be acceptable?

What do you think?

What factors might influence whether a firm decides to join a cartel?

Economics in context Price fixing in Korea

The Korean Fair Trade Commission (FTC) recently took a series of actions against alleged price fixing. Supporters of these interventions claim that stricter enforcement of the fair-trade law is the correct move to defend the rights of consumers. Critics argue that the FTC is imposing too many fines without clear evidence of price fixing.

The latest controversy occurred when the FTC imposed a combined fine of 667.9 billion won ($577.5 million) on six liquefied petroleum gas suppliers, accusing them of colluding to keep prices unfairly high for six years between 2003 and 2008.

It was the largest fine ever levied by the FTC. Earlier in July, the FTC imposed a fine of 260 billion won on US-based mobile chipmaker Qualcomm Inc for 'abusing its monopoly market status' in the local chip market.

Annual combined fines levied by the FTC from 2005 to 2008 for alleged price fixing remained between 100 billion won and 300 billion won.

This year, however, combined fines are expected to easily exceed 1,000 billion won, reflecting that the FTC is waging a war against price fixing in earnest.

A wide range of industries, including soft drink manufacturers, hospitals, airlines, credit ratings agencies, banks, and telecommunications companies, has been sanctioned this year as part of the FTC's attack on price fixing.

When fining companies, the European Union can levy 10 per cent of the 'total sales', while Korea can levy 10 per cent of 'sales only related to price-fixing activities'.

? **Questions**

Why do you think the FTC might have started to become more interventionist when it comes to price fixing?

What determines whether a potential fine of up to 10 per cent of sales is a reasonable deterrent?

However, the basic problem with cartels is that it is in the interest of individual firms to cheat! By producing more than the amount agreed with the other members of the cartel (the quota), an individual firm can make more profit at the expense of its 'associates'. On the other hand, if everyone is cheating, then the market supply gets ever higher, and this brings the price down; the group as a whole therefore ends up worse off. Cartels may therefore self-destruct even if it is in their interests to keep together.

In Figure 13.5a, the industry profit-maximizes at the price P1 and the quantity Q1. This determines the price and quantity that should be set. Each member of the cartel is given a quota: for example, q1 to be produced at the set price (see Figure 13.5b). Each member is making an abnormal profit. However, the individual firm is not profit-maximizing; it

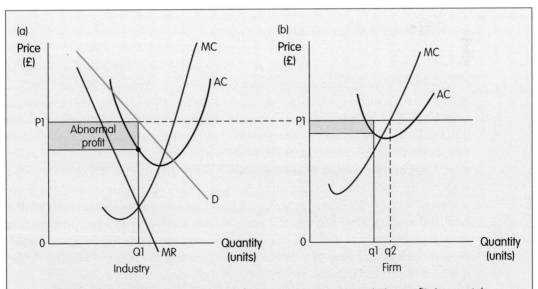

Figure 13.5 (a) The industry price and output outcomes to maximize profits in a cartel; (b) The price and output outcomes for a member of a cartel.

would profit-maximize when the price equals the marginal revenue at the quantity q2. Therefore there is an incentive for an individual firm to produce more to increase its own rewards. However, if all of the members of the cartel were to do this, then it would drive up industry output and bring down the industry price, moving the industry as a whole away from its profit-maximizing position.

To make a cartel work, it therefore requires the member firms to trust each other, and, if necessary, to be able to check easily how much each member is producing and at what price. Policing the agreement becomes very important; otherwise, it is likely to fall apart.

What do you think?

What factors are likely to lead to a price-fixing agreement occurring?

If you were the government, under what circumstance might you allow a price-fixing agreement?

In the UK until 2001, manufacturers of certain products, such as pharmaceuticals and books, were allowed to set the price at which they were sold in shops rather than retailers being allowed to determine their own prices (this was called resale price maintenance). What arguments might have been used to justify such price fixing?

Under the Competition Act 1998, cartels in the UK are illegal. Any business found to be a member of a cartel can be fined up to 10 per cent of its UK turnover. Under the Enterprise Act 2002, it is a criminal offence for individuals dishonestly to take part in the most serious types of cartel. Anyone convicted of the offence could receive a maximum of five years' imprisonment and/or an unlimited fine.

■ Prisoner's dilemma

The 'Prisoner's dilemma' is a famous model of game theory. This model analyses the effects of interdependence on decision-making. It is called the 'Prisoner's dilemma' because it is based on a scenario in which two thieves are arrested. They are interviewed separately and have to decide whether or not to confess to the crime. Their decision depends on what they think the other prisoner is going to do. The best idea would be for both of them to deny the charges, because the police would not be able to prove anything. However, what if one prisoner decides to confess to get lenient treatment? In this case, the police would come down heavily on the other. So should one confess just in case? But if one confesses and the other does so as well, then both prisoners will be convicted; if they had both said nothing, then they could have got away with it. What each prisoner does depends on his or her view of what the other person is likely to do. This, in turn, depends on issues such as the degree of trust between the prisoners, the extent to which each feels that he or she understands the other person, past behaviour, and their assumptions about how rational each other is.

In the economics version of this scenario, there are two firms, X and Y, operating in a market. Each firm can decide to produce at a high level of output and sell it at a low price,

Table 13.1   A pay-off matrix for two firms

Firm X output (£m)		Firm Y output (£m)	
		High	Low
Firm X output (£m)	High	£1m, £1m	£3m, £0
	Low	£0, £3m	£2m, £2m

or it can sell a low level of output at a high price. If both firms restrict output, then this is the most desirable situation for each of them, because the limited amount available in the market generates high prices and high profits for both. However, each firm will be worried that if it holds back, the other one will flood the market and win all of the sales at a lower price. This suspicion is likely to lead both firms to flood the market because of their fear of what the other will do. The result is that the market price ends up extremely low because supply is so high and both firms do badly. If only they could trust each other and collude, then they would do much better.

Table 13.1 shows the financial results of each possible outcome: the left-hand amount is the outcome for firm X and the right-hand amount is the outcome for firm Y. If both X and Y produce high levels of output, then they will gain only £1 million each, because prices will be very low with so much output; if they both restrict output, then they could earn £2 million each. If one goes high whilst the other holds back, the former will win the market with lower prices and the latter will get nothing.

The interesting questions here are:

- What determines whether firms will collude with each other?
- One factor may be the track records of the different firms—have they stuck to their promises in the past?
- Is there a way of getting a commitment up front to show that they really want the agreement to work?
- Can the agreement be effectively policed so that any cheating is easily identified?

Price war

If the firms in an oligopolistic market do not agree to collude, then they may compete. The most aggressive form of competition is a price war (also called predatory pricing), whereby one firm undercuts the others in an attempt to remove them from the market. The ability of a business to survive a price war depends on how much the price needs to be cut and its own resources compared with the finances of its competitors. Although customers may benefit in the short term from lower prices in a price war, in the long term the firm that wins may exploit its market power and push up prices even higher than they were originally.

■ Summary

Oligopolistic markets are very common. They involve a few dominant firms. The price and output outcomes in an oligopoly depend on the behaviour of the firms involved; this, in turn, can depend on their assumptions about what the other firms will be doing. Oligopolistic firms are often involved in complex strategic planning in which they try to determine what other firms might do.

Case study Sony price war

In July 2010, Sony entered the e-reader price war, cutting the price of its digital reading devices in the USA just one week after market leader Amazon and book retailer Barnes and Noble had cut prices on their e-readers.

The pricing moves by the three companies came as Apple's iPad computer threatened to gain a significant market share, with sales expected to more than double to 5 million units, up from 2.2 million last year.

The Japanese electronics company cut the price of its most expensive version of its e-reader, the Daily Edition, to $299.99, down from $349.99. Amazon's Kindle DX came down in price to $379 from $489. Barnes and Noble started the price cuts by lowering the price of its Nook to $199. At the time of these changes, Amazon had about 60–65 per cent of the market, with Sony second at 30–35 per cent.

Although the iPad, with a starting price of $499, costs more than either the top-end Kindle or Sony's most expensive e-reader, it has a colour screen, and can also play video and browse the web.

Sony claimed that it was not concerned about competition from Apple's iPad, but said that reducing the price of a consumer electronics product was normal once the product had been on the market for some time. In fact, Sony said that it welcomed the iPad, because it helped to build the market as a whole.

❓ Questions

- Analyse the reasons why Sony might have cut the price of its e-reader.
- How low do you think prices will go in this market?
- How important do you think the price is when determining the market share of firms in this market?
- Do you think that the success of the iPad will help other manufacturers to succeed as well?

Checklist

Now that you have read this chapter, try to answer the following questions.

☐ Can you explain the meaning of oligopoly?

☐ Do you understand the significance of interdependence in an oligopoly?

☐ Can you outline different models of behaviour in an oligopoly?

☐ Can you explain the meaning of cartel?

Review questions

1 In what ways does an oligopoly differ from perfect competition?

2 In what ways does an oligopoly differ from a monopoly?

3 Why is the kinked demand curve kinked?

4 What is meant by game theory?

5 Are firms in an oligopoly most likely to collude or compete?

Key learning points

- An oligopoly occurs when a few firms dominate a market.

- The price and outcome results in an oligopoly depend on the assumptions that are made regarding the way in which firms behave toward each other (for example, whether they compete or collude).

- Oligopoly highlights the significance of interdependence in business. One firm's decisions about how much to produce and what price to charge are linked to its assumptions about how other firms will behave.

References

Hall, R. and Hitch, C. (1939) 'Price theory and business behaviour', *Oxford Economic Papers*, 2(1): 12–45

Sweezy, P.M. (1939) 'Demand under conditions of oligopoly', *Journal of Political Economy*, 47(4): 568–73

Learn more

To learn out more about game theory and the strategies that firms might adopt, visit the Online Resource Centre. To learn more about non-price competition, read Chapter 14.

 Visit our Online Resource Centre at http://www.oxfordtextbooks.co.uk/orc/gillespie_econ2e/ for test questions and further information on topics covered in this chapter.

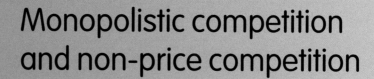

» 14 Monopolistic competition and non-price competition

We have now examined the following market structures: perfect competition; monopoly; and oligopoly. Another form of market structure is monopolistic competition. In this chapter, we examine the features of monopolistic competition, and the implications of this market structure for customers and firms.

LEARNING OBJECTIVES

By the end of this chapter, you should be able to:

✔ explain the key features of monopolistic competition;

✔ consider the efficiency of monopolistic competition;

✔ outline non-price forms of competition that are experienced in many markets;

✔ outline Porter's five forces analysis;

✔ understand how firms might try to influence these forces.

■ Introduction

Monopolistic competition occurs in a market in which there are many firms competing and each one offers a differentiated product. There are, for example, many thousands of cafes and restaurants in the UK. Whilst they all compete in the same market, there are differences between them: for example, they have different menus, different themes, and different locations. These factors can influence your decision when choosing between them; this means that the cafes involved have some control over their market and the ability to decide what prices to charge.

Firms in monopolistic competition face a downward-sloping demand curve. If they increase the price, they will lose some customers (but not all) to competitors; if they reduce prices, they should gain some customers from competitors (but not all). As in a

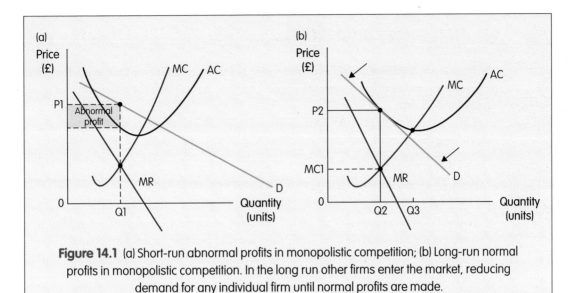

Figure 14.1 (a) Short-run abnormal profits in monopolistic competition; (b) Long-run normal profits in monopolistic competition. In the long run other firms enter the market, reducing demand for any individual firm until normal profits are made.

monopoly, the marginal revenue is below the demand curve and diverging; to sell more, the price has to be lowered on the last unit and all of the ones before.

Firms in monopolistic competition are assumed to be profit-maximizers. This means that they will produce the highest output at which marginal revenue equals the marginal cost (see Figure 14.1a). The difference between this type of market and a monopoly is that there are no barriers to entry. This means that if firms are making abnormal profits in the short run, then this will attract other firms into the industry. This will cause the demand for any one firm's products to fall. It will cause an inward shift of the firm's demand curve until only normal profits are made (see Figure 14.1b).

If losses were being made, then firms would leave the industry, so demand for a particular firm's products would increase until normal profits were made.

Put into practice

Draw a diagram that illustrates a firm in monopolistic competition making a loss in the short run and then, following the departure of other firms, the firm making normal profits in the long run.

In the long run in monopolistic competition, a firm is:

- allocatively inefficient because the price that it charges is greater than the marginal cost (P2 > MC1 in Figure 14.1b); and

- productively inefficient because the firm does not produce at the minimum of the average cost curve (Q2 not Q3 in Figure 14.1b).

▧ Non-price competition

Non-price competition occurs when firms compete by methods other than using the price. Non-price competition is commonly used by firms to try to boost their demand and make it less price elastic.

The marketing mix, or the 'four Ps' (see Figure 14.2), describes the key elements in marketing that affect a customer's decision to purchase a product.

The four Ps are as follows.

- **Price** This involves not only the price, but also the payment terms—for example, whether you can pay over time and how payments can occur.

- **Product** This encompasses all of the different elements of a product, including the features, the specifications, the after-sales service, and the brand. For example, Apple has long been admired for the design of its products; Dyson won a significant market share in the vacuum cleaner market with its innovative technology.

- **Promotion** This includes all of the different ways in which a firm communicates about its product, such as advertising, the sales force, sponsorship, public relations activities, and sales promotions (for example, offers and competitions).

- **Place** This refers to the distribution of the product—that is, how it gets to the market. For example, whether it is sold through wholesalers and retailers or direct to customers.

If a firm is not competing on price, then it can use other elements of the marketing mix to win customers. For example, firms might do the following.

- Firms may use their promotional activities to develop a strong brand image. Companies such as Virgin, Microsoft, Nike, and Coca-Cola all have very strong brand names.

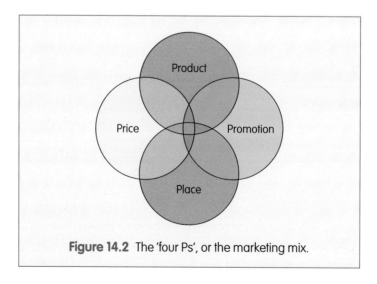

Figure 14.2 The 'four Ps', or the marketing mix.

Customers associate these names with certain values. This brand image has been created by the way in which the company advertises, the quality of its products, the way in which its employees behave, and the types of sponsorship that its undertakes. By differentiating their products, firms may develop their customers' brand loyalty, which means that new entrants to the market will have to fight harder to get buyers to switch to them. Brand loyalty also means that the customer may be less sensitive to price (that is, demand is more price inelastic) and that customers would be more likely to accept new products launched by a business. This can make product launches cheaper and more likely to be successful.

Economics in context   Sonic branding

Every day, all of us hear small sections of music that remind us of particular brands. The sound when Microsoft Windows starts; Nokia's ringtone; and Intel's four-note theme: all are examples of what is now called 'sonic branding'. These short pieces of sound are called *Ohrwurms*, or 'earworms', by the Germans—because they worm their way into your brain!

The most famous sonic brand of them all is Intel's four-note 'bong', which was composed in 1994 and has been heard more than a billion times since. The tune was composed by Walter Werzowa.

? Questions

Can you think of any other sonic branding examples or famous jingles?

What other marketing activities help to build the brand recognition for companies such as Intel?

What do you think?

How do you think the following brands differ?

a. Costa, Starbucks, and Café Nero

b. Pepsi and Coca-Cola

c. French Connection and Next

d. Nike and Umbro

e. The *Daily Telegraph* and The *Daily Mail*

- Firms may develop the product to create a unique selling point—that is, something that makes it stand out from the competition. This could be the recipe for the product or a special feature, such as rapid delivery times or an extended warranty.

- Firms may develop more distribution channels to make the product more widely available and easier for customers to buy.

Top global brands 2009

Rank	Company	Sector	Brand value ($m)
1	Coca-Cola	Beverages	68,734
2	IBM	Computer services	60,211
3	Microsoft	Computer software	56,647
4	GE	Diversified	47,777
5	Nokia	Consumer electronics	34,864

Source: Interbrand.

 Questions

How do you think you would value a brand?

Analyse the benefits of having a well-recognized brand to a company such as Coca-Cola.

Can you think of brands that have risen or fallen in importance in recent years? Why do you think this has happened?

Can you think of strong brands in your country that are not global brands? Why do you think this is?

What do you think?

The markets for many consumer products, such as DVD players and digital cameras, are very competitive. Is it better to compete in these markets on price or using other factors?

■ Porter's five forces analysis of market structure

We have now considered four different types of market: perfect competition; monopoly; oligopoly; and monopolistic competition. Each one has its own characteristics, and its own price and output outcomes. A comparison of these helps us to predict what might happen in different markets and to consider what policies we might want to introduce as a government.

In 1985, Michael Porter, a business analyst, produced his study of market structure. According to Porter, the likelihood of making profits in an industry depends on the following five factors (known as Porter's five forces—see Figure 14.3).

• **The likelihood of new entry** This refers to the extent to which barriers to entry exist. The more difficult it is for other firms to enter a market, the more likely it is that existing firms can make relatively high profits. In a monopoly, for example, these would be high, whereas in a competitive market, it would be easier to enter.

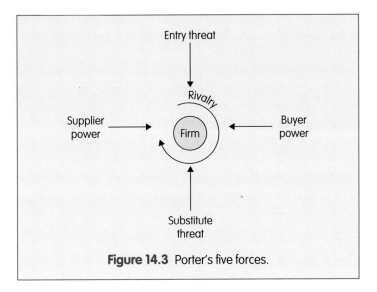

Figure 14.3 Porter's five forces.

Economics in context   Audio novels

In 2006, the world's first audio-only novel was launched, responding to the fast growth of down-loadable books. *Sex on Legs* was a 75,000-word novel written and read by Brian Luff, and was made available at http://www.audible.co.uk

Mr Luff had no contract with a traditional book publisher. New technology has made the book 'publishing' industry much easier for anyone to enter.

❓ Question
Can you think of markets in which sales via the Internet are high?

- **The power of buyers** The stronger the power of buyers in an industry, the more likely it is that they will be able to force down prices and reduce the profits of firms that provide the product. Buyer power will be higher if:
  - there are relatively few buyers;
  - the buyers can easily switch to other providers; or
  - the buyers can threaten to take over the firm.
- **The power of suppliers** The stronger the power of suppliers to an industry, the more difficult it is for firms within that sector to make a profit. Suppliers will be more powerful if:
  - there are relatively few of them (so that the buyer has few alternatives);
  - switching to another supplier is difficult and/or expensive; or
  - the supplier can threaten to buy the existing firms.

- **The degree of rivalry** This measures the degree of competition between existing firms. The higher the degree of rivalry, the more difficult it is for existing firms to generate high profits. Rivalry will be higher if:
  - there are a large number of similar-sized firms (rather than a few dominant firms);
  - the costs of leaving the industry are high (for example, because of high levels of investment), which means that existing firms will fight hard to survive because they cannot easily transfer their resources elsewhere; or
  - the level of capacity underutilization is high—if there are high levels of capacity being underutilized, then the existing firms will be very competitive to try to win sales to boost their own demand.
- **The substitute threat** This measures the ease with which buyers can switch to another product that does the same thing: for example, aluminium cans rather than glass bottles.

Using Porter's analysis, an industry is likely to generate higher profits if:

- the industry is difficult to enter;
- there is limited rivalry;
- buyers are relatively weak;
- suppliers are relatively weak; and
- there are few substitutes.

On the other hand, profits are likely to be low if:

- the industry is easy to enter;
- there is a high degree of rivalry between firms within the industry;
- buyers are strong;
- suppliers are strong; and
- it is easy to switch to alternatives.

The implication of Porter's analysis for managers of firms is that they should examine these five factors before choosing an industry into which to move. They should also consider ways of changing the five factors to make them more favourable. For example:

- if firms merge together, then this can reduce the degree of rivalry;
- if firms buy up distributors (this is called forward vertical integration), then they can gain more control over buyers; and
- firms may differentiate their product, perhaps by trying to generate some form of unique selling proposition (USP) that makes it stand out from the competition.

The five forces will change over time as market conditions alter. For example, the Internet has made it easier for customers to compare prices and therefore this increases buyer power in many markets, including travel and consumer products, such as fridges and televisions. The Internet has also made it easier for producers to access customers, making it easier to enter many markets, such as finance, book retailing, and clothes retailing. As ever, the business world is not static and the conditions in any industry will always be changing to some extent.

Case study The UK chocolate market

The chocolate market in the UK is dominated by the three large international companies Cadbury's, Mars, and Nestlé, which together account for approximately 75–80 per cent of the retail market in chocolate confectionery.

This, however, is not unusual: with the process of globalization of markets and concentration having taken place throughout the world, in common with international markets in general, it is the case that most domestic markets for volume sales of chocolate confectionery are concentrated into a few large companies. There are concerns about the diminution of competitive pressures that this causes, but it is still the case that, in the UK as well as elsewhere, there are ongoing market competition and market opportunities. On the one hand, competition between the three large companies ensures that their products remain innovative, strongly promoted, and keenly priced. On the other hand, there are continuing opportunities for smaller companies operating in niche markets, such as organic, low fat, and other quality aspects of chocolate products.

Chocolate manufacturers attract and keep customers through promotion as follows.

- The manufacturers expand product ranges to meet consumers' needs—for example, to meet the recent trend in demand for low-fat, reduced-calorie or sugarless products.

- The manufacturers use brand promotion or branding, creating a brand identity so that the brand name is recognized and understood immediately.

- Price competition ensures that the manufacturers' products offer excellent value for money compared with others, including snacks.

- The manufacturers use generic promotion, such as the International Cocoa Organization (ICCO)/Common Fund for Commodities (CFC) project in Japan that focused on the health benefits of cocoa rather than an individual product.

- The manufacturers look for new and emerging markets, such as Asia and Eastern Europe, in which chocolate consumption is low and there is potential growth.

The following are examples of the use of promotion in the chocolate market.

- Attitudes can be changed by promotion. The Chocolate Manufacturers Association of the USA has a strategy for promotion that includes: reminding consumers that chocolate fits into a healthy, happy lifestyle; maintaining a positive media atmosphere for chocolate; promoting health information on chocolate to the media; and promoting chocolate to the retail trade.

- Various promotions and surveys have taken place, aimed at people's perceptions and attitudes toward giving, receiving, and eating boxed chocolate.

- Spain has seen a fall in exports and in domestic consumption due to a change in consumer habits. The promotional campaign had the slogan: 'Life is short, let's make the most of it, let's learn to appreciate the full flavour of chocolate.'

- In Italy, manufacturers have benefited from a boom period with increasing chocolate consumption, and various campaigns have promoted the taste of chocolate, its mood-enhancing and energy-giving properties, and its efficacy against allergies, migraines, and cholesterol. Producers are looking to play upon its nutritional qualities in future campaigns.

Sources: Graham (1997); ICCO (1998; 1999)

? Questions

- Outline the ways in which chocolate companies compete through non-price competition.
- What niches do you think exist in the chocolate market?
- Do you think that such non-price competition is desirable?
- How competitive do you think the chocolate market really is?
- What do you think are substitutes for chocolate?

Checklist

Now that you have read this chapter, try to answer the following questions.

- ☐ Can you explain the key features of monopolistic competition?
- ☐ Are you able to consider the efficiency of monopolistic competition?
- ☐ Can you outline non-price forms of competition that are experienced in many markets?
- ☐ Do you understand Porter's five forces model?

Review questions

1 How does monopolistic competition differ from perfect competition?
2 How efficient are firms in monopolistic competition?
3 What are common forms of non-price competition?
4 What are Porter's five forces and how do they affect the structure of an industry?
5 How can firms try to influence the five forces?

Key learning points

- In markets that are monopolistically competitive, there are many competitors, but each firm attempts to differentiate its products.
- In monopolistic competition, firms face a downward-sloping demand curve.
- In the short run, firms in monopolistic competition may make a loss or abnormal profit; in the long run, firms make normal profits due to entry or exit.
- Price changes are relatively easy for competitors to follow and therefore firms often use non-price methods of competing, such as advertising.
- The structure of a market may be analysed using Porter's five forces analysis.

References

Graham, L. (1997) 'What's going on in chocolate consumption, and promotion in the US', International Cocoa Organization, CC/14/4

International Cocoa Organization (1998) 'Faire campagne pour le chocolat [On the campaign trail for chocolate]', *Plantations, Recherche, Développement*, 5(5): 371; available online at http://www.icco.org

_____ (1999) 'Boxed chocolate: Campaign for boxed chocolate in its second year', *The Manufacturing Confectioner*, 79(5): 30–1; available online at http://www.icco.org

 Visit our Online Resource Centre at http://www.oxfordtextbooks.co.uk/orc/gillespie_econ2e/ for test questions and further information on topics covered in this chapter.

15

Barriers to entry and price discrimination

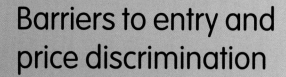

In the previous few chapters, we have examined different market structures. For firms to make abnormal profits in a market in the long run, barriers to entry must exist. This chapter outlines different barriers to entry that can exist. It also examines the way in which firms can use their monopoly power to charge different prices to different customer groups, which is known as price discrimination.

LEARNING OBJECTIVES

By the end of this chapter, you should be able to:

✔ understand the meaning and significance of barriers to entry;

✔ be able to explain the different forms of barrier to entry;

✔ explain the meaning of price discrimination;

✔ outline the conditions for effective price discrimination;

✔ analyse the benefits of price discrimination.

▨ Introduction to barriers to entry

The monopoly power of a firm or group of firms can be sustained only if there are barriers to entry. Otherwise any abnormal profits that they earn will be competed away by new firms entering the market. Firms that operate within a market with barriers to entry are protected from the effects of competition, and the impact of this on price and output. In some cases, the barriers may exist because the government has granted exclusive rights to provide a service. In other instances, firms will set out themselves to devise ways of preventing others from coming in. In its competition policy, a government must decide whether barriers to entry do exist in a market and whether customers suffer as a result.

Even if barriers to entry do exist, they can be removed or reduced over time: for example, with the signing of treaties opening up new markets, or with new technology making it easier or cheaper for others to enter a market.

Types of barrier to entry include the following.

- **Legislation** A firm's monopoly power may be protected by law. For example, it may gain a patent; this prevents other firms from making, using, or selling its invention for a given period.

  It generally takes three to five years to obtain a patent. Patent protection gives firms 20 years' protection. IBM spends over $5 billion per year on research and development to develop its products and new technology. It earns over $1.2 billion by licensing its intellectual property—for example, selling the rights to use its technology.

  Alternatively, barriers to entry exist if a government controls an industry itself and passes legislation to prevent other firms from competing in it.

Economics in context   **Registering a patent**

The following is information from the Patent Office.

To be patentable your invention must be the following.

- **Be new** The invention must never have been made public in any way, anywhere in the world, before the date on which an application for a patent is filed.

- **Involve an inventive step** An invention involves an inventive step if, when compared with what is already known, it would not be obvious to someone with a good knowledge and experience of the subject.

- **Be capable of industrial application** An invention must be capable of being made or used in some kind of industry. This means that the invention must take the practical form of an apparatus or device, a product such as some new material or substance, or an industrial process or method of operation.

Patents are one form of protection for intellectual property. Others include trade marks for logos and designs, and copyright for books and music. Well-known legal cases relating to intellectual property include the following.

- *James Dyson v Hoover* This was an action by Dyson against Hoover for allegedly infringing a Dyson patent for bagless vacuum cleaners.

- *Elvis Presley Enterprises Inc v Sid Shaw Elvisly Yours* This case concerns the rights of well-known celebrities to exploit their names as trade marks.

- *Michael Baigent, Richard Leigh v The Random House Group Ltd (The Da Vinci Code case)* This case was concerned with the alleged infringement by Dan Brown in his book *The Da Vinci Code* of the claimants' copyright in their work *Holy Blood, Holy Grail*.

- *R Griggs Group Ltd and Others v Ross Evans, Raben Footwear Pty Ltd (The Doc Martens case)*
  This case relates to the question of beneficial ownership or ownership in equity of all aspect of the copyright in a logo.

Source: UK Patent Office

 Question

What do you think are the benefits of protecting intellectual property rights through systems such as patents?

 Web

For more information on the UK Patent Office, visit **http://www.patent.gov.uk**

Economics in context **GSK**

GlaxoSmithKline (GSK) is a leading global pharmaceutical company. According to its website:

> Our scientists are working hard to discover new ways of treating and preventing diseases. By combining the wide-ranging talents of our R&D employees with our leading-edge science resources, we are dedicated to bringing more medicines of value to patients.
>
> Our product pipeline is diverse and changes over time as new medicines progress from discovery to development, and ultimately to approval where they become available to patients.
>
> But this process requires time and investment. It takes about 12–15 years, and costs over £500 million to discover and develop a new medicine or vaccine, so we need to be determined and innovative to help new molecules progress into medicines.

Source: GlaxoSmithKline website

 Questions

Why might the patent system be essential for GlaxoSmithKline?
How might research and development create a competitive advantage for GlaxoSmithKline?

- **The learning experience** Existing firms have the benefit of experience when operating in an industry. They know what to do, how to do it, how not to do it, and how to put things right. They have the contacts, and an understanding of what works and what does not work. This means that they will benefit from this experience, and tasks can be completed more effectively and efficiently. This makes it more difficult for new entrants to compete. Remember how difficult it was when you first learned to drive; now you can change gears without even thinking. A learner driver will find it difficult to compete with your skill. The same is true when a firm considers entering a new market; it must be aware of the expertise of those already in it and how this can give them a competitive advantage.

The management consultancy Boston Consulting Group argued that the learning (or experience curve) was so significant that it should drive business strategy. By growing and dominating a market, a business can achieve significant cost advantages over competitors because of its greater experience in operating in that environment.

- **Technology** Existing firms may have a technological advantage that new entrants cannot easily imitate. This may be a way of producing or organizing things that others do not know how to imitate.

- **Internal economies of scale** If there are high levels of economies of scale in an industry, then those firms that are producing on a larger scale will have much lower unit costs than new entrants, which are likely to be producing on a smaller scale. It will therefore be difficult to enter a market that has a high minimum efficient scale (MES) relative to demand and there is a significant cost disadvantage in operating below the MES (see Chapter 9). In this situation, if a firm does enter the market, it is most likely to focus on a niche; this enables it to charge a higher price for a specialist product.

- **Entry costs** The initial costs of starting up in an industry can be high: for example, to buy equipment or to promote the product nationally. This can make entry prohibitive for small firms. For example, imagine the costs involved in establishing a national network (or even an international network) for a mobile phone operator.

- **Fear of retaliation** If existing firms have reacted in a hostile way to new entrants in the past (for example, by starting a price war), then this sends out a signal to others that may deter them from entering.

- **Brand loyalty and product differentiation** Existing firms in an industry will try to make their products different, in the eyes of the consumer, from competitors' products. If they can do this successfully, then they can generate brand loyalty; this makes it difficult for potential entrants because it will be more difficult for them to win new customers.

- **Control supplies or distribution** If a firm can gain control of the major supplier or a significant distributor, then this can make it difficult for newcomers to get into the market. In the UK, in the 1980s, the main brewers controlled most of the pubs in the UK. This made it almost impossible for new brewers to get their beers to customers. This market was later investigated by the government, and brewers were forced to sell off some of their pubs, and open them to 'guest beers'.

The higher the level of barriers to entry, the more protected existing firms are from competition; this means that they have more power over the market and are more likely to be able to earn large abnormal profits in the long run.

Economics in context   Airlines

Following their alliance, British Airways, American Airlines, and Iberia offered to give up landing and take-off slots at airports in London and New York following an investigation by regulators at the European Commission. The three Oneworld alliance members offered this to end the Commission's inquiry into their cooperation on transatlantic routes.

Virgin Atlantic's Richard Branson described the proposals as 'woefully inadequate'.

The six pairs of take-off and landing slots offered were at London Heathrow or London Gatwick airports on routes to Boston, New York, Dallas, and Miami. British Airways, American Airlines, and Iberia have also said that new entrants would be able to join the frequent-flyer programmes that they operate on the relevant routes.

The European Commission argues that these proposals will enable other airlines to start operating transatlantic routes by lowering the barriers to entry and that the slots surrendered will compensate for the fact that the three airlines are no longer in competition. It explained that the slots on offer were equivalent to 42 flights a week between London and US cities. But Virgin Atlantic argued that British Airways and American Airlines would still control 100 per cent of the international routes in and out of Dallas, 80 per cent of those in Boston, 70 per cent of those in Miami, and 68 per cent of those in Chicago.

? Questions

In what ways might the Oneworld alliance act as a barrier to entry?

Do you think Virgin Atlantic was right to complain about this alliance?

What problems might British Airways, American Airlines, and Iberia face now that they operate as an alliance?

■ Price discrimination

If barriers to entry do exist in a market, then firms may have some form of monopoly power and be price makers. This may enable them to price-discriminate. Price discrimination occurs when a firm offers the same product to different customers at different prices. For example, a nightclub might charge different prices depending on what time of the evening or what day you enter; the price of a train ticket may vary depending on what time of day you travel.

By price-discriminating, a firm can increase its own profits; at the same time, it reduces the amount of consumer surplus (utility that is not paid for). In our earlier analysis of monopoly, the firm profit-maximized at the price P1 and the quantity Q1 in Figure 15.1, when the marginal revenue equalled the marginal cost. It charged one price for all of its units. If it were able to price-discriminate, then it might sell some of these units for a higher price. For example, imagine that the output Q2 was sold at the price P2, whilst

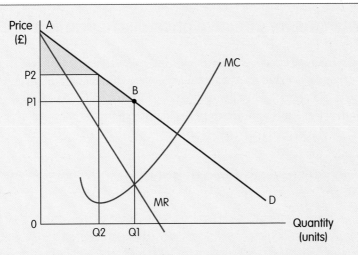

Figure 15.1 Price discrimination. A single-price monopolist would charge the price P1 for Q1 units. The consumer surplus would then be equal to the area ABP1. A price discriminator may charge the price P2 for Q2 units and the price P1 for Q1 – Q2 units. The revenue (and therefore profit) is then increased and the consumer surplus is reduced to the shaded areas.

the remainder (Q1 – Q2) was sold at P1 (see Figure 15.1). The firm is now earning more revenue from its sales and therefore more profits. At the same time, consumer surplus has been reduced from ABP1 to the shaded areas in Figure 15.1. Price discrimination therefore enables the firm to make more profits, but the customer is worse off.

Economics in context   Petrol prices

Travellers driving from the north of England to holiday spots in the south experience a significant increase in petrol prices, according to the AA. Average petrol prices in southern Britain are now almost 2 pence a litre higher than in northern Britain. This particularly hits those needing to fill up in the West Country—one of the top holiday locations.

The most expensive petrol in 2010 was to be found in London, where prices average 118.7 pence a litre. The cheapest was in north-west England, and in Yorkshire and Humberside.

Interestingly, when it comes to petrol pricing, Asda is the only national supermarket that sets the same prices in all outlets across the country; all of the others price according to local conditions.

? Question

If prices of petrol are higher in the south of Britain than the north, what does this suggest about the price elasticity of demand in this region? Why?

Conditions for effective price discrimination

To price-discriminate effectively, a firm must be able to identify different demand conditions: for example, demand may be different between different groups of customer. It will then charge a higher price when demand is price inelastic and a lower price when demand is price elastic. This leads to different prices in different market segments.

Economics in context **The price of games characters**

In the online game *EverQuest*, people pay more for male games characters than for females. In *EverQuest*, players can become a powerful warrior, a sorcerer, or a monk of either sex. More than 90 per cent of the players of *EverQuest* are male, but only 80 per cent of the characters in the game are male and so some people are gender-swapping. Players who want to gain powers quickly can buy high-level players. The price of male characters is greater than the price of female characters, suggesting a sexist approach. Typically, a female character is worth $41 less than a male.

? Question

The insurance rates for male and female drivers are different. Why do you think this is?

To be successful, a policy of price discrimination requires the following.

- The first requirement is that buyers in one market cannot switch easily to another market—that is, that those being asked to pay a high price cannot switch to the low-price market (because this would undermine the policy).

  Markets can be separated in many ways, such as the following.
- **Time** This means that people pay different prices at different times of day (for example, peak and off-peak travel).
- **Age** For example, old-age pensioners or children pay less than other people on the bus; their age can be verified by travel cards.
- **Region** For example, charging different prices for the same model of car or the same beer in different parts of the world; the transport costs to buy the cars in the cheaper market and bring them back can ensure that it is not worth trying to buy in the lower-priced market.
- **Status** For example, some firms may have customer clubs or loyalty schemes, and charge different rates to members and non-members.
- **Income** The price charged may vary according to how much you earn. Some private schools offer bursaries to subsidize students who come from low-income backgrounds. However, for this to work, the business must be sure that it can tell accurately what people earn; otherwise, everyone will pretend to be on a low income to try to obtain a bursary!

- The second requirement for effective price discrimination is that the price elasticity of demand is different—that is, that demand is more price inelastic in one market segment than another, enabling prices to be increased in some sections of the market and reduced in others. The fact that demand conditions vary enables different prices to be charged. The higher price will be in the more price-inelastic segment(s) of the market, because this will increase revenue (see Chapter 4).

In Figure 15.2, the demand and marginal revenue in the two markets (A and B) have been added together at each price (that is, horizontally summated) to give the total market demand and the market marginal revenue. The profit-maximizing output, as ever, occurs when the marginal revenue equals the marginal cost. This determines the profit-maximizing output level for the market as a whole. For each market, the marginal revenue must be equal to MR1. If the marginal revenue in one market were greater than in another, then it would make sense to switch output to the one in which the extra revenue is higher, because this would boost profit. To sell this output, the price would need to fall in this market, and this would reduce the marginal revenue. This should continue until the marginal revenue is the same in both markets. Thus, to profit-maximize, the marginal revenue in market A must be equal to the marginal revenue in market B.

Given that the marginal revenues are equal in both markets, the relevant price and output in each one can then be identified. The price will be higher in the price-inelastic market and lower in the price-elastic market (PA > PB in Figure 15.2).

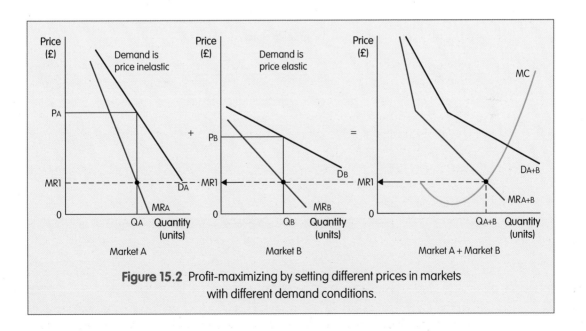

Figure 15.2 Profit-maximizing by setting different prices in markets with different demand conditions.

▪ Perfect price discrimination

Perfect price discrimination occurs when a different price is charged for every single unit of the product. This is also called 'first-degree price discrimination'. A perfect price discriminator charges the customer the maximum that he or she is willing to pay for every single unit. In this case, the marginal revenue curve is the same as the demand curve and consumer surplus is removed entirely. In practice, the difficulty for firms in doing this lies in identifying exactly how much customers genuinely value each item. Ask them and they may not tell you the truth!

In perfect price discrimination, a firm will profit-maximize when the marginal revenue equals the marginal costs; in this case, this is where the marginal cost curve crosses the demand curve. The total revenue earned is the whole area under the demand curve. In Figure 15.3, the total costs are the area AC1EQ1O. This highlights that revenue is higher than costs with price discrimination; this can mean some products are provided that could not be provided by a single price monopolist. A firm charging a single price for all of its units could not make a profit in this situation. The price could never cover the unit costs. In perfect price discrimination, the revenue will be higher and could cover the costs: for example, the area OFGQ1 may be greater than AC1EQ1O.

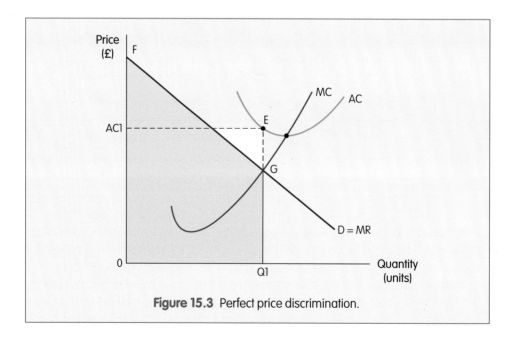

Figure 15.3 Perfect price discrimination.

■ The benefits of price discrimination

Price discrimination increases a firm's profits and reduces consumer surplus. The increase in profits may be seen as undesirable (an abuse of monopoly power); however, it may provide more funds for investment and innovation, leading to lower costs in the long term.

Price discrimination may also enable some goods and services to be produced that would not otherwise be provided. By price-discriminating, a firm may be able to make enough profits to want to stay in the industry when otherwise it would make a loss and leave.

Economics in context   The South African World Cup

South Africa had almost 22 per cent unemployment and had an average income of $10,400 in 2008. When the 2010 South African World Cup tickets went on sale, a proportion of tickets were available to South African residents only. These cost about one third of the ticket prices for non-locals.

? Question

Do you think it was fair to charge less to South Africans for World Cup tickets?

 Case study Price discrimination

[A]ny well-run business would seek to charge each customer the maximum price he'd be willing to pay—and they do . . .

The first [strategy] is what economists call 'first-degree price discrimination', but we could call it the 'unique target' strategy: to evaluate each customer as an individual and charge according to how much he or she is willing to pay. This is the strategy of the used-car salesman or the estate agent. It usually takes skill and a lot of effort: hardly surprising, then, that it is most often seen for items that have a high value relative to the retailer's time—cars and houses, of course, but also souvenirs in African street stalls, where the impoverished merchant will find it worth bargaining for some time to gain an extra pound.

Now, however, companies are trying to automate the process of evaluating individual customers to reduce the time it takes to do so. For instance, supermarkets accumulate evidence of what you're willing to pay by giving you 'discount cards', which are needed to take advantage of sale prices. In return for getting a lower price on certain items, you allow the stores to keep records of what you buy, and then in turn offer you vouchers for discounts on products. It doesn't work perfectly, because supermarkets can only send 'money off' vouchers, not 'money on' vouchers. 'Money on' vouchers have never been a success.

The second approach, the 'group target' strategy, is to offer different prices to members of distinct groups. Who could complain about reduced bus fares for children and the elderly? Surely it must be reasonable for coffee shops to offer a discount to people who work nearby and for tourist attractions to let locals in for a lower rate? It often seems reasonable because people in groups who pay more are usually people who can afford more, and that's because people who can afford more are usually people who care less about the price. But we shouldn't forget that this is a convenient coincidence. Companies trying to increase their profits and get the maximum value out of their scarcity are interested in who is willing to pay more, rather than who can afford to pay more. For instance, when Disney World in Florida offer admission discounts of more than 50 per cent to local people, they're not making a statement about the grinding poverty of the Sunshine State. They simply know that for a reduced price, locals are more likely to come regularly. But tourists will probably come once, and once only, whether it is cheap or expensive.

. . . The same is true of discounts at coffee bars for local workers. The AMT bar in Waterloo station will knock 10 per cent off the cost of your coffee if you work locally. This isn't because the local workers are poor: they include top Whitehall mandarins and the extravagantly remunerated employees of the gigantic oil company, Shell. The discount reflects the fact that local workers are price-sensitive despite being rich. Commuters who pass through Waterloo in a hurry see only one or two coffee bars and are willing to pay high prices for convenience. Local workers pop out of the office at 11 a.m. for coffee, and could walk in any direction. They can buy from several cafes, all equally convenient, all of which they will have had a chance to sample. They are bound to be more price-sensitive, even if they are rich.

The 'individual target' strategy is difficult, partly because it requires a lot of information, and partly because it tends to be very unpopular. Despite the difficulties, however, it's so profitable that companies always explore new ways to do it. The 'group target' strategy of discounts for students or locals is less effective, but easier to put into action, and usually it's socially acceptable. Either will deliver more profits than simply treating all customers as a homogeneous mass.

. . . Supermarkets have turned price targeting into an art, developing a vast array of strategies to that end. Above the main concourse of Liverpool Street station, there's a Marks and Spencer 'Simply Food' store, catering for busy commuters on the way in and out of London. Knowing what we do about scarcity value, we shouldn't be surprised to find that this shop isn't cheap—even compared with another branch of M&S merely 500 metres or so away, at Moorgate.

. . . Try to spot other odd mix-ups next time you're in the supermarket. Have you noticed that supermarkets often charge 10 times as much for fresh chilli peppers in a packet as for loose fresh chillies? That's because the typical customer buys such small quantities that he doesn't think to check whether they cost 4p or 40p. Randomly tripling the price of a vegetable is a favourite trick: customers who notice the mark-up just buy a different vegetable that week; customers who don't have self-targeted a whopping price rise.

Source: Harford (2005)

? Questions

- What is meant by first-degree price discrimination? Why would this pricing approach appeal to firms? Why is it difficult for them to implement?
- What does Harford mean by the 'group target' strategy of price discrimination? Can you think of other examples of this approach?
- Of what other examples of price discrimination can you think?
- Do you think that price discrimination should be allowed? Should it be encouraged?

Checklist

Now that you have read this chapter, try to answer the following questions.

☐ Can you explain what is meant by barriers to entry?

☐ Can you outline different forms of barrier to entry?

☐ Can you explain the significance of barriers to entry in relation to the profits that may be earned in an industry?

☐ Can you explain the meaning of price discrimination?

☐ Can you outline the conditions for effective price discrimination?

☐ Can you analyse the benefits of price discrimination?

Review questions

1 Of what types of barriers to entry can you think?

2 Are barriers to entry a good thing?

3 What is meant by a price-inelastic demand?

4 If a business is price-discriminating, will the price be higher or lower in the more price-inelastic market segment?

5 Is price discrimination a good thing?

Key learning points

- Price discrimination occurs when different prices are charged for the same product.

- Price discrimination reduces consumer surplus, but increases producer surplus.

- Price discrimination may enable some products to be produced that it would not be financially feasible to produce otherwise.

- When price-discriminating, a higher price is charged where demand is more price inelastic.

- With perfect price discrimination, consumer surplus is reduced to zero.

Reference

Harford, T. (2005) *The Undercover Economist*, Little, Brown Book Group Ltd, London

Learn more

Effective price discrimination relies on there being different price elasticities of demand in the various markets. To make sure that you understand the determinants of the price elasticity of demand, check your understanding of Chapter 4.

 Visit our Online Resource Centre at http://www.oxfordtextbooks.co.uk/orc/gillespie_econ2e/ for test questions and further information on topics covered in this chapter.

Business objectives

In this chapter, we examine the different forms of business in the UK, and consider the advantages and disadvantages of each one. We also consider business objectives. Traditionally, economists have assumed that the overriding objective of a firm is to maximize profits. In this chapter, we consider some alternative business objectives, and the impact of these in terms of price and output decisions. In particular, we examine issues relating to growth of firms.

LEARNING OBJECTIVES

By the end of this chapter, you should be able to:

✔ analyse different business objectives, and the impact of these on price and output decisions by firms;

✔ explain the different forms of integration;

✔ analyse the reasons why firms integrate in different ways;

✔ outline different strategies for growth;

✔ outline the key objectives and features of competition policy.

✔ understand the idea of corporate social responsibility.

■ Business objectives

The classical assumption in economics is that managers will aim to maximize profits. This means that firms will produce an output where the marginal revenue equals the marginal costs. At this level of output, no further profit can be made, and so there is the largest possible positive difference between the total revenue and the total costs.

Managers are expected to pursue profit for the following reasons.

- This will generate the highest possible financial rewards for the owners of the business, such as the shareholders. If managers fail to satisfy shareholders, then they may lose their jobs.
- Profit is a source of internal finance that can be used for expansion. Alternatives to profit include borrowing (which incurs interest charges) or, if it is a company, selling more shares (which can mean that the existing shareholders lose some of their ownership).
- Profit is a common benchmark of success, and so enables managers to meet their own ego needs and measure their own effectiveness relative to others.
- Managers' salaries may be connected to profits: the more profits they make, the more they may earn.
- High profits may lead to more demand for the shares and an increase in the share price, which will please shareholders.

However, the profit-maximizing assumption has some limitations—not least the difficulties that managers have knowing exactly what the revenues and costs would be at different levels of output. Without perfect knowledge, it is unlikely that managers could identify the actual profit-maximizing price and output, even if they were trying to do so.

Furthermore, a business is actually made up of many different interest groups, all of whom may be pursuing slightly different objectives: for example, the marketing department, the production department, the human resources department, the finance department, and the administrative staff (see Figure 16.1). The finance department may well be focused on profit, but the marketing team may be more concerned with the level of sales,

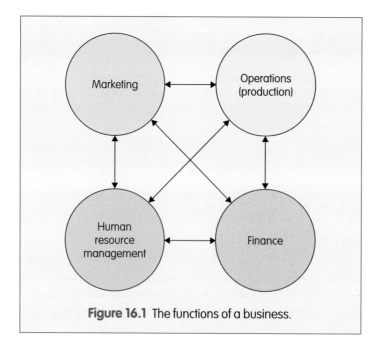

Figure 16.1 The functions of a business.

even if boosting sales requires higher expenditure and less profit. The human resources department may be reluctant to make people redundant, even if this increases efficiency and profit.

All of these different interest groups will be bargaining and negotiating over every decision made within a business; it is therefore likely that the actual pricing and output decisions that are made are a compromise between them. A business may well 'satisfice' its different stakeholders rather than profit-maximize. This idea was put forward by Simon (1947), and stems from Cyert and March (1963); it suggests that managers are satisfying different needs and trying to balance their demands.

There may also be a difference between the objectives of the managers and the owners. For example, the owners may want high profits so that they can receive higher dividends, whereas the managers may want the following.

- Some managers may want to control larger departments or want faster growth. They may be more interested in the scale of their operations and the power that they have than they are in achieving the most profitable outputs.

- Some managers may have environmental or social concerns that lead to more expensive production methods or not producing in the least-cost location.

- Some managers and employees may be interested in job security and the quality of their working life. They may wish to be paid more, even if profits are reduced.

Economics in context   **When money is not everything**

Dame Anita Roddick, who made her fortune selling ethical body and beauty products, decided in 2005 to cash in her 18 per cent share of the company and give away half of her £100 million fortune, saying: 'I don't want to die rich.' Anita Roddick set up The Body Shop in 1976 in Brighton. 'The worst thing is greed, the accumulation of money. I don't know why people who are extraordinarily wealthy are not more generous. I think the rich have to look after the poor,' she said.

? Question
To what extent do you think that firms should give away their profits?

Other objectives

As we have seen, there are many groups within an organization, all with their own agenda. Although shareholders are the owners of a company and are likely to want the business to maximize profits, managers may not necessarily pursue the objectives that the shareholders want. There are a number of theories that economists have developed about possible objectives other than profit-maximization. The following are two possible alternative theories.

Sales revenue maximization

According to Baumol (1959), managers may want to maximize the revenue earned from sales even if profits are not maximized (although a minimum level of profit must be made to satisfy the owners). For example, a firm may invest heavily in advertising to boost revenues, and may end up with lower profits than it could have achieved otherwise because of the advertising costs. Managers may want high revenues because:

- it means that the business has a higher profile, which gives the managers a sense of achievement (and may be good for their future careers if they move on to other firms); and
- their salaries may be linked to the firm's income rather than its profit.

To maximize revenue, a firm should produce at a level of output where the marginal revenue is zero. At this output, no extra revenue can be earned. This occurs at the output Q3 in Figure 16.2. Notice how the focus is on revenues, not costs.

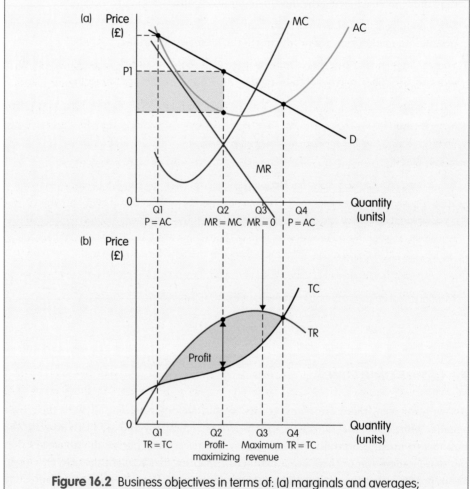

Figure 16.2 Business objectives in terms of: (a) marginals and averages; and (b) total costs and total revenues.

Growth maximization

According to Marris (1964), managers may seek to make the business as large as possible in terms of its output, provided that they do not make a loss and that they meet some minimum profit requirement to satisfy investors. The reason why growth may be important is to make the business more difficult to take over. By increasing the size of the organization, managers are possibly protecting their own jobs by making the firm more expensive to buy and therefore less likely to be bought. Growth also makes the business more visible because it is selling a lot of products and therefore the organization has a higher profile. Once again, this may be good for the managers' own careers. The Royal Bank of Scotland in the 1990s and 2000s undertook a rapid expansion plan led by Sir Fred Goodwin that raised his profile and that of the company.

The highest possible level of output at which a firm can produce without making a loss is where the average revenue (price) equals the average cost. This is shown at the output Q4 in Figure 16.2.

▨ Integration

One way of achieving rapid growth is to join with other firms; this is known as 'integration'. Integration occurs when firms join together. This may be in one of the following forms.

- **A takeover or an acquisition** This occurs when a firm or individual buys control of another business—for example, in 2005, News Corporation bought MySpace for $580 million, and in 2006, Google bought YouTube for $1.65 billion.
- **A merger** This occurs when two firms join to create one new business.

Expanding via integration is known as 'external growth', as opposed to 'internal growth' or 'organic growth', which occurs when firms grow by developing their existing business. External growth can lead to rapid and dramatic increases in the scale of a business. Internal growth tends to be slower and therefore possibly easier to manage. Growth through mergers and takeovers has been common in many industries—particularly global ones, such as pharmaceuticals, banking, car production, and brewing—as firms pursue a larger scale to try to achieve a stronger competitive position.

▨ Merger versus takeover

In a merger, the owners of both companies become the owners of the new organization. In a takeover, the owners of the victim company give up their shares in return for cash or shares in the purchaser. A takeover is also called an acquisition.

A merger is a voluntary joining of two or more organizations. This has the advantage of information being freely shared, whereas in a hostile takeover, information may not be so readily available. However, a merger may not be possible because the owners of one of the firms may not want to join with the other. This means that the other firm may have to buy control of the organization. Equally, the owners of one organization may want to control another rather than share control of it, and so may insist on a takeover.

Economics in context   The growth of General Electric

General Electric (GE), one of the biggest companies in the world, has grown rapidly through acqui-sitions. Its businesses include financial services, plastics, health care, and broadcasting. It spends billions of dollars per year buying companies and has over 200 people working full-time in its acquisitions team. By comparison, at Procter and Gamble, another large multinational, the business development team consists of only the chief executive and his chief financial officer.

Deals at GE are judged on quantitative criteria (for example, can they achieve a given rate of return?) and qualitative criteria (for example, do they fit with the overall strategy?). The company measures performance regularly after the deal to discover what works and what does not work.

❓ Question
What problems can you imagine might occur when one firm grows by taking over another one?

■ Types of integration

The different types of integration are shown in Figure 16.3 and are described as follows.

• Horizontal integration occurs when two or more firms at the same stage of the same production process join together—for example, Morrisons bought Safeway in 2003 (both are supermarkets); in 2008, the Co-operative bought Somerfield supermarkets for £1.57 billion; in 2010, Geely cars bought Volvo for £1.14 billion.

Horizontal integration offers benefits such as:
• greater market share and greater market power; and
• internal economies of scale—for example, the combined business will buy on a larger scale than each of the individual firms would have done before the integration and this should lead to purchasing economies of scale.

Given that the firms are in the same industry, managing the combined business should be easier than taking over a business in a different sector entirely. Managers should understand the production process, and customer needs and wants.

• **Vertical integration** occurs when one firm joins with another at a different stage of the same production process. The following are some examples.
   • A film company may buy a cinema chain (this is forward integration because the firm is moving nearer to the final customer).

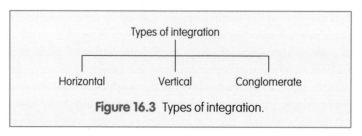

Figure 16.3 Types of integration.

- A petrol company may buy an oil refinery (this is backward integration because it goes back toward the raw materials). BP, for example, is a very vertically integrated business involved in the exploration, extraction, refining, and sale of petrol.

By vertically integrating, a firm can cut out the profit margins of the other intermediaries. This may lead to a lower final price for the buyer (or higher profit margins for the firm itself). In the case of backward vertical integration, a firm may be able to control supply more effectively (for example, it may have more control over costs, design, and delivery). With forward vertical integration, the firm can ensure access to the market.

- Conglomerate integration occurs when one firm joins with another in a different market entirely—for example, Mars owns a food business, a vending business, and a pet food company!

This type of growth may reduce a firm's risks, because if demand declines in one market, then it may be increasing in another. However, from a management point of view, it will be complex managing organizations operating in different markets.

What do you think?

Is it better for a firm to specialize in one product market or to operate in several different ones?

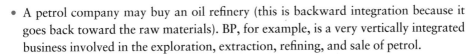

Vertical integration

In 2009, PepsiCo Inc agreed the takeover of two of its bottle makers in a deal worth $7.8 billion.

The world's second-largest soft drinks manufacturer said that the acquisition of Pepsi Bottling Group Inc and PepsiAmericas Inc would lead to annual savings of $300 million by 2012. The buyout would lead to speedier decision-making and would help it to bring products to market more quickly.

The previous arrangement separated bottling and distribution from product development and marketing, but according to PepsiCo chairman and chief executive officer Indra Nooyi:

While the existing model has served the system very well, it is clear that the changing dynamics of the North American liquid refreshment beverage business demand that we create a more flexible, efficient, and competitive system that can drive growth across the full range of PepsiCo beverage brands . . . The fully integrated beverage business will enable us to bring innovative products and packages to market faster, streamline our manufacturing and distribution systems, and react more quickly to changes in the marketplace, much like we do with our food business.

Pepsi could now control how its products were distributed, priced, and ideally even displayed in retail outlets.

 Questions

Analyse the possible advantages to Pepsi of taking over its bottling companies.

Why might Pepsi have kept product development and marketing separate from bottling in the past?

■ Problems of integration

The following are some of the problems of integration.

- **In the case of a takeover, the buyer will have to entice shareholders to sell their shares** This can be expensive and will usually mean that the buyer has to offer more than the current market price of the shares. The buyer will therefore need to improve the performance of the business following the takeover, simply to cover the premium paid to buy the company.

- **When organizations join together, there may be a culture clash** The culture of an organization refers to the values, attitudes, and beliefs of the employees within it. In other words, it is 'the way we do things around here'. When firms join together, their employees' views of how things should be done may be very different, and this can lead to conflict and underperformance. The problems of culture clashes are often underestimated by managers engaging in integration.

- Diseconomies of scale When two firms join together, the size of the business may make it difficult to run. Managers may struggle to control a larger-scale business due to coordination and communication problems. Managing more people, producing more products, and dealing with more suppliers and distributors make the management process more complex. There are also often problems with motivation in larger firms because employees feel more distant from managers. They do not feel as noticed or as important as individuals, and this can lead to less effort, and problems with attendance and work rate.

To try to control a larger business efficiently, managers may introduce the following.

- Budgeting systems may be used to set targets, and to review financial income and expenditure. This should help to keep control of the larger business and coordinate decision-making.

- Management by objectives may be introduced; this is a system in which all managers agree targets with their subordinates and review these regularly. This helps to ensure that everyone knows what they are trying to achieve and why.

Economics in context   **Kraft and Cadbury**

In 2010, Kraft, the US food giant, announced its takeover of Cadbury, the UK confectionery business. To win the deal, Kraft had to increase its offer to 840 pence a share—valuing the company at £11.5 billion ($18.9 billion). Kraft said that the deal would create a 'global confectionery leader'.

However, there were fears of job cuts at Cadbury UK operations as a result of the agreed takeover. The offer consisted of 500 pence in cash, with the rest made up of Kraft shares. Kraft borrowed £7 billion ($11.5 billion) to finance the deal.

'We believe the offer represents good value for Cadbury shareholders . . . and we will now work with the Kraft Foods's management to ensure the continued success and growth of the business,' said Cadbury chairman Roger Carr.

The deal is a significant increase on earlier Kraft bids, which were flatly rejected by the Cadbury board as 'derisory'.

Kraft's previous offer valued the company at £10.5 billion—a bid that Cadbury chairman Roger Carr said was an attempt to 'buy Cadbury on the cheap'.

Kraft also said it expected 'meaningful cost savings' as a result of the merger.

? Questions

What benefits might Kraft gain from taking over Cadbury?

What problems might Kraft experience from the takeover?

Why did Kraft increase its bid for Cadbury and what difficulties might this have caused the business?

▨ Strategies for growth

According to Ansoff (1957), the growth strategies of a business can be analysed under the following four categories (see Table 16.1 for the Ansoff matrix).

- **Market penetration** This occurs when firms sell more of their products within their existing markets. For example, they might advertise more, modify their products, or cut the price to boost their sales. By modifying the marketing mix, a firm can try to boost its sales.
- Market development This occurs when a firm aims its products at new market segments. For example, a firm might try to sell its products in new countries, or it might target new age ranges or new users.
- **New product development** This involves developing new products to sell to existing customers—for example, a new variety of a brand of drinks, such as Coca-Cola with lemon, with lime, without caffeine, or with vanilla.
- Diversification This strategy involves developing new products and selling in markets that are new to the business. This is the riskiest strategy in terms of management, because it involves unknown areas for the managers.

Table 16.1 Growth strategies for a business

		Products	
		Existing	New
Markets	Existing	Market penetration	New product development
	New	Market development	Diversification

What do you think?

Do you think that it is better to grow by joining with another business or to grow independently?

Do you think that growth strategies may mainly be driven by the personal objectives of managers?

Economics in context | Pilkington and Nippon Glass

A few years ago, the UK glass manufacturer Pilkington agreed to be taken over by Japan's Nippon Sheet Glass. The 180-year-old UK glassmaker employed almost 24,000 people, and had factories in Birmingham and Doncaster, as well as its head office in St Helens in the north-west. Under the cash deal, Nippon Sheet offered 165 pence per share. It raised some of the money through borrowing.

The main aim of this horizontal integration was to benefit from major cost savings. For example, the head offices could be combined. It also meant that the new business would be in a stronger position to compete against the world's largest glass company, Asahi of Japan, which had around 20 per cent of the market; Pilkington had around 19 per cent of the market and Nippon had only 3 per cent. The deal was also a good fit geographically, with Pilkington stronger in Europe and the USA, and Nippon stronger in Asia. Nippon had focused on supplying the Japanese car industry, so the deal with Pilkington opened up new markets for it. In particular, it was hoped that it would save Nippon's contract with Toyota. Toyota had threatened to end the contract because Nippon did not have the global coverage that it wanted.

? Questions

Outline the possible benefits of this takeover deal.

What might be the problems of a takeover such as this?

To what extent should the UK government worry about UK firms being taken over by foreign firms?

▪ Social objectives

Some organizations have very explicit social aims and do not seek to make a profit. These may be public sector organizations, charities, or other non-profit organizations, such as sports clubs. The National Health Service (NHS), for example, is very conscious of the costs of treatment and the opportunity costs of resources; managers also have control of huge budgets. However, because the product is not marketed and charged for, the NHS does not measure its success in terms of profits. Similarly, libraries, museums, and galleries may need to be assessed in very different ways. And what about local football clubs, schools, social services, and the defence sector? All of these have a range of performance criteria other than profits.

■ The principal–agent problem

In many companies, the owners (who are called the 'principals') are not the same as the managers. In many companies, for example, the shareholders invest in the business, but hire managers (as their 'agents') to run it on a day-to-day basis. There is a divorce between ownership and control. This approach has advantages in that those with money hire specialists who are good at managing, but who may not have the funds themselves to establish a business. However, a possible consequence of this may be that the objectives pursued by the managers differ from those of the owners. The owners are most likely to be interested in financial returns either through dividends or through an increase in the share price. However, they do not have perfect information and may not know at any time what would lead to the highest profits. They are likely to be guided by the managers, who may not always be seeking the maximum profit. For example, as we have seen, managers may be interested in growing the business because this makes them feel more important; alternatively, they may have particular projects that interest them, such as developing a new product. The principal–agent problem arises because of the difference between those owning a business and those running it on a daily basis. The directors are elected by shareholders to look after their interests, but they may also lack the same information as managers or may side with managers as they come to see issues from their own perspective.

To try to control the managers, shareholders elect a board of directors that meets regularly and monitors the managers' behaviour. The directors act as the watchdogs of the shareholders (see Figure 16.4).

The divorce between ownership and control is not an issue if the owners and the managers are the same people—for example, if the business is a sole trader. The divorce between ownership and control may also not be a problem if managers buy up the shares in a business to gain control; this is a called a 'management buyout'.

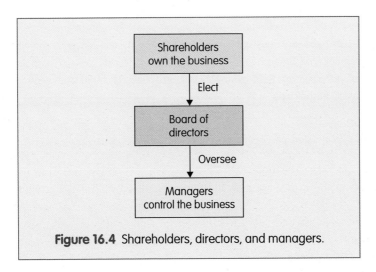

Figure 16.4 Shareholders, directors, and managers.

What do you think?

Can the problem of divorce between ownership and control ever be overcome? What would you recommend?

Economics in context

The dangers of the principal–agent difference

The dangers of the difference between the principal and agents can be seen by cases in which managers abuse their position at the expense of their owners. The following are two examples of this.

In 2005, US prosecutors indicted Conrad Black on various charges, including racketeering, obstruction of justice, and money laundering. Lord Black and three executives were accused of using almost $84 million (£49 million) of Hollinger International funds. Lord Black and three former Hollinger executives were also charged with 11 counts of fraud in the USA, linked to a $2.1 billion (£1.2 billion) sale of hundreds of Canadian newspapers. Lord Black and his co-defendants stood accused of having cheated both Hollinger International's US and Canadian shareholders, and tax authorities in Canada, in three fraudulent schemes between 1998 and 2002. Conrad Black was released in 2010.

In 2001, Enron, a huge US company that went bankrupt, was investigated by the US financial regulator, the Securities Exchange Commission (SEC). It turned out that millions of dollars of debt had been hidden from investors. Some of the senior executives were taken to court on charges of fraud. Jeffrey Skilling, the former chief executive, for example, faced 35 charges, including conspiracy and fraud. It was alleged that he had attempted to fool investors into believing that Enron was a healthy company, whilst he and other executives received high rewards. Kenneth Lay, former chairman, faced seven charges. Enron started as a producer of energy in 1985 following the merger of two companies, Internorth and Houston Natural Gas. It later became a major 'market maker' in the USA, buying and selling energy. In just 15 years, it grew from very little to become the USA's seventh-largest company, employing 21,000 staff in over 40 countries. *Fortune* magazine named Enron 'America's most innovative company' for six consecutive years from 1996 to 2001. Enron ended up with $31.8 billion (£18 billion) of debts, its shares became worthless, and its employees all lost their jobs.

 Question

How do you think investors ensure that managers pursue their interests?

Marks and Spencer

Marks and Spencer boss Sir Stuart Rose had the warmest of welcomes when he took the chief executive job five years ago. He has been one of the best-known British business leaders—so why are shareholders celebrating the fact he is scaling back his role?

Not because he has failed his investors. For a number of years after stepping in to fight off a takeover bid from Sir Philip Green in 2004, Sir Stuart was lauded by investors and retail experts alike.

He is credited with refocusing and re-energizing the business, giving it cachet among younger, more fashion-savvy customers, and making it more profitable.

He even managed to bring full-year profits back to the magical level of £1 billion—something not seen since the company's real heyday in 1997.

But all that praise melted away when Sir Stuart announced he would add the role of chairman to his chief executive duties.

Sir Stuart did not have to look too far back to see how things change for Marks and Spencer heroes who take on both the top roles. In the 1990s, Sir Richard Greenbury, the first to take the company to the magic billion profit level, found himself reviled in his final year in the roles. The next man to hold both positions was the Belgian Luc Vandevelde. Hailed as the saviour of the struggling chain, he ended his time there under a barrage of questions as to his commitment to the company. Now Sir Stuart himself has suffered the same turn in sentiment.

At the recent annual general meeting, shareholders voted by almost 38 per cent against him remaining as chairman and chief executive.

There is plenty to celebrate of Sir Stuart's time as head of M&S . . . They will remember the trouble that M&S was in when he arrived from Arcadia in 2004, losing market share to hipper and cheaper rivals, and struggling to argue a case for remaining independent against repeated approaches from rival retailer—and former friend—Sir Philip Green.

His turnaround strategy involved taking control of women's fashion brand Per Una, selling non-core businesses, and injecting glamour into its brand by using celebrities such as Twiggy and Antonio Banderas in its advertising. It proved highly successful.

Sir Stuart handed over the chief executive baton in the new year to Marc Bolland, but even then, he promised shareholders he would stay on as part-time chairman to ensure a smooth transition.

Analysis of share register

Ordinary shares: As at 3 April 2010, there were 217,541 holders of ordinary shares whose shareholdings are analysed below.

	Number of holdings	Percentage of total shareholders	Number of ordinary shares	Percentage of ordinary shares
Range				
1–500	108,735	49.98	21,582,412	1.36
501–1,000	43,817	20.14	32,780,554	2.07
1,001–2,000	33,458	15.38	47,897,697	3.03
2,001–5,000	22,468	10.33	68,859,124	4.35
5,001–10,000	5,709	2.62	39,645,480	2.51
10,001–100,000	2,714	1.25	62,120,241	3.93
100,001–1,000,000	452	0.21	152,384,856	9.63
1,000,001–HIGHEST	188	0.09	1,157,046,217	73.12
Total	217,541	100.00	1,582,316,581	100.00

Source: Marston (2009).

 Questions

Why might Sir Stuart Rose want to be chairman and chief executive?

What are the possible problems that this might cause?

Looking at the analysis of the share register from the company's 2010 accounts, what does this tell us about:

- the number of shareholders in the company?
- the most common number of shares owned by shareholders?
- the relative power of the largest 188 shareholders?

Case study The purpose of business

There is much debate over the role of business in society. Some people think that a business should focus on meeting the needs of its investors and that everything else is something of an irrelevance; this is known as the 'shareholder view'. Others believe that an organization needs to take all of its stakeholders into account when making decisions; this is known as the 'stakeholder concept'. Organizations such as the Co-operative Bank are known to be stakeholder-friendly. It regularly surveys its customers to make sure that the actions of the bank fit with the customers' own values. This has led to the decision not to lend to organizations involved in animal testing or ones that produce equipment that can be used for torture. Many companies pride themselves on their donations to charity, investment in the community, and environmentally friendly policies. However, Milton Friedman, the famous economist, believes that socially responsible actions such as this only make sense if they actually benefit the investors. According to Friedman (1970):

> In a free-enterprise, private-property system, a corporate executive is an employee of the owners of the business. He has direct responsibility to his employers. That responsibility is to conduct the business in accordance with their desires, which generally will be to make as much money as possible while conforming to the basic rules of the society, both those embodied in law and those embodied in ethical custom . . .

Whilst individual managers may wish to act socially responsibly in their own time, this is very different from using investors' money to do this. Paying more to specific suppliers that you have used for a long time may be a generous act, but does it actually help the business? Keeping on employees even when they are not needed may be the act of a kind employer rewarding loyalty, but is it profit-maximizing? Reducing pollution beyond the level required by law may be praiseworthy according to some environmental groups, but is it the right action of a manager who is only the 'agent' of the investors? Of course, says Friedman, if these 'socially responsible' actions do actually benefit the business in the long term (perhaps through more loyal employees or suppliers), then they should be undertaken and supported.

According to Friedman:

> It may well be in the long-run interest of a corporation that is a major employer in a small community to devote resources to providing amenities to that community or to improving its government. That may make it easier to attract desirable employees, it may reduce the wage bill or lessen losses from pilferage and sabotage or have other worthwhile effects.

Overall, Friedman claims:

> There is one and only one social responsibility of business—to use its resources, and engage in activities designed to increase its profits so long as it stays within the rules of the game, which is to say, engages in open and free competition without deception or fraud.

❓ Questions

- Summarize Friedman's views in your own words.
- To what extent do you agree with Friedman's view about the 'one and only one social responsibility' of a business?

Checklist

Now that you have read this chapter, try to answer the following questions.

☐ Can you analyse different business objectives, and the impact of these on price and output decisions by firms?

☐ Do you understand the idea of corporate social responsibility?

☐ Can you explain the different forms of integration?

☐ Can you analyse the reasons why firms integrate in different ways?

☐ Can you outline different strategies for growth?

☐ Can you outline the stakeholder view of a business?

Review questions

1 If a firm is seeking to maximize sales revenue, what will determine its price and output? Explain your answer.

2 If a firm produces to maximize growth without making a loss, what will determine its price and output? Explain your answer.

3 Is horizontal integration better than vertical integration?

4 Does the idea of pursuing corporate social responsibility conflict with maximizing profits?

5 What other measures of business performance might you use as well as, or instead of, profit?

Key learning points

- Traditional economics assumes that firms profit-maximize. In fact, there is a range of possible objectives (such as growth maximization and sales revenue maximization). Different objectives lead to different price and output outcomes.

- Corporate social responsibility occurs when firms accept obligations to society over and beyond their legal obligations—for example, obligations to the environment and the local community.

- There are many forms of integration, and each type may have its own motives and business logic.

- Business strategy can focus on the decision of which markets to compete in and which products to offer.

- Managing firms after external growth can be difficult due to culture clashes, and difficulties in communicating and coordinating. This is why many mergers and takeovers underperform after the integration.

- Managers may believe that they have responsibilities to several stakeholder groups, not just shareholders.

References

Ansoff, H.I. (1957) 'Strategies for diversification', *Harvard Business Review*, 35(2): 113–24

Baumol, W. (1959) *Business Behaviour, Value, and Growth*, Macmillan, New York

Cyert, R.M. and March, J.G. (1963) *Behavioral Theory of the Firm*, Prentice Hall, New Jersey

Friedman, M. (1970) 'The social responsibility of business is to increase profits', *The New York Times Magazine*, 13 September

Marris, R. (1964) *The Economic Theory of 'Managerial' Capitalism*, Macmillan, London

Marston, R. (2009) 'Sir Stuart Rose's legacy at M&S', BBC News, available online at http://news.bbc.co.uk/1/hi/business/8366635.stm

Schumpeter, J.A. (1950) *Capitalism, Socialism, and Democracy*, 3rd edn, Harper and Row, New York

Simon, H.A. (1947) *Administrative Behaviour*, Macmillan, New York

Learn more

- To learn more about takeovers and mergers, visit the Online Resource Centre. To learn more about monopolies, you can read Chapter 12.

- The issue of corporate social responsibility, and the relationship between managers and an organization's stakeholders, are key issues in business today. To learn more about the issues involved in this debate, visit the Online Resource Centre.

 Visit our Online Resource Centre at http://www.oxfordtextbooks.co.uk/orc/gillespie_econ2e/ for test questions and further information on topics covered in this chapter.

»17 The labour market

Labour is a vital resource in business. An understanding of the labour market will help us to understand why wage levels differ between jobs and regions, and what determines the number of people working in a particular industry. In this chapter, we consider the determinants of supply and demand for labour, and examine how changes in wages bring about equilibrium in the market.

LEARNING OBJECTIVES

By the end of this chapter, you should be able to:

✔ understand why labour is a derived demand;

✔ explain the factors that affect the demand and supply of labour;

✔ explain the profit-maximizing condition for hiring labour;

✔ understand the role of a trade union;

✔ explain the factors influencing the powers of trade unions.

■ The labour market

Most of us are interested in the wages that we might earn in different jobs. What is also interesting is how the wages vary between industries and why the earnings of, say, a cleaner can be so different from those of a merchant banker. We all think that nurses, police, and firefighters do a valuable job, and yet their pay is relatively low. Some footballers seem to play relatively few games per season and yet earn vast sums of money. In this chapter, we look at the labour market and consider why wages differ so much, and examine the impact of changes in market conditions.

■ The supply of and demand for labour

In a free market, the wages of employees will be determined by the supply of and demand for labour in a given industry. In just the same way that the price adjusts to bring about equilibrium in the product market, the wage will adjust to bring about equilibrium in the labour market. So, to understand why some jobs pay so much more than others, we must examine the supply and demand of labour.

■ Labour supply

The supply of labour depends on the number of people willing and able to work, and the number of hours that they are willing to work at a given wage.

The supply of labour to a particular industry will depend on the following.

- **The level of wages** The higher the wages being paid, then the more people are likely to want to work in an industry, all other things being unchanged. This will cause a movement along the supply curve for labour (see Figure 17.1a).
- **The value of the benefits available from the government if people are unemployed** If these benefits are relatively low, then there will be more incentive for people to work. This will increase the supply of labour at any wage level and shift the supply curve of labour to the right (see Figure 17.1b).
- **The training period** If there is a long training period for a particular industry (perhaps because the work requires highly specialist skills, such as being a surgeon), then this will reduce the number of employees who can work in this sector at any moment and shift the supply of labour to the left.
- **The overall appeal of the job** If the job itself is unappealing (perhaps because working conditions are unpleasant or even dangerous—think of night work, working on an oil rig, or being a firefighter), then this will reduce the supply of labour to it.

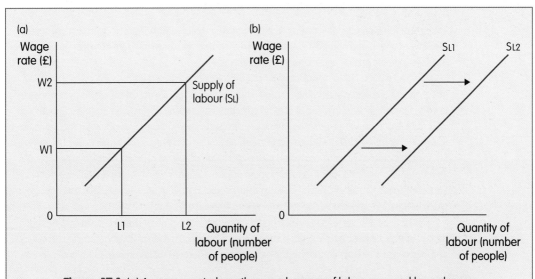

Figure 17.1 (a) A movement along the supply curve of labour caused by a change in the wage rate; (b) A shift in the supply of labour curve means that more (or less) is supplied at each and every wage rate.

- **The labour force** This will determine the overall size of the labour pool and therefore the number that can work in any industry. The working population will depend on what the working age is (for example, at what age people leave school and at what age they retire), and demographic factors such as birth and death rates, and migration rates. Out of this labour force, the number of people willing to work will depend on the unemployment benefits available relative to the wages offered.

- Trade unions Trade unions represent employees and bargain with management to protect their interests. Unions may take industrial action (such as a strike) as a bargaining tool. In some countries, unions can affect the supply of labour by restricting jobs to union members.

- **The time period** In the immediate run, the supply of labour will be fixed. You will have a certain number of employees available. In the short and medium terms, you can attract people with the right skills into your industry from other sectors. Over time, however, people can be trained to accept jobs and this will increase supply.

What do you think?

What job do you want to pursue as a career? Why?

Why might the quantity of labour supplied not increase if the wage goes up?

Economics in context — Wanted: secret service officer

The following is an extract from an advert for an operational officer for the UK Secret Intelligence Service.

The role of the Operational Officer is to plan and execute covert intelligence operations overseas. Working in London and abroad, Operational Officers gather the secret intelligence which government needs to promote and defend UK national interests.

The work calls for men and women who combine exceptional interpersonal skills with a strong intellect and a high degree of personal integrity. The successful Operational Officer will be someone able to influence and persuade others, and to do so across cultural and linguistic boundaries. Candidates who are bilingual or who come from ethnically diverse backgrounds are welcome for the particular skills and insights they bring. Regardless of their background and experience, Operational Officers will be energetic and resourceful, motivated by the challenge of solving complex problems. Resilience is important, as is the ability to deliver results under pressure, often in difficult and stressful environments. To become an Operational Officer requires a keen interest in international issues and a curiosity about other cultures, along with an appetite for living and working overseas.

Successful candidates for this special and demanding role will need a strong academic record to degree level or beyond, a history of personal achievement and influence in extra-curricular activities, and experience of independent travel. They will also have a demonstrable commitment to public service.

❓ Question

Do you think that the supply of labour for this position is likely to be high or low? Why?

Economics in context Union membership

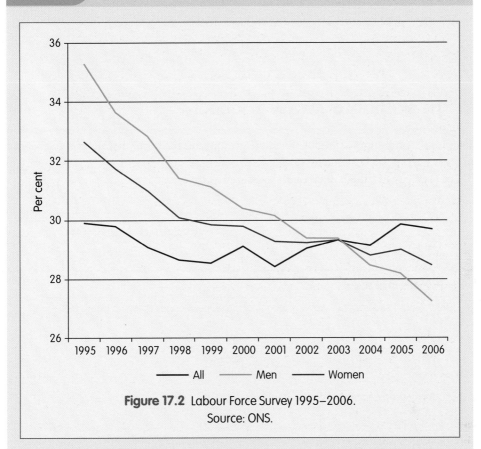

Figure 17.2 Labour Force Survey 1995–2006.
Source: ONS.

Trade union membership, as a percentage of the workforce, has fallen over the last 15 years to around 28 per cent.

There are regional differences in the proportion of employees who are union members. Union density ranged from 21.4 per cent in the south-east to 38.9 per cent in the north-east.

Source: Labour Force Survey (Autumn quarters)

? Questions
Why do you think people join unions?
Why do you think membership has been falling?
Why might membership vary between regions?

Put into practice

• For what jobs would you be able to apply tomorrow?

• For what jobs would you need extensive training before you could apply?

The elasticity of supply of labour

The elasticity of supply of labour shows how responsive the supply of labour is to changes in the wage rate, all other factors being unchanged.

The elasticity of supply of labour is measured as follows:

$$\text{Elasticity of supply of labour} = \frac{\text{Percentage change in the quantity of labour supplied}}{\text{Percentage change in the wage rate}}$$

Put into practice

Calculate the elasticity of supply of labour for the wage changes shown in Figure 17.3.

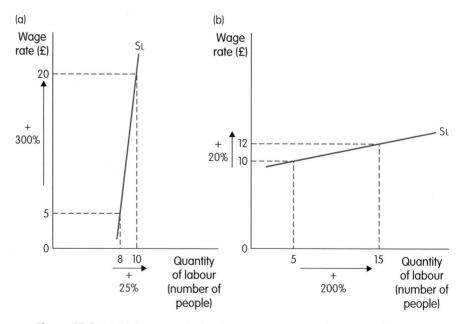

Figure 17.3 (a) A labour supply that is not responsive to changes in the wage rate (the supply of labour is wage-rate inelastic); (b) A labour supply that is responsive to changes in the wage rate (the supply of labour is wage-rate elastic).

The elasticity of supply of labour depends on factors such as the following.

- **The geographical mobility of labour** This refers to how easy it is for people to change location to get a job. This depends on:
  - the availability of information (do employees know that jobs are available in the first place?);
  - the costs of moving—for example, transport costs, removal costs, and the costs of finding accommodation in different areas (house prices in some areas can be a major barrier to location);
  - the upheaval involved in moving—for example, changing children's schools, interrupting their education, and leaving friends and family; and
  - the willingness of people to take risks and move to a new area.
- **The occupational mobility of labour** This refers to how easy it is for employees to change professions if wages change. This depends on factors such as the training involved, the qualifications needed, the skills required, and the awareness of the availability of jobs.

What do you think?

What do you think makes people go out to work?

Economics in context   An ageing population

One of the key issues facing European business in the future is the increasing average age of the population. This means that firms will need to consider how to recruit older workers and how to retain their younger ones. It also means that many organizations will have to review their pension arrangements. Their existing pension schemes are simply not viable. In recent years, nearly all large firms have ended their final-salary pension schemes. These give employees a proportion of their final salary during every year of their retirement; the amount of pension that they receive depends on how many years they had worked. In 2005, Rentokil was the first company to end this scheme, not only for new employees, but also for existing ones. It had to do this because the gap between its pension liabilities and assets was over £350 million.

? Question

How might an ageing population affect a firm's approach to recruitment and the management of staff?

■ The demand for labour

The demand for labour measures the number of employees that a firm is willing and able to employ, all other things being unchanged.

The demand for labour is a 'derived demand'. This means that employees are demanded because there is a demand for the final good or service. The demand for employees is derived from the demand for the product. Employees are needed to produce the output, so an increase in the demand for the product increases the demand for labour.

The demand for labour is determined by the value of each employee's output. This is measured by the marginal revenue product of labour (MRPL). The MRPL depends on how much output is produced by an additional employee and the value of that output when it is sold—that is:

Marginal revenue product of labour (MRPL) = Marginal product (MP)
× Marginal revenue (MR)

For example, if an additional employee produces ten units that can sell for £5, then the marginal revenue product of labour is £50.

The demand for labour will depend on the following.

- **Wages** At higher wages, fewer employees will be demanded because they are more expensive, all other things being unchanged. This is shown by a movement along the demand-for-labour curve and a change in the quantity of labour demanded.

- **The stock of capital equipment and technology** The level of investment in capital goods will affect the productivity of employees and therefore their MRPL. Better capital equipment and technology should enable staff to produce more, and this will lead to an increase in their MRPL.

- **Working practices and management approaches** Better management and better ways of organizing people can lead to improvements in the levels of output produced by employees.

- **Training** If employees are better trained, then they should be more productive and this will increase their MRPL.

- **Skills** The more skilled employees are, the more productive they may be.

> **What do you think?**
>
> What do you think influences the level of investment within an industry or economy?

The MRPL is downward-sloping because:

- the marginal product (extra output) of extra employees falls due to the law of diminishing returns (see Chapter 9); and

- the marginal revenue (extra revenue) generated from selling units will either:
  - fall if the products are sold in monopoly markets (this is because the price has to be lowered to sell more—see Chapter 10); or
    - be constant if the product is sold in perfectly competitive markets in which the price is constant (see Chapter 11).

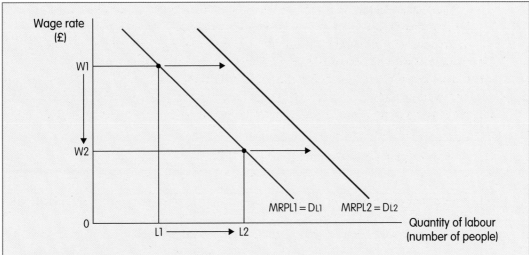

Figure 17.4 A movement along versus a shift in demand for labour. A change in the wage rate leads to a movement along the demand curve for labour. A change in other factors, such as productivity or demand for the product, shifts the demand curve.

Changes in the wage rate are shown as a movement along the demand-for-labour curve. Changes in any of the other factors above will lead to a shift in the curve as the value of the MRPL for any number of employees changes. The difference between a movement along, and a shift in, the MRPL is shown in Figure 17.4.

■ The wage elasticity of demand for labour

The wage elasticity of demand for labour measures how sensitive the demand for labour is in relation to changes in the wage level. It is calculated as follows:

$$\text{Elasticity of demand for labour} = \frac{\text{Percentage change in the quantity demanded of labour}}{\text{Percentage change in the wage rate}}$$

The demand for labour is wage inelastic if the percentage change in the quantity demanded is less than the percentage change in the wage level (see Figure 17.5a). The demand for labour is wage elastic if the percentage change in the quantity demanded is greater than the percentage change in the wage rate (see Figure 17.5b).

The elasticity of demand for labour will depend on the following.

• **How easy it is to replace labour with other factors of production** For example, is it easy to replace people with machines? The easier it is to replace staff, the more elastic the demand for labour will be. When economies are industrializing, the elasticity of demand for labour can be relatively high, because there is plenty of scope for investment in capital equipment to do the work that people are doing at present.

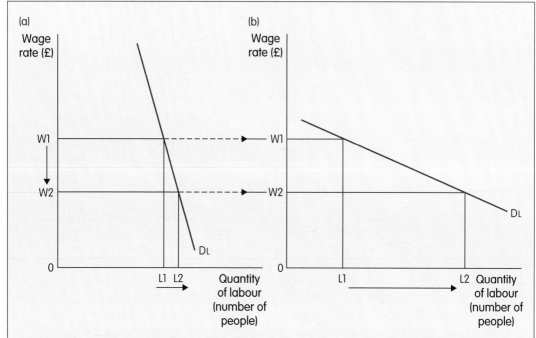

Figure 17.5 The impact of a change in wages: (a) wage-inelastic demand; and (b) wage-elastic demand. In (a), a given percentage change in the wage rate leads to a smaller percentage change in the quantity demanded of labour. In (b), a given percentage change in the wage rate leads to a larger percentage change in the quantity demanded of labour.

- **The price elasticity of demand for the final product** An increase in the wage rate will increase a firm's costs and therefore the price of the product; this will lead to a fall in sales. The greater the price elasticity of demand for the product, the greater the fall in sales, and therefore the greater the fall in the number of staff needed—that is, the more elastic demand is for labour.

- **Wages as a proportion of total costs** If wages are a high proportion of total costs, then an increase in wages will significantly increase the overall costs. This is likely to lead to a relatively large fall in the quantity of labour demanded—that is, the demand for labour will be wage elastic.

- **Time** Over time, it will be possible to find alternative ways of producing with less labour and so demand for labour will be more wage elastic in the long run than in the short run.

Put into practice

a. The wage rate increases by 10 per cent. The quantity of labour demanded falls by 20 per cent.
  - What is the elasticity of demand for labour?
  - What would happen to the quantity of labour demanded if the elasticity of demand were to stay the same and the wage rate to increase by 2 per cent?

b. The price elasticity of demand for a product is –0.1.
   • Is this price inelastic or elastic?
   • Does this mean that demand for labour in this industry is likely to be elastic or inelastic? Why?

▩ Wages in a perfectly competitive labour market

In a perfectly competitive labour market, there are many buyers of labour. The level of wages in an industry is determined by the supply of labour and demand for labour.

If the wage were set at a wage rate above the equilibrium—for example, the wage W2 in Figure 17.6—then this would lead to an excess supply of labour. More people would be willing and able to work at this high wage rate than the quantity demands. In a free market, the wage rate would fall, leading to an increase in the quantity of labour demanded and a fall in the quantity supplied. This process continues until equilibrium is reached at W1, where the quantity of labour supplied equals the quantity demanded. At this point, there is no incentive for the wage rate to change. If the wage rate was originally at W3, which is below the equilibrium rate, then there would be excess demand. The number of workers willing and able to work at this wage is less than the number demanded. In a free market, this will lead to an increase in the level of wages until it reaches W1, where the market is in equilibrium.

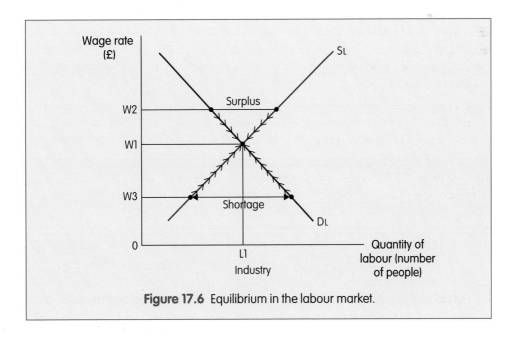

Figure 17.6 Equilibrium in the labour market.

The firm's decision to hire employees

A firm in a perfectly competitive labour market is small relative to the industry. It can hire as many employees as it wants and it will not have any noticeable impact on the overall demand for labour in the industry. This means that the firm is a wage taker: it can hire as many people as it wants at the given wage. This means that the extra cost of an employee is the wage (the marginal cost of labour equals the wage rate), as shown in Figure 17.7.

A profit-maximizing firm will employ workers up until the point at which the marginal revenue product of an employee is equal to the marginal cost of employing that worker—that is, the extra amount of revenue that they generate is equal to the extra cost of employing them.

If the marginal revenue product of labour is greater than the marginal cost of labour, then the extra revenue generated by hiring someone is greater than the extra cost of employing them—that is, profits increase by employing that person, so they will be hired.

If the marginal revenue product of labour is less than the marginal cost of labour, then the extra revenue earned by hiring someone is less than the extra cost of hiring them—that is, profits will fall if that person is employed, so they will not be recruited

The area w1Bl10 in Figure 17.7 shows the wages earned by employees. A profit-maximizing employer hires l1 employees (i.e. where MRPL = MC). The area Aw1B represents the surplus (the difference between the marginal revenue product of labour and the marginal cost of labour) earned by the firm.

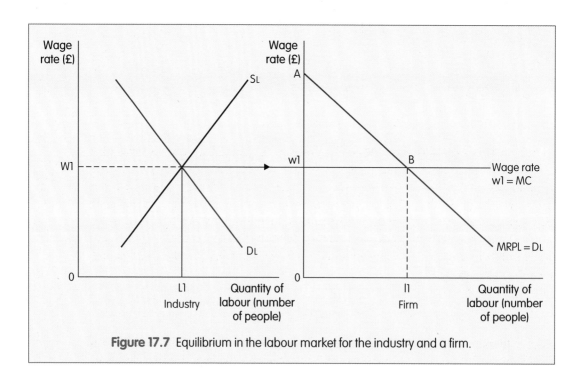

Figure 17.7 Equilibrium in the labour market for the industry and a firm.

Economics in context Music

In 2010, U2 were the world's biggest-selling band over the past 12 months, earning $130 million (£84.9 million), according to http://www.Forbes.com. The Irish group had recently staged their global tour to support their album *No Line on the Horizon*.

Rank	Band/artist	2010 earnings
1	U2	$130m (£84.9m)
2	AC/DC	$114m (£74.5m)
3	Beyonce Knowles	$87m (£56.8m)
4	Bruce Springsteen	$70m (£45.7m)
5	Britney Spears	$64m (£41.8m)
6	Jay-Z	$63m (£41.1m)
7	Lady Gaga	$62m (£40.5m)
8	Madonna	$58m (£37.9m)
9	Kenny Chesney	$50m (£32.6m)
10	Black-Eyed Peas/Coldplay	$48m (£31.3m)

? Questions

What determines the earnings of bands?

Do you think that the earnings of U2 are reasonable?

■ Changes in demand and supply of labour

The effect of an increase in demand for labour

Imagine that the market is at equilibrium at the wage W1 and the quantity of labour L1 (see Figure 17.8). If there is then an outward shift in the demand for labour (perhaps due to an increase in demand for the product), then this will lead to an excess demand at the given wage. This, in turn, will lead to an increase in wages. As wages increase, the number of people willing to work will increase (that is, there will be an increase in quantity supplied) and the quantity of labour demanded will fall. This will continue until a new equilibrium is reached with higher wages, and more people employed at the wage W2 and the quantity of labour L2.

The effect of an increase in the supply of labour

Imagine that the market is at equilibrium at the wage W1 and the quantity of labour L1 (see Figure 17.9). If there is then an outward shift in supply (perhaps due to a change in

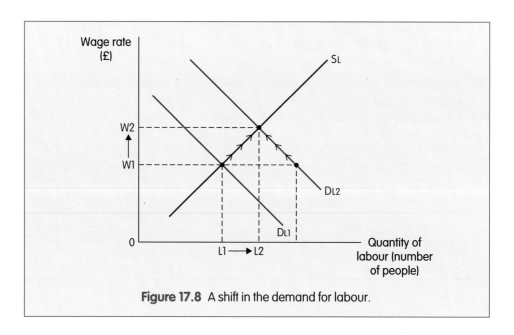

Figure 17.8 A shift in the demand for labour.

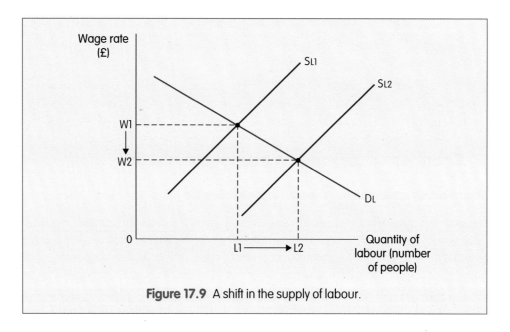

Figure 17.9 A shift in the supply of labour.

income tax rates that makes working more financially rewarding), then this will lead to an excess supply at the old wage rate. This, in turn, will lead to a fall in the wage rate. As this happens, the quantity of labour supplied will fall, whilst the quantity demanded will rise. This will continue until a new equilibrium is reached with a lower wage rate, and a higher number of people employed at the wage W2 and the quantity of labour L2.

Wages in football

Premier League clubs spent 67 per cent of their revenues, or £1.3 billion, on player wages during season 2008–09, according to a report by the accountants Deloitte.

Chelsea topped the wages bill, at £167 million, while Manchester City's wage bill soared from £54 million to £83 million.

Premier League clubs' operating profits fell by more than half to £79 million, their lowest level since 1999–2000, with Germany's *Bundesliga* overtaking it to become the world's most profitable league.

The wages ratio in the Football League was 86 per cent as a whole and 90 per cent in the Championship.

Rank	Club	Wage bill 2008–09 (2007–08)
1	Chelsea	£167m (£172m)
2	Man Utd	£123m (£121m)
3	Liverpool	£107m (£90m)
4	Arsenal	£104m (£101m)
5	Man City	£83m (£54m)

The effects of recession on demand meant that revenue growth at Premier League clubs was restricted to 3 per cent—leaving it just short of the the £2 billion level, at £1.981 million. The result of the high wage levels is that profit margins are very thin or non-existent; with the tightening of credit, that is really making that problem come into sharp focus and those debt levels start to hurt.

Only ten of the 20 top league clubs made an operating profit in 2008–09—one fewer than a year before.

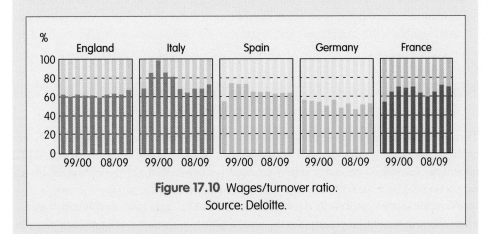
Figure 17.10 Wages/turnover ratio.
Source: Deloitte.

Premier League clubs' net debt at the end of the 2008–09 season had increased to £3.3 billion from £3.2 billion the year before. Almost two-thirds, or more than £1.9 billion, of the total net debt related to Arsenal, Chelsea, Liverpool, and Manchester United.

 Questions

What determines the earnings of an individual footballer?

Do you think that footballers get paid too much?

Wage differentials

If all labour markets were perfectly competitive, then all employees would be paid the same. This is because if the wages were higher in one industry than another, then the employees in the lower-paid industry would move to the higher-paid one, attracted by the greater rewards. This would decrease the supply of labour in the lower-paid sector and bring up the equilibrium wage in that market (see Figure 17.11a), whilst increasing the supply of labour in the highly paid sector and reducing the equilibrium wage in that market (see Figure 17.11b). This process continues until the wages are equal and there is no further incentive to move.

This assumes that:

- the movement of employees between industries is easy (that is, there is no immobility);
- employees are aware of what is being paid elsewhere and want to move to gain the highest possible wage; and
- employees have equal abilities, and there are no barriers to prevent them moving and entering another industry.

In reality, wage differences obviously do exist, for the following reasons.

- Movement between industries is limited by geographical and occupational immobility. For example, there can be significant differences in the workforce in terms of skills and natural abilities; this can prevent employees moving easily from one market to another.
- Jobs differ significantly in terms of working conditions and job satisfaction; this naturally affects people's willingness to do them.
- Ignorance can be a factor, because employees may lack the information about what jobs are available elsewhere and so wage differences may continue.

These reasons mean that some people earn considerably more than others. If, for example, the supply of labour is limited (perhaps because of the need for special skills, talents, or specialized training) and/or demand for labour is high, then the equilibrium wage rate is likely to be high (see Figure 17.12a). If, however, the supply of labour is high (perhaps because it is an unskilled job) and the demand for labour is low (perhaps because it does not generate high revenues for the firm), then the wage rate will be much lower (see Figure 17.12b).

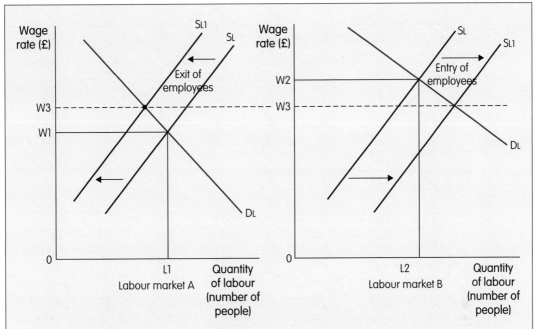

Figure 17.11 Shifts in supply bringing about equilibrium between labour markets. Consider two labour markets that are in equilibrium: market A is in equilibrium at the wage rate W1 and the quantity of labour L1; market B is in equilibrium at the wage rate W2 and the quantity of labour L2. If there was perfect mobility, then employees would leave market A and enter market B, attracted by the higher wages. The supply curve for labour in market A would shift to the left; the supply curve for labour in market B would shift to the right. This process would continue until the wages were equal and there was no further incentive for movement.

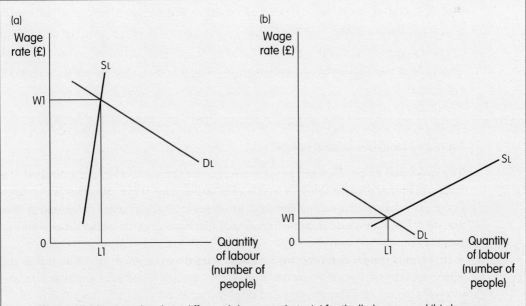

Figure 17.12 Wage levels in different labour markets: (a) football players; and (b) cleaners.

What do you think?

Men and women still tend to follow very different career paths. Approximately 25 per cent of female employees undertake administrative or secretarial work, whilst men are most likely to be managers, senior officials, or in skilled trades. Why do you think this is?

Economics in context

Bankers' earnings

Despite making a loss, the Royal Bank of Scotland (RBS) announced that more than a hundred of its top bankers were awarded bonuses of at least £1 million last year. The bank insisted that its £1.3 billion bonus pool was the lowest it could offer staff even though the bank reported a £3.6 billion loss for last year.

This announcement by the bank, in which the taxpayer has an 84 per cent stake, caused much controversy. The RBS bonus payments equate to an average of £80,000 each for the 16,800 investment banking staff, on top of an average salary of £80,000. Stephen Hester, brought in as chief executive during the October 2008 bailout by the government, waived his bonus for 2009, which could have been as high as £2.4 million.

Hester insisted that RBS needed to pay bonuses to its investment bankers to keep the best staff and to ensure that its shares could eventually be sold at a profit to the taxpayer. He insisted that the bank was paying its bankers less than rivals and made what he described as a 'best guess' that the bank's profits would have increased by up to £1 billion if it had been able to pay bigger bonuses: 'Some of our best-performing people are leaving in their thousands.'

He insisted that the bank was using 27 per cent of its revenue in the investment bank to pay staff—the lowest ratio in the industry. The equivalent ratio at Barclays, which reported record profits of £11.6 billion, was 38 per cent and Hester conceded that the RBS ratio was likely to rise next year.

Source: The *Guardian*, 26 February 2010

 Question

Do you think that Stephen Hester is right to say that paying bonuses to key bank staff is essential?

Monopsony in the labour market

The analysis so far has assumed a competitive labour market in which an individual firm is able to hire as many employees as it wishes at the given wage rate. This is because a firm is so small relative to the industry that however many people it employs, it does not affect the industry demand for labour and therefore does not affect the equilibrium wage rate.

However, in some markets, one or more firms may dominate the recruitment and employment of staff. In this case, the employer has what is called monopsony power, and this will alter the equilibrium wage and employment level.

Imagine that there is one employer in an industry facing an upward-sloping labour supply curve. To employ more, the employer must offer higher wages; the firm is not significant in the industry, so has to offer more to recruit more staff. We assume that this higher wage will have to be offered to the additional employee and all previous employees. The extra cost is therefore higher than is suggested by the supply curve for labour.

Imagine you hire one person for £10 an hour, then increase the wage to £11 to recruit a second. The marginal cost of labour is now the additional £11 plus the £1 to the first employee—that is, the marginal cost is £12. As more employees are recruited, the marginal cost will diverge from the supply curve (which basically shows the average cost of employees—that is, the wage rate paid to each one). This is illustrated in Table 17.1 below.

Table 17.1 Illustration of monopsony in the labour market

Number of employees	Wage rate per hour (£)	Total cost of labour per hour (£)	Marginal cost per hour (£)
1	10	10	–
2	11	22	12
3	12	36	14
4	13	52	16
5	14	70	18

Put into practice

Explain why the marginal cost of the fifth worker in Table 17. above is £18 when the average cost (the wage) is only £14.

A profit-maximizing employer will employ staff up to the level at which the marginal revenue product of labour (MRPL) equals the marginal cost of labour. This is where L1 employees are employed at a wage rate of W1. Employees beyond L1 are not employed because the extra cost (taking account of the fact that wages would have to be increased not only to the additional worker, but all those before) exceeds the value of their additional output.

As we might expect, the effect of monopoly power is to push down wages below the level that they would achieve in the free market (W2); also, fewer people are employed (L1 compared to L2). The shaded area in Figure 17.13 represents the difference between the wage that each worker is receiving and the value of his or her additional output.

If employees were well organized, perhaps in a trade union, they would try to recover some of the area that represents a 'zone of bargaining'. If employees could exert their power and be rewarded fully for the additional revenue that their extra output generates, then each one would be paid a wage suggested by the MRPL curve. Their ability to do this depends on their power, which in turn depends on factors such as the effect of any strike action and how easy it would be to replace them.

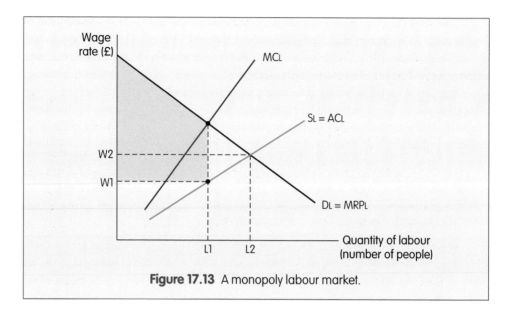

Figure 17.13 A monopoly labour market.

 Economics in context **BAA strike**

Staff at six UK airports owned by BAA recently voted three to one in favour of striking in a dispute over pay. Heathrow, Stansted, Southampton, Glasgow, Edinburgh, and Aberdeen airports would have to close if the strikes were to go ahead, according to BAA, because key staff such as firefighters were due to take part.

The Unite union said it was fighting against a 'measly' pay offer worth up to 1.5 per cent. Of the 3,054 staff who voted, 74.1 per cent had said 'yes' to strike action. A total of 6,185 staff were balloted.

The vote was put to firefighters, security officers, engineers, and workers in various support roles.

❓ Question

What factors do you think will determine whether or not BAA agrees to higher pay demands from the union?

Problems with the marginal revenue product model of wage determination

Whilst using supply and demand analysis in the labour market provides some very useful insights into why certain jobs pay more than others, it does not fully explain wage levels in a mixed economy. This is because of the following reasons.

- In some sectors—particularly the service sector—the actual productivity of an employee cannot easily be measured. What is the productivity of a receptionist, a welfare officer, or a security guard? If it is difficult to measure the marginal revenue product, this may limit the value of demand and supply analysis.

- The output of some employees has no market value—for example, librarians, teachers, and priests—and so their marginal revenue product cannot be valued.

- There are many markets. Whilst the theory of supply and demand may work, actually analysing the determinants of wages can be difficult because there are so many different labour markets. The demand for taxi drivers in London is very different from the demand in Dundee. The supply of motorbike couriers in the south-east of England may be different from the supply in Wales. 'The' labour market is therefore made up of millions of labour markets, each with its own supply and demand conditions.

- In the public sector, the government determines the wage rate rather than market forces (although it is likely to compare public sector pay with private sector pay). In these cases, the wages that are determined by supply and demand will probably influence the wages paid for these jobs, but market analysis does not effectively explain what happens.

▩ Minimum wages

On 1 April 1999, the UK government introduced a national minimum wage (NMW). This set an hourly rate below which employers could not go. There are three rates: a development rate for those under the age of 18; one for employees between the ages of 18 and 21; and one for those aged 22 and over.

The arguments for the NMW are that:

- it ensures a 'living' wage—that is, one that is perceived as fair;

- it should mean that fewer people have to receive benefits and this should help to shift the aggregate supply function in the economy to the right; and

- it should help to reduce the inequality between the low-income and high-income groups.

The arguments against the NMW include that:

- it raises costs and may reduce firms' profits, which may reduce funds for investment (the higher costs may also lead to higher prices for consumers); and

- it creates unemployment by raising the price of labour.

In Figure 17.14, imagine that the labour market is at equilibrium at the wage W0 and the quantity of labour L0. If a minimum wage above equilibrium is introduced, then the quantity of labour supplied is L1, but the quantity demanded is L2. Those who are in work are earning more, but the total number in work is reduced.

The impact of overall earnings depends on the wage elasticity of demand for labour. If demand for labour is wage elastic, then the higher wage leads to a proportionately

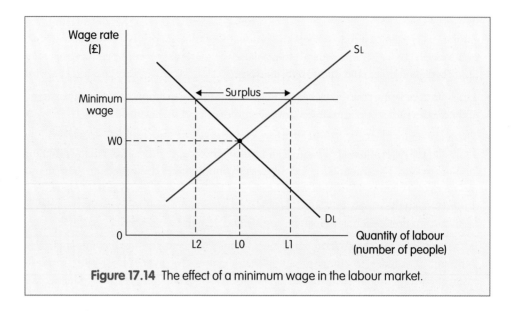

Figure 17.14 The effect of a minimum wage in the labour market.

higher fall in the quantity demanded and overall earnings decrease for those in jobs (see Figure 17.15a). If demand is wage inelastic, then the higher wage leads to a proportionately lower fall in the quantity demanded and overall earnings increase for those in jobs (see Figure 17.15b).

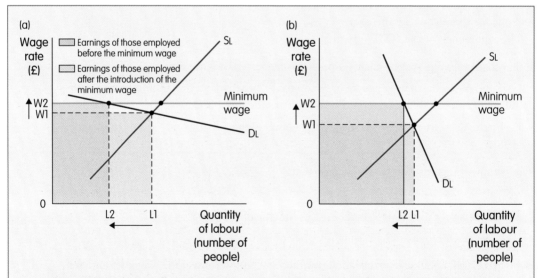

Figure 17.15 (a) The effect of a minimum wage when demand for labour is wage elastic (the introduction of a minimum wage above equilibrium leads to a fall in the overall earnings of those employed); (b) The effect of a minimum wage when demand for labour is wage inelastic (the introduction of a minimum wage above equilibrium increases the earnings of those employed).

Economics
in context Minimum wages

April 2009 was the tenth anniversary of the introduction of the national minimum wage (NMW) in the UK. On 1 April 1999, the adult and youth development rates were introduced for the first time, and this was followed by a rate for 16- and 17-year-olds in 2004.

In 1998, a year before the NMW was introduced, nearly 1.3 million employees (5.6 per cent) were paid below the 1999 NMW rate, while in 2008, there were 288,000 (1.1 per cent) paid below the NMW.

The impact of the NMW in 1999 can clearly be seen with the percentage of employees being paid below it falling from 5.6 per cent to 2.1 per cent in the year of its introduction. There was a further decrease in 2000, after which the percentage has remained broadly the same, at just over 1 per cent.

Although low-pay estimates attempt to measure the number of jobs that are paid below the NMW, it should be noted that the estimates cannot be used as a measure of non-compliance with the legislation. This is because it is not possible to determine from the survey data whether an individual is eligible for the minimum wage. For example, it is not possible to identify people such as apprentices and those undergoing training who are exempt from the minimum wage rate or are entitled to lower rates. If employees receive free accommodation, employers are entitled to offset hourly rates.

 Question

What do you think should determine how high the minimum wage is?

Case study Earnings in the UK

The median[1] weekly pay[2] for full-time employees in the UK in 2005 was £431. For women, it was £372. According to the *Annual Survey of Hours and Earnings* published by the Office for National Statistics (ONS), the top 10 per cent of the earnings distribution earned more than £851 per week, while the bottom 10 per cent earned less than £235. Obviously, earnings varied between regions. Full-time weekly earnings in London were £556, significantly higher than in other regions, where they ranged from £386 in the north-east to £450 in the south-east.

The occupations with the highest earnings in 2005 were 'Health professionals' (median pay of full-time employees of £1,021 a week), followed by 'Corporate managers' (£663), and 'Science and technology professionals' (£633). The lowest paid of all full-time employees were 'Sales occupations', at £245 a week.

[1] The median is the value below which 50 per cent of employees fall.
[2] Pay refers to gross pay (before tax) of full-time employees on adult rates whose pay for the survey week was unaffected by absence; annual and weekly earnings include overtime.

Earnings also differed between the public and private sectors. The monetary difference between the median level of full-time earnings in the public sector (£476 per week in April 2005) and the private sector (£412 per week) has widened over the year to April 2005; in 2004, the figures were £456 and £403, respectively.

? Questions

- Explain the possible reasons for the differences in earnings between regions and between jobs.
- Why do you think earnings differ between the private and public sectors?
- How could a government make earnings more equal? Do you think that it should do this?

Checklist

Now that you have read this chapter, try to answer the following questions.

- ☐ Do you understand that labour is a derived demand?
- ☐ Can you explain the factors that affect the demand and supply of labour?
- ☐ Can you explain the profit-maximizing condition for hiring labour?
- ☐ Can you explain why wages might differ between jobs?

Review questions

1 Why is the demand for labour downward-sloping?
2 To what extent does labour productivity determine the demand for labour?
3 What is the effect on the market wage of an increase in the supply of labour?
4 Why are merchant bankers paid so much in comparison with teachers?
5 Is having a national minimum wage a good thing?

Key learning points

- The demand for labour is derived from the demand for the final product.
- Profit-maximizing firms employ workers up to the point at which the marginal revenue product of labour equals the marginal cost of labour.
- A monopsony occurs when there is a major employer in an industry.

- The wage and employment decisions depend on the nature of the labour market.

- In some markets, productivity may be difficult to measure; in other markets, there is no saleable output.

Learn more

There are many different forms of labour market. In the UK, for example, the National Health Service (NHS) employs a high proportion of doctors and nurses. To learn more about these labour markets, visit the Online Resource Centre.

 Visit our Online Resource Centre at http://www.oxfordtextbooks.co.uk/orc/gillespie_econ2e/ for test questions and further information on topics covered in this chapter.

Macroeconomics

Introduction to macroeconomics

In the previous chapters, we have focused on microeconomic issues. For example, we have examined the demand for labour in a particular industry or the structure of a specific market. In this chapter, we outline the issues involved in macroeconomics. These are then developed in the following chapters.

LEARNING OBJECTIVES

By the end of this chapter, you should be able to:

✔ explain the meaning of macroeconomics;

✔ explain government economic objectives;

✔ explain government policy instruments;

✔ explain the possible conflicts of government economic objectives.

▪ Introduction

In the previous chapters, we have been studying microeconomic issues. We have looked at the demand for and supply of a particular product, and examined the different structures that can exist in various types of market. This form of analysis helps us to explain issues such as:

- why the price of a particular product is high or low;
- why someone working in one industry gets paid more than someone working elsewhere; and
- why firms in some industries can earn more profits than others.

These are all microeconomic issues.

However, we may also want to examine the economy on a larger (or macro) scale. For example, we may be interested in the general price level in an economy rather than the price of one product. We may want to examine the average wage rate in the economy as a whole or the total amount being produced in a country rather than focus on one industry. Macroeconomics tackles all of these issues. Building on the analysis covered in microeconomics, macroeconomics takes more of an overview and focuses on big issues that affect the economy as a whole.

In microeconomics, we developed an understanding of a series of concepts and models, such as supply and demand analysis, and marginal cost and marginal revenue. We were then able to apply this understanding to a range of markets and market structures. We saw how supply and demand conditions affect the price of oil, housing, labour, and concert tickets. Using our economic tools, we could analyse many different markets to understand changes within them. The same is true in macroeconomics.

In the following chapters, we will develop an understanding of many different areas of the economy, such as households, government, and firms. We will put this understanding together to build a model of the economy that includes areas such as the money market, the labour market, the capital goods market, and the market for final goods and services. We will analyse how a change in interest rates, taxation, or government spending affects all of these markets, and we will be able to trace the effect through to the impact on national income, growth, prices, employment, the government's budget, and the trade position. In essence, we will be building a model of the whole economy, and learning how the different elements fit together and interact with each other. The analytical tools that you gain will allow you to analyse any economy in the world and to appreciate some of the fundamental issues within them.

By the end of these chapters on macroeconomics, you should be able to form a view on the policies that any government should consider adopting given the position of its economy. However, you will also come to realize how difficult it is actually trying to control an economy made up of millions of households and firms, all with their own objectives, constraints, expectations, and experiences. Sometimes, policy decisions do not lead to the result that you expected—especially when you are dealing with as many different relationships as there are within any economy.

Of course, economic change has a real impact on people's lives. It affects whether they have a job, what they do, whether they can afford to buy a house, whether they have a good standard of living, and whether they can afford to start a family. Economic analysis is therefore important to governments because they have a responsibility for the state of the economy and are often assessed on their economic performance. In fact, how well the economy is doing is a very important factor in determining how people vote. A government will set objectives and then try to influence the economy to achieve these, using its policy tools.

▩ Government economic objectives

Typical government objectives include achieving the following.

- **Economic growth** Economic growth measures how much the income of an economy is growing over time. This is often seen as a very important target for governments. This is because, with more income in the economy, people can afford more products and may have a better quality of life. Interestingly, however, there is some debate over whether having more money does necessarily lead to a better standard of living (if you work an 80-hour week, you may earn more, but not enjoy life much). This debate is discussed in Chapter 20. Nevertheless, most governments still try to make sure that their economies are growing. Economic growth can provide more income, more jobs, and economic progress.

- **Stable prices** In most economies, prices in general increase by a small percentage each year. For most firms and people, this is not a major problem; they can plan for it and take it into account when setting their own prices or bargaining for their wages. However, sometimes prices can increase at very fast rates. This can become a problem in many ways. For example, some people will find that they cannot afford products and will be worse off, and the country's products are likely to be expensive when they try to sell them abroad, which could limit sales. This is why governments usually try to keep prices relatively stable. An increase in the general price level is known as inflation, and governments usually try to keep this at a low and predictable rate. The causes, consequences, and possible cures of inflation are examined in Chapter 28.

- **Low levels of unemployment** If people are unemployed, then they are not working. This means that they are not generating output and are not earning money. This is a waste of resources and is also a drain on a government's own income, because it will probably have to pay benefits to the unemployed people. Unemployment can also lead to frustration and discontent with the government, and so, not surprisingly, the government will usually try to reduce it! The causes, consequences, and cures of unemployment are examined in Chapter 26.

- **A favourable balance of trade** All countries are involved in trade. They buy goods and services from abroad (these are called imports), and they sell products overseas (these are called exports). The amount that a country buys and sells abroad depends on many factors, such as the relative price of products, their quality, and the incomes in the different countries. As we shall see in Chapter 29, by trading abroad, a country can consume outside its own production possibility frontier (PPF). A government is therefore likely to encourage trade, but may want to make sure that the imports and exports are reasonably balanced. If there are too many imports, then this leads to money leaving the economy; if there are too many exports, then this may mean that foreign governments retaliate because money is flowing out of their economies. Governments will monitor their country's balance of trade and ensure that it is at an appropriate level.

Whilst these are the four main economic objectives that governments have, there will be others. For example, the government may be interested in the distribution of income in its economy and the relative income of different regions.

What do you think?

How well is your economy doing at the moment in terms of the economic objectives above?
Can you think of other economic objectives that a government might set?

Economics in context

Macroeconomic indicators for OECD countries

	Average 1997–2006	2009	2010	2011
Real GDP growth	2.8	−3.3	2.7	2.8
Unemployment rate (as % labour force)	6.5	8.1	8.5	8.2
Inflation	2.8	0.6	1.6	1.3
Government budget position (as % GDP)	−2.1	−7.9	−7.8	−6.7

Source: Based on OECD (2010) *OECD Economic Outlook*, Vol. 2010/1, OECD Publishing.

The Organization for Economic Cooperation and Development (OECD) is an organization of 32 leading economies.

❓ Question

What do you think of the economic performance of the OECD economies in the table above?

What do you think?

Which of the four main objectives outlined above should be the government's priority? Why?

■ Policy instruments

To achieve its objectives, a government may use economic tools such as the following (see Figure 18.1).

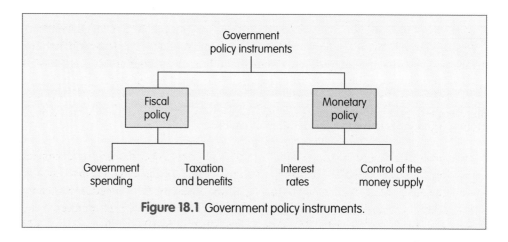

Figure 18.1 Government policy instruments.

- Fiscal policy This involves changing the level of government spending and taxation rates.
- **Monetary policy** This involves controlling the money supply within an economy and changing interest rates.

By changing the different elements of fiscal and monetary policy, the government will try to influence the total level of demand in the economy (this is called aggregate demand) or the total level of supply in the economy (this is called aggregate supply). For example, the government might:

- cut corporation tax, leaving firms with more money to invest (here, fiscal policy is affecting demand in the economy);
- increase its own spending in areas such as health and defence to generate more demand (again, raising demand);
- make it cheaper for people to borrow money by lowering interest rates (this is an example of monetary policy);
- make it cheaper and easier for firms to borrow money to invest in new equipment (again monetary policy); or
- reduce unemployment benefits to encourage more people to work and increase the supply of labour (this is fiscal policy affecting aggregate supply).

Monetary and fiscal policy are examined in more detail in Chapters 27 and 25, respectively.

What do you think?

How important are changes in interest rates to you?

Policy debates

Inevitably, using government policy to affect the economy is quite complex and not a precise science. If we cut income tax, for example, and expect people to spend more, then we may be surprised and find that they decide to save it! Instead, they may spend it much later than we thought they would, so the impact does not occur at the right time. Alternatively, at the time that we cut taxes, other changes in the economy may offset the expected benefits of this. Changes in economic policy can therefore have unpredictable effects.

As well as the practical problems of intervention, economists often differ in their diagnosis of a problem and their views of how best to solve it. Common areas of debate include the following.

- How much should the government intervene in the economy? Can it effectively control the many different aspects of demand and supply, using a range of policy instruments? If so, the government can attempt to 'fine-tune' the economy. Or is it better to use only a few key instruments to try to bring about broad changes in the nature of the economy? In the 1950s and 1960s, there was a belief in the UK that fine-tuning could work. More recently, many economists have favoured a broader, less interventionist approach, but there is still much disagreement about what this means in practice. The recent global economic crisis has also led many economists and politicians to revert to a more interventionist approach to try to stimulate the economy.

- Which policy instruments are the most effective? Is it better to rely mainly on fiscal policy or monetary policy, or are they both as effective as each other? To boost demand in the economy, does a tax cut work better than reducing the cost of borrowing? Again, there is much debate here and views change over time. Generally, in the last decade, the UK government has favoured interest rates as the main policy tool to influence the economy, but obviously continues to use a range of other spending, tax, and benefit programmes to support this. More recently, much greater levels of government spending have been necessary in many economies to boost demand levels.

■ Policy conflicts

Even if it were clear which policy instruments were best, life would still be difficult for governments! This is because achieving all of their economic objectives at the same time may prove problematic. For example, to reduce unemployment, a government may want to encourage more spending in the economy (perhaps through lower taxes and lower interest rates). However, as we saw in our microeconomic analysis, an increase in demand may lead to higher prices, which could cause higher inflation: achieving one target has been at the expense of another. Similarly, if an economy were importing too much, then one possible solution to this would be to slow the economy's growth; with less growth in income, the amount of imported products that people were buying would probably fall. However, the consequence of this would be less demand, as well as more unemployment within the economy. Again, achieving one goal has had a negative effect on others. Of course, by using the right combination of policies, it may be possible to achieve all of the goals—or at least reach an acceptable compromise. However, the government may have to decide what the priority at any moment is and on its general focus in terms of policy instruments.

Case study The UK economy

Overview

The world economy is being buffeted by several shocks. The United Kingdom, like most OECD economies, is in a deep recession (which means that the national income is falling and there is negative growth). House prices are falling after an extended period of large increases which left many households overextended. Financial conditions are tight and the financial market crisis has threatened the stability of the financial system. External conditions are also highly unfavourable. The recovery is likely to be slow, and unemployment is expected to climb significantly. Both monetary and fiscal policies have been changed to cushion the severe downturn with the interest rate now at historically low levels.

The health service

Since 2000, many aspects of the health-care system have been reformed. A large increase in spending has improved outcomes in many respects, but measures of productivity of health-care provision fell up to 2005, although these measures are not yet comprehensive, and other measures of NHS value for money have improved. Reforms need to continue, and indeed accelerate to ensure that the NHS remains sustainable as the growth of spending slows, and in the long term as the population ages.

Financial system

A well-regulated and supervised financial system is necessary to promote long-term growth and macroeconomic stability. During the credit cycle, some UK banks made . . . substantial losses. Stronger banking regulation is required and supervision needs to become more effective. The framework to manage systemic risks needs to be developed further.

Unemployment

The unemployment rate could reach close to 10 per cent by 2010. Over the last few years, with low unemployment levels, spending on active labour market programmes has been comparatively low. As unemployment has risen significantly, the government's further policy initiatives in this area are warranted, particularly those focused on the younger unemployed. The proportion of people on disability pensions remains high. More also needs to be done to promote productivity growth.

Source: CIA Factbook

? Questions

- Summarize the UK economic position in 2010.
- Why do you think house prices were falling?
- How do you think monetary and fiscal policies might be changed in this situation?
- What do you think the possible consequences of high unemployment in the UK might be?
- Why did the health system need reforming?
- Why do you think better regulation of the banks is essential for the UK?
- What is the position of the UK now compared to when this article was written in 2010? What do you think has brought about the changes?

@ Web

For more information from the CIA on economies, visit **http://www.cia.gov/cia/publications/factbook**

Checklist

Now that you have read this chapter, try to answer the following questions.

- ☐ Can you explain the meaning of macroeconomics?
- ☐ Can you explain government economic objectives?
- ☐ Can you explain what is meant by government policy instruments?
- ☐ Can you explain possible conflicts of objectives?

Review questions

1 How does microeconomics differ from macroeconomics?

2 What are the four main economic objectives of a government and why do they matter?

3 Explain how the economic objectives of a government might conflict.

4 Do you think that one economic objective is more important than another?

5 Explain the difference between monetary and fiscal policy.

Key learning points

- Macroeconomic analysis focuses on the economy as a whole rather than one market within it.

- Typical economic objectives include stable prices, economic growth, a favourable trade situation, and low unemployment.

- The government uses policies such as monetary and fiscal policy to achieve its economic objectives.

- Achieving all of the government's objectives simultaneously may be difficult; at times, there may be a conflict of objectives.

Learn more

To learn more about the performance of the UK economy over recent years, visit the Online Resource Centre.

 Visit our Online Resource Centre at http://www.oxfordtextbooks.co.uk/orc/gillespie_econ2e/ for test questions and further information on topics covered in this chapter.

Equilibrium in the economy

In this chapter, we examine how equilibrium in the economy is brought about. To do this, we consider what is known as the circular flow of income and the conditions necessary for equilibrium in the economy. In microeconomics, we examined supply and demand in one particular market. In macroeconomics, we consider the aggregate, or total, supply and demand for the whole economy.

LEARNING OBJECTIVES

By the end of this chapter, you should be able to:

✔ distinguish between injections and withdrawals;

✔ explain the conditions necessary for equilibrium in the economy and how the economy moves toward equilibrium;

✔ explain the factors that can influence aggregate demand;

✔ analyse the multiplier effect caused by a change in aggregate demand;

✔ explain the factors that can influence aggregate supply.

■ Introduction

We will begin our study of macroeconomics by considering how equilibrium in an economy is determined—that is, what determines how much an economy is producing and earning. This analysis will help us to understand macro issues such as economic growth, unemployment, and the impact of government policy changes. Obviously, some economies generate more income than others. The USA, for example, earns much more than Papua New Guinea. This chapter examines the reasons why an economy settles at a particular level of income; with this understanding, we can then consider how a government might increase the income of a country.

Equilibrium in the economy

In microeconomics, we saw that equilibrium in a particular market occurs when demand equals supply. In macroeconomics, equilibrium in the economy as a whole will occur when the total (or 'aggregate') planned demand in the economy for all goods and services equals the total (or 'aggregate') supply of these products. Thus, for equilibrium in the economy, we have:

Aggregate demand (AD) = Aggregate supply (AS)

To analyse how and why equilibrium occurs in an economy, we first consider the circular flow of income, which highlights how spending and income flow around an economy, and how equilibrium is reached.

The circular flow of income

Imagine a simple economy in which there are only firms and households. Firms are producing output. Households are employed by firms and earning income, which is then spent buying goods and services. This is called a two-sector economy because it contains only firms and households. In this scenario, the value of the output produced by producers equals the income earned by households. For example, if the economy produces £100 of goods, then the money for this is earned as income in some form by households (either as wages, rental on land or capital goods, or profit). In the simplest of models, this is then spent on buying the goods and services produced by the firms; this spending is known as consumption spending (C). Money flows around the economy from firms to households, and back again—hence the term 'circular flow' (see Figure 19.1). In this

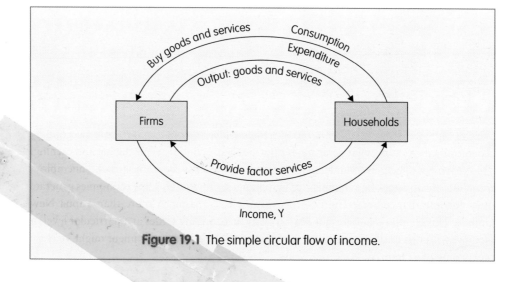

Figure 19.1 The simple circular flow of income.

situation, we can see that the output of the final goods and services, the income earned, and the expenditure are all equal:

Output (Q) = Income (Y) = Expenditure (E)

Of course, this is a very limited model in which there are only two sectors and everything that is produced is sold. What we can now do is to extend the analysis by adding in other sectors of the economy (namely, the foreign sector and the government); this will introduce the concepts of injections and withdrawals into the circular flow of income.

▓ Injections (J)

Injections (J) into the economy represent spending on final goods and services in addition to households' spending. These represent demand for goods and services in addition to consumption spending (C). Injections include the following.

- **Investment (I)** This is spending on capital goods by firms. It includes the purchase of new equipment and machinery, which will be used to produce more in the future. Investment also includes stockbuilding: if stocks increase, then firms are assumed to have invested in these (intentionally or not).

- **Government spending (G)** This is spending by the government on final goods and services, such as health and education.

- **Exports (X)** This represents the spending from abroad on an economy's final goods and services. If UK output is sold to US buyers, for example, this is export demand.

So, in summary, in addition to consumption spending in this economy, we have:

Injections (J) = Investment (I) + Government spending (G) + Exports (X)

All of these injections are assumed to be unrelated to the level of output or income, as shown in Figure 19.2. They are, therefore, exogeneous (or autonomous) of the level of

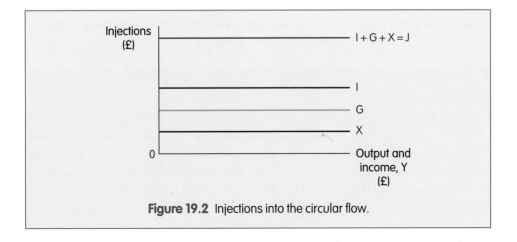

Figure 19.2 Injections into the circular flow.

income. This means that they are determined by factors other than the level of national income; the following are some examples of the influences on these factors.

- The level of investment in an economy (I) may be influenced by the cost of borrowing (interest rates) and expectations of future profits (which may be influenced by how the economy will do in the future), rather than the level of national income at the moment. Cheaper borrowing is likely to encourage more investment as is the expectation of higher profits, perhaps, as an economy recovers. (Investment is examined in greater detail in Chapter 24.) The level of investment depends on the returns that managers think will occur in the future rather than what the level of income is now. The economy may be doing badly, but managers may invest more in facilities and equipment if they think that it will grow quickly in the future.

- The level of government spending on final goods and services in an economy (G) may be influenced by government policy, and its view about the appropriate levels of government intervention and expenditure. A government may decide that it wants to boost demand and increase its spending, or it may decide to reduce demand by cutting its spending; these decisions depend on government policy and may depend on what it thinks is going to happen in the future. There is no definite, predictable relationship between the level of government spending and the current level of national income; the likely position of the economy in the future, rather than where it is now, determines government spending because changes in spending take so long to bring about and take effect. The government spending (G) considered is on final goods and services; it does not include transfer payments (that is, payments such as benefits) because these simply redistribute income rather than create new demand. (Government spending is examined in greater detail in Chapter 25.)

- The level of spending on our exports (X) may be affected by income levels abroad and the exchange rate; it is not determined by the current level of UK income. Just because the UK earns more, for example, does not mean that it exports more; this depends on how much overseas buyers are earning. The influences on a country's level of exports are examined in greater detail in Chapter 29.

Planned injections refer to the amount that the government, firms, and foreigners intend to spend in a given period on final goods and services in an economy. These factors increase the level of aggregate demand in an economy.

What do you think?

On what do you think the government spends money?

What do you think are the main influences on the amount of government spending in an economy?

What do you think would make firms invest more in capital equipment?

Put into practice

Which of the following statements are true and which are false?

a. Injections are determined by the level of national income.

b. An increase in injections increases aggregate demand.

c. Lower interest rates might encourage spending and boost aggregate demand.

d. Higher exports increase injections into the economy.

■ Withdrawals (W)

In a four-sector economy, injections add to the demand of households. However, not all of households' income will be spent on goods and services. This is because of withdrawals. Withdrawals (W) represent income that has been earned by households, but which is not spent on final goods and services in this economy. Withdrawals include the following.

- **Savings (S)** This is income earned by households that is saved rather than spent. People may save by putting money in the bank, for example, or by putting some of their salary into a pension scheme. In general, we would expect more to be saved as income increases. The determinants of consumption and savings are examined in greater detail in Chapter 23.

- **Taxation (T)** This represents revenue taken from firms and households by the government; it is withdrawn from the circular flow and therefore is not spent by them. There are many forms of taxation, such as taxes on income and company profits. Taxation is examined in greater detail in Chapter 25.

- **Imports (M)** This is spending on foreign goods and services. This means that this spending leaves this economy to be spent elsewhere. It is withdrawn from this economy. The influences on a country's level of imports are examined in greater detail in Chapter 29.

So, in summary, we have:

Withdrawals (W) = Savings (S) + Taxation (T) + Imports (M)

Withdrawals are 'leakages' from the economy and reduce the level of demand in the domestic economy.

Unlike injections, withdrawals are assumed to be directly related to income (that is, they are a function of income), as shown in Figure 19.3. This is because, as income increases, the following occurs.

- The level of savings tends to increase because households can afford to save.

- The amount paid in tax will increase—for example, people will earn and spend more, so the government will gain more tax revenue from this.

- The amount spent on foreign goods and services will increase. With more income, households will spend more, and some of this spending will be on foreign goods and services. This spending will therefore leave the UK economy.

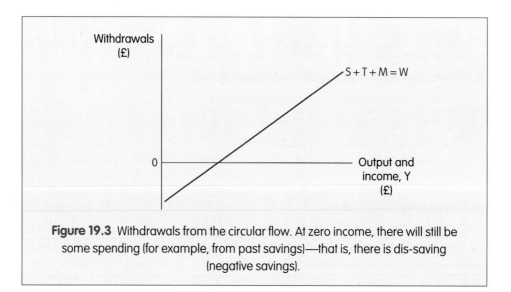

Figure 19.3 Withdrawals from the circular flow. At zero income, there will still be some spending (for example, from past savings)—that is, there is dis-saving (negative savings).

Put into practice

List as many types of tax as you can.

Why do you think all of these taxes exist? For what do they pay?

The circular flow of income including injections and withdrawals is shown in Figure 19.4.

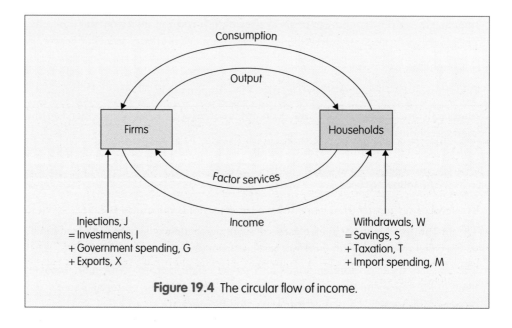

Figure 19.4 The circular flow of income.

Put into practice

Which of the following statements are true and which are false?

a. An increase in withdrawals decreases aggregate demand

b. An increase in savings increases withdrawals

c. An increase in exports increases withdrawals

d. A decrease in taxation reduces withdrawals.

Chinese exports

China's exports jumped by 46 per cent in February 2010 compared with the previous year. The increase was higher than analysts' expectations of a rise of between 35 per cent and 40 per cent. This was helped by the value of the currency, which made Chinese goods relatively cheap. This big rise in exports came despite factories across the country being closed for up to five days over the Chinese New Year.

China's imports also rose strongly, increasing by 44.7 per cent. This was helped by an increase in government spending, some of which was on foreign goods.

The rise in imports reduced China's trade surplus (the value of exports minus the spending on imports) to a one-year low of $7.6 billion (£5 billion) for February.

? Questions

What factors other than the cheap currency might have influenced the increase in China's exports? What else as well as the government spending might have increased imports?

Adding in injections and withdrawals: Planned and actual

Let us now return to our simple economy with output and income of £100, but now assume that planned withdrawals are £40. This means that, of the £100 produced, £40 of this will not be demanded because households are saving, paying this in tax, or spending this money abroad. The economy is clearly not in equilibrium unless there is £40 of planned injection—that is, the £40 worth of products that households do not require are wanted by someone else (for example, the government, firms, or foreigners).

If the planned injections do equal the planned withdrawals, then the £40 worth of products produced, but not bought by domestic households, are bought by another group, such as the government. In this case, the aggregate demand in the economy will equal the aggregate supply and the economy will be in equilibrium. So, for equilibrium in the economy, we have:

Planned injections $(I + G + X)$ = Planned withdrawals $(S + T + M)$

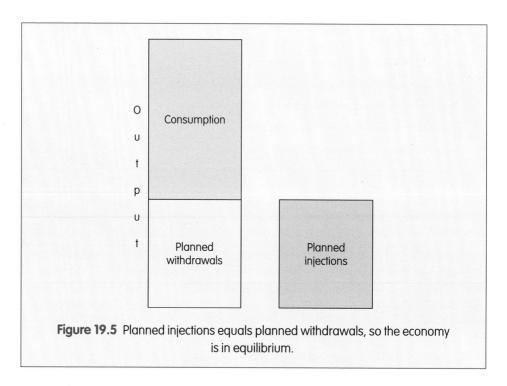

Figure 19.5 Planned injections equals planned withdrawals, so the economy is in equilibrium.

The planned injections equal the planned withdrawals, so all of the output that is not demanded by households is bought by other sectors and the economy is in equilibrium (see Figure 19.5). Aggregate demand equals supply.

NOTE Individual elements of injections and withdrawals do not need to be equal (that is, the planned S does not have to equal the planned I), but the overall planned injections must equal the overall planned withdrawals for equilibrium.

■ Getting to equilibrium: The adjustment process

Imagine that planned injections are too low compared with planned withdrawals. This will mean that there is not enough demand in the economy. The amount that households do not buy is not completely bought by, say, the government or foreigner buyers. Firms will have to increase their stocks unexpectedly because there is unsold output. In the next time period, they will cut back on output, because the demand had been lower than expected; this means that less income is earned in the economy. This will not affect the level of injections because they are assumed to be exogeneous of income. However, with less income, there will be less in planned withdrawals, because savings, taxation, and import spending will fall with less income. This process will continue, with income falling leading to lower planned withdrawals, until the levels of planned injections and planned withdrawals are equal. Changes in output and income therefore lead to a change in the level of the planned withdrawals, until the planned injections and the planned withdrawals are equal, and the economy is in equilibrium, as shown in Figure 19.6.

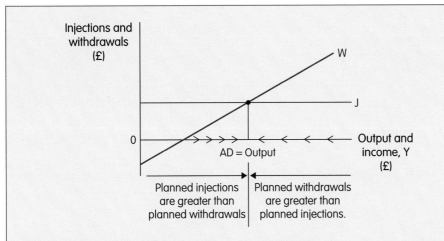

Figure 19.6 Planned injections and planned withdrawals. When planned injections are greater than planned withdrawals, there is too much demand in the economy; firms will increase their output to meet the higher levels of demand. When planned withdrawals are greater than planned injections, there is too little demand in the economy; firms will reduce their output.

On the other hand, if planned injections are too high compared with planned withdrawals, then there will be too much demand in the economy. The demand from the sectors other than households is greater than the output available that is not bought through consumption. Firms will have to de-stock (that is, use up more of their stocks than they intended). In the next time period, they will increase their output because demand was so high, leading to more income in the economy. This will not change the level of injections (because they are exogenous), but will change the level of planned withdrawals. These will increase with more income. This process continues, with firms increasing output, which increases income and therefore withdrawals, until equilibrium is reached where the planned injections and the planned withdrawals are equal.

Equilibrium in the economy is therefore brought about by changes in output and income in the economy until the planned injections equal the planned withdrawals.

Put into practice

- If planned injections are £300 million and planned withdrawals are £100 million, is the economy in equilibrium or not?

- If not, is equilibrium income higher or lower than the present income? Explain your answer.

From this analysis, we can see that if the level of planned injections in an economy increases, then the level of income will increase until the planned injections once again equal the planned withdrawals, as shown in Figure 19.7. At this output, the aggregate demand equals aggregate supply.

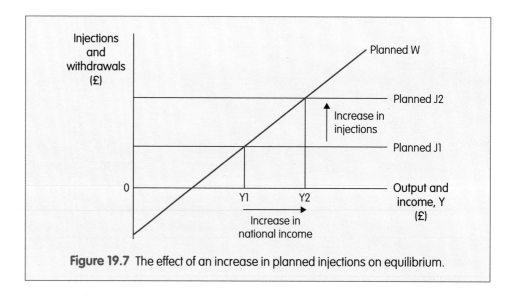

Figure 19.7 The effect of an increase in planned injections on equilibrium.

Government policy that aims to increase national income might therefore focus on increasing planned injections into the economy. For example, the government may do the following:

- offer incentives to encourage firms to expand or undertake more research and development boosting;
- increase its own government spending, perhaps by investing more in education; or
- promote UK goods and services abroad or influence the value of the exchange rate to boost exports.

What do you think?

What type of incentive might a government offer to increase private investment by firms?
What other government actions might encourage investment?

Economics in context   US deficit

In 2010, the US government deficit (that is, the difference between its spending and its revenue) was set to reach $1,350 billion according to US Congress estimates. This was nearly 10 per cent of national income.

❓ Question

Is the effect of a government deficit an injection into or a withdrawal from the economy?

Table 19.1   Changes in injections and withdrawals

Change	Meaning	Effect
An increase in investment	Higher injections	Higher aggregate demand
An increase in exports	Higher injections	Higher aggregate demand
An increase in imports	Higher withdrawals	Lower aggregate demand
An increase in savings	Higher withdrawals	Lower aggregate demand
A decrease in government spending	Lower injections	Lower aggregate demand
A decrease in taxation revenue	Lower withdrawals	Higher aggregate demand

Put into practice

Which of the following statements is true and which are false?

a. For equilibrium in a four-sector economy, savings must equal investment.

b. An increase in exports boosts aggregate demand.

c. An increase in taxation rates reduces aggregate demand.

d. If planned injections are greater than planned withdrawals, national income will fall.

e. If planned injections equal planned withdrawals, the economy is in equilibrium.

f. If aggregate demand increases, national income will increase.

 UK savings ratio

According to the Office for National Statistics (ONS), the UK economy shrank by 1.6 per cent in the last quarter of 2008. That was the biggest fall in gross domestic product (GDP) since 1980. There was also a large jump in the percentage of household income being saved, leading to the highest 'savings ratio' since 2006. The savings ratio increased from a negative number in the first quarter of 2008 to almost 5 per cent by the end of the year, as people saved for hard times. The savings ratio was affected by people borrowing less, and consumers cutting their spending on credit cards and other types of borrowing. A series of interest rate cuts by the Bank of England in the year, taking rates to a record low, had dramatically lowered the cost of some mortgages. Some of the benefits of the lower mortage costs were then being saved.

This was unusual for the UK, where the savings ratio had been falling for many years.

? Questions

Why do you think the UK savings ratio had increased?

What happens to aggregate demand if the savings ratio increases?

▨ The aggregate demand schedule

How an economy reaches equilibrium can also be analysed using aggregate demand and supply schedules.

Aggregate demand (AD) is equal to the total planned demand for final goods and services in an economy, and is written as follows:

$$AD = C + I + G \times X - M$$

where:

- C is the consumption (this is the demand for goods and services by households);
- I is the investment (this is the demand for goods and services by firms);
- G is the government spending on goods and services; and
- X − M equals the exports minus the imports (this represents the overall demand for domestic goods and services resulting from international trade).

In Figure 19.8a, the level of aggregate demand is shown relative to national output and income. The schedule begins at the point F; it is assumed that even if national income were zero, there would still be some spending. For example, households, firms, or the government would use past savings to keep spending. As income increases, the aggregate demand increases, because of greater consumption spending; out of each extra pound earned, households will want to spend a proportion of this on goods and services in this economy.

Equilibrium

Equilibrium occurs when the aggregate demand is exactly equal to the output produced. What is being produced is being demanded, so there is no excess demand or supply. This is shown where the aggregate demand schedule crosses the 45° line (this line represents all of the combinations at which demand equals supply)—that is, the equilibrium national income and output is Y1 (see Figure 19.8a). At this level of output, the planned injections must equal the planned withdrawals (see Figure 19.8b), as shown earlier.

At outputs below Y1, the level of aggregate demand is more than national output. This is because the planned injections are more than the planned withdrawals. Over time, firms will produce more output because of the high level of aggregate demand until Y1 is reached. With the higher levels of output and income, the level of planned withdrawals will increase, and at Y1, they equal the level of planned injections.

At outputs above Y1, the aggregate demand is less than national output. This is because the planned injections are less than the planned withdrawals. Firms will reduce output because demand is too low over time until Y1 is reached. As income falls towards Y1, the level of planned withdrawals falls, until it equals planned injections at Y1 and equilbirum occurs.

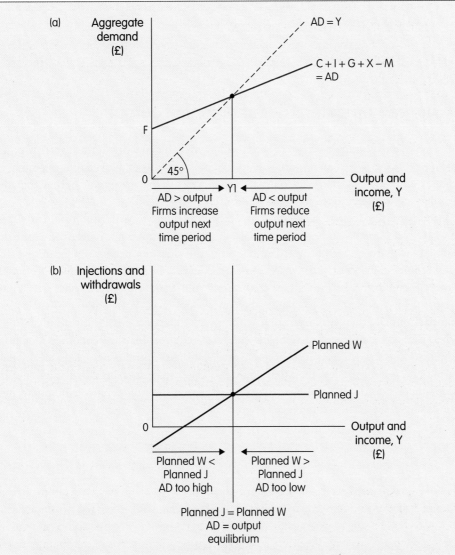

Figure 19.8 Equilibrium output using: (a) aggregate demand analysis; and (b) injections and withdrawals. In (a), the aggregate demand curve slopes upwards because with more income households spend more, and so consumption increases. At zero income, there will still be spending, for example by the government.

Put into practice

Suppose that Y1 is the equilibrium output.

• Below Y1, are the planned injections more or less than the planned withdrawals, or equal to them?

- Above Y1, are the planned injections more or less than the planned withdrawals, or equal to them?

- At Y1, are the planned injections more or less than the planned withdrawals, or equal to them?

Aggregate demand and potential output

Full employment occurs when all of those willing and able to work at the given real wage rate are working. When all resources in an economy are fully employed, it is operating at what is known as its potential output; this represents the maximum output that the economy can produce given its existing resources.

If the aggregate demand schedule is AD1, then the economy is in equilibrium at Y1; in this case, Y1 happens to be the potential output of the economy. However, whilst the economy will always move toward equilibrium, this does not necessarily mean that this equilibrium is always at this level of potential output. In fact, the economy will often settle in equilibrium below its potential output and therefore governments will try to boost the level of demand to change the equilibrium level. If an economy is below its potential output, then it is operating within the production possibility frontier (PPF). When the aggregate demand is below the level required for the economy's potential output, this is known as a recessionary, or deflationary, output gap. This means that output and income are less than they could be. The 'gap' is measured by the amount by which the aggregate demand has to increase to reach the full employment equilibrium (for example, the vertical difference between AD2 and AD1 in Figure 19.9).

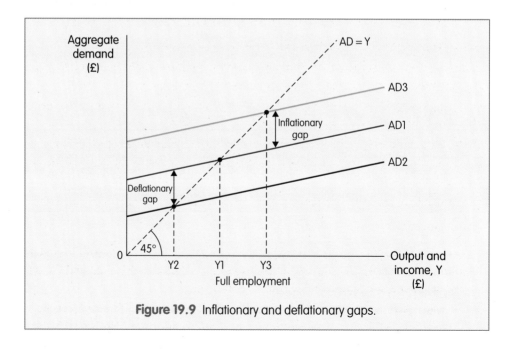

Figure 19.9 Inflationary and deflationary gaps.

An inflationary output gap occurs when the aggregate demand is above the level required for potential output. The 'gap' is measured by the amount by which the aggregate demand has to decrease to reach the potential output (for example, the vertical distance between AD3 and AD1 in Figure 19.9). It is called an inflationary gap because, with excess demand, there will be upward pressure on prices—the economy cannot easily meet this level of demand and so firms are likely to put up prices. If there is a sustained increase in prices, this is known as inflation. The causes and consequences of inflation are examined in greater detail in Chapter 28.

Economics in context   US trade deficit

In 2010, the US trade deficit increased to $42.3 billion due to increased demand for imported cars, computers, and clothing. This means that import spending exceeded export earnings by this amount. The deficit with China alone was $22.3 billion.

? Question

Is the effect of a trade deficit to increase or decrease aggregate demand?

■ Reflationary policies

Reflationary (or expansionist) fiscal policies occur when the government increases the level of aggregate demand in the economy. To do this, a government could use demand-side policies (that is, policies aimed specifically at changing aggregate demand) such as:

- increasing its own spending on goods and services (increasing G);
- reducing taxes to increase the incomes that customers and firms keep rather than give to the government, which should lead to greater spending (increasing C and I);
- reducing taxes placed on goods and services, which should also encourage spending in the economy (increasing C);
- reducing interest rates, which makes borrowing cheaper and therefore should increase spending. It should also discourage savings, because the rewards for doing so are less (increasing C and I); and
- encouraging banks to lend, enabling more borrowing and spending.

An increase in the aggregate demand can be seen by:

- a change in the slope of the aggregate demand schedule—if the rate of income tax were cut, this would mean that more is likely to be spent out of each pound and the AD schedule would pivot upwards (see Figure 19.10); and
- an upward shift of the AD schedule—this occurs if, at every level of income, demand increases perhaps because of an injection of more government spending. As can be seen

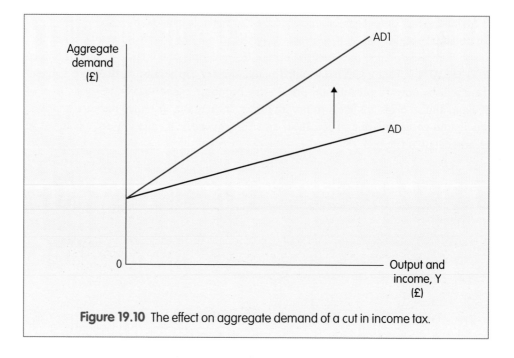

Figure 19.10 The effect on aggregate demand of a cut in income tax.

in Figure 19.11, this leads to a new equilibrium at Y2. The increase in the aggregate demand has led to a greater increase in national income. This is due to the multiplier effect.

Put into practice

Do the following increase or decrease aggregate demand? Explain your answer.

- Higher taxes
- Lower interest rates
- More government spending
- More savings
- More imports
- Fewer exports

▧ The multiplier effect

The multiplier effect explains how an initial increase in the planned injections into the economy increases national income by more than the initial amount of injection. For example, an increase in government spending by £1 million may increase national income

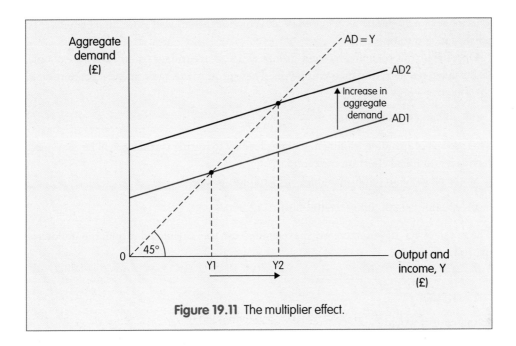

Figure 19.11 The multiplier effect.

by £5 million; in this case, the multiplier is five (5). The size of the multiplier shows how much output in the economy will increase relative to the initial increase in demand.

■ How does the multiplier work?

Imagine that a government decides to spend £1 million on new schools and hospitals. This means that the construction companies and architects involved in these projects will be earning £1 million. A proportion of these earnings will be spent domestically and a proportion will be saved. The amount spent on domestic products will depend on the marginal propensity to consume domestically. The marginal propensity to consume domestically (MPCD) measures the amount of extra income that is spent on domestic goods and services:

$$\text{Marginal propensity to consume domestically} = \frac{\text{Change in consumer spending domestically}}{\text{Change in income}}$$

If the MPCD is 0.8, for example, then out of the extra income of £1 million, the extra spending domestically is £800,000. This £800,000 will be spent on a range of goods and services, such as materials and equipment. This spending will generate income that is earned by subcontractors, employees, and the providers of a range of other services.

These different groups will also spend a proportion of their earnings domestically and save the rest. If the MPCD is 0.8 again, then this will mean that they spend:

$0.8 \times £800,000 = £640,000$

This money might be spent on materials and components, as well as electrical goods, cars, meals out, and so on.

Once again, this spending by some groups will lead to earnings by others—for example, dealerships, retailers, and their employees. These groups will again spend a proportion of their income—in this case:

$$0.8 \times £640,000 = £512,000$$

This process of spending leading to income, leading to further spending, will be continued, having a multiplied effect on the economy.

So the effect of an initial spending of £1 million will be:

$$£1,000,000 + £800,000 + £640,000 + £512,000 + \ldots$$

The total effect of an increase in spending can be calculated using the following expression:

$$\frac{1}{1 - \text{MPCD}}$$

In this case, it would be:

$$\frac{1}{(1 - 0.8)} = \frac{1}{0.2} = 5$$

Thus any initial increase in spending will have five times the effect on the output; the multiplier has a value of 5. Therefore an initial increase in spending of £1 million will lead to an overall increase of £5 million—which is the sum of the series:

$$£1,000,000 + £800,000 + £640,000 + £512,000 + \ldots$$

■ The size of the multiplier

The size of the multiplier depends on the size of the marginal propensity to consume domestically. The higher the marginal propensity to consume domestically, the greater will be the size of the multiplier, because more of consumers' income is spent domestically at each stage of the process. For example, if the MPCD is 0.9, then the size of the multiplier will be:

$$\frac{1}{1 - 0.9} = \frac{1}{0.1} = 10$$

This means that an increase in spending of £1 million will lead to an overall increase in national income of £10 million. This is because, at each stage in the process, a greater proportion of income is spent, leading to a larger overall increase in demand.

A discussion of the determinants of the marginal propensity to consume domestically can be found in Chapter 23.

The impact of a higher marginal propensity to consume on the multiplier can be seen in Figure 19.12.

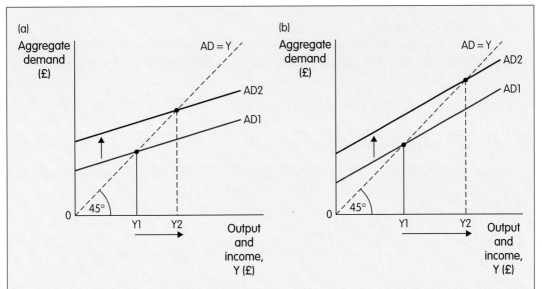

Figure 19.12 The effect of an increase in the aggregate demand when: (a) the marginal propensity to consume is low; and (b) the marginal propensity to consume is high. The aggregate demand schedule in (b) is steeper than in (a) due to the higher marginal propensity to consume; the multiplier effect of a given increase in the aggregate demand is greater in (b).

What do you think?

What do you think influences how much you spend out of each pound that you earn?

Put into practice

- If the proportion of each pound spent in the UK were 0.6, what would the size of the multiplier be?
- What if only 0.5 were spent in the UK out of each pound?

▓ The multiplier in an open economy

A closed economy is a theoretical situation in which there is no trade with other economies—that is, no exports or imports. In an 'open' economy, there is trade between economies. The value of the multiplier will be less in an open economy than in a closed economy. This is because, out of each pound earned, a proportion will be spent on foreign goods and services. Spending will leak out of the economy. Less spending will occur within the economy, reducing the multiplier effect domestically. In a closed economy, by comparison, all of the spending will stay within the economy, thereby increasing the size of the multiplier and boosting the overall effect.

What do you think?

In recent years, there has been more international trade. There are fewer barriers to trade between countries. What effect do you think this has on the size of the multiplier?

Put into practice

What is the impact on the size of the multiplier of each of the following?

- More spending out of each pound on imports
- More saving out of each pound
- A higher rate of income tax

The paradox of thrift

The paradox of thrift highlights the possible consequences of attempts to save more in an economy. Imagine a two-sector economy with only households and firms. For equilibrium, as we know, the planned withdrawals will equal the planned injections. In a two-sector economy, this means:

Planned savings = Planned investment

If households start to save more (to be 'thrifty'), this increases the level of planned withdrawals, which reduces aggregate demand. This leads to a fall in national income and equilibrium will occur once planned savings again equal the planned investment. Assuming that the injections have not changed, this means that households end up saving a bigger proportion of a smaller income and the absolute level of savings would be the same. (Hence the paradox: attempts to save more do not actually lead to more savings.)

Using a simple savings function, imagine that savings are at 0.2 of income and planned investment is £500 million:

$S = 0.2Y$

$I = £500$ million

For equilibrium:

$S = I$

So:

$0.2Y = £500$ million

$$Y = \frac{£500 \text{ million}}{0.2} = £2,500 \text{ million}$$

Say households now save more and the savings function becomes:

$S = 0.5Y$

Then, for equilibrium:

$0.5Y = £500$ million

$$Y = \frac{£500 \text{ million}}{0.5} = £1,000 \text{ million}$$

What we can see is that households are saving a greater proportion of their income (0.5 rather than 0.2), but as a result, income has fallen to such a level (£1,000 million rather than £2,500 million) that the absolute level of savings remains £500 million.

Put into practice

- If planned investment remains at £500 million, but savings increase so that $S = 0.8Y$, what is the equilibrium level of national income?
- What if the savings were to fall to become $S = 0.1Y$?

Case study Japan

From the 1960s onwards, Japan grew extremely quickly and became a major world economic power. Close links between the government and its industry, a strong work ethic, and high levels of investment in high technology gave the country a competitive edge. Japan became the third-largest economy in the world after the USA and China. For three decades, Japan's economic growth has been spectacular: a 10 per cent average in the 1960s; a 5 per cent average in the 1970s; and a 4 per cent average in the 1980s. The UK average for that whole period was around 2–2.5 per cent per year.

However, growth in Japan slowed considerably in the 1990s and averaged just 1.7 per cent. This was partly due to contractionary policies by the government, such as reduced spending and higher taxation. The government was concerned that demand was growing too fast and one problem emerging was too much speculation in property. This was driving up the price of property, and leading to excessive borrowing and spending by firms and households. Unfortunately, intervention by the government led to a collapse in the economy and a loss of confidence. This in turn affected investment and spending levels.

Between 2000 and 2003, the Japanese government tried to revive economic growth, but was largely unsuccessful. Growth was further hampered by the slowing of the US, European, and Asian economies. This meant that Japan could not export as much. Exports are a significant element of Japanese aggregate demand. Also, households and firms seemed to be reluctant to borrow or spend because they were worried about the future. At one point, the government reduced the cost of borrowing to 0 per cent to stimulate spending. Demand was so low in Japan during these years that firms started putting their prices down in order to gain any sales. Prices in general were lower at the end of the year than at the start—an unusual occurrence for most economies.

In 2004 and 2005, growth in the economy did begin to improve. Confidence began to return, stimulating spending and investment. However, the country entered into recession in 2008, with 2009 marking a return to near 0 per cent interest rates. A sharp downturn in business investment and global demand for Japan's exports in late 2008 pushed Japan further into a recession.

Japan's huge government debt, estimated to have reached 192 per cent of GDP in 2009, and an ageing and shrinking population are two major long-run problems.

Source: CIA Factbook

❓ Questions

- Distinguish between injections into, and withdrawals from, an economy. What influences each of these?

- With reference to this case study, how have changes in injections or withdrawals affected the Japanese economy?

- What does the case highlight about the possible role of expectations in an economy?

- Interest rates in Japan have been 0 per cent. Why might this be expected to stimulate spending in an economy? What are the interest rates in your country at the moment?

- What factors do you think will determine how quickly the Japanese economy grows in the future?

Checklist

Now that you have read this chapter, try to answer the following questions.

☐ Can you explain the conditions necessary for equilibrium in the economy?

☐ Can you distinguish between injections and withdrawals?

☐ Can you explain how the economy moves toward equilibrium?

☐ Can you explain the factors that can influence aggregate demand?

☐ Can you analyse the multiplier effect caused by a change in aggregate demand?

☐ Can you explain the factors that influence the size of the multiplier?

Review questions

1 What are the conditions necessary for equilibrium in an economy?

2 What factors might affect the level of injections in an economy?

3 What is the effect of an increase in injections on the level of national income?

4 What factors might lead to a decrease in aggregate demand?

5 What factors would increase the size of the multiplier?

Key learning points

- Equilibrium in an economy occurs when the aggregate demand equals the aggregate supply.

- Equilibrium in an economy occurs when the planned injections equal the planned withdrawals.

- Equilibrium in an economy occurs when Planned $I + G + X$ = Planned $S + T + M$.

- If the planned injections are greater than the planned withdrawals, then there is excess demand in the economy and national income will rise until equilibrium is restored.

- If the planned injections are less than the planned withdrawals, then there is too little demand in the economy and national income will fall until equilibrium is restored.

- The aggregate demand measures the total planned expenditure on final goods and services in an economy, expressed as $C + I + G + X - M$.

- An increase in the aggregate demand can set off the multiplier process, which leads to a greater increase in national income.

- The size of the multiplier depends on the marginal propensity to consume domestically.

- The paradox of thrift means that attempts to save more may lead to a higher proportion of a smaller income being saved rather than a higher level of savings.

Learn more

If you want to learn more about the relationship between injections and withdrawals, and the difference between actual and planned withdrawals, visit the Online Resource Centre.

 Visit our Online Resource Centre at http://www.oxfordtextbooks.co.uk/orc/gillespie_econ2e/ for test questions and further information on topics covered in this chapter.

»20 National income and the standard of living

In the previous chapter, we examined how an economy reached equilibrium. In this chapter, we examine how national income is actually measured and whether it can be used as a good indicator of a country's standard of living. Governments often seek to increase the income per person in their economies; this chapter considers whether or not this is a useful objective.

LEARNING OBJECTIVES

By the end of this chapter, you should be able to:

✔ explain the meaning of national income and how it is measured;

✔ discuss the value of national income as a measure of the standard of living;

✔ explain the Gini coefficient.

■ Introduction

National income measures the value of final goods and services produced in an economy in a given period—usually a year. Final goods and services include all of the intermediate products used in producing them. The final value of a car, for example, includes the value of all of the components and materials used in its production. Measuring the value of final goods and services therefore includes the value of all of the products used to make them. Naturally, there is a large amount of interest in how high the level of national income is in an economy. If national income is high, then this suggests that there will be jobs and that the standard of living in a country will be high, because people will be earning more (assuming we believe that earning more improves our standard of living). On the other hand, a low national income will be associated with poverty and unemployment. In this chapter, we consider how national income is measured and whether it is, in fact, a good measure of the standard of living.

Measuring national income

As we saw in the previous chapter, the value of what has been produced in an economy must have been earned by one or other of the factors of production. If £100 million of output has been produced, then this money has been earned by one of the factors of production such as employees, owners, suppliers or landlords. Therefore we can measure either the value of the output produced or the income earned by the different factors of production. Alternatively, we can measure the amount spent in an economy.

Here, however, we have to make adjustments—for example, if we spend less than is produced, then firms will end up with unexpected stocks; provided that we include this stockbuilding as a form of spending, then the total expenditure will also equal the output, which will also equal the total income.

National income can, therefore, be measured in the following different ways.

- **Output** This can show the value of the output of different sectors of the economy, such as agriculture, manufacturing, and services.

- **Expenditure** This shows the spending by all of the different sectors of the economy, such as households, the government, and foreign buyers, on a country's final goods and services.

- **Income** This represents all of the earnings in the economy—for example, income earned by companies (corporations), employees, and the self-employed.

However national income is measured, it will give the same answer—that is:

Output = Expenditure = Income

Whichever method we choose to measure national income, there are different indicators that we can use, including the following.

- **Gross domestic product (GDP)** This measures the value of final goods and services produced within an economy over a given period—usually a year. It shows how much has been earned within a country's national boundaries.

- Gross national product (GNP) This measures the value of final goods and services earned by a country's national citizens, as opposed to the amount of money earned within a country, over a given time period—usually a year. Some of the income measured by the GDP is earned by overseas producers or individuals who are not based in the UK. This money will leave the UK. At the same time, UK citizens and firms abroad will be earning money there and this will be counted as part of the GNP.

Thus we have:

GNP = GDP

– Income earned by overseas firms and households located within an economy

+ Income earned by the country's households and firms working abroad

This can also be written as:

GNP = GDP + Net property income from abroad

where

Net property income from abroad
= UK earnings abroad – Foreign earnings within the UK

- **Net national product (NNP)** Some of the national income earned in a year is simply spent on replacing the depreciation of assets rather than genuinely adding new output to the economy. If, for example, you are buying equipment to replace old machines that have stopped working, then you are not increasing the productive capacity of the economy. Depreciation refers to the wear and tear of assets.

Thus we have:

Net national product (NNP) = GNP – Depreciation

- **GNP at market prices and factor cost** If we measure the value of spending on final goods and services, then these prices will include taxes placed on them by the government (which increase the price) and government subsidies (which reduce the price). The prices in the market do not therefore reflect the income (or cost) of the factors of production. To measure the value of the output at 'factor cost', you need to adjust the market prices.

Thus we have:

GNP market prices – Indirect taxes + Subsidies = GNP factor cost

---

Economics in context   UK GDP

GDP at 2009 market prices	£m
Household consumption	875,234
Non-profit institutions consumption	35,334
General government spending	327,466
Gross fixed capital formation (investment)	208,499
Change in stocks (investment)	–14,694
Exports	388,838
Imports	421,315

? Questions

What is the major element of spending in the UK?

What do the data above show about the UK trading position?

Economics in context   Data

GDP statistics in the USA are calculated every month of the year on the fifth floor of a modern office building in Washington, DC, where government economists review a large pile of data compiled by the Bureau of Economic Analysis, a part of the US Department of Commerce. For a whole day, the group is placed under 'lockup'. Phones have to be handed in and all Internet access is shut down; those entering and leaving the building are strictly limited. The work involves analysing 10,000 streams of data that describe recent economic activity in the USA. The goal is to arrive at a single figure for GDP. By tradition, no one in the room says the final number aloud—a throwback to the old days, apparently, when there was a fear of hidden microphones.

? Question

Why do you think it is so crucial that the GDP statistics are kept private until the day on which they are supposed to be officially announced each month?

■ Real national income versus nominal

If the income of an economy has increased by, say, 2 per cent, then this is an increase in nominal income, but does not necessarily mean that firms and households are better off. This is because we need to know what is happening to the price level. If prices are growing by 2 per cent as well, then, in real terms, the economy is no better off: the nominal growth in income is cancelled out by the growth in prices. Nominal increases in income simply mean that the absolute number has increased. The real GDP and the real GNP measure the national income taking account of what is happening to prices. They show the purchasing power of a given level of income.

Economics in context   Office for Budget Responsibility

When the new coalition government came to power in the UK in 2010, it created an Office for Budget Responsibility (OBR). The OBR was established as an independent body to ensure that the public sector financial figures are based on reasonable economic assumptions and explain where the numbers come from. It should mean that figures about the economy can be relied on and are not manipulated for political gain. In the words of George Osborne, chancellor of the exchequer:

> We have changed the way Budgets are written, by establishing a new Office for Budget Responsibility, which will stop any chancellor fiddling the figures ever again in our history.

 Question

Why might a government want to manipulate national income statistics?

National income and living standards

The standard of living in an economy is often measured by the real GDP per capita. The GDP is used (rather than the GNP) because it shows the income being earned in a region, regardless of who is earning it.

The real GDP per capita measures the national income per person adjusted for inflation—that is, in real terms, how much individuals earn. A higher average real income per person suggests a higher standard of living because, on average, people have more purchasing power.

The real GDP per capita is defined as:

$$\text{Real GDP per capita} = \frac{\text{Real GDP}}{\text{Population}}$$

However, this measurement simply shows an average figure—for example, £25,000 per person. A more detailed examination of a country's standard of living might consider the distribution of income in an economy. It might be possible to have a relatively high average income per person, for example, but then find that most of the income is being earned by relatively few people, whilst the rest live in poverty.

To analyse the distribution of income in an economy, we can use the Lorenz curve and the Gini coefficient.

The Lorenz curve and the Gini coefficient

The Lorenz curve shows the distribution of income within an economy (see Figure 20.1). The horizontal axis measures the percentage of the population from the poorest to the richest. The vertical axis measures the percentage of national income that they receive.

If income were distributed equally in an economy, then the Lorenz curve would be a straight line: 20 per cent of households would earn 20 per cent of national income; 60 per cent would earn 60 per cent; and so on. This would lead to a 45° line from the origin and this is called the line of absolute equality. In practice, the Lorenz curve will be below the 45° line. This is because the bottom 50 per cent of the population might earn only 20 per cent of the country's income.

The Gini coefficient measures the ratio of the area between the Lorenz curve and the 45° line to the whole area below the 45° line (see Figure 20.1).

If the income is equally distributed, then the Lorenz curve would be the 45° line and so the Gini coefficient would be equal to 0. The more unequal the distribution of

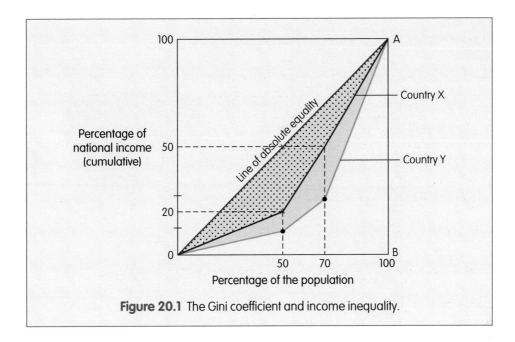

Figure 20.1 The Gini coefficient and income inequality.

income, the larger the Gini coefficient. The largest value that the Gini coefficient can have is one (1).

NOTE The Gini coefficient is sometimes expressed as a percentage between 0 per cent and 100 per cent.

In Figure 20.1, the Gini coefficient would be measured as follows:

$$\text{Gini coefficient} = \frac{\text{Shaded area}}{\text{Area OAB}}$$

From this, we can see that country Y would have a higher Gini coefficient than country X. This is because there is greater inequality: for example, in country X, 70 per cent of the population have 50 per cent of the country's income, whereas in country Y, they have a lower percentage.

Put into practice

If the Gini coefficient is 0.9, does this suggest that income is fairly distributed or not? Explain.

Income inequality: Gini coefficients

Country	1992–2007
Hong Kong, China (SAR)	43.4
Singapore	42.5
USA	40.8
New Zealand	36.2
Italy	36
UK	36
Australia	35.2
Spain	34.7
Greece	34.3
Ireland	34.3
Switzerland	33.7
Belgium	33
France	32.7
Canada	32.6
Netherlands	30.9
Luxembourg	30.8
Austria	29.1
Germany	28.3
Finland	26.9
Norway	25.8
Sweden	25
Japan	24.9
Denmark	24.7

- From the data above, which country has the least and which has the most income inequality? Why might this be?

- What could the government do about this? Do you think it should do something about it?

Economics in context   UK income distribution

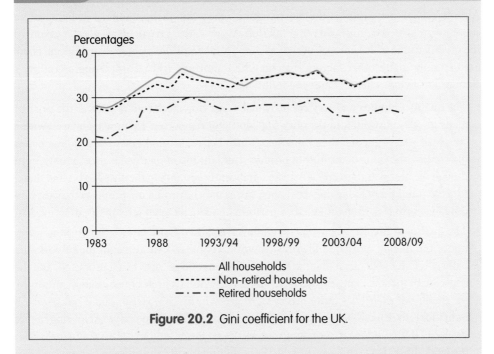

Figure 20.2 Gini coefficient for the UK.

In 2008–09, after direct taxes and cash benefits were taken into account, the level of inequality as measured by the Gini coefficient was 34 per cent for all households in the UK. This figure has remained almost unchanged since 2005–06.

During the past decades, income inequality for all households in the UK increased substantially, from 28 in 1983 to 34 in 2008–09. However, this trend has not been continuous. During the late 1980s and the late 1990s, income inequality increased, while it decreased in the first half of the 1990s, and between 2001–02 and 2005–06. Since 2005–06, the level of inequality was relatively stable.

Changes in inequality can be related to the overall trends in the economy of the country. During periods of economic growth, the Gini coefficient tends to rise, while it falls or grows very slowly during economic recessions. This is due primarily to households at the top of the distribution benefiting more from growths in income from employment and from investments, while households at the bottom of the distribution rely on more stable sources of income, such as benefits and pensions.

Source: Office for National Statistics

 Question

Analyse the reasons why the Gini coefficient tends to increase when the economy is shrinking.

■ Other factors affecting living standards

Although GDP per capita is the most common measure of the standard of living of an economy, many economists do not think that this provides a particularly good measure of the quality of life in economies, even if account is taken of the income distribution. There are certainly many other factors that may be important when considering a country's standard of living. These include the following.

- **The quality of goods and services provided** Over time, technology reduces the price of many goods—just think of the price of a laptop or flat-screen TV now compared with a couple of years ago, and then think how much better the quality is. These falling prices may reduce the value of the output produced and the income earned in an economy, even though the design and functions may be significantly better than they used to be, and therefore the standard of living may be higher. Firms may be producing products that are supposedly worth less, even though they perform at a much higher level than earlier models.

- **The quality of life** In recent years, people have shown more interest in working fewer hours and having more of a life outside work. People talk more about their 'work–life balance'. This could mean that the amount of goods and services being produced, and the consequent income being earned fall, but that individuals prefer this situation and enjoy the quality of their lives more. More GDP growth, by comparison, may put stress on individuals to deliver the required output, and make life less enjoyable. Achieving higher levels of GDP could mean more hours at work and fewer holidays. This could mean that the work–life balance shifts away from the home and toward the office or factory, and that satisfaction falls even if the GDP per person rises. Greater stress leading to more health care may increase incomes, but are we better off? More walking to work may reduce spending on transport, but with a healthier lifestyle and less pollution, are we actually worse off?

- **Non-marketed items** If work is undertaken but not paid for, then it will not be recorded in the official national income statistics. For example, if you hire a plumber, then this work will be paid for and will increase the recorded national income. If, however, you were to do the plumbing work yourself, then it would not be recorded or counted. Changes in the amount of work that people do for themselves will, therefore, distort comparisons of standards of living over time and between countries.

- **The 'black economy'** This refers to all of the work that may be done in an economy but which is not declared because people want to avoid paying tax to the government. By definition, this income cannot be counted officially, even though it may be relatively high—particularly in some countries in which there is a culture of not declaring earnings to the government.

- **Environmental issues** Faster economic growth may be at the expense of damage to the environment. Although we may be richer, we may find that factors such as higher levels of pollution and global warming make growth undesirable.

- **Wealth** Income shows the stream or flow of earnings over a given period—usually a year. Wealth measures the value of all of the assets owned by a country at a given moment. It is known as a stock concept. The income of an economy may be low during a particular year, but because of previous earnings, its wealth may be high. Its citizens may benefit from this stock of assets accumulated in the past. This means that a country may have a lower income, but still have a high standard of living due to past wealth.

Traditionally, governments have been eager to increase the real GDP per person. This has been regarded as an important goal of government and a measure of its success or failure. Nowadays, some people argue that the government should not focus on increasing the real GDP per person, but should look at other targets. Many economists have developed their own measures of economic welfare rather than relied on the GDP per person. For example, Nordhaus and Tobin (1972) have produced a measure called the net economic welfare (NEW). This adjusts the GNP by deducting economic 'bads' (such as pollution), adding the value of non-marketed activities, and including the value of leisure. Similarly, Friends of the Earth suggests that an index of sustainable economic welfare (ISEW) is used instead. This attempts to:

> measure the portion of economic activity which delivers genuine increases in our quality of life— in one sense 'quality' economic activity. For example, it makes a subtraction for air pollution caused by economic activity, and makes an addition to count unpaid household labour—such as cleaning or child-minding. It also covers areas such as income inequality, other environmental damage, and depletion of environmental assets.

Obviously, with these other indicators, there is plenty of room for debate over what to include and the relevant weighting of the different factors.

Recently in the UK, there has also been increasing interest in measuring how happy people are within a country rather than simply measuring their income.

Economics in context — Gross national happiness in Bhutan

The remote Himalayan kingdom of Bhutan is the only country in the world that puts happiness at the centre of government policy. The government must consider every policy for its impact, not only on gross domestic product, but also on 'gross national happiness' (GNH). For example, the capital, Thimpu, has no advertising, because this is felt to promote consumerism. Bhutan has even banned plastic bags and tobacco on the grounds that they make the country less happy.

 Questions

Do you think that a UK government should ban tobacco? Do you think that it would be able to do so?

In 1999, Tony Blair, then UK prime minister, stated:

> Money isn't everything. But in the past governments have seemed to forget this. Success has been measured by economic growth—GDP—alone. Delivering the best possible quality of life for us all means more than concentrating solely on economic growth. That is why sustainable development is such an important part of this government's programme. All this depends on devising new ways of assessing how we are doing.

In 2006, David Cameron, then leader of the Conservative Party and who would go on to become prime minister in 2010, said:

> We should be thinking not just what is good for putting money in people's pockets but what is good for putting joy in people's hearts. When politicians are looking at issues they should be saying to themselves, 'How are we going to try to make sure that we don't just make people better off but we make people happier, we make communities more stable, we make society more cohesive?'

Trying to achieve greater happiness has important implications for government policy. The following are some examples.

- Research suggests that one main reason why higher incomes do not automatically lead to happiness is that we tend to compare ourselves with people who are richer than we are. Therefore, even if we become better off, we do not necessarily get any happier. To produce a happier society, the government would need to reduce the gap between the rich and the poor. It can do this by redistributing wealth from the rich to the poor.

- Advertising may be a major cause of unhappiness because it makes some people feel less well off, and often promotes greed and envy. Perhaps advertising should be controlled to make us feel better.

- Research suggests that happiness is likely to be higher if more people get married and stay married. Marriage is typically so good for your happiness and general well-being that it adds an average of seven years to the life of a man and around four years for a woman. In this case, the government could use the tax and benefit system to make marriage more economically attractive.

What do you think?

Do you think that people are more or less happy than they were 100 years ago? Why?
What do you think influences people's happiness?
To what extent do you think that government policy should aim to increase happiness rather than income?
If you were in government, what laws would you introduce to make people happier?

Case study Human development

Human development is a development paradigm that is about much more than the rise or fall of national incomes. It is about creating an environment in which people can develop their full potential, and lead productive, creative lives in accord with their needs and interests. People are the real wealth of nations. Development is thus about expanding the choices people have to lead lives that they value. And it is thus about much more than economic growth, which is only a means—if a very important one—of enlarging people's choices.

Fundamental to enlarging these choices is building human capabilities—the range of things that people can do or be in life. The most basic capabilities for human development are to lead long and healthy lives, to be knowledgeable, to have access to the resources needed for a decent standard of living, and to be able to participate in the life of the community. Without these, many choices are simply not available and many opportunities in life remain inaccessible.

This way of looking at development, often forgotten in the immediate concern with accumulating commodities and financial wealth, is not new. Philosophers, economists, and political leaders have long emphasized human well-being as the purpose, the end, of development. As Aristotle said in ancient Greece, 'Wealth is evidently not the good we are seeking, for it is merely useful for the sake of something else.'

In seeking that something else, human development shares a common vision with human rights. The goal is human freedom. And in pursuing capabilities, and realizing rights, this freedom is vital. People must be free to exercise their choices, and to participate in decision-making that affects their lives. Human development and human rights are mutually reinforcing, helping to secure the well-being and dignity of all people, building self-respect, and the respect of others.

> The basic purpose of development is to enlarge people's choices. In principle, these choices can be infinite, and can change over time. People often value achievements that do not show up at all, or not immediately, in income or growth figures: greater access to knowledge, better nutrition and health services, more secure livelihoods, security against crime and physical violence, satisfying leisure hours, political and cultural freedoms, and sense of participation in community activities. The objective of development is to create an enabling environment for people to enjoy long, healthy, and creative lives.
>
> Mahbub ul Haq, Founder of the Human Development Report

Source: United Nations Development Programme (2009)

❓ Questions

- Based on the extract above, do you think that natonal income is a useful indicator for governments to use to measure the standard of living or as a goal for economic policy?
- What targets other than national income do you think the government should set to improve human development?
- How well do you think your country does in terms of human development? Why?

Checklist

Now that you have read this chapter, try to answer the following questions.

- ☐ Can you explain the meaning of national income and how it is measured?
- ☐ Can you discuss the value of national income as a measure of the standard of living?
- ☐ Can you explain the Gini coefficient?

Review questions

1 How does income differ from wealth?
2 How does the gross domestic product differ from the gross national product?
3 If the Gini coefficient is close to one (1), is the income distribution fairly equal or not?
4 To what extent do national income figures reflect the standard of living in a country?
5 Should the government focus on increasing the happiness of its people?

Key learning points

• National income can be measured in terms of output, income, or expenditure.
• The gross domestic product (GDP) measures the income generated in a country. The gross national product (GNP) measures the income of a country's citizens.
• Real national income adjusts the nominal income for inflation.
• The standard of living in an economy is often measured by the real national income per person. However, this ignores the distribution of income.
• The Gini coefficient measures how equally income is distributed in an economy.
• The standard of living will depend on many factors apart from income, such as the quality of goods and environmental issues.

References

Gini, C. (1921) 'Measurement of inequality and incomes', *The Economic Journal*, 31(121): 124–6
Nordhaus, W. and Tobin, J. (1972) 'Is growth obsolete?', in National Bureau of Economic Research (ed.) *Economic Growth*, General Series No. 96E, Columbia University Press, New York
United Nations Development Programme (2009) *Human Development Report: Overcoming Barriers: Human Mobility, and Development*, Palgrave Macmillan, New York

Learn more

In this chapter, we have focused on income rather than wealth. To learn more about the difference between these, and for more information on inequality in the UK and other countries, visit the Online Resource Centre.

 Visit our Online Resource Centre at http://www.oxfordtextbooks.co.uk/orc/gillespie_econ2e/ for test questions and further information on topics covered in this chapter.

Economic growth and the economic cycle

In Chapter 19, we explained how an economy moves toward its equilibrium level of income. The level of consumption, and injections and withdrawals in an economy determine whether it ends up in equilibrium. However, this level of national income is not static and will change over time. In fact, a key government economic objective is usually to increase the country's income over time. In this chapter, we examine the causes of economic growth, including productivity, research and development, and entrepreneurship. We also consider the pattern of economic growth over time, which is known as the economic cycle.

LEARNING OBJECTIVES

By the end of this chapter, you should be able to:

✔ outline the key stages and features of the economic cycle;

✔ explain the possible causes of the economic cycle;

✔ understand the meaning and significance of productivity;

✔ understand the meaning and significance of research and development;

✔ understand the meaning and importance of entrepreneurship;

✔ consider the possible problems of economic growth.

▪ Introduction

The level of national income is an important influence on a country's standard of living although, as we saw in the previous unit, it is not its only determinant. Increasing national income and achieving economic growth are a common economic objective.

Economic growth can be measured by an increase in the real output or income of an economy over time. This may be measured in terms of the whole economy, or in terms of output or income per person. Economic growth is usually measured in terms of the percentage change in gross domestic product (GDP) or GDP per capita compared to the year before.

Economic growth creates more income in the economy. This can lead to a higher average income per person (although the income may not actually be distributed equally). This is often linked to a higher standard of living. Greater earnings can contribute to greater welfare and a more content nation.

Remember, however, that a fast rate of growth is often achieved by economies that are industrializing quickly and starting from a relatively low base. More mature economies may have higher incomes per person, but relatively slow economic growth.

▓ Types of growth

When examining economic growth, it is sometimes helpful to distinguish between actual and potential growth.

- **Actual growth** is the rate at which the economy is actually growing. It is measured by the annual percentage increase in national income.

- **Potential growth** measures how much the economy could grow were all of its resources to be employed fully—that is, it represents an increase in the capacity of the economy.

The difference between the two can be seen using a production possibility frontier (PPF). The movement from X to Y represents actual growth in the economy because more is produced; in this case, resources are being used more fully rather than there being increase in capacity (see Figure 21.1a), so this is not an increase in potential output.

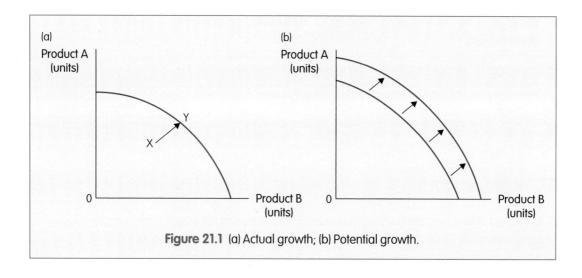

Figure 21.1 (a) Actual growth; (b) Potential growth.

Actual growth may be caused by a boost in aggregate demand or the removal of inefficiencies in the markets for factors of production that make reallocating between industries easier.

Potential growth is shown by an outward shift of the PPF (see Figure 21.1b). This represents potential growth because the economy is increasing what it can produce, whilst still utilizing all of its resources fully. Potential growth may be caused by:

- an increase in resources—for example, a population increase, net migration, and a more skilled workforce would increase the labour input; or

- improvements in technology or the way in which resources are used (for example, better management techniques).

An output gap occurs if there is a difference between an economy's actual and potential output.

- If an economy is operating below its potential output, then there is a negative output gap. The actual output of the economy is below what it could be.

- If the actual output of the economy is above the potential output, then there is a positive output gap. This would occur if firms were operating above their usual capacity levels—perhaps running additional shifts or working additional overtime hours.

Economics in context | **OECD output gap**

	Average 1997–2006	2009	2010	2011
Real GDP growth	2.8	–3.3	2.7	2.8
Output gap (% of potential output)	0.2	–5.1	–3.8	–2.6

Source: Based on OECD (2010) *OECD Economic Outlook*, Vol. 2010/1, OECD Publishing.

? Questions

Why did the real GDP growth become negative in 2009?
How might this affect different groups within the economy?
What is the significance of a positive or negative ouput gap?

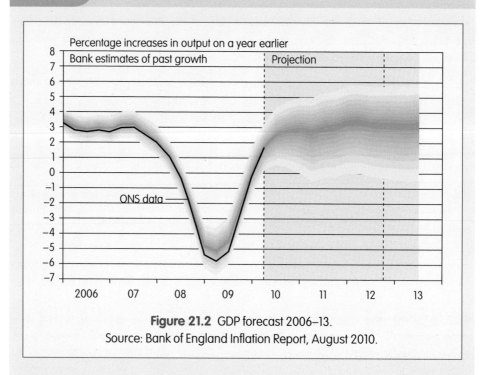

Figure 21.2 GDP forecast 2006–13.
Source: Bank of England Inflation Report, August 2010.

Figure 21.2 above is called a fan diagram and shows the possible growth rates of the UK economy in the future. The darker the shading, the more likely this outcome is.

From the shading, looking back, you can see how close the Bank of England's estimates were compared with what actually happened.

? Questions

Why is there uncertainty about the future growth rate of the UK economy?
Why do these forecasts matter?

■ What can a government do to promote growth?

To promote potential growth (that is, to increase the capacity of the economy), a government could use supply-side policies.

These aim to boost the supply of resources such as labour, capital, land, and entrepreneurship, in the economy and shift the aggregate supply to the right (see Figure 21.3).

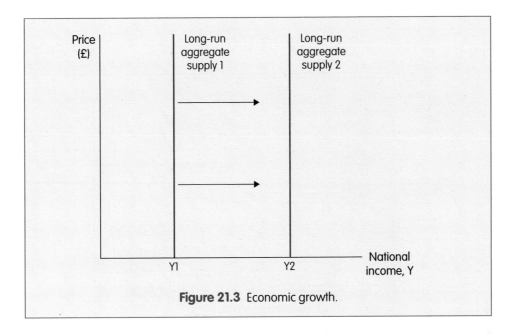

Figure 21.3 Economic growth.

The aggregate supply shows the amount producers are willing and able to produce in an economy. At full employment in an economy, it is perfectly price inelastic. For example, to increase aggregate supply the government might provide tax incentives to encourage more people to work, thereby reducing the number of people in the labour force but not working. Alternatively, it might increase the labour force by increasing the retirement age, or it might provide tax credits or subsidies for investment.

Economics in context Retirement age

In 2010, the French government approved a law that would raise the retirement age from 60 to 62. The Bill ended the right to retire at the age of 60, which had been the case since 1982.

In the UK, the government announced that it wanted to scrap the default retirement age of 65 from October 2011. Previously, a UK employer could force an employee to retire at the age of 65 without paying any financial compensation. The only obligation was to hold a meeting with the member of staff to discuss plans at least six months before his or her 65th birthday.

The UK government hopes that the change will encourage people to work for longer. This could help to reduce the government deficit as more people continue to pay tax. But some employers are worried that it will make managing the workforce more difficult.

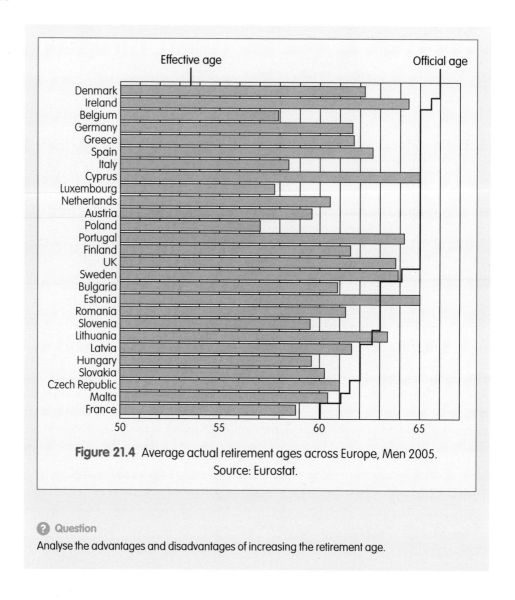

Figure 21.4 Average actual retirement ages across Europe, Men 2005.
Source: Eurostat.

? Question

Analyse the advantages and disadvantages of increasing the retirement age.

What is certainly important in terms of government policy is providing a stable economic environment in which businesses feel confident about investing and households are willing to spend, confident of employment in the fture.

The government might also try to improve the quality of resources. This could be through training, or by encouraging research and development to promote new products and processes. Supply-side policies are examined in more detail in Chapter 22.

Economics in context   Growth

In its first Budget statement, the new coalition government in the UK in 2010 stated:

> If growth is to be balanced and sustainable, it needs to be based on an expansion in the private sector, not the public sector, and UK businesses need an environment which helps them compete in a global marketplace. The measures in this Budget are intended to give businesses the confidence to invest for the long term, and to reduce the burden of tax and regulation. They aim to encourage firms to create new jobs and to help those out of work back into the labour market. Where small businesses continue to have problems accessing finance, measures in this Budget are designed to address this. This Budget also helps to create the right incentives for building a sustainable low-carbon economy, and for attracting private sector investment in the UK's infrastructure. This Budget seeks to make sure that all parts of the UK benefit from sustainable economic growth, especially those regions most dependent on public sector employment.

Source: HM Treasury, Budget 2010

? Questions

What do you think is meant by 'sustainable economic growth'?

Analyse the ways in which the UK government set out to help achieve sustainable growth.

The zero-growth option

Although economic growth can bring benefits for society in that people, on average, have more income, it also brings with it problems, as we saw in our analysis of measuring the standard of living in an economy. For example, it may lead to more stress for individuals, who are pushed to work harder, and may well lead to a worse quality of life. It may also damage the environment and lead to the loss of non-renewable resources, such as oil reserves. Fast growth may mean that these resources will be used up at a faster rate, leaving fewer for future generations. Greater growth may also lead to greater inequality as some people gain more than others, thereby widening the differences between them.

Given that such problems can result from economic growth, some economists have called for a zero-growth policy by major economies. However, this may well be too extreme a solution; typically, economists would want a marginal solution. The best level of growth would be where the social marginal benefit of growth equals the social marginal cost. The problem lies in fully identifying and measuring the social costs and benefits.

What do you think?

Do you think that zero growth is an option?

▪ The economic cycle

The economic cycle shows the pattern of economic growth that tends to occur in economies over time. Whilst there may be an underlying steady long-run trend, most economies experience an economic cycle that is measured by changes in national income. Over time, the stages through which economies typically go are growth, boom, recession, and slump, as shown in Figure 21.5. Whilst increasing national income is often an aim of government, so is stabilizing its growth path. Instability and uncertainty tend to make planning difficult and to deter investment. Firms may become wary of investing if they are not sure whether an economy is going to be doing well or not. Similarly, households may save more if there is greater uncertainty. If a government can provide stability, then it can actually help the economy to grow faster in the long run.

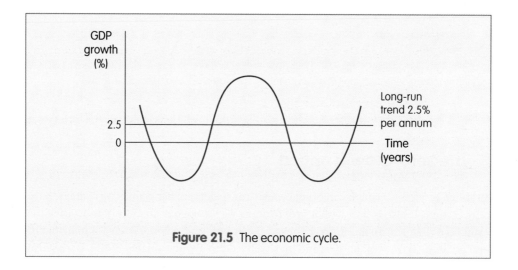

Figure 21.5 The economic cycle.

▪ The stages of the economic cycle

The four main stages of the economic cycle are as follows.

- **A boom** A boom is characterized by high rates of economic growth. The GDP will be growing relatively quickly. This should lead to relatively low levels of unemployment. Firms will have busy order books and may have to turn business away because they cannot keep up with demand. Prices may begin to rise due to demand growing so quickly that output cannot keep pace.

Economics in context Marriage and national income

In the late 1990s, the proportion of marriages ending in divorce within four years fell to around 90 per 1,000. This might have been due to a change in morals and values, but was more likely due to a booming economy. Recessions put strain on marriages, because couples find it hard to cope financially; in a boom, relationships tend to be better, so the number of divorces is lower. Also, in a boom, property prices tend to rise, making it more difficult to be able to afford to separate and have to two houses.

 Questions

What types of product are likely to experience most growth in a boom?

Are these products income elastic or income inelastic?

- **A recession (or downswing)** A recession occurs when there is a period of two successive quarters of negative economic growth. This means that the economy is shrinking. The GDP is growing at a negative rate.

  A recession is usually characterized by:
  - increasing levels of unemployment;
  - low levels of profits, reducing the amount of internal funds available for investment;
  - unused capacity;
  - downward pressure on prices to try to stimulate demand;
  - less income, leading to less demand in the economy and equally less spending on imports;
  - more business closures;
  - less tax revenue for the government (because fewer people are earning and fewer products are being sold). At the same time, the government is likely to be paying more in subsidies and benefits, so overall, the government's financial position will be weakened and this may require more government borrowing.

- **A recovery (or upswing, or upturn)** In the recovery phase, demand begins to pick up, reducing firms' excess capacity and improving employment levels. With more demand for products, the demand for factors of production increases, which begins to pull up prices and wages. Machinery begins to be replaced or updated, and business confidence picks up, leading to more investment.

- **A slump (or depression)** In a slump, economic growth is slow and unemployment is high. There is downward pressure on prices (deflation) and profits, and business confidence is low. The point at which the slump flattens out is called the 'lower turning point' of the economic cycle. The 'upper turning point' is in the boom.

Whilst this general pattern of growth outlined in the economic cycle may typically be followed, there will be differences over time in:

- for how long each stage lasts; and
- how large each stage is—for example, how big the slump or boom is.

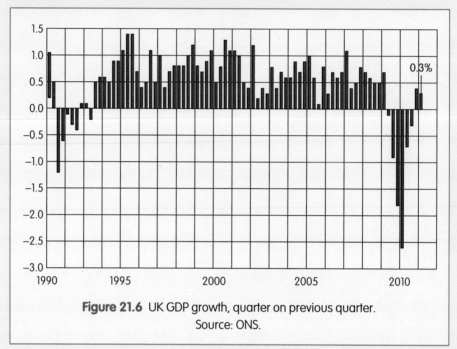

Figure 21.6 UK GDP growth, quarter on previous quarter.
Source: ONS.

? Questions

In 2009, the UK was in recession, as were many other economies around the world. Discuss the possible reasons why this might have happened.

Discuss the possible effects of a recession on firms, households, and governments.

During his Labour Party conference speech in 2000, Gordon Brown said: 'We will not put hard-won economic stability at risk. No return to short-termism. No return to Tory boom and bust.' He went on to argue: 'Why did the Tory Party give Britain 20 years of stop–go, 20 years of boom and bust? It is Labour that is now the party for stability and growth.' How successful was he in upholding this statement?

In fact, different economists have identified several different economic cycles. These include the following.

- **The classical trade cycle** This describes a pattern of boom and slump in which there is often around eight to ten years between one boom and another.
- **The Kuznets cycle** This is named after Simon Kuznets, a Nobel prizewinner, who identified a cycle of activity in the construction industry that took between 15 and 25 years.

- **The Kondratieff cycle** This highlighted that, as well as a ten-year cycle, there was a major underlying cycle that takes 50 to 60 years to complete—that is, that there can be cycles within cycles.

What do you think?

How might different stages of the economic cycle affect a firm's marketing decisions?

What causes the economic cycle?

The causes of the economic cycle include the following.

- **Expectations** Changes in the expectations of firms and households can have a major effect on the state of the economy. If an economy is growing relatively fast and confidence is high, then firms may be more likely to invest, because they are more optimistic about future levels of demand. Households are more likely to spend because they are more confident about their employment and earning prospects. If expectations are positive, then this is likely to generate greater spending by firms and households, and this helps to stimulate further growth in the economy. However, at some point, households and firms may decide that growth cannot continue and may become more pessimistic. As this happens, spending falls, bringing about a recession. Changes in expectations may cause, or certainly exaggerate, the underlying economic cycle.

What do you think?

If you were in government, how could you influence people's expectations about the economy?

- **Stock levels** Stocks include raw materials, components, semi-finished goods, and finished goods waiting to be sold. They are also called inventory. Changes in stock levels can affect demand in the economy. When an economy starts to grow faster, managers may be reluctant to increase output in the short term in case the boom does not last. They will not want to invest and employ more people only to find that demand falls again. They are more likely to keep production at the same level as before and run down their stock levels. However, if demand does keep growing, then firms will now have too few stocks and managers will have to expand production. They may need to increase their production capacity, not only to meet the new higher level of demand, but also to replace the stocks that will have been run down. This leads to a relatively high increase in spending, which leads to even faster growth in the economy. This can create a boom in the economy.

Once demand starts to grow more slowly, managers are likely to be reluctant to reduce their production levels immediately, because it may be only a temporary decline. Rather than make people redundant and reduce capacity, firms are likely to maintain the existing output level in the short term. Given that demand is lower, producing at the old level leads to increasing levels of stocks. However, if demand continues to be low, then, in the long run, managers will cut back output. Because they have been building up stocks, they can now reduce output significantly. This leads to a large fall in demand for resources and may push the economy into a recession.

The sluggishness of managers to react to changes in demand therefore exaggerates the changes in demand, and creates booms and slumps.

Economics in context **Flexible production**

A business trend in the last 20 years has been to make production more flexible so that firms can respond more quickly to changes in demand and can hold less stock at any moment. The aim is to get demand to match supply as instantly as possible, so that producers produce 'just in time'. Toyota is famous for its just-in-time approach: it only ever starts making a car when an order is there. Zara, the fashion retailer, also produces just in time, which means that it holds much less stock of any one item. It works closely with suppliers so that it can increase the number that it has of any product very quickly. However, by working just in time, it does not get caught with large levels of unsold stock and can change its product range very rapidly.

 Questions

How can a firm make its production more flexible so that it can adjust quickly to demand changes? What do you think are the advantages and possible disadvantages of producing just in time? What problems might there be in introducing this approach?

- **Government policy** Governments will often intervene to try to stabilize the economy. However, policies that are intended to stabilize the economy can actually end up de-stabilizing it! This is because it is difficult for the government to fine-tune the economy effectively and attempts to do so may make things worse. One reason for this is that the information that the government uses to make decisions is inevitably out of date. By the time the government has determined what it thinks the level of national income actually is, the economy will have moved on. Policies intended to correct a particular problem may therefore not be relevant because the economic situation has changed.

  This problem is made worse because economic policy changes take time to work through the economy and the effects are not always predictable. For example, a tax cut may not lead to an increase in spending if households decide to save the extra dispos-able income.

  Imagine that the government thinks that the economy is at the point X in Figure 21.7 and therefore needs a boost in aggregate demand. It might then introduce reflationary

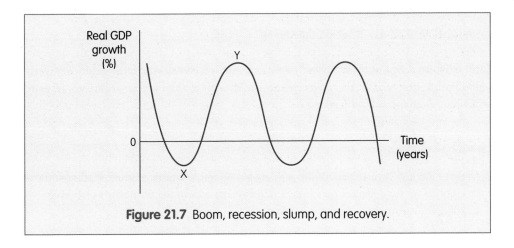

Figure 21.7 Boom, recession, slump, and recovery.

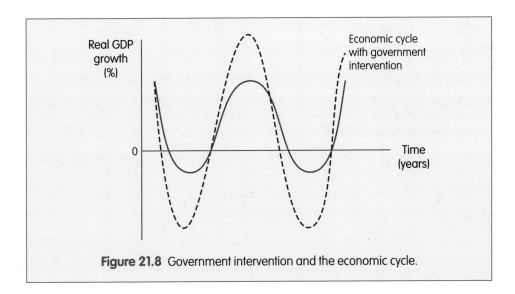

Figure 21.8 Government intervention and the economic cycle.

policies. However, by the time the policies begin to have an effect, the economy may be at the point Y, in which case, the boost to aggregate demand leads to too much demand in the economy, causing excessive growth and then demand-pull inflation. Government attempts to reduce fluctuations in demand may therefore end up exaggerating them (see Figure 21.8).

Put into practice

If the government were to think that the economy was in a recession, what type of policies would it adopt?

▤ Indicators of the economic cycle

As we have seen, one of the problems of government intervention is the difficulty of knowing when to intervene. If the government gets it wrong, then intervention can actually make the economic situation worse.

Leading indicators

To help to identify how the economy is going to change, analysts examine leading indicators; changes in these factors may indicate future changes in the economy as a whole.
Leading indicators include the following.

* **Consumer confidence surveys** If consumers become more confident, then they are more likely to spend in the future.
* **New car registrations** This is often an indicator of confidence, because new cars are a significant expenditure.
* **Recruitment advertising** An increase in the number of jobs being advertised highlights that firms are feeling positive and are looking to expand.
* **Mortgage applications** Mortgages are loans that households take out to buy a house. If the number of applications for these increases, then this, again, reveals something about the confidence of households.
* **Share prices** An increase in share prices suggests that there is more demand to own companies. This suggests that investors believe that demand is going to be high in the future.

Coincident indicators

Coincident indicators are indicators that happen as the cycle occurs—for example, changes in the real GDP and retail sales.

Lagging indicators

Lagging indicators are indicators that alter after changes in the economic cycle. For example, unemployment tends to lag behind the cycle. When a recession starts, firms are often reluctant to let staff go in case they need to rehire them; it takes time for firms to decide to make redundancies, so the number of job losses lags behind changes in the economic position.

Put into practice

Can you think of any more possible leading, coincident, or lagging indicators?

Case study Iceland

In 2008, many economies started to shrink in size. Iceland was particularly badly affected and even two years later was having to cope with high rates of unemployment. The country's banking sector had been involved in high-risk lending, and several banks had to close when individuals and firms were unable to repay them. As a result, there had been a loss of jobs, followed by a credit crunch when households and firms could not borrow easily. The uncertainty about the economy also deterred spending and investment. In 2009, there were 2,000 people unemployed in the country. A year later, there were 16,000. For most of the last 20 years, unemployment had been around 1 per cent of the labour force; now it was nearer 8 per cent. The government admitted that it had not expected this increase and did not have the services in place for unemployment on this scale. The Red Cross, a charity, had to step in to help—for example, offering counselling.

The country was also burdened with high levels of debt to countries such as the UK and the Netherlands, which had provided support in the middle of the crisis. The amount owed was the equivalent of £10,000 for every Icelandic taxpayer.

However, indicators suggested that a recovery was on its way and that the worst might be over.

? Questions

- Which stage of the economic cycle was the Icelandic economy in during 2010?
- Discuss the social consequences of the economy being in this position.
- What might have caused the high levels of unemployment in the economy?
- 'Indicators suggested that a recovery was on its way and that the worst might be over.' What indicators might suggest a recovery was on its way?
- What actions do you think a government might take to help the economy recover?
- At what stage of the economic cycle is your economy at the moment? Explain your reasoning.

Checklist

Now that you have read this chapter, try to answer the following questions.

- ☐ Do you understand the difference between actual ouput and potential output?
- ☐ Do you understand what is meant by an output gap?
- ☐ Can you outline the key stages and features of the economic cycle?
- ☐ Can you explain the possible causes of the economic cycle?
- ☐ Can you consider the possible problems of economic growth?

Review questions

1 What is the economic cycle?

2 What is the difference between actual and potential growth?

3 What is the difference between a boom and a recession? How might these stages affect a firm?

4 How can a government promote faster economic growth?

5 What might cause the economic cycle?

Key learning points

- National income growth does not follow a steady path, but tends to occur in cycles.

- The government often intervenes to stabilize growth in the economy, but mistimed intervention can create further instability.

- Leading indicators may be useful to identify future changes in the economy.

- Growth may bring a higher average income per person, but this does not necessarily mean that the quality of life is better or that growth is desirable.

- Growth in an economy occurs when income increases. This may lead to a higher standard of living, but there are many other factors that have to be considered to assess the quality of life.

- Potential growth in an economy can be shown by an outward shift of its production possibility frontier.

Learn more

To learn more about the economic cycle and economic growth in the UK over the last 20 years, visit the Online Resource Centre.

 Visit our Online Resource Centre at http://www.oxfordtextbooks.co.uk/orc/gillespie_econ2e/ for test questions and further information on topics covered in this chapter.

Aggregate demand, aggregate supply, and the price level

In this chapter, we examine the interrelationship of aggregate supply and aggregate demand in the economy. Using supply and demand analysis, we can examine the impact of changes in the aggregate demand and the aggregate supply, and consider the consequences of this in terms of the equilibrium price and output, and employment.

LEARNING OBJECTIVES

By the end of this chapter, you should be able to:

✔ explain the shape of the aggregate demand curve relative to price;

✔ explain the shape of the aggregate supply curve relative to price;

✔ explain equilibrium in the economy in terms of aggregate supply and aggregate demand;

✔ examine the effect of changes in the aggregate supply and the aggregate demand in terms of price and output outcomes.

■ Introduction

In our earlier analysis of aggregate demand in Chapter 19, we focused purely on the impact of changes in demand on output levels. For example, investigating the change in the aggregate demand using 45° diagrams simply showed the effect of demand changes on output; we did not consider the price level in any detail. In reality, any change in demand affects both output and prices. We now look at both aggregate supply and aggregate demand in the economy, and include changes in price in the analysis.

■ Aggregate demand

The aggregate demand is the quantity of final goods and services that individuals and organizations in an economy are willing and able to buy at each and every price, all other things being unchanged. It is the total level of desired spending by households, firms, governments, and overseas buyers.

The aggregate demand curve is downward-sloping relative to price, meaning that more products are demanded in the economy as the price falls (see Figure 22.1). This is due to the following reasons.

- **The income effect** When the price level falls, this increases the real wealth of households. With lower prices, households and firms have more purchasing power, and can buy more. Therefore the quantity demanded increases.

- **The substitution effect** When the UK price level falls, there is a substitution effect. With lower prices, individuals and organizations are more likely to buy UK products than foreign products, thereby increasing the quantity demanded domestically.

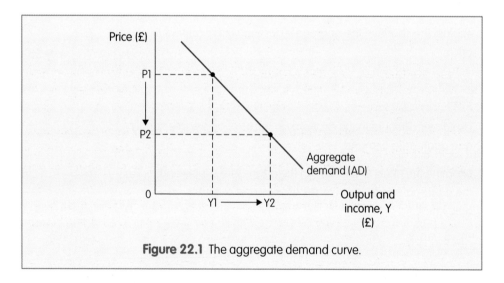

Figure 22.1 The aggregate demand curve.

The level of aggregate demand at any price will depend on factors such as:

- households' incomes—all thing being equal, customers will usually spend more if their incomes are higher;

- households' and firms' expectations (which will affect their spending)—if households are confident that they will keep their jobs, and even anticipate a promotion or pay increase, they may spend more now; similarly, expectations affect levels of investment by firms;

- government spending—this is an injection into the economy and an expansionary government programme can boost demand; and

- the level of spending on exports and imports—an increase in demand for exports will increase demand, whilst more spending on imports should reduce it.

Changes in these factors will change the level of injections into an economy and shift the aggregate demand curve; more or less will be demanded at each and every price.

Put into practice

Which of the following would increase aggregate demand? Explain your answers.

- An increase in investment
- A decrease in government spending
- A decrease in spending on exports
- A fall in import spending
- An increase in taxation rates
- A fall in the amount saved out of each extra pound

▪ Aggregate supply

The aggregate supply is the quantity of final goods and services that firms in an economy are willing and able to produce at each and every price, all other things being unchanged. The level of aggregate supply will depend on the following.

- **The price level** The amount supplied should increase if the price increases, because firms can afford to use less efficient methods of production and to pay more for resources. The effect of a change in the price level on supply in an economy is shown as a movement along the supply curve.

- **The level of technology and innovation in an economy** Improvements in technology may enable more to be produced at each price. This causes an outward shift in aggregate supply.

- **The size of the labour force and its skills** A better-trained and larger workforce should be able to produce more than a smaller, unskilled workforce. Immigration into an economy could increase the labour force, as could changes in the working age and retirement age.

- **The amount and state of capital equipment** The amount and quality of machinery, plant, and equipment will clearly influence the amount that can be produced at any moment.

- **The skill of management to combine resources and use them effectively**

- **The degree of entrepreneurship in an economy** This will influence the amount and quality of innovation, generating new ways of doing things and greater efficiency.

An increase in price leads to a movement along the short-run aggregate supply curve. A higher price means that firms can afford to produce more and can cover their costs. This means that the aggregate supply curve will slope upwards, as shown in Figure 22.2.

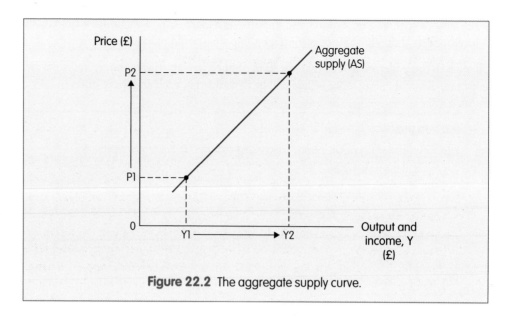

Figure 22.2 The aggregate supply curve.

A change in the other factors will shift the aggregate supply curve; with a larger or a better-trained workforce, for example, the aggregate supply curve will shift to the right (see Figure 22.3)—more will be supplied at each price. This is known as an increase in supply.

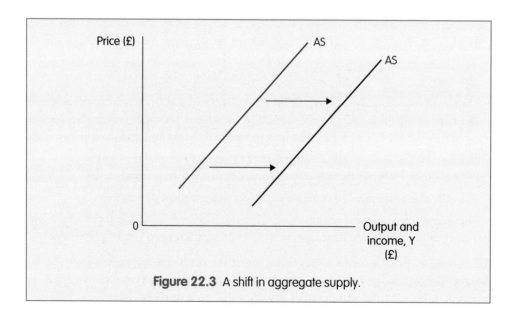

Figure 22.3 A shift in aggregate supply.

Put into practice

What factors would shift the aggregate supply curve to the left?

Equilibrium in the economy

Equilibrium in the economy will occur at the price and output for which the aggregate demand equals the aggregate supply. This occurs at the price P1 and output Y1 in Figure 22.4. If the price were higher than this, then there would be excess supply, driving the price down to an equilibrium solution at P1. If the price were below this, then there would be excess demand, pulling the price up until equilibrium is reached at P1. Just as we saw in our microeconomic analysis, the price changes to equate supply and demand. The difference here is that we are dealing with the aggregate supply, the aggregate demand, and the general price level for the economy as a whole, rather than the supply, demand, and price level in one specific market (Figure 22.4).

As in our micro equilibrium analysis, we can see that an increase in demand leads to a higher price and quantity in the market, whilst a fall in demand leads to a lower price and output in the short run (Figure 22.5).

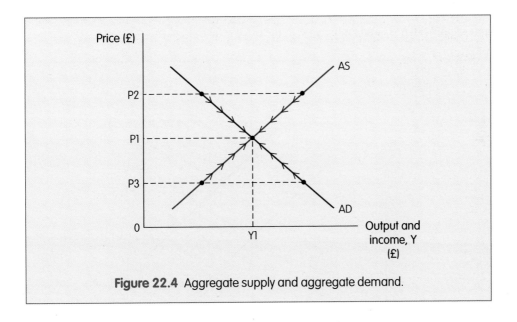

Figure 22.4 Aggregate supply and aggregate demand.

The short-run and long-run aggregate supply curve

In the short run, we assume that wages are fixed in an economy. In the long run, we assume that wages are flexible, although there is considerable debate amongst economists

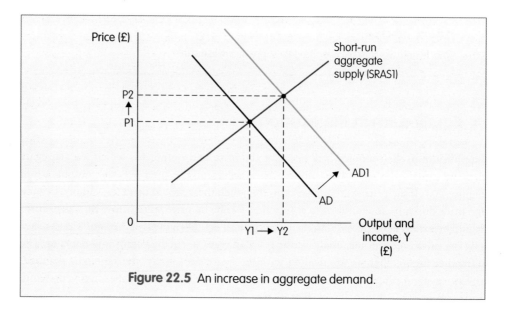

Figure 22.5 An increase in aggregate demand.

about how long the long run actually is. The importance of wage flexibility can be seen in the analysis below.

Imagine that an economy is at long-run equilibrium at P1Y1 in Figure 22.6. An increase in aggregate demand in the short run will lead to a movement along the short-run aggregate supply (SRAS1) and an increase in the price level to P2Y2.

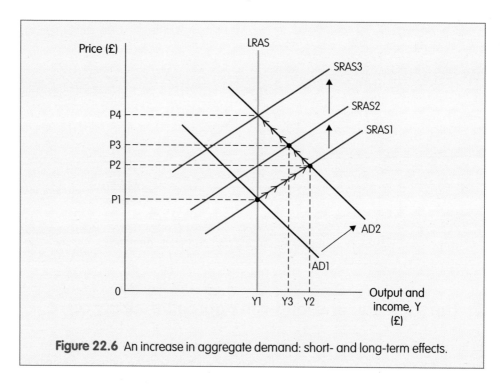

Figure 22.6 An increase in aggregate demand: short- and long-term effects.

In the short run, wages are assumed to be fixed—possibly because employees are locked into contracts and/or because they do not immediately notice that prices have gone up. Most of us buy a relatively limited range of goods and so do not necessarily appreciate the overall rate of inflation immediately. This means that we may suffer from money illusion—that is, we may not realize what inflation rates actually are. If prices are higher, but money (or nominal) wages are not, then, in real terms, employees are cheaper (so more are hired)—which is one reason why more products can be supplied.

Over time, however, employees will notice the higher prices and demand higher wages; wages will be pulled up by the increased demand for labour and the higher price level as contracts are renegotiated. This will increase a firm's costs and shift the short-run aggregate supply curve upwards. In the medium term, this might shift to SRAS2 and the new equilibrium would be P3Y3. In the long term, the wages would increase to compensate completely for the higher prices, further shifting the aggregate supply to SRAS3 and a new long-run equilibrium of P4Y1. This means that the long-run aggregate supply curve is vertical at LRAS. Higher aggregate demand in the long term has led to higher prices and higher wages, meaning that in real terms nothing has changed. The economy remains at its potential output, but with higher prices. More demand has simply created inflation over time, although in the short and medium terms it has increased output and reduced unemployment.

Now imagine that the economy is in long-run equilibrium at P1Y1 again, but this time aggregate demand falls (see Figure 22.7). In this situation, prices will fall, but if

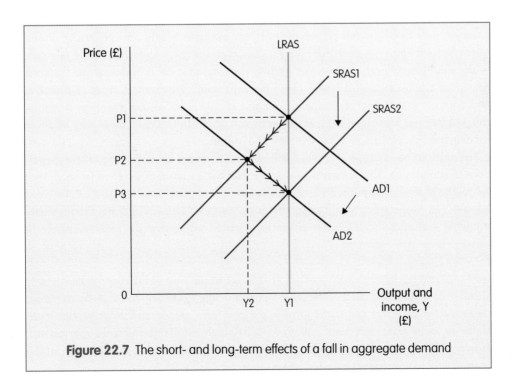

Figure 22.7 The short- and long-term effects of a fall in aggregate demand

wages are fixed, in the short term, employees are more expensive in real terms and likely to be laid off (or at least to have overtime cut). This would reduce the quantity supplied and the economy moves along the SRAS1 to P2Y2. In the long term, there will be a fall in money wages as:

- employees realize prices are lower and so are more willing to accept lower wages as they renegotiate their wages; and

- there is pressure from an excess supply of labour.

This leads to short-run aggregate supply shifting to the right to SRAS2 until an equilibrium of P3Y1 is reached. Wages have fallen, reducing the real wage to its original level, and the economy is back at its potential output with full employment. The long-run effect of a fall in aggregate demand has been a fall in prices, but no long-term change in output. Again, it can be seen that the long-run aggregate supply is vertical; changes in aggregate demand change prices, but not output.

However, there is the question of how long the long run is and whether markets truly adjust in this way. The key is the labour market and how flexible money wages are. If they adjust quickly both up and down, then the economy should reach the long-run situation rapidly and the economy is on the long-run aggregate supply most of the time. This is the position of monetarist or new classical economists, who think that the economy is always at or close to full employment and supply is vertical. In this situation, demand-side policies are not especially effective, and governments should concentrate on supply-side policies and on shifting the long-run supply of the economy to the right.

If, however, the labour market does not clear rapidly, then for long periods of time the economy may be below full employment. If, for example, wages are very sticky downwards because employees will not take pay cuts, then the real wage would never fall back to the equilibrium level. In this case, even in the long run, the economy could be stuck below full employment and supply could be very elastic. This is the Keynesian position, which argues that the vertical supply curve might only ever occur in the very, very long run, but by then, according to Keynes, 'we are all dead'! In this case, there may be a role for demand-side policies to boost demand and output.

For much of our analysis, we will use Figure 22.8, which highlights the different positions of economists. Keynesians would argue that the economy is likely to be stuck well below the potential output with an elastic supply curve (that is, in Figure 22.8, between Y1 and Y2). Monetarists would argue that supply is price inelastic and that the aggregate supply is vertical as at Y3; most economists would argue that we are somewhere in between these two extremes.

NOTE In reality, we are really looking at changes in the rate of inflation rather than at absolute changes in the price level—that is, a fall in aggregate demand is likely to reduce the rate at which prices and wages grow in the long term, rather than their absolute level. Similarly, an increase in demand is likely to lead to higher inflation and wage-rate growth. However, these figures do provide a simplified illustration of what is happening in the economy to demonstrate the underlying issues.

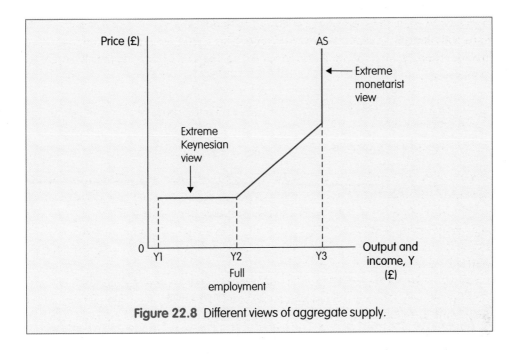

Figure 22.8 Different views of aggregate supply.

The effects of a shift in the aggregate demand on the economy

Aggregate demand may shift due to changes in consumption, injections, or withdrawals. An outward shift may occur, for example if:

- consumption increases;
- investment increases;
- government spending increases;
- export spending increases; or
- savings fall;
- taxation revenue falls;
- import spending falls.

When the long-run aggregate supply is relatively price elastic, then an increase in the aggregate demand will have a relatively greater effect on output and income than prices. For example, in Figure 22.9, an increase in the aggregate demand from AD1 to AD2 increases the output from Y1 to Y2, but the price level only increases from P1 to P2.

If long-run aggregate supply is more price inelastic, a given increase in the aggregate demand has an increasingly greater effect on prices compared to output. When the aggregate demand increases from AD3 to AD4 (see Figure 22.9), prices increase from P3 to P4, and output increases from Y3 to Y4.

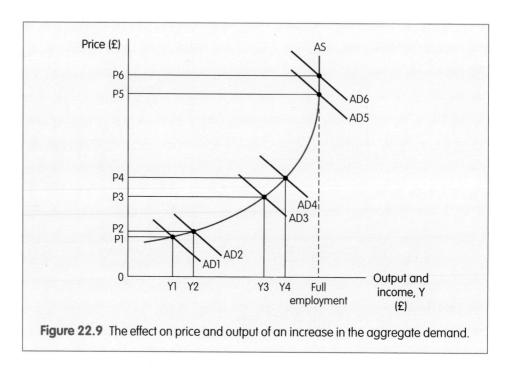

Figure 22.9 The effect on price and output of an increase in the aggregate demand.

When the long-run aggregate supply is totally price inelastic, an increase in the aggregate demand increases the price level, but does not change output. An increase in the aggregate demand from AD5 to AD6 leads to a price-level increase from P5 to P6.

The effect of a shift in aggregate supply: Short-run and long-run effects

Just as aggregate demand can shift, so can aggregate supply. Imagine that there is an increase in costs—perhaps due to employees demanding higher wages or higher imported costs of materials. This shifts the short-run aggregate supply upwards, and leads to a higher price and lower income in the economy in the short run (see Figure 22.10). Employment should fall, putting downward pressure on wages. If money wages fall, this reduces costs, shifting the short-run supply back out, and the economy moves back down to the original equilibrium at P1Y1. There has been short-term unemployment, but no long-term effects.

However, the question again is how long it takes to get back to the long run. Would a government faced with high unemployment be tempted to boost aggregate demand, shifting this out and leading the economy back to its potential output, but with higher prices at P3 (see Figure 22.11)?

It may also be the case that changes in supply conditions affect the potential output—that is, the long-run equilibrium in the economy. For example, if the cost of oil were to increase, this would reduce the profitability of many production processes and thereby reduce the potential output in the economy. In this case, the economy may, over time, end up at a position such as Y rather than X, and the long-run aggregate supply will have shifted inwards (see Figure 22.12).

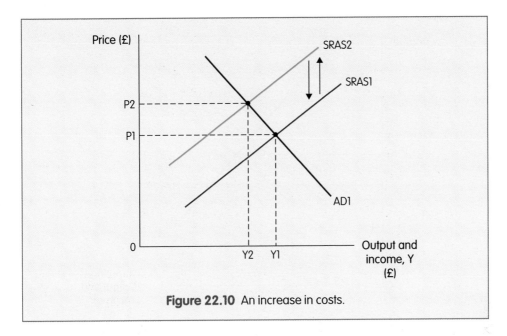

Figure 22.10 An increase in costs.

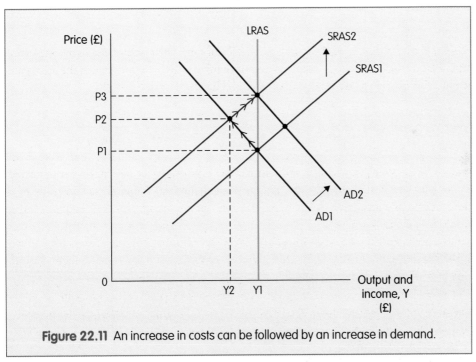

Figure 22.11 An increase in costs can be followed by an increase in demand.

Change in the underlying resources of the economy can also change an economy's potential output and shift the long-run aggregate supply. Imagine, for example, that there was an increase in net immigration, leading to a larger workforce. This should lead to lower wages, which shifts the long-run aggregate supply to the right—leading to a long-run equilibrium, with lower prices and higher output.

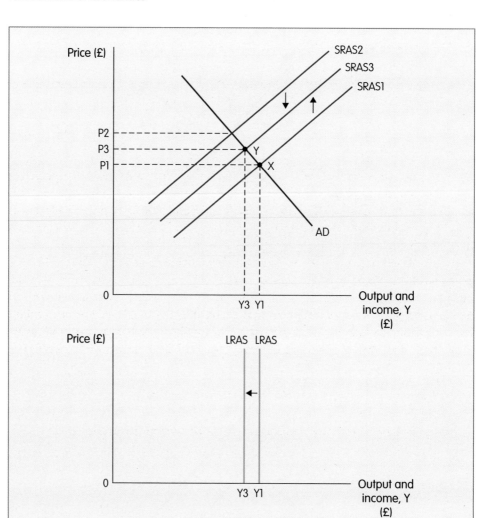

Figure 22.12 Change affecting potential output.

The price of oil

In the 1970s, the price of oil increased significantly, making energy much more expensive. This also made many pieces of capital equipment uneconomic to run. The effect of this was to shift the aggregate supply to the left.

? Question

Illustrate this, using an aggregate supply and demand diagram, and show the effect of this shift on the equilibrium price and output in the economy.

■ Government policy and the level of national income

To influence the equilibrium of the economy, the government may use demand-side or supply-side policies.

Demand-side policies

Demand-side policies are policies used by the government to control the level of aggregate demand. For example, expansionist policies may include lowering the tax rates to boost spending, or an increase in government spending. Contractionary policies would aim to reduce aggregate demand—for example, by increasing interest rates to encourage saving to earn higher rewards.

The impact of a change in the aggregate demand in terms of its relative effect on price and output therefore depends on the price elasticity of supply. This, in turn, depends on how close the economy is to full employment. The nearer an economy is to its potential output, the more likely it is that expansionist demand-side measures simply lead to inflation and not to increases in output. If supply is price elastic, then an increase in demand is much more effective in terms of boosting output than it is in affecting prices.

Put into practice

Illustrate the impact of a fall in the aggregate demand on the equilibrium price and output.

Supply-side policies

As we saw in Chapter 19, supply-side policies focus on changing the aggregate supply, and influencing the amount supplied in the economy at each and every price. Supply-side policies will be aimed at shifting the long-run aggregate supply to the right (see Figure 22.13). For example, the government may want to increase the potential output of the economy.

Supply-side policies could include the following.

- **Increasing the quantity of resources available** For example, a lowering of the school leaving age would increase the size of the available workforce. An introduction of an immigration system to limit the number of people entering a country, by comparison, would limit the growth of the workforce.

- **Increasing the quality of those resources** For example, a better-trained workforce would be more productive.

- **Increasing the efficiency in the way in which they are used** For example, if resources are managed more effectively, then they can produce more.

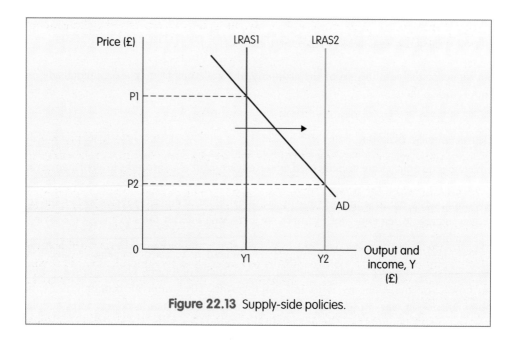

Figure 22.13 Supply-side policies.

Supply-side measures might include the following.

- **Labour market measures** The government may invest in training schemes to provide employees with the skills that they need for the jobs that are available. In some cases, employees lack the appropriate skills, which prevents them from getting jobs or being as productive as they could be.

  The government may also change the tax and benefit system to boost the rewards of working relative to being unemployed.

  The government may introduce labour market reforms to help the labour market to work more efficiently. For example, it may reduce trade union power to enable more flexible working practices, and to enable firms to hire people and change the number of people working for them more easily.

What do you think?

Is a more flexible labour market a good thing?

- **Intervening in the capital goods market** For example, the government may provide incentives for firms to invest in capital equipment and technology, to enable them to produce more efficiently and more effectively.
- **Intervening in the product markets to encourage competition** For example, many governments have privatized industries and opened markets up to greater competition. The

aim of such policies is to create an incentive for greater efficiency and to bring about pressure from investors to improve performance.

Problems with supply-side policies

The problems with supply-side policies include the following.

- To create flexibility in the labour market, fewer employees may be offered permanent contracts and these short-term employees will therefore be less secure in their jobs. In an attempt to create a more flexible workforce, managers are less willing to guarantee jobs for life or to offer long-term contracts. They want flexible contracts that enable them to increase or decrease supply as demand dictates. This may be good for the firm, but not for employees.

- In an attempt to encourage people to work, those who are unemployed will become worse off—for example, the government may reduce the benefits available to those who are unemployed. This will widen the gap between the rich and the poor, and may be seen as unfair.

- An increase in supply is valuable only if the demand is there; otherwise, it simply creates excess capacity.

Economics in context   **Supply-side policies**

Supply-side policies focus on increasing the supply of goods and services in the economy. Supply-side policies came to prominence in the 1980s when they were advocated in the UK by Margaret Thatcher and in the USA by Ronald Reagan. The traditional approach to the economy of managing demand was seen to have failed and so the emphasis was now placed on supply-side issues.

? Question

Are supply-side policies likely to be more of a priority than demand-side policies when the economy is at, near, or well below full employment?

Demand-side versus supply-side policies

The effectiveness of demand-side and supply-side policies depends on the position of the economy and the price elasticity of supply. If the level aggregate demand is at AD1 in Figure 22.9, for example, then, an increase in aggregate demand (a demand-side policy) leads to an increase in output, but little increase in prices, because the economy has so much capacity.

If, however, the economy is at its potential output, then an increase in demand would lead to an increase in the price level (demand-pull inflation) without any increase in output (for example, the aggregate demand increases from AD5 to AD6 in Figure 22.9). If the economy were at its potential output, then an increase in the aggregate supply would be more effective than an increase in the aggregate demand.

As the economy approaches full employment, successive increases in the aggregate demand have successively more effect on the price level compared to output—that is, demand-side polices become increasingly less attractive.

Obviously, a view of where the economy is at any moment (for example, whether it is near full employment or not) will have a big influence on whether demand-side or supply-side policies are recommended.

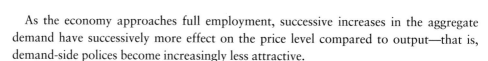

Case study US government policy

Guiding principles

President Obama's central focus is on stimulating economic recovery, and helping America emerge a stronger and more prosperous nation. The current economic crisis is the result of many years of irresponsibility, both in government and in the private sector. As we look toward the future, we must confront the many dimensions of this crisis while laying the foundation for a new era of responsibility and transparency.

Creating jobs

President Obama's first priority in confronting the economic crisis is to put Americans back to work. The American Recovery and Reinvestment Plan signed by the president will spur job creation while making long-term investments in health care, education, energy, and infrastructure. Among other objectives, the recovery plan will increase production of alternative energy, modernize and weatherize buildings and homes, expand broadband technology across the country to computerize the health-care system. The recovery plan will save or create about 3.5 million jobs while investing in priorities that create sustainable economic growth for the future.

Keeping Americans in their homes

Millions of hard-working, responsible families are at risk of losing their homes as home prices fall and jobs are threatened. The Making Home Affordable Refinancing program will expand access to refinancing for up to 4 to 5 million families who are . . . unable to refinance because their homes have lost value. The Making Home Affordable Modification program has a $75 billion commitment to support loan modifications so that up to 3 to 4 million borrowers at risk of foreclosure can keep their homes. President Obama's programs to prevent foreclosures will help bolster home prices, and will provide direct support to up to 9 million homeowners to refinance for lower payments or have their mortgages modified to prevent foreclosure. President Obama also launched MakingHomeAffordable.gov, where borrowers can learn basic facts about mortgages, homeownership, and resources available.

Bringing stability to financial markets

This crisis has taught us the real impact that financial markets and institutions can have on working families. President Obama has worked to get credit flowing again so that small businesses can rebuild and hire workers, and families can afford to send their children to college. At the same time, the president has demanded accountability and transparency both on Wall Street and in Washington, taking steps to ensure that banks use taxpayer assistance to support lending and create sustainable economic growth. For the long term, the president will create a new regulatory framework that holds market players responsible for their actions and stops fraudulent practices before they take hold.

Source: http://www.whitehouse.gov/issues/economy

? Questions

- Show the effects of a fall in aggregate demand on an economy, using aggregate supply and demand analysis. What determines the relative impact on prices compared to income?

- Show the likely effects of Obama's policies if they are successful, using aggregate supply and demand analysis.

- Obama wants to 'get credit flowing again'. How might this be achieved and why is it important?

- In what ways do you think an economic crisis might be 'the result of many years of irresponsibility, both in government and in the private sector'?

Checklist

Now that you have read this chapter, try to answer the following questions.

☐ Can you explain the shape of the aggregate demand curve relative to price?

☐ Can you explain the relationship between the short-run and long-run aggregate supply curves?

☐ Can you explain equilibrium in the economy in terms of aggregate supply and aggregate demand?

☐ Can you examine the effect of changes in the aggregate supply and the aggregate demand in terms of price and output outcomes?

Review questions

1 How might an increase in the aggregate demand affect the equilibrium price and output in the economy?

2 What factors cause a shift to the right in the aggregate supply curve?

3 Why might the aggregate supply be price inelastic?

4 How do supply-side policies differ from demand-side policies?

5 Should demand-side policies always be used rather than supply-side policies when a government intervenes in an economy?

Key learning points

- Equilibrium in an economy occurs when the aggregate demand equals the aggregate supply.

- The aggregate demand is downward-sloping in relation to price. A higher price level for a given level of income reduces the quantity demanded.

- The short-run aggregate supply is upward-sloping in relation to price.

- The long-run aggregate supply is vertical.

- An increase in the aggregate demand will usually lead to an increase in price and output. The relative impact on price compared to output depends on the price elasticity of the aggregate supply.

Reference

Keynes, J.M. (1936) *General Theory of Employment, Interest, and Money*, Harcourt, Brace, and Co, New York (first published by Macmillan, Cambridge University Press for the Royal Economic Society)

Learn more

Supply-side policies have a significant impact on the level of income in an economy and on economic growth. To learn more about supply-side policies that have been introduced in the UK, visit the Online Resource Centre.

 Visit our Online Resource Centre at http://www.oxfordtextbooks.co.uk/orc/gillespie_econ2e/ for test questions and further information on topics covered in this chapter.

Consumption  » 23

The level of aggregate demand in an economy is made up of consumption spending, investment, government spending, and export and import spending. In this chapter, we examine the factors that affect consumption spending in particular. In the following chapters, we examine the other elements of aggregate demand.

LEARNING OBJECTIVES

By the end of this chapter, you should be able to:

✔ explain the factors that influence levels of consumption;

✔ analyse the impact of a change in consumption spending.

▓ Introduction

We all like to spend money and, in so doing, we are consuming goods and services, and creating demand in the economy. This spending generates output and employment. Consumption, in macroeconomics, measures the total planned level of demand in the economy by households for final goods and services. Consumption spending is the largest element of the aggregate demand and therefore changes in households' spending can have a major impact on an economy. Economists are naturally interested in what determines the total level of consumption in the economy because this is such an important element of the aggregate demand and therefore has a big influence on how well an economy is doing.

Economics in context

UK consumption spending

UK household consumption 2009	£m
Net tourism	8,408
Food and drink	80,893
Alcohol/tobacco	30,507
Clothing/footwear	46,882
Housing	196,394
Household goods/services	44,780
Health	13,420
Transport	128,220
Communication	18,557
Recreation/culture	98,319
Education	12,458
Restaurants/hotels	91,883
Miscellaneous	104,513
Total	875,234

? Questions

What is the major item of consumption expenditure in the UK?

Analyse two factors that you think might increase or decrease the level of consumption in an economy.

■ The Keynesian consumption function

According to the economist John Maynard Keynes (1936), the level of consumption in an economy is given by the following equation (see Figure 23.1):

$$C = a + bYd$$

where:

- 'C' is the level of consumption spending;
- 'a' is the level of autonomous consumption—that is, the amount of spending that there would be even if incomes were zero. This is known as 'dis-saving' because households must be borrowing or using up past savings;

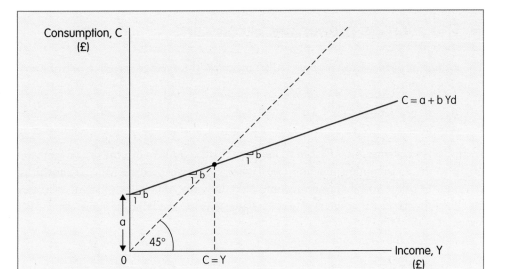

Figure 23.1 The consumption function. Here, 'b' is the gradient of the consumption function; out of each extra pound, 'b' is consumed.

- 'b' is the marginal propensity to consume (MPC)—that is, the amount of extra spending out of an extra pound. For example, if the MPC is 0.8, then this means that 80 pence out of each extra pound are spent on the consumption of final goods and services.
  The MPC is given by:

  $$\frac{\text{Change in consumption spending}}{\text{Change in income}}$$

  A change in the size of the MPC will alter the slope of the consumption function and therefore the aggregate demand schedule;

- 'Yd' is the disposable income, which consists of income from employment and self-employment, pensions, investment income, and cash benefits *less* income tax, local taxes, and employees' National Insurance contributions (NICs). It represents the household income available to be spent or saved.

According to this equation, there is a direct relationship between the level of disposable income earned by households and the amount that they spend on consumption.

What do you think?

How much do you think you spend out of each extra pound that you get?
Do you think that this is more or less than your friends? Why?

▨ The average propensity to consume

The average propensity to consume (APC) measures the average spending out of every pound of income:

$$APC = \frac{C}{Yd}$$

At any level of income, the APC can be measured by the gradient of a ray drawn from the origin to the consumption function (see Figure 23.2), whereas the MPC is shown by the gradient of the consumption function. Note how the APC falls as income increases (as shown by the fact that the rays become flatter); as income falls, the value of the APC approaches the MPC.

Imagine that the consumption function is

$$C = 100 + 0.8Yd$$

Out of each extra pound, we spend 80 pence; there is an autonomous element of spending of £100. If we earn only £1 of disposable income, then the consumer spending will be £100 + £0.80—that is, a total spending of £100.80 out of £1. The APC is 100.8. Due to the autonomous element, we are spending a lot, even though income is low, making the APC high. The average spending is much higher than the marginal spending.

As income increases, the autonomous element becomes far less significant and the key factor of our spending becomes the MPC. For example, if income is £10,000, then:

$$C = £100 + (0.8 \times £10,000) = £8,100$$

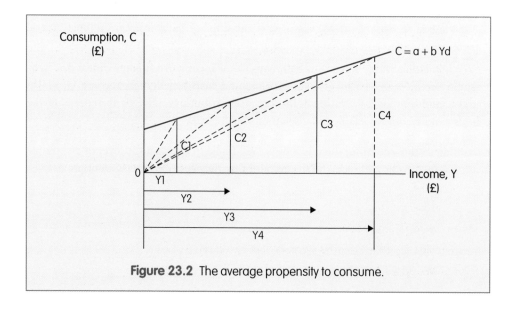

Figure 23.2 The average propensity to consume.

Therefore:

$$APC = \frac{£8,100}{£10,000} = 0.81$$

The APC is now close to the MPC. The average spending is closer to the spending out of each extra pound. The autonomous element of consumption becomes almost irrelevant at high levels of income.

Put into practice

Imagine that C = £10 billion + 0.5Yd

What is the MPC and the APC when:

- disposable income is £100 billion?
- disposable income is £200 billion?

Other influences on consumption spending

Whilst Keynes may have highlighted important determinants of consumption—especially current income—there are many other factors that can also influence households' spending. These may include the following.

- **The distribution of income in the economy** Lower-income groups tend to have a higher MPC than higher-income groups. If you give an extra pound to a poor person, then they are likely to spend it; a rich person is more likely to save it, because they have already bought many goods and services. If income is redistributed from the richer to the poorer, then the MPC in the economy will rise.

- **The availability and cost of credit** If it is easy and cheap to borrow, then households are more likely to spend money, so consumption will rise even if incomes have not increased. Think of all of the different ways in which you can borrow money, and you will realize how much spending is financed this way and how important credit is in the UK economy.

Put into practice

There are numerous ways of borrowing money, such as overdrafts, loans, student loans, credit cards, and mortgages.

- Can you think of any more?
- How much do you owe?
- Could you borrow more if you were to want to do so?
- How easy would it be?

Total UK personal debt

The total personal debt in the UK at the end of April 2010 stood at £1,460 billion. Individuals owed more than what the whole country produced in a year.

Average household debt in the UK was about £8,761 (excluding mortgages). This figure increases to £18,252 if the average is based on the number of households who actually have some form of unsecured loan.

The average household debt in the UK is around £57,915 (including mortgages).

 Questions

Why do you think UK households borrow so much?

Do you think that this is a good thing?

What do you think?

Do you think that it is the banks' responsibility to check whether people can easily afford to repay a loan or not?

- **Wealth effects** If households become wealthier—perhaps due to an increase in house or share prices—then this can allow them to borrow more to spend. Often, this will be spent on items such as holidays, cars, and other income-elastic products.

- **The age distribution in the economy** In general, people will tend to spend more than their income when they are younger (for example, when they are just starting out in a job). We will tend to spend less than our income in our middle years (when we are building up savings) and more than our income in later life (when we are running down savings) (see Figure 23.3). The importance of the stage in the life cycle on consumption spending was highlighted by Ando and Modigliani (1957). The UK has an ageing population, for example, which means that there may be more dis-saving.

- **Expectations** If consumers believe that the economy is going to grow rapidly, then they may be more willing to spend now, because they believe that their income is going to increase later on. This means that it is not only current income that affects spending, but also future expected income.

- **The permanent income theory** This model was developed by Friedman (1957) and states that what matters to consumers when determining spending is not their present income, but rather their 'permanent income'. A household's permanent income depends on its view of what it will earn over its whole lifetime. Temporary unemployment may reduce the current level of income considerably (which, according to Keynes, would lead to a significant fall in spending), but its impact on the overall lifetime income is far less significant, assuming that the household thinks that the unemployment will not last

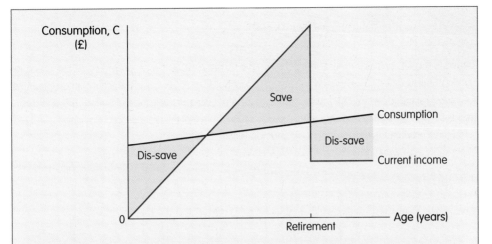

Figure 23.3 Consumption in relation to age. Over our working lives, our income will, hopefully, increase until retirement. Our consumption patterns may be far more stable than this, so there will be periods of dis-saving and saving.

long. Equally, a one-off bonus would not lead to a significant increase in present spending, because when this one-off increase is considered in the context of the whole lifetime's income of a household, its effect is less significant. According to the permanent income hypothesis, changes in disposable income that are not expected to last will not have much effect on current spending.

This has implications for government policy. A tax cut to boost spending will not affect consumers' view of their permanent income if they think that the tax cut is only for the short term. To have a real effect, the government would need to convince households that the tax cut would be large enough and long enough to have an impact on their average lifetime earnings.

What do you think?

What are the main influences on how much you spend?

Case study Saving in the UK

People in the UK are saving less than at any time in the past 40 years, according to the Office for National Statistics (ONS). The household saving ratio in the UK in 2008 was 1.7 per cent of total resources, the lowest recorded since 1970 and well below the 7.6 per cent average for that period. The ONS Social Trends survey reveals that housing, water, and fuel now represent the biggest area of spending. In 1970, the highest proportion was spent on food and non-alcoholic drinks.

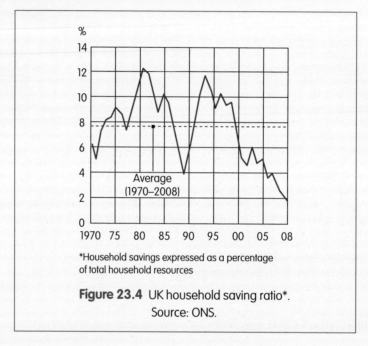

*Household savings expressed as a percentage of total household resources

Figure 23.4 UK household saving ratio*.
Source: ONS.

This does not necessarily mean that the amount of food and non-alcoholic drinks purchased has fallen, but rather implies that expenditure on other goods and services has risen more rapidly.

Other categories showing large falls in the proportion of total spending between 1970 and 2008 were clothing and footwear, from 10 per cent to 5 per cent, and alcoholic drinks and tobacco, from 8 per cent to 3 per cent.

But from 1998 to 2008, the proportion of total domestic household expenditure spent on services exceeded that for goods.

Other categories that showed an increase over the period were:

• transport—increasing from 11 per cent to 15 per cent;

• miscellaneous goods and services—which include personal care, social protection, insurance, and financial services—up from 7 per cent to 13 per cent; and

• recreation and culture, from 9 per cent to 11 per cent.

People's perceptions and expectations towards their financial well-being affect their likelihood of saving, according to the ONS. Between 2006 and 2008, people who had not been saving during the past 12 months were more likely to save in the next 12 months if they expected improvements in their financial situation.

Household spending: Selected comparisons

	1971	1991	2006
Alcohol, tobacco	100	92	89
Housing, water, fuel	100	139	160
Communication	100	307	956
Recreation, culture	100	279	783
Restaurants, hotels	100	167	211
Tourism abroad	100	298	763

Index: 1971 = 100

Source: ONS.

Over the past decade, economic growth in the UK has been driven by the accumulation of unsustainable levels of private sector debt and rising public sector debt. This pattern of unbalanced growth and excessive debt has helped create the exceptional economic and fiscal challenges that the government must address, to restore the economy to sustainable, balanced, and private sector-led growth.

By 2008, household debt had risen to 100 per cent of GDP, as households borrowed heavily to purchase increasingly expensive property. Companies also took on rising levels of debt, reaching 110 per cent of GDP by 2008. Within the financial sector, the accumulation of debt was even greater. While rising debt was an international phenomenon, it was more pronounced in the UK than in most other countries. It has been estimated that the UK has become the most indebted country in the world.

Source: Budget 2010

? Questions

- Why do you think UK households are saving less?
- What do you think is causing a change their consumption patterns?
- Is debt a good or bad thing?
- Growth in the UK has been built on an 'accumulation of unsustainable levels of private sector debt and rising public sector debt'. Why do you think this has occurred?
- What is meant by 'private sector-led growth'?
- Why do you think that 'the UK has become the most indebted country in the world'?

Checklist

Now that you have read this chapter, try to answer the following questions.

- ☐ Can you explain the factors that influence levels of consumption?
- ☐ Can you analyse the impact of a change in consumption spending?

Review questions

1 Why does an understanding of consumption spending matter?

2 What, according to Keynes, is the most important determinant of consumption spending?

3 How might a fall in interest rates affect consumption spending?

4 To what extent does it matter whether consumption is mainly determined by permanent income rather than current income?

5 Why might expectations play an important role in the level of consumption in an economy?

Key learning points

* Consumption is an important element of aggregate demand.

* The level of consumption in an economy may be influenced by a range of factors, including current income, estimates of permanent income, interest rates, expectations of the price level, the availability of credit, and the age distribution.

* An increase in consumption increases the aggregate demand.

References

Ando, A. and Modigliani, F. (1957) 'Tests of the life cycle hypothesis of saving: Comments and suggestions', *Oxford Institute of Statistics Bulletin*, XIX(May): 99–124

Friedman, M. (1957) *A Theory of the Consumption Function*, National Bureau of Economic Research, Princeton, NJ

Learn more

This chapter has focused on the consumption function; this is clearly interrelated with the savings function. To learn more about this relationship, visit the Online Resource Centre.

 Visit our Online Resource Centre at http://www.oxfordtextbooks.co.uk/orc/gillespie_econ2e/ for test questions and further information on topics covered in this chapter.

Investment

Investment is an important element of the aggregate demand. It is of particular importance because it is the most volatile element of the aggregate demand, and therefore an understanding of it is vital if a government is to be able to influence the level of aggregate demand effectively and influence the growth path of the economy. Investment is also important because it affects the level of aggregate supply in the economy. In this chapter, we examine the influences on the level of investment in an economy, and the consequences of it changing on the equilibrium price and output, and employment.

LEARNING OBJECTIVES

By the end of this chapter, you should be able to:

✔ analyse the determinants of investment spending;

✔ explain the impact of a change in investment spending on national income;

✔ explain the instability caused by the accelerator–multiplier model.

■ Introduction

Investment occurs when firms make a decision to allocate resources into projects that will generate future returns—for example, investing in a new machine or a new information technology system. Investment involves sacrificing existing, present consumption for future expected benefits.

Investment may be in the following.

- **Fixed capital** This involves the purchase of assets that are expected to be used for a long period—for example, transport, factories, and production equipment.

- **Working capital** These are short-term assets that will be used up in the production process—for example, stocks and materials.

Investment spending is an injection into the economy and is a particularly volatile element of aggregate demand, as well as an influence on aggregate supply.

▨ Gross and net investment

The types of investment include the following.

- **Gross investment** This measures the total investment in an economy in a period.
- **Depreciation investment** This is investment undertaken to replace equipment or machinery that has worn out. Depreciation investment simply maintains the level and quality of the capital stock.
- **Net investment** This is new investment that increases the capital stock in the economy.

Therefore we have:

Gross investment = Net investment + Depreciation investment

or

Net investment = Gross investment − Depreciation investment

NOTE Although, in the media, 'investment' often refers to buying shares or putting money into a pension scheme, these represent savings to an economist. 'Investment', to an economist, refers to capital goods.

▨ Factors affecting the level of investment in an economy

The amount of investment in an economy will depend on the following.

- **The initial cost of capital projects and availability of funds** Some projects may be attractive in terms of the possible rewards that they offer, but may not be affordable at the present time if firms do not have, or cannot raise, the necessary finance. Therefore the availability and cost of finance are an important issue. Following the global recession of 2008–09, one of the problems facing businesses was the difficulty raising finance for investment projects, because banks were worried about taking risks.
- **The expected returns from the investment** What are the expected costs and revenues from the project, and therefore what profits does the firm expect to be earned and over what period? These estimates of revenues and costs are, of course, only a forecast of the future net inflows. As a result, investment decisions inevitably have an element of risk and uncertainty. An investment into an oil project, for example, involves estimates of what the world oil price will be many years into the future—this involves a high degree of risk in terms of the accuracy of the forecast. The likely returns on a project will depend on firms' views about the likely level of sales, which are likely to be linked to economic growth and also to the likely inflation rates. The importance of expectations in the investment decision explains why this element of aggregate demand can be so

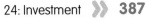

volatile. Changes in our views of what might happen in the economy will affect the expected profits and therefore investment spending.

- **The alternatives available** A decision to invest in one project means that resources are being allocated to this area and away from something else. A decision is therefore being made about the best way in which to use resources and this involves an opportunity cost. If, for example, the returns available in other countries or in financial savings such as shares are high, then this is likely to reduce the level of investment in the UK.

- **Risk and culture** Any investment project will involve risk, because the outcomes are not certain. Different managers and organizations may have different perceptions of the risk of any particular project, and will have different attitudes to taking risks. This may affect their willingness to pursue a particular investment. If a country has a culture that is risk-taking, then this might affect the level of investment in one country compared to another. National culture can also be important in other ways. Japanese and German investors have tended to be more long-termist than UK firms; this means that they were willing to wait longer for the eventual rewards. This was partly because their investors tended to be linked to the firm in some way (such as being their suppliers) and so were willing to wait for the long-term benefits in which they would share. In the UK, investors do not tend to be directly linked to the business and look for shorter-term rewards. This has tended to reduce the number of projects in which UK firms might invest compared with those available to Japanese firms, because investors are less willing to wait for their returns.

- **Non-financial factors** When considering an investment, a firm may be interested in the expected profits, but it may also take into account non-financial factors. What will the investment do to the brand image? How will stakeholders in the firm react to the investment? Will it fit with any proposed policy on issues such as corporate social responsibility? Does it fit with the corporate strategy? Investing in a new product area may in itself appear profitable, for example, but may not fit with a corporate strategy that intends to focus on existing business areas. In recent years, for example, many firms have become more concerned with the environmental impact of their activities and this has diverted investment away from some projects that are perceived to be environmentally unfriendly. On a national scale, firms may be concerned about factors such as political stability when deciding whether or not to go ahead with a project.

- **Government policy** Changes to the tax system can provide incentives for firms to invest. For example, tax credits may enable firms to reduce their tax bill if they invest more in research and development; a reduction in corporation tax increases likely returns on a project, encouraging investment.

The importance of investment

Investment is an injection into the economy and is important for the following reasons.

- Investment tends to be very volatile, partly because it depends so much on expectations. Sudden changes in investment can lead to instability in the economy. The economist Keynes referred to firms's expectations as 'animal spirits' and highlighted how easily a decision to invest may change.

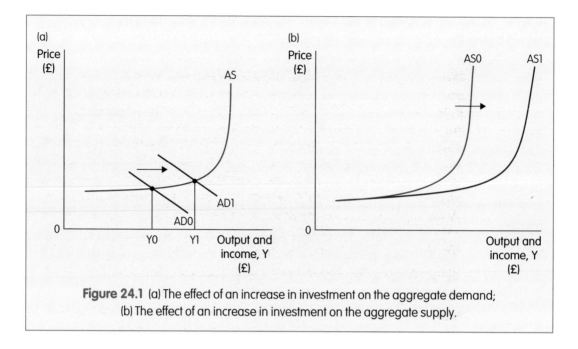

Figure 24.1 (a) The effect of an increase in investment on the aggregate demand;
(b) The effect of an increase in investment on the aggregate supply.

- Investment affects both the aggregate demand (because it involves spending) and the aggregate supply (because it increases the productive capacity of the economy and therefore, in the long run, the amount that can be produced) (see Figure 24.1). Investment is an injection into the economy and so an increase in it will boost the level of the aggregate demand. However, more investment will also increase the productive capacity of the economy and shift the aggregate supply over time.

Put into practice

Using an aggregate supply and aggregate demand diagram, show the effect of an increase in demand and an increase in aggregate supply due to an increase in investment.

Put into practice

Expectations are an important influence on investment decisions.

- How do you think the government can influence firms' expectations?
- In what other ways do you think expectations can influence an economy?

The marginal efficiency of capital

The marginal efficiency of capital (MEC) shows the rate of return on an additional investment project. This return can be compared with the cost of borrowing to decide

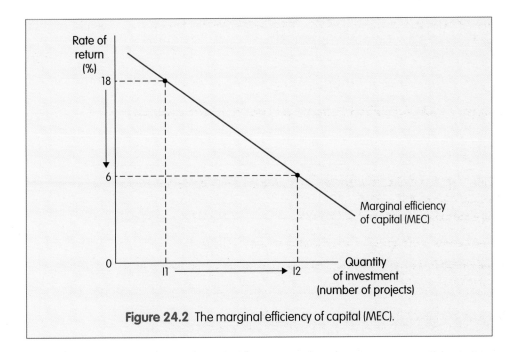

Figure 24.2 The marginal efficiency of capital (MEC).

whether or not to invest in a project. If the return on the project (that is, the MEC) is greater than the rate of interest (which is the cost of borrowing), then the project should go ahead on financial grounds. If the return is less than the cost of borrowing, then the project should not go ahead (for example, you should not invest in a project expected to generate returns of 8 per cent if the cost of borrowing is 9 per cent). Therefore, a profit-maximizing firm should invest up to the point at which the MEC equals the extra costs of borrowing (the interest rate). This is another example of the marginal condition under which, to maximize returns, managers undertake an activity up to the point at which the extra benefit equals the extra cost.

In Figure 24.2, for example, project I1 is expected to achieve returns of 18 per cent; project I2 is estimated to achieve returns of 6 per cent. If the cost of borrowing is 6 per cent, then all of the projects up to and including I2 are worth doing. The projects beyond I2 are not financially attractive, because the expected return (MEC) is less than the cost of borrowing.

Changes in the interest rate therefore lead to movements along the MEC schedule. Higher interest rates usually lead to less investment as fewer projects become viable. The extent to which investment changes depends on the interest elasticity of demand for capital goods.

Put into practice

- What do you think the equation for the interest elasticity of demand for capital goods would be?

- If demand for capital goods is very sensitive to interest rate changes, does this mean that it is interest elastic or interest inelastic?

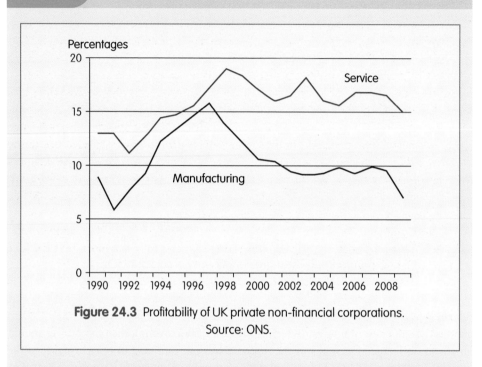

Corporate profitability

Figure 24.3 Profitability of UK private non-financial corporations.
Source: ONS.

The overall profitability of UK private non-financial corporations on average in 2009 was 11.6 per cent.

The net annual rates of return on investment within the services and manufacturing sectors have settled into a fairly stable picture over the course of this decade. Service industries are averaging a net annual return of around 16 per cent against the capital employed. Manufacturing industries, which tend to be more capital intensive, have averaged a net annual return of around 10 per cent against the capital employed.

 Questions

Explain the meaning of profitability (as opposed to profit).

What factors might affect profitability in an economy?

Why is it important for firms to assess the profitability of a project?

With what might managers compare the likely profitability of a project?

Why is the service return on capital employed usually higher than the manufacturing return?

Shifts in the marginal efficiency of capital

The MEC will move position if every project is expected to earn higher or lower returns. This may be due to more optimistic expectations about the future level of sales; this, in turn, may be due to a belief that the economy is going to grow faster. This would lead to an upward shift in the MEC as higher returns are expected on each project (see Figure 24.4).

In the media, you will often see reports on levels of business confidence and the views of business people about whether they think that orders will increase or not in the future. These surveys are a way of assessing business confidence. The level of business confidence is an extremely important factor in determining the level of investment in an economy. Given that people's confidence can change quite easily (for example, if the government is having problems or if there is an external shock, such as a natural disaster or a change in the oil price), investment levels can change quite dramatically due to shifts in the MEC. This can have a large impact on the aggregate demand.

The MEC might also shift due to changes in technology or the level of capital in the economy. An increase in the expected returns on projects will lead to more investment at any level of interest rate.

What do you think?

What do you think influences firms' expectations of the future economic environment?

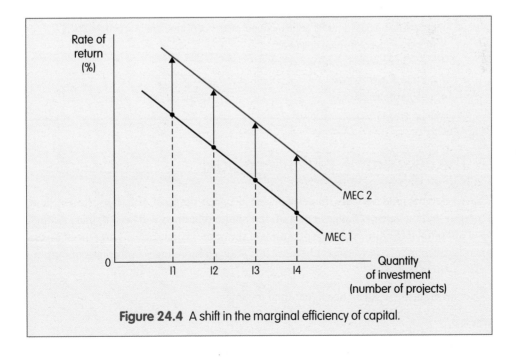

Figure 24.4 A shift in the marginal efficiency of capital.

Economics in context

Expectations

In July 2010, Japanese business confidence hit its highest level for two years, according to a central bank survey. The survey of more than 11,000 manufacturers found that optimism about Japan's economy outweighed pessimism for the first time since June 2008. Firms predicted rising profits and increased investment. It comes as the world's third-largest economy battles to recover from its worst slump in decades. However, the outlook for the Japanese economy remained uncertain. The country's new prime minister said that the country was at 'risk of collapse' under its huge debts.

Japan's central bank announced a scheme to offer 3 trillion yen (£22 billion; $33 billion) in low-interest loans in an effort to push forward economic growth. It also set targets to reduce its national debt, the biggest in the industrialized world. However, the government gave no specific ideas of how it will reach its long-term goal of balancing its budget.

? Question

Why does business confidence matter to an economy?

Put into practice

a. There will be a movement down a given marginal efficiency of investment schedule when:
  • managers become more optimistic.
  • managers become more pessimistic.
  • the rate of interest falls.
  • the rate of interest rises.

b. There will be an outward shift in the marginal efficiency of investment schedule when:
  • managers become more optimistic.
  • managers become more pessimistic.
  • the rate of interest falls.
  • the rate of interest rises.

The accelerator–multiplier model

The accelerator model shows the relationship between the level of net investment in an economy and the rate of change of output. It assumes that firms will need to increase their level of capital if the rate of change of output in the economy increases. This type of investment is called induced investment because it is induced by changes in the level of output.:

We assume that

Net investment = a × Change in national income

where

• 'a' is the accelerator coefficient.

Imagine that demand is growing by a constant amount each year. To be able to meet this demand, firms will need to invest more each year. Because the growth is constant, the amount of net investment remains the same each year (assuming a constant capital-to-output ratio).

For example, if a firm needs £2 million of capital equipment to be able to increase capacity by £1 million, then if demand grows by £5 million every year, firms will invest £10 million per year to be able to produce at this higher level. The level of net investment (that is, ignoring spending on updating and maintaining old equipment) will be constant each year at £10 million and this will increase the capacity of the economy by a constant amount.

If, however, demand begins to grow by more each year, then, to keep pace with this increasing rate of demand, firms must increase their annual level of net investment. This, in turn, boosts the aggregate demand and helps to stimulate even more spending due to the multiplier process. If this increased spending leads to a larger increase in demand than the year before, then this, again, increases the level of net investment to keep pace with it and a growth spiral has been created.

For example, if demand grows by £5 million one year, £6 million in the second year, and £7 million in the third year, then firms will want to invest £10 million, then £12 million, and then £14 million. The level of net investment is increasing because the growth in demand is accelerating (see Figure 24.5).

However, this investment–demand spiral is vulnerable to collapse. For example, if the demand grows again, but by less than the year before (for example, by £4 million rather than £5 million), then firms will need to invest to have the additional capacity to produce this output, but their investment will be at a lower level than the previous year. In this example, investment will fall to £8 million from £10 million. Because the rate at which demand has grown has slowed up, the amount of net investment will be less than before. This leads to

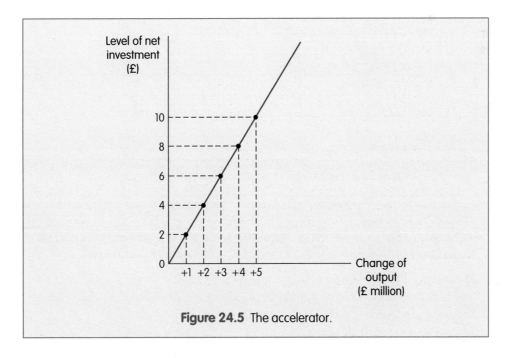

Figure 24.5 The accelerator.

a fall in the aggregate demand and sets off a downward multiplier. This may send the economy into a period of even slower growth and therefore another fall in net investment.

The accelerator model shows the link between net investment and the rate of growth of demand in the economy. It shows why the level of net investment in an economy may fall compared with the year before, even if the economy is still growing. It is the rate of growth that is most important. Given that changes in net investment can set off the multiplier, it also highlights how significant swings in the aggregate demand can be caused by initial changes in the rate of growth of the economy. A small fall in the rate of growth of the economy leads to a fall in net investment, which can set off a downward multiplier and create much slower long-term growth.

According to the accelerator model, an increased level of net investment can only be achieved by accelerating increases in demand in the economy; this is not sustainable, which is one reason why economies swing from booms to slumps.

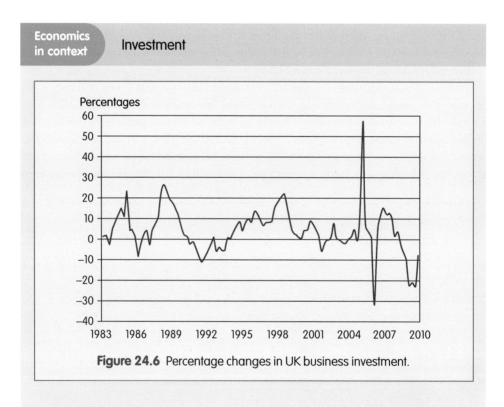

Economics in context   Investment

Figure 24.6 Percentage changes in UK business investment.

UK business investment for the first quarter of 2010 was around 7.8 per cent higher than the previous quarter. However, it remained 7.7 per cent lower than the same period last year.

? Questions
Analyse the factors that might change the level of business investment in the UK, as shown above.
Analyse the possible consequences of a fall in business investment.

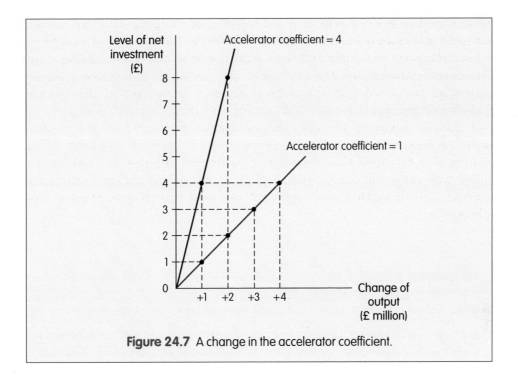

Figure 24.7 A change in the accelerator coefficient.

Limitations of the accelerator model

The limitations of the accelerator model include the following.

- Some firms will have excess capacity and therefore will not need to undertake net investment to meet an increase in demand.
- Technology may change and this will change the accelerator coefficient—for example, less net investment may be required to meet a given increase in output. The effect of a change in the accelerator coefficient can be seen in Figure 24.7.
- There may be bottlenecks and constraints in the producer (capital goods) industry that prevent or delay the net investment from going ahead.

Put into practice

- Can you remember the equation for the multiplier?
- On what does the size of the multiplier depend?

Cost–benefit analysis

Cost–benefit analysis is a technique used mainly by governments when assessing an investment project. It is a technique that tries to quantify the external costs and external benefits involved in any project. It is often used by governments, which are not only interested in the private costs and benefits of any activity, but also want to consider the full social impacts of any project. For example, it may be used when assessing a new council-house development. The government may also ask private firms to undertake such an analysis when dealing with a major project with important social effects, such as a new airport terminal.

A cost–benefit analysis involves estimating the monetary value of external costs, such as pollution, congestion, noise, and the impact of a project on wildlife. It will also try to value external benefits, such as the benefits to society of improving the public transport system. Measuring such external costs and benefits can be difficult to do, but is likely to lead to different decisions being made from those that a private firm would make.

Economics in context   **Traffic speed systems**

In the 1990s, a cost–benefit analysis of traffic light and speed cameras was commissioned by the Home Office, working with the Association of Chief Police Officers (ACPO) Traffic Committee. The terms of reference were:

> to provide a detailed and rigorous cost–benefit analysis in relation to traffic light and speed cameras by identifying and quantifying the whole range of relevant factors, and producing a comprehensive and clear account of the analysis process.

The types of cost and benefit considered relevant included:

- the costs of purchasing, installing, operating, and maintaining the cameras;
- the costs to the courts and the Crown Prosecution Service (CPS) resulting from the use of the cameras;
- the costs of associated publicity campaigns;
- savings in human life and injury, as well as those associated with reduced damage to property;
- savings experienced by the police and emergency services as a result of attending fewer traffic collisions;
- savings experienced by the health service as a result of dealing with fewer road accident victims;
- fine income generated as a result of camera use; and
- improved traffic flow, reduced journey times, and an 'improved environment'.

Source: http://rds.homeoffice.gov.uk/rds/prgpdfs/fprs20.pdf

 Question

In 2010, a number of councils in the UK removed their traffic speed cameras because financial cutbacks meant that they could not afford to maintain them. Do you think that speed cameras should be maintained?

Terminal 5 at Heathrow

The decision to go ahead with Terminal 5 at Heathrow was reached only after 27,000 letters from the general public, and after 46 months of public enquiry to consider all of the different costs and benefits. The terminal covers 26 hectares, around the same area as Hyde Park. Building it involved shifting 6.5 million m³ of earth and building a 13.5 km tunnel network underneath the runways.

Previously, the number of passengers using Heathrow was 67 million; the new terminal created room for 30 million more.

❓ Question

What kinds of external costs and benefits might have been considered when deciding whether or not to invest in Terminal 5?

Case study Building Dubai

Dubai is a truly extraordinary city where almost anything has seemed possible. Despite being in the desert, it is home to the first ski resort in the Middle East, and it has the world's tallest building, a seven-star hotel, and an underwater hotel!

Thirty years ago, Dubai was little more than a fishing village, but it has become one of the world's fastest-growing cities. In 2005, its economy grew by almost 17 per cent. This incredible growth was financed by its oil reserves and massive investment from abroad, which was attracted by the lack of direct taxes. The investment has funded enormous construction projects. The city has attracted multinational companies and has also become a major tourist destination. This spending has had a multiplier effect within the economy.

However, growth came at a price. The roads are often blocked with traffic and throughout the city there have been numerous ongoing construction projects. This growth has increased the cost of living to residents and visitors—so much so that the authorities had to cap rent increases to 15 per cent per year.

Following huge investment and consequent growth, the global recession came as a major shock to the country, with many construction companies having to halt their projects. One high-profile business, Dubai World, had massive debt and had to launch a restructuring programme for $26 billion of this in 2009 to try to reorganize repayments; this worried many investors, who had thought that the company would be backed by the government. Despite such problems, Sheikh Mohammad bin Rashed al-Maktoum, the emirate's ruler, insisted that Dubai's economy was now 'one of the world's most solid and stable' because of its diversity, its resources, and its strategic planning.

❓ Questions

- Why might the lack of direct taxes attract overseas investment? What else determines the level of investment in an economy?
- What is the effect of high levels of investment in an economy? Use aggregate demand and aggregate supply diagrams to illustrate your answer.
- Do you think that economic growth can be too fast?
- What factors would influence companies looking to invest further in Dubai now?

Checklist

Now that you have read this chapter, try to answer the following questions.

- ☐ Can you analyse the determinants of investment spending?
- ☐ Can you explain the impact of a change in investment spending on national income?
- ☐ Can you explain the instability caused by the accelerator–multiplier model?

Review questions

1 Why are expectations such an important influence on the level of investment in an economy?

2 What is the likely effect of a fall in interest rates on the level of investment in an economy?

3 Should private firms take account of external costs and benefits when making an investment decision?

4 What is meant by the multiplier effect?

5 In what way can the accelerator–multiplier model help to explain the economic cycle?

Key learning points

- Investment depends in part on expectations of the future and can be volatile.

- Changes in investment lead to changes in the aggregate demand.

- The marginal efficiency of capital shows the expected return on investment projects.

- Profit-maximizing firms will invest up to the point at which the interest rate equals the marginal efficiency of capital.

- An increase in interest rates is likely to decrease the level of investment and therefore the level of the aggregate demand in an economy, all other things being unchanged.

- The accelerator shows the relationship between net investment and the rate of change of national income. According to the accelerator, an increase in net investment requires the economy to grow at an increasing rate.

- A cost–benefit analysis uses social costs and benefits rather than private costs and benefits when assessing an investment.

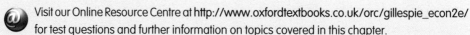 Visit our Online Resource Centre at http://www.oxfordtextbooks.co.uk/orc/gillespie_econ2e/ for test questions and further information on topics covered in this chapter.

Fiscal policy

Fiscal policy refers to decisions made by a government regarding its spending, taxation, and benefits policies. Changes in these policy areas can affect the level of aggregate demand and aggregate supply, and therefore the equilibrium levels of price and output, and employment. In this chapter, we examine the elements of government fiscal policy and analyse the importance of it in terms of the economy as a whole.

LEARNING OBJECTIVES

By the end of this chapter, you should be able to:

✔ understand the key elements of government spending;

✔ outline the different elements of taxation;

✔ analyse the impact of changes in taxation;

✔ assess the fiscal stance of a government.

■ Introduction

Fiscal policy involves the use of changes in government spending, and the taxation and benefit systems to influence the economy. Fiscal policy can be used to affect the level of both aggregate demand and aggregate supply. At times in the past, the priority of fiscal policy in the UK has been to try to fine-tune the level of the aggregate demand. However, in the first decade of the 21st century, the UK government left the control of demand to the Bank of England via interest rates; fiscal policy was used more to influence the aggregate supply. The global recession of 2008 and 2009 brought fiscal policy back to the fore, and an expansionist fiscal policy was regarded as essential to try to sustain demand levels in economies around the world.

First of all, in this chapter, we examine forms of government spending and taxation, and then we consider how fiscal policy can influence demand and supply.

▮ Government spending

The government in the UK is made up of central and local government. Central government is responsible for the national provision of some goods and services, such as the National Health Service (NHS) and the police force. Local government is responsible for regional, city-based or town-based services, such as street cleaning and local amenities (for example, swimming pools).

Government spending covers a wide range of goods and services, including:

- defence;
- social security benefits (for example, government payments to people if they are ill or unemployed);
- education; and
- repayments on previous borrowing.

Governments need to spend money to intervene to solve the market failures and imperfections that arise in the free market. For example, government spending may be needed to provide public and merit goods, to subsidize greater production of positive externalities, or to reduce instability in some markets with a buffer stock system. The government may also intervene to try to bring an economy out of a recession and to stabilize economic growth.

To finance its spending, the government raises funds from the following sources.

- **Taxation revenue** (see below) The government can raise revenue via taxes placed on products, households, and firms. When considering a tax system, it is important to examine the range of taxes, the thresholds at which taxes have to be paid (for example, at what level of income do households start paying income tax?), and the rates of taxation.
- **Borrowing** This might refer to borrowing from banks and individuals, for example. The government sells what are called bonds, or securities. These are 'IOU's that last for a variety of periods. Government bonds pay interest and are paid back on a specified date. Some government bonds are short term and some are long term. The interest rate that has to be paid depends on the number of years to maturity, the rates available elsewhere, and the risk associated with it.

Economics in context   Government intervention in Malaysia

In Malaysia in 2010, the government allocated RM230 billion for development expenditure under the Tenth Malaysia Plan. The allocation comprised 55 per cent for the economic sector, 30 per cent for the social sector, 10 per cent for the security sector, and 5 per cent for general administration.

The key points of the Tenth Malaysia Plan were as follows.

- The gross national income per capita is targeted to increase to RM38,850, or US$12,140, by 2015. This requires achieving real gross domestic product (GDP) growth of 6 per cent per annum. Growth will be led by the service sector.

- The government will focus on efforts to develop non-physical infrastructure, including human capital development, such as skills development and strong innovation capabilities. Focus will be given to skills development programmes, research and development activities, and venture capital funding geared towards promoting a higher level of innovation in the country.

The key areas for growth are: (i) oil and gas; (ii) palm oil and related products; (iii) financial services; (iv) wholesale and retail; (v) tourism; (vi) information and communications technology (ICT); (vii) education services; (viii) electrical and electronic; (ix) business services; (x) private health care; (xi) agriculture; and (xii) greater Kuala Lumpur.

② Questions

What economic benefits might there be in having a clear government plan?

Why might the Malaysian government be trying to develop the country's infrastructure?

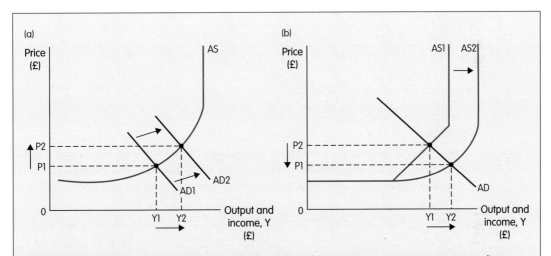

Figure 25.1 (a) Fiscal policy and the aggregate demand (an increase in government spending can increase the aggregate demand; price and output increase); (b) Fiscal policy and the aggregate supply (a change in the tax and benefit system can increase the aggregate supply (e.g. by increasing the incentive to work); this increases output and decreases the price level.

An increase in government spending is an injection to the economy, and increases the aggregate demand and sets off the multiplier (see Figure 25.1a).

Fiscal policy may also be used to provide incentives to increase the aggregate supply (see Figure 25.1b).

■ Taxation

Taxes are charges levied on individuals and organizations in an economy. Taxation is used to achieve the following.

- **To raise revenue to finance government spending**
- **To influence firms' and households' behaviour** For example, by making some goods more expensive, taxation can lead to households switching to other products or changing their consumption patterns (for example, taxes placed on fuel may reduce energy usage, whilst taxes on tobacco may reduce consumption).

Economics in context   Taxing chopsticks

The Chinese government introduced a 5 per cent tax on disposable wooden chopsticks in 2006 to help to preserve its forests. The country produces around 45 billion pairs of chopsticks per year. The Chinese government also raised consumption taxes to help the environment, and to reduce the gap between the rich and the poor. Taxes on yachts, luxury watches, golf clubs, energy-inefficient cars, and wooden floor panels increased by 5–20 per cent.

 Question

How else could the Chinese government reduce inequality in its country?

Types of taxes include the following.

- **Direct taxes** These are taxes placed on households' incomes and firms' profits, such as the following.
  - **Income tax** The primary forms of taxable income are earnings from employment, income from self-employment and unincorporated businesses, income from property, bank and building society interest, and dividends on shares. Income tax has different rates according to the amount of money being earned.
  - **National Insurance contributions (NICs)** These act like a tax on earnings, but their payment entitles individuals to certain ('contributory') social security benefits.
  - **Corporation tax** This tax is charged on the global profits of UK-resident companies. Firms not resident in the UK pay corporation tax only on their UK profits.
  - **Capital gains tax (CGT)** Introduced in 1965, CGT is charged on gains arising from the disposal of assets by individuals and trustees. Capital gains made by companies are subject to corporation tax (see above). As with income tax, there is an annual threshold below which CGT does not have to be paid.
  - **Inheritance tax (IHT)** This tax applies to transfers of wealth on or shortly before death that exceed a minimum threshold.
  - **Council tax** This is a largely property-based tax. Domestic residences are banded according to an assessment of their market value; individual local authorities then determine the overall level of council tax, while the ratio between rates for different bands is set by central government.
  - **Business rates** These taxes are levied on non-residential properties, including shops, offices, warehouses, and factories.
- **Indirect taxes** These are incurred when items are purchased. The producer is legally obliged to pay these taxes, but adds them onto the price to try to pass them on to the customer.

- **Value added tax (VAT)** This is a proportional tax paid on all sales. Before passing the revenue on to HM Revenue and Customs (HMRC), however, firms may deduct any VAT that they paid on inputs into their products; hence it is a tax on the value added at each stage of the production process, not simply on all expenditure. A reduced rate applies to some products such as domestic fuel, children's car seats, contraceptives, certain residential conversions and renovations, certain energy-saving materials, and smoking-cessation products. A number of goods are either zero-rated or exempt. Zero-rated goods have no VAT levied upon the final good and firms can reclaim any VAT paid on inputs as usual. Exempt goods have no VAT levied on the final good sold to the consumer, but firms cannot reclaim VAT paid on inputs.
- **Excise duties** These are levied on three major categories of good: alcoholic drinks; tobacco; and road fuels. They are levied at a flat rate (per pint, per litre, per packet, etc.); tobacco products are subject to an additional *ad valorem* tax of 24 per cent of the total retail price (including the flat-rate duty, VAT, and the *ad valorem* duty itself).
- **Licences** The main licence is vehicle excise duty (VED), levied annually on road vehicles.
- **Air passenger duty** On 1 November 1994, an excise duty on air travel from UK airports came into effect (flights from the Scottish Highlands and Islands are exempt).
- **Landfill tax** Landfill tax was introduced on 1 October 1996 to charge for the disposal of waste in landfill sites.
- **Climate change levy** The climate change levy came into effect on 1 April 2001. It is charged on industrial and commercial use of electricity, coal, natural gas, and liquefied petroleum gas, with the tax rate varying according to the type of fuel used. The levy is designed to help the UK move towards the government's domestic goal of a 20 per cent reduction in carbon dioxide emissions between 1990 and 2010.

Economics in context   Taxation revenue

	Revenue (£ bn)	% Tax revenue
Income tax	156.7	28.7
National insurance	97.7	17.9
VAT	82.6	15.1
Corporation tax	44.9	8.2
Council tax	24.6	4.5
Tobacco duties	8.2	1.5
Alcohol duties	8.5	1.6
Betting and gaming duties	1.5	0.3

Source: HM Treasury Pre-Budget Report 2008.

 Questions

What else do you think the government could or should tax?

Can you think of how tax revenue is used by government?

Economics in context — Tax freedom days

The Adam Smith Institute calculates Tax Freedom Day by comparing the government's tax revenue with the net national income (NNI). In 2010, tax is 40.9 per cent of NNI, which means that people in the UK have worked for the first 149 days of the year for the taxman, only breaking free on May 30.

Days required to pay parts of tax burden in 2010 were:

- income tax—41 days;
- National Insurance—27 days;
- VAT—21 days;
- excise duties—13 days;
- corporation tax—12 days;
- council tax—7 days;
- business rates—7 days;
- stamp duty—3 days;
- miscellaneous—18 days;

 Questions

What are the possible consequences of increasing taxes?

Which tax would you remove if you had a choice? Why?

Economics in context — Taxing the mining companies

In Australia, the government recently proposed a new 40 per cent tax on what it defines as the 'super profits' of the mining industry. Mining companies had been benefiting from significant increases in commodity prices.

Australia's prime minister highlighted that major parts of the two biggest mining companies listed in Australia, Rio Tinto and BHP Billiton, were held by foreign shareholders. As a result, many of the benefits of Australian resources have gone to non-Australians. Some argue that this type of tax deters investment into this sector. The Australian government argues that investment will not be impeded because the tax is applied to profits over and above what is necessary to fund reinvestment.

 Question

Do you think that the mining businesses should be taxed when they make high profits as a result of increases in commodity prices?

What do you think?

Some analysts argued that the banks should face an additional tax in 2010 to help to compensate for their role in causing the recession. Do you think that this was a good idea?

Marginal and average tax rates

The marginal rate of tax is the extra tax paid when an additional pound is earned. For example, 40 pence may be paid on each extra pound of income earned.

The marginal rate of tax is calculated as:

$$\text{Marginal rate of tax} = \frac{\text{Change in tax paid}}{\text{Change in income}}$$

The average rate of tax is calculated as:

$$\text{Average rate of tax} = \frac{\text{Total tax paid}}{\text{Total income}} \times 100$$

that is, the average amount of tax paid per pound.

Example

Imagine, for example, that a tax system is 0 per cent tax on every pound up to £999 of income and then 40 per cent tax on every pound earned above this. This means that if £1,000 is earned, then:

● the marginal rate of tax (the extra tax on the last pound) is 40 per cent;

● the average rate of tax is

$$\frac{\text{Total tax paid}}{\text{Total income}} \times 100 = \frac{£0.40}{£1,000} \times 100 = 0.04\%$$

Because the amount of tax-free income relative to the actual earnings is low, the average tax rate is low.

If an individual were earning £1 million, then the tax paid would be 40 per cent on the taxable amount of £999,001. The total tax paid would be £399,600.40. The average rate of tax would then be:

$$\left(\frac{£399,600.40}{£1,000,000}\right) \times 100 = 39.96\%$$

Put into practice

An individual can earn up to £5,000 with 0 per cent income tax. The marginal rate of tax after that is 25 per cent.

- What is the total tax paid if the individual earns:
  - £20,000?
  - £50,000?
- What is the average rate of tax if the individual earns:
  - £20,000?
  - £50,000?

▨ Taxation systems

The following are the different types of taxation system (see Figure 25.2).

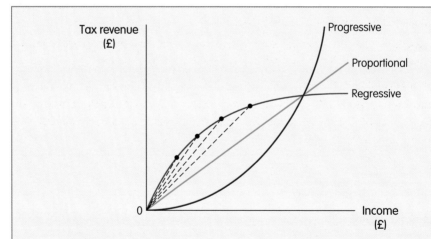

Figure 25.2 Progressive, proportional, and regressive taxation systems.
In a progressive taxation system, the average rate of tax increases as income increases. In a regressive taxation system, the average rate of tax decreases as income increases. In a proportional taxation system the average rate of tax is constant. Note: the average rate of tax is shown by the gradient of rays from the origin. The gradient falls for a regressive system, for example.

- **Progressive** In a progressive taxation system, the average rate of tax increases as people earn more money. The income tax system in the UK is progressive; as people earn more, they move into higher marginal tax brackets. The increasing marginal tax rate pulls up the average amount of tax paid per pound.

- **Regressive** In a regressive tax system, the average rate of taxation falls as income increases. This can occur if, for example, the same amount of tax is paid regardless of individuals' or firms' income levels. For example, you might pay £10 VAT on an item whether your income is £10,000 or £50,000. On average, therefore, the more income you have, the lower the tax paid per pound earned.

- **Proportional** A proportional tax occurs when the percentage of their income that people pay in tax stays constant whatever they earn—that is, the average rate of tax is constant.

What do you think?

Some economists and politicians have argued for a flat rate of income tax rather than having different tax bands with increasing rates of tax. Would you recommend this?

An effective taxation system should have the following features.

- **Understandable** Individuals and organizations should be able to understand how their tax is calculated or they will think that it is unfair.

- **Cost-effective to administer** If a taxation system is too complex, then too much will be spent administering it and collecting the tax, thereby wasting resources.

- **Difficult to avoid paying**

- **Non-distortionary** It should not alter market signals in an undesirable fashion—for example, it should not discourage the production or consumption of a product below the socially efficient level.

Economics in context — VAT

VAT is generally paid when you buy goods or services. However, there are various items for which you do not have to pay any VAT, such as most food, children's clothing, newspapers, and magazines.

The table below shows the standard rates of VAT in the European Union at the time of writing (noting that the standard rate of VAT in the UK rose to 20 per cent from 17.5 per cent in January 2011).

Country	VAT (%)	Country	VAT (%)	Country	VAT (%)
Austria	20	Germany	19	Netherlands	19
Belgium	21	Greece	23	Poland	22
Bulgaria	20	Hungary	25	Portugal	20
Cyprus	15	Ireland	21	Romania	19
Czech Republic	20	Italy	20	Slovakia	19
Denmark	25	Latvia	21	Slovenia	20
Estonia	20	Lithuania	21	Spain	16
Finland	22	Luxembourg	15	Sweden	25
France	19.6	Malta	18	UK	20

Source: European Commission.

 Question

What do you think the effect of an increase in VAT is likely to be in the economy? Should the UK increase its VAT to 25 per cent, like Denmark?

■ A 'fair' tax system

The fairness of a taxation and benefit system can be measured in terms of the following.

- **Horizontal equity** This occurs if people in the same situation pay the same amount of tax.
- **Vertical equity** This occurs if taxes are regarded as fair between different income groups. Obviously, what is regarded as fair is very controversial and people will have very different opinions on what they think a taxation system should involve.

What do you think?

Do you think the present tax system in your country is fair? Does it work well?

■ Using taxation as a government policy instrument

The factors to consider when assessing the effectiveness of taxation as a government policy instrument include the following.

- Taxing people and firms can reduce their earnings, but cannot directly increase their income. This can only be done if the taxation revenue is redistributed in some way. It is therefore important to consider not only what taxes are charged, but also what is done with the money raised.

- There is always an incentive for tax avoidance and tax evasion.
  - **Tax avoidance** occurs when individuals or firms take legal steps to avoid paying as much tax—for example, by finding loopholes in the system.
  - **Tax evasion** is illegal and means that people are trying to get out of paying the tax that they are meant to pay.

Economics in context

Richard and Judy

Richard and Judy, who were well-known TV presenters a few years ago, won a battle with HMRC in 2006 to have themselves classified as 'entertainers'. Due to oddities of the tax law, this allowed them to offset their payments to their agent (around £500,000 per year) against tax and claim a rebate on the tax that they had already paid since the 1990s. The 29-page ruling confirmed that they were entertainers. Jeremy Paxman, by comparison, could not claim such a rebate, because he is a television interviewer. This is an example of tax avoidance rather than tax evasion (which is when individuals or firms act illegally).

? Question

What factors would the government want to consider when deciding how many resources to invest in catching people who evade their taxes?

- Increasing tax rates can have a disincentive effect. For example, increasing income tax can lead to there being less incentive for people to work (or at least to work more hours) because the amount that they earn is relatively little after tax. This is known as the poverty trap. On the other hand, a tax cut can have an incentive effect and, according to Laffer (see Wanniski, 1978), may increase tax revenue, as explained below.

The Laffer curve

Professor Art Laffer advised President Reagan in the USA between 1981 and 1984. He highlighted that the total tax revenue depends on the tax rate and the income being earned; if cutting the tax rate encourages people to work and thereby increase incomes, then this can increase tax revenues—an effect known as the Laffer curve (see Figure 25.3).

If the average rate of tax were zero, then no tax revenue would be raised. As the average rate of tax increases, more tax revenue is raised. However, if the tax rate is set too high, then this might discourage people from working and firms from investing, therefore

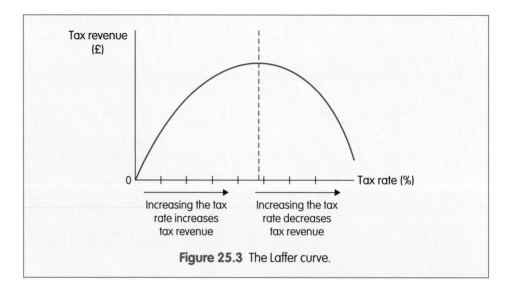

Figure 25.3 The Laffer curve.

reducing the income and the tax revenue being earned. Laffer argued that the USA at that time had reached a point at which the tax rate was too high and was acting as a disincentive to firms and households to earn more. A tax cut would encourage more earnings and lead to an increase in revenue.

What do you think?

At the moment, the government can use the money raised from any tax on whatever it decides. Some economists argue for hypothecation, whereby the tax from a particular source must be used for a specific purpose. For example, road tax would have to be spent on road improvements, or the revenue from National Insurance would have to be used for the health service.

Do you think that hypothecation would be a good idea?

Why do you think it has not been adopted?

■ Types of benefit

The impact of fiscal policy is not only to do with the tax system or government spending on final goods and services; it also depends on the government's spending on benefits. Types of benefit include the following.

- **Means-tested benefits** These are benefits that are paid to people on low incomes, such as income support.
- **Universal benefits** These are available to everyone, such as State Pension.
- **Benefits in kind** These are not direct monetary payments, but provide free or subsidized goods or services, such as health care and education.

These payments are known as transfer payments; they are transferring money from one group to another (for example, taxpayers to non-taxpayers), and are not in return for final goods and services.

Fiscal drag

Fiscal drag occurs when individuals pay more tax because their nominal incomes have increased and this has moved them into higher tax brackets, even if in real terms their incomes have not increased. Imagine that someone receives a 2 per cent pay increase and inflation is also at 2 per cent. In real terms, this person is not better off; his or her real income has not changed—he or she can buy only the same amount of products. However, if the government does not move the tax brackets in line with inflation, then it is possible that this person may move from one tax bracket to another because of the increase in his or her nominal earnings. This means that he or she would end up paying more tax.

To avoid fiscal drag (if it wants to!), the government should move up the levels at which people enter different tax bands in line with inflation.

The public sector net cash requirement

The public sector net cash requirement (PSNCR) used to be known as the public sector borrowing requirement (PSBR). It measures the amount that the government has to borrow in a given year to meet its spending requirements. It occurs if the government spends more than it earns in revenue. The PSNCR can be measured in absolute terms (that is, billions of pounds) and also in relative terms, as a percentage of national income.

To finance its PSNCR, the government will need to borrow money. It can do this by borrowing from the Bank of England or by selling government securities. Government securities include Treasury bills and government bonds.

- **Treasury bills** are short-term loans to the government (they are paid back within three months).
- **Government bonds** are long-term loans (for example, they are paid back several years later).

Selling bonds incurs an interest charge, because the government will have to offer an inducement to get firms and households to lend to it.

▨ The national debt

The national debt is the total amount of money that a government owes. If a government has a deficit in a given year, then this will increase the national debt. The debt needs 'servicing'—that is, the government will have to decide on how much it wants to pay off, if any, in a given year.

What do you think?

Is the government wrong to borrow?

Economics in context — UK government debt and deficit

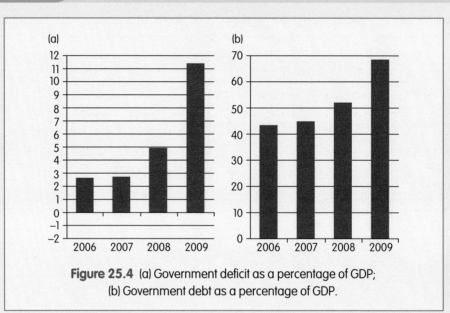

Figure 25.4 (a) Government deficit as a percentage of GDP;
(b) Government debt as a percentage of GDP.

In 2009, the UK recorded a general government deficit of £159.2 billion, which was equivalent to 11.4 per cent of GDP.

At the end of December 2009, general government debt was £950.4 billion, equivalent to 68.1 per cent of GDP.

 Questions

Why do governments have deficits?

Is debt a bad thing?

Debt

In 2010, the credit ratings agency Moody's downgraded the Irish Republic's sovereign bond rating to Aa2 from Aa1. This means that Moody's does not think that lending money to the Irish government is as safe as it was before: there is considered to be an element of risk of non-repayment.

Ireland suffered a severe contraction in GDP since 2008, causing a sharp decline in tax revenue. Moody's said that the banking and property sectors, which had driven the economy before the global economic downturn, would not contribute strongly to overall growth in coming years. It also pointed to the country's increasing levels of debt as a reason for the downgrade. The effect of this downgrading will be to increase the cost of raising finance.

? Question

Should the Irish government have avoided debt?

 Greece

Greece was admitted to the eurozone in 2001, and there were concerns even then about the strength of the Greek economy and whether problems there might causes strains later on. In 2010, the huge Greek deficit meant that confidence in the government and the country's finances led to downward pressure on the euro (the currency used by many European countries), causing major euro partners such as Germany to stress its willingness to support the Greek government if necessary. In 2009, Greece's budget deficit reached 12.7 per cent of GDP, causing great concern in the bond market (which trades government debt), in which traders worried about the ability of the government to repay its borrowings.

The panic was reduced in February when the European Commission endorsed the Greek government's plan to cut the deficit to 3 per cent of GDP by 2012.

The Greek government needs the confidence of the markets to be able to borrow again to meet its interest payments. To reduce the deficit, a severe austerity programme needed to be introduced—for example, cutting civil service jobs and reforming the pension scheme (before the crisis, pensioners in Greece could expect to receive earnings of 96 per cent of their previous salary).

? Questions

What might determine the success of the Greek government in reducing its deficit?
Why were other European Union countries eager to see Greece get control of its deficit?

■ Automatic and discretionary fiscal policy

Some changes in fiscal policy occur automatically as the level of income in the economy changes. In a boom, for example, more people will be employed and more people will be spending. This will increase tax revenue. At the same time, unemployment benefits will

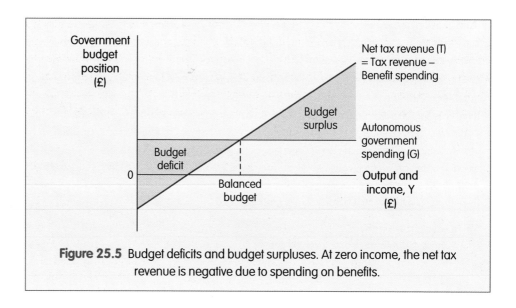

Figure 25.5 Budget deficits and budget surpluses. At zero income, the net tax revenue is negative due to spending on benefits.

not be needed as much, so government spending will fall. Therefore, in a boom, a government's fiscal position will automatically improve because income will be higher, but spending will be lower, as shown in Figure 25.5. Similarly, in a deficit, a government's fiscal position will automatically worsen. With any given tax rate, less tax revenue will be generated in a slump and more will be spent on unemployment benefits.

In Figure 25.5, G – T shows the difference between the government's spending and revenue (the PSNCR).

Discretionary fiscal policy occurs when the government makes a deliberate attempt to change the level of economic activity. For example, it might:

- introduce new taxes and benefits, or withdraw existing ones;
- change the thresholds at which taxes are paid and change the rate of tax; or
- increase its spending in addition to any automatic changes in expenditure.

■ Fiscal stance

A government's fiscal stance shows whether it is adopting an expansionist or deflationary policy. You cannot tell this simply by looking at the size of the PSNCR. This is because the budget position will not only depend on the discretionary decisions of the government, but will also be automatically affected by the level of national income. To identify the fiscal stance of a government, it is important to remove the automatic effects of national income changing in order to measure the discretionary changes.

Automatic changes to the government's fiscal position are shown as we move along a given budget line. If the government deliberately changes the tax rate or deliberately changes its levels of spending, then this is discretionary fiscal policy. This can be seen by a shift or pivoting of the line, as shown in Figure 25.7. As we can see from Figure 25.6a, an increase in government spending has increased the deficit at Y2 from B – A to C – A. Also, Figure 25.6b shows how a cut in the rate of tax increases the deficit at Y2 from A – B to A – C.

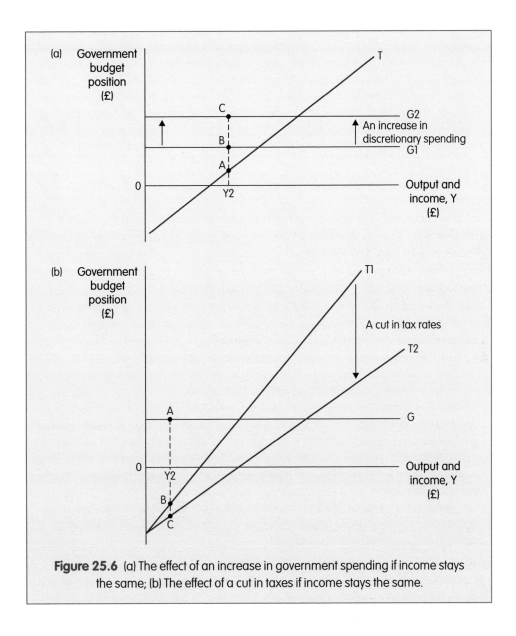

Figure 25.6 (a) The effect of an increase in government spending if income stays the same; (b) The effect of a cut in taxes if income stays the same.

The Greek deficit

Attempts by the Greek government to convince its citizens of the need for austerity measures to cut its deficit met with riots in the streets. In Athens, demonstrators marched outside the government building where they were debating the cuts and called on the parliamentary 'thieves' to come out. Other protesters set fire to a bank building.

The deficit had grown during ten years of spending. A change of approach was clear with the announcement on 2 May 2010 of loans from the International Monetary Fund (IMF) and the European Union worth a total of €110 billion ($144 billion), plus an austerity plan to cut spending and raise more revenue. The government has announced major cuts in pay in the public sector, higher taxes, and plans to reduce the budget deficit from 13.6 per cent of GDP in 2009 to less than 3 per cent by 2014. However, this will almost certainly deepen the recession that is already hitting Greece, with a drop in GDP in 2010 of at least 4 per cent and a further fall expected in 2011. The Greek government needed to take action because its lack of financial controls was making it increasingly difficult to borrow and this was leading to real concerns about the government's ability to govern.

 Question

What difficulties are likely to be faced by the Greek government when making these cuts?

Economics in context **Global deficits**

On 26 and 27 June 2010, the leaders of the G20 countries met in Canada to consider how to protect the global economic recovery while also dealing with the large public sector deficits of most of the countries attending. (The G20 is an organization set up in 1999 for important industrialized and developing economics to discuss key economic issues.)

These deficits have increased significantly as a result of the recession of 2008–09, which reduced tax revenues and resulted in more people claiming benefits, and because of the expansionary fiscal policies adopted to bring countries out of recession.

However, the leaders were divided on how much to cut their deficits now. Some, such as the new coalition government in the UK, wanted to cut the deficit quickly in order to regain control of finances and avoid a lack of confidence in the government's ability to finance the debt. Others, such as the Obama administration in the USA, wanted to cut the deficit more slowly so as not to put the recovery in jeopardy. Nevertheless, cuts were generally agreed, although agreement about the timing was more vague.

However, if all countries cut their spending, this could lead to a second global recession (a double dip). Also, higher taxes and reduced government spending may make consumers nervous, reducing their spending as well as deterring investment.

 Question

Faced with deficits after a severe recession, some governments wanted to reduce their spending dramatically and fairly suddenly. Others wanted to wait to make cuts. What approach do you think is right?

Economics in context

Japanese debt

Following the global recession, Japan was at 'risk of collapse' under its huge debt mountain, according to the incoming government in 2010. The newly elected prime minister said: 'Our country's outstanding public debt is huge . . . our public finances have become the worst of any developed country.' After years of borrowing, Japan's debt is twice its gross domestic product. For 20 years, the government has been borrowing to spend, hoping to revive the stagnant economy, amassing the biggest debt-to-GDP ratio in the industrialized world.

The Japanese government is effectively the only borrower in Japan and raises all of the money that it needs from the savings of its own citizens.

Government debt	200% GDP
Government deficit	8% GDP
External surplus	2.5–3.5% GDP
GDP growth	3%
Inflation	1.5%
30-year bond yield	2%

Source: Daiwa (2010).

Some 95 per cent of the government's debts are held by Japanese investors and the government can currently borrow for 30 years at a mere 2 per cent interest rate. But Japan does have serious medium-term problems related to its ageing population.

As more and more Japanese citizens retire in the next few years, they are likely to start selling their government bonds to pay for their retirements.

This means that Japan will need to start borrowing from the rest of the world and the government may find it difficult to convince foreign lenders to let it borrow at such a low interest rate.

❓ Questions

What problems can high levels of debt cause a government?

What might cause high debt levels for a government?

Do high levels of debt mean that the government is undertaking an expansionist policy?

▪ Changing taxes versus changing spending to affect the aggregate demand

When using fiscal policy, a government may use changes to the taxation system or changes in government spending to influence aggregate demand. Changes in government spending directly affect the aggregate demand. By comparison, reducing direct taxes increases disposable income, but the impact on the aggregate demand will depend on how much of the extra income is spent and how much is saved. A spending of £100 by the government will have a greater multiplier effect than giving £100 back to households because some of the latter will be saved and only a proportion will be spent—for example, only £80 may be spent. Also, by using spending, the government can target specific industries or regions quite easily.

On the other hand, taxes can usually be changed more quickly than spending programmes, can target specific products or forms of income, and are likely to have a faster effect on the economy. Changes in spending usually involve changing major government projects, which can take years to bring about. Furthermore, the government may have committed itself to particular projects and levels of spending. It may not be easy to alter these commitments.

Put into practice

If the government were trying to boost the aggregate demand, what changes might it make to the taxation system?

The effectiveness of fiscal policy

The effectiveness of fiscal policy depends on the following.

- **The accuracy of government forecasting** Intervention will depend on where the government thinks that the economy is at any moment and where it thinks it is heading. If either of these estimations is wrong, then fiscal policy may not remedy the problems effectively; it may even make them worse!

- **The impact of any policy changes** The government may base a policy on a set of assumptions about the behaviour of households and firms, only to find that they do not react in the expected way or at the expected time. Not only are delays likely between the economy changing position and the government realizing this, but delays are also likely when it comes to agreeing a policy response to this change. For example, it may take years to get agreement to increase spending in the economy significantly. There will also be a delay in the policy change taking effect. For example, an income tax cut may not lead to an immediate increase in consumer spending; households may wait for a while before deciding to increase consumption. This is particularly likely if consumption is linked to permanent income rather than current income (see Chapter 23).

- **Funding desired spending** A government may wish to inject more money into the economy, but lack the necessary funds to do so. If the deficit is already high, then further borrowing could lead to extremely high interest rates to achieve the necessary funding, and a government may worry about the burden of debt and interest repayments.

- **Other factors** As ever, the economy is never static. Whenever you plan a particular action, the success of your policies may be blown off course by changes in other elements of demand or supply.

Economics in context

Economic forecasting

Highlighting the problems for a government of intervening in an economy, the economist John Kenneth Galbraith said: 'The only function of economic forecasting is to make astrology look respectable.'

? Question

If economic forecasting is often wrong, is there any point in forecasting in the first place?

- **The funding of government spending may also create problems** It is possible that fiscal policy by the government may lead to less private sector investment. This is called 'crowding out'. Crowding out can occur because, with higher levels of government spending, the Bank of England does not need to keep interest rates as low as it otherwise would to maintain the desired level of demand overall in the economy. As a result, the higher interest rates may deter private sector investment because borrowing is more expensive. The effect of this depends in part on the sensitivity of investment to changes in the interest rate. Also, if the government attracts private finance by selling bonds, then these funds will not be available for other private sector projects; these projects have been 'crowded out', because the government has absorbed the funds that were needed to go ahead with them.

■ Supply-side fiscal policy

This involves the use of fiscal policy to influence the aggregate supply in the economy; the methods for achieving this include the following.

- In the labour market, the methods include:
  - offering individuals funding to help them with training and developing their skills;
  - helping the unemployed to get back into work—for example, with retraining schemes;
  - guaranteeing a minimum wage to encourage people to work;
  - reducing income taxes to act as another incentive; and
  - avoiding a poverty trap—that is, the situation that occurs when the benefits given up and the taxes incurred when an individual starts to work mean they are worse off than when they were unemployed.

- In the goods market, the methods include:
  - encouraging firms to invest by using tax incentives to undertake research and development to develop new products, and new production processes; and
  - helping start-ups with advice and financial aid, thereby encouraging new businesses, and increasing the supply of goods and services in the economy.

Put into practice

Show the effect of an increase in the aggregate supply on the equilibrium price and output in the economy.

Case study The UK Budget deficit

The most urgent task facing this country is to implement an accelerated plan to reduce the deficit. Reducing the deficit is a necessary precondition for sustained economic growth. To continue with the existing fiscal plans would put the recovery at risk, given the scale of the challenge. High levels of debt also put an unfair burden on future generations.

For the first time, the government's fiscal policy decisions have been based on independent forecasts for the economy and public finances. The Office for Budget Responsibility (OBR), in its Pre-Budget Forecast, has confirmed that, without further action to tackle the deficit:

- public sector net borrowing would remain at 4 per cent of GDP in five years' time, having been above 5 per cent of GDP for six consecutive years—unprecedented in the post-war period;
- the structural deficit would be 2.8 per cent of GDP in 2014–15, while the structural current deficit would be 1.6 per cent; and
- debt would still be rising in 2014–15 to 74.4 per cent of GDP, with annual debt interest payments set to reach £67 billion in that year.

This Budget takes urgent action to eliminate the bulk of the structural deficit through plans for additional consolidation of £40 billion per year by 2014–15. These plans include:

- £32 billion per year by 2014–15 from spending reductions, which includes £30 billion of current spending reductions and no further reductions in capital spending beyond those already announced;
- as part of these spending reductions, £11 billion of welfare reform savings designed to reward work and protect the most vulnerable, including adopting the Consumer Prices Index for the indexation of benefits, tax credits, and public service pensions from April 2011. The Budget also announces a two-year freeze in public sector pay, except for those earning less than £21,000 a year; and
- £8 billion per year from net tax increases, which includes an increase in the main standard rate of VAT to 20 per cent, and the standard and higher rate of insurance premium tax (IPT) to 6 per cent and 20 per cent from 4 January 2011.

By 2014–15, 80 per cent of the additional consolidation measures set out in this Budget will be delivered through spending reductions. (The Budget is the annual financial plan of the government, setting out changes in benefits, spending, and taxes.)

Source: Budget 2010 HM Treasury www.directgov.uk

? Questions

- Why did the government in the UK in 2010 think that 'The most urgent task facing this country is to implement an accelerated plan to reduce the deficit'?
- In what ways do high levels of debt also put an unfair burden on future generations?
- Discuss the possible consequences of the ways in which the government set out to reduce its deficit.
- Do you think that cutting spending is better than increasing taxes as a way of reducing the deficit?

Checklist

Now that you have read this chapter, try to answer the following questions.

- ☐   Do you understand the key elements of government spending?
- ☐   Can you outline the different elements of an effective taxation system?
- ☐   Can you analyse the impact of changes in taxation?
- ☐   Are you able to assess the fiscal stance of a government?

Review questions

1   What is meant by fiscal policy?
2   How does the government raise revenue?
3   Can you tell a government's fiscal stance from its budget position?
4   Can cutting tax rates increase tax revenue?
5   What factors might limit the effectiveness of fiscal policy?

Key learning points

- Fiscal policy involves the use of government spending and taxation to influence the economy.
- Fiscal policy can be used to influence the aggregate supply and the aggregate demand.
- Fiscal policy acts as an automatic stabilizer on the economy; discretionary changes can also be used to try to influence the state of the economy.
- Fiscal drag occurs when the tax bands do not change in line with inflation or growth in the economy.
- A budget deficit occurs when government spending is greater than income over a year.
- The national debt measures the total borrowing of the government.

Reference

Wanniski, J. (1978) 'Taxes, revenues, and the "Laffer curve"', *The Public Interest*, 50(Winter): 3–16

Learn more

To learn more about the UK government's budget position, visit the Online Resource Centre.

 Visit our Online Resource Centre at http://www.oxfordtextbooks.co.uk/orc/gillespie_econ2e/ for test questions and further information on topics covered in this chapter.

Unemployment 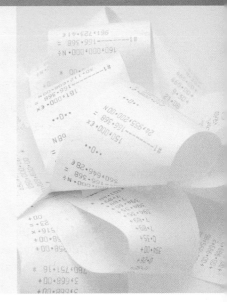 »26

Reducing unemployment is often seen as one of the major economic objectives of governments. This chapter examines the causes and problems of unemployment, and considers how it can be reduced.

LEARNING OBJECTIVES

By the end of this chapter, you should be able to:

✔ explain the possible causes of unemployment;

✔ outline the costs of unemployment;

✔ examine ways of reducing unemployment.

▨ Introduction

Unemployment is a measure of the number of jobless people who want to work, are available to work, and are actively seeking employment. It can be measured in different ways, including the following.

- **The claimant count** This is the number of individuals who are actually claiming unemployment-related benefits at any moment. This is a relatively straightforward figure to gather, but may be misleading because governments can change the conditions under which people can claim such benefits. It is therefore open to abuse by governments because, to reduce unemployment, they can simply make claiming more difficult!

- **The Labour Force Survey (LFS)** This measure of unemployment is based on interviews with people to determine those who want to work, but who are not employed. This is now the official way of measuring unemployment in the UK.

Of the two measures, the claimant count is always the lower of the two, because some unemployed people are not entitled to claim benefits or choose not to do so. When employment is high, the gap between the LFS and the claimant count will tend to widen. This is because some jobless people who were not previously looking for work start to do so. By actively looking for work, they are counted under the LFS, but do not feature in the claimant count unless they also begin to claim benefits, which is not necessarily made easy for them.

UK unemployment

Considering that gross domestic product (GDP) fell by 6 per cent during the recent recession, the increase in unemployment in the UK was smaller than would have been predicted based on historical experience. However, even larger decreases in GDP during the current recession led to smaller increases in unemployment in Germany, Japan, and a number of other Organisation for Economic Co-operation and Development (OECD) countries, than in the UK. At the other extreme, Spanish and US employers responded to smaller falls in output by aggressively cutting workforces.

 Question

What might determine how managers respond to a recession in terms of job losses?

▉ Causes of unemployment

There are several causes of unemployment. These include the following.

- **Cyclical (or demand-deficient) unemployment** This occurs when demand is low throughout the economy. For example, there may be a recession with negative GDP growth. Demand for labour is a derived demand, so if demand for goods and services is generally low, then this will lead to less demand for employees and more unemployment.

- **Structural unemployment** This occurs when the structure of an economy changes. For example, an industry may lose its international competitiveness with the arrival of new global competitors. With the decline of a particular industry, some of those who are employed in it will lose their jobs. It may not be easy for these individuals to find alternative employment because they may have the wrong skills to work in other industries or may not easily be able to move to where the jobs are. These employees will need retraining. In the UK, for example, there has been a significant decline in many manufacturing sectors as other countries have come to dominate these markets.

- **Seasonal unemployment** This occurs in seasonal industries, such as staffing ski resorts and fruit picking. When the relevant season is over, people in that industry may be unemployed (unless they find work elsewhere). This does not usually involve large numbers of people. Seasonally unemployed workers are likely to find jobs again in the following season, so this type of unemployment is not usually a major concern.

- **Frictional (search) unemployment** This occurs when people have left one job and are looking for another. This may not be a concern if employees find another job easily. As long as people are passing through this period of frictional unemployment, this is not a major cause for concern; the problems occur if they get stuck and do not find work. As time goes on, it becomes increasingly difficult for employees to get re-employed.

- Classical (real wage) unemployment This occurs when the real wage remains too high for equilibrium. This will lead to an excess supply of labour (more people want to work than are demanded because of the relatively high real wages). Real wages may be too high because employees continue to demand high wages even when prices are falling. The downward stickiness of nominal wages in this situation (because employees resist nominal pay cuts) leads to higher real wages. Real wages may also be too high if trade unions push the wages above the equilibrium rate. This unemployment should put downward pressure on money wages to reduce the real wage, but this may take time to take effect. The extent to which real wage unemployment exists depends on whether you think that money wages are flexible upwards and downwards, or whether you think that factors such as negotiated contracts and trade unions mean that money wages can stay away from the real wage equilibrium for some time.

Economics in context

Unemployment rates across the world, 2007 and 2010

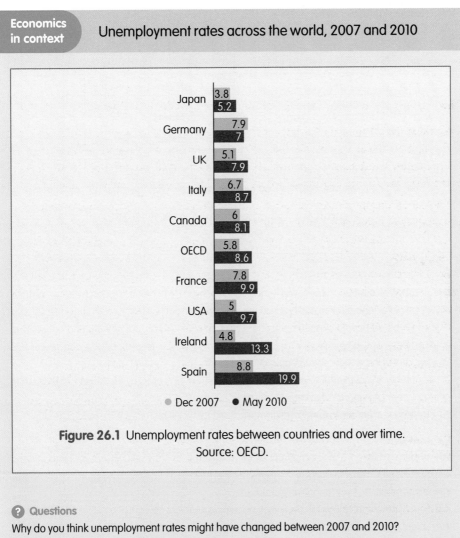

Figure 26.1 Unemployment rates between countries and over time.
Source: OECD.

❓ Questions

Why do you think unemployment rates might have changed between 2007 and 2010?
Why might unemployment rates vary between countries?

What do you think?

What do you think is the major cause of unemployment in the UK at the moment?

Economics in context   UK unemployment

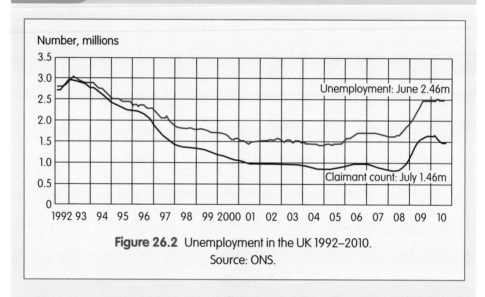

Figure 26.2 Unemployment in the UK 1992–2010.
Source: ONS.

The number of people unemployed in the UK reached 2.51 million in March 2010—around 8 per cent of the labour force, according to the Labour Force Survey.

The number of people classed as economically inactive—those out of work and not seeking employment—was 8.19 million. This is the highest level since records began and represents 21.5 per cent of the working-age population.

The number of people out of work for more than a year increased by 85,000 to 772,000, while unemployment among 16–24-year-olds rose by 11,000 to 926,000.

The number of people in employment was around 28.9 million.

? Questions

Why is there a difference in the chart above between the unemployment figures and the claimant count?

Why might someone be economically inactive?

What might have caused the relatively high unemployment rates in 2010?

Why might the proportion of long-term unemployed and youth unemployment be of particular interest to economists?

Economics in context

Unemployment rate

	% Labour force 2007	2008	2009	2010	2011
USA	4.6	5.8	9.3	9.7	8.9
Japan	3.8	4.0	5.1	4.9	4.7
Euro area	7.4	7.5	9.4	10.1	10.1
OECD	5.6	6.0	8.1	8.5	8.2

Source: Based on OECD (2010) *OECD Economic Outlook*, Vol. 2010/1, OECD Publishing.

 Questions

Analyse the possible reasons for the differences in unemployment rates between countries in the table above.

Choose any one country or area above and analyse the possible causes of the change in unemployment over time.

Put into practice

Which of the following statements are true and which are false?

a. Cyclical unemployment may be caused by high levels of aggregate demand.

b. A fall in export demand might cause cyclical unemployment.

c. To reduce structural unemployment may require retraining.

d. High real wages are associated with excess demand for labour.

Voluntary and involuntary unemployment

Another way of categorizing unemployment is to distinguish between voluntary unemployment and involuntary unemployment.

- **Voluntary unemployment** is made up of those people who are looking for work, but are not yet willing or able to accept work at the given real wage rate. They are in the labour force, but are not willing or able to accept a job at that real wage. This is shown by the difference at any real wage between the job acceptance and the labour force curves. The job acceptance curve shows the number of people who are willing and able to accept a job at a given real wage rate. It increases as the real wage increases because people will be less willing to wait around in the labour force as the rewards of taking a job increase.

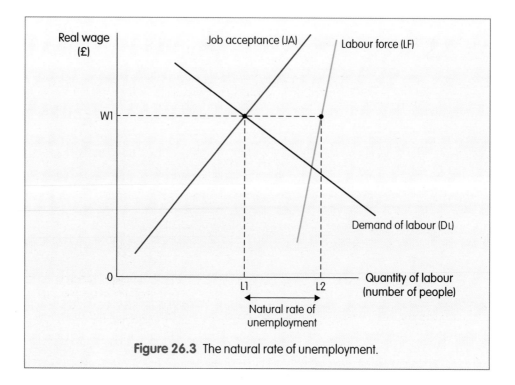

Figure 26.3 The natural rate of unemployment.

The labour force curve shows the number of people in work or looking for work at each real wage; this will also be slightly upward-sloping because, as the real wage increases, it is an incentive for more people to start looking for work. In Figure 26.3, the difference between L2 and L1 represents voluntary unemployment. When the labour market is in equilibrium, this level of unemployment is known as the 'natural level of unemployment'.

- **Involuntary unemployment** measures the number of people who are willing and able to work at the given real wage, but who are not in employment. This is because there is a lack of jobs available. This is due to a lack of demand in the economy.

If, for example, the real wage is too high at W2, then L4 – L3 in Figure 26.4 represents employees who are willing and able to work, but are not demanded. This is involuntary unemployment.

L5 – L4 represents voluntary unemployment at this real wage.

What do you think?

A detailed analysis of unemployment would examine the level and rates of unemployment in different categories, such as men and women, and between regions.

What other categories would you analyse?

Why might this analysis be useful?

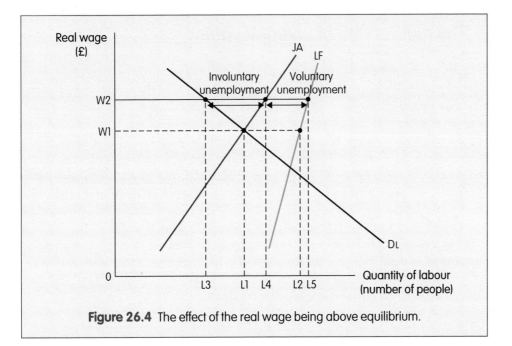

Figure 26.4 The effect of the real wage being above equilibrium.

Economics in context   Unemployment benefits

In 2009, the benefits that were available to people who were unemployed in the UK included the following.

- **Jobseeker's Allowance (JSA)** This was the main benefit for the unemployed. To qualify, you had to be actively seeking work, under the State Pension age (60 for women and 65 for men), and either not working or working less than 16 hours a week. The allowance varied between £47.95 and £94.95 a week, depending on your circumstances.
- **The New Deal programme** This was designed to give people on benefits the help and support that they need to look for work, including training and preparing for work.
- **Income support** This was designed for those who could not work full-time.
- **Council Tax Benefit** It was possible to get up to a 100 per cent reduction on your council tax bill.
- **Tax credits** Tax credits are payments from the government. If you are responsible for at least one child or young person who normally lives with you, you might qualify for **Child Tax Credit**.
- **Disability Living Allowance (DLA)** This was for children and adults who need help with personal care or who have walking difficulties because they are physically or mentally disabled.
- **Carer's Allowance** This was a taxable benefit to help those who look after a disabled person.
- **Housing Benefit** If you were out of work and needed financial help to pay all or part of your rent, you were able to get Housing Benefit.

? Questions

What would be the economic effects of removing benefits such as the ones listed above?
How might a government decide on an appropriate level of benefits?

The natural rate of unemployment

Even when the economy is in long-run equilibrium, at full employment, there will still be voluntary unemployment. This level of unemployment is called the natural rate of unemployment (or full-employment unemployment). It represents the level of unemployment when all of those who are willing and able to work at the given real wage are working. This unemployment may be because people are simply between jobs or have no intention of working at the moment. To reduce the natural rate of unemployment, supply-side policies must be used. These can increase the number of people who are willing and able to accept a job at each real wage. This shifts the job acceptance curve to the right and nearer to the labour force curve (see Figure 26.5). The natural rate of unemployment has fallen from L2 – L1 to L4 – L3 because the real wage has fallen from W1 to W2.

The natural rate of unemployment is the long-run equilibrium rate of unemployment; this means that there is no pressure for wages or prices to change. At the given real wage, the economy is settled for the long term. Some economists call the natural rate the non-accelerating inflation rate of unemployment (NAIRU).

What do you think?

Do you think that it is the government's responsibility to reduce unemployment?
How low should the government try to get unemployment to be? What is the best way of achieving this?

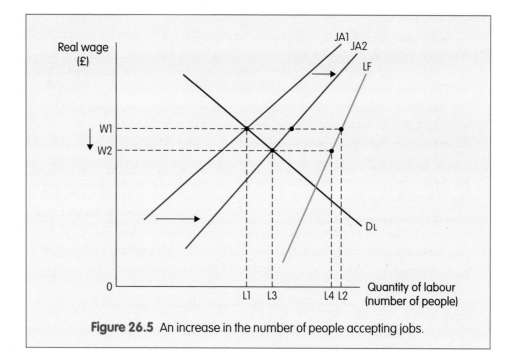

Figure 26.5 An increase in the number of people accepting jobs.

The level of voluntary unemployment in an economy will depend on many factors, such as the level of benefits, the real wage, union power, and productivity. It also depends on how many peple are in the labout force, and how many are willing and able to accept a job. One interesting phenomenon following a period of unemployment is known as hysteresis. This occurs in the labour market if the occurrence of unemployment in the short term increases the long-term natural rate of unemployment. If people have been out of work for some time, they may lose the skills required as the world of work changes and/or they may lose the desire to work. They may also stop searching for jobs if this has proved unsuccessful in the past. The result is an increase in the level of voluntary unemployment.

■ Government intervention to reduce unemployment

Demand-side policies

By using demand-side policies, the government can boost the aggregate demand and provide jobs for those who are involuntarily unemployed—that is, individuals who have the necessary skills and who want to work, but for whom there are no jobs available.

Demand-side policies include:

• cutting direct taxes to boost spending by firms and households;

• increased government spending; and

• reducing interest rates to stimulate borrowing and spending.

Demand-side policies raise the level of demand in the economy; to produce more, firms need to employ more labour, so the demand for labour shifts to the right (see Figure 26.6). Voluntary unemployment falls from L1 – L2 to L3 – L4.

Put into practice

Which organization has control of the interest rate in the UK? What are its objectives?

Supply-side policies

In the case of voluntary unemployment, the problem is not a lack of jobs; rather, it is a question of whether individuals have the required skills to work or want to accept a job. If the government were to intervene to increase spending to provide more jobs, then this would not solve the problem. What is needed here is help for individuals to get work that is actually there already—that is, supply-side policies.

To reduce voluntary unemployment, the government might do the following.

• The government could invest in training to provide the skills that people need to get jobs in other industries.

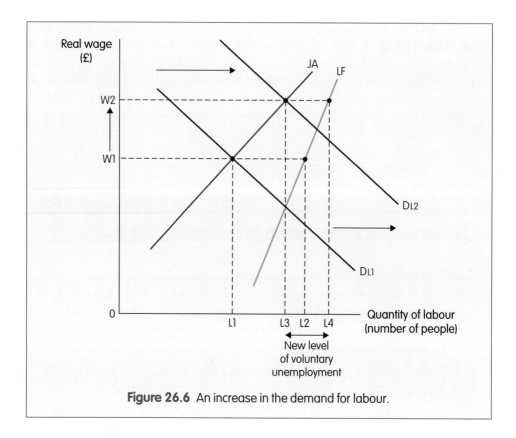

Figure 26.6 An increase in the demand for labour.

- It could change the benefits and tax system to make being unemployed less of an option—that is, to force people to accept a job by making the gains from being unemployed very low. The replacement ratio measures the levels of benefits available relative to the wages that can be earned when working. If this ratio increases, this may encourage more people to be in the labour force (because the benefits even if you are unemployed are higher), but at the same time, it may reduce the number accepting a job (because there is less incentive). This increases the amount of voluntary unemployment.

- The government could reduce the tax wedge. Taxes drive a wedge between the pay that employees receive and their take-home pay. In Figure 26.7, the equilibrium wage is W1. However, because the firm has to pay National Insurance Contributions (NICs) for employees, the actual cost to the firm is W2. After tax, the employee will receive only W3. At this wage, the amount of voluntary unemployment will be L2 – L1. If the tax wedge could be reduced, then the level of voluntary unemployment would be less (L4 – L3).

- The government could provide more information so that employees know what jobs are available; this could increase the mobility of labour.

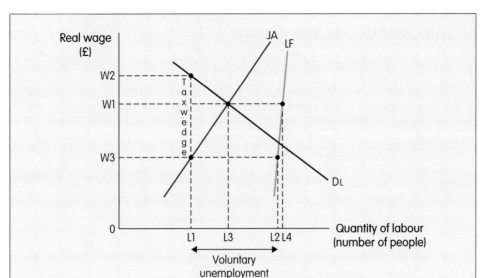

Figure 26.7 The tax wedge.

What do you think?

Should the government reduce the retirement age to create more jobs for younger people?

Economics in context US unemployment

In 2010, the US economy was on target to grow strongly, but unemployment was expected to remain high, according to the US Federal Reserve (the US central bank, known as the 'Fed').

The Federal Reserve expected economic growth of between 2.8 per cent and 3.5 per cent in 2010, but the unemployment rate was expected to remain between 9.5 per cent and 9.7 per cent in 2010. Even though the USA exited the recession last year, the Fed said that unemployment would remain high while both consumers and firms were still cautious about increasing their spending.

Already, under the US government stimulus package, $179 billion (£113 billion) had been spent on increased government projects—ranging from road-building schemes to job training initiatives and health care.

Some $93 billion (£59 billion) worth of tax cuts for both individuals and companies had also been granted.

? Questions

Which types of unemployment are the US policies aimed at reducing?

Explain why the policies of the US government migtht be expected to reduce unemployment. Use diagrams to support your analysis.

Why do you think they do not seem to have been effective?

The costs of unemployment

One of the the main problems with unemployment is that it is inefficient. If there are unemployed resources in the economy, then fewer goods and services are being produced than it is possible to produce. The economy is productively inefficient and is operating within the production possibility frontier (PPF)—for example, at the point X in Figure 26.8.

High levels of unemployment in an area are also likely to mean the following.

- There will be less income in a given region because fewer people are working. This, in turn, means less spending on local goods and services; this can then lead to more unemployment. This lowers living standards in the region due to a downward multiplier effect.

- There will be more social problems because people have more free time and lower incomes. It may, for example, lead to more crime.

- There will be more spending by the government on benefits, such as unemployment benefits.

- There will be less income for the government from taxation. The government will earn less from direct taxation because people are not earning and indirect taxation revenue will also fall because people are not spending as much. With less income and higher spending, the government's budget position will worsen.

- Less investment may occur if firms lose confidence in the economy and so do not want to put money into longer-term projects until unemployment is seen to fall.

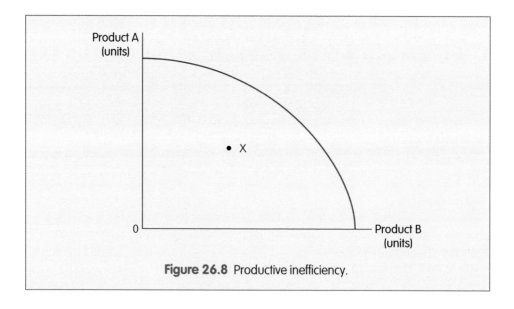

Figure 26.8 Productive inefficiency.

The costs of unemployment can be divided into the following.

- **Private costs** These are the costs for the individual, such as lower morale and lower income.
- **Social costs** These are the costs that affect society as a whole—for example, higher levels of unemployment deter future investment in an area. This can reduce economic growth. High unemployment can also lead to higher crime levels, which can prove disruptive to society.

Economics in context   Unemployment

Severe economic downturns can have pernicious and long-lasting effects on the labour market by lengthening the average duration of unemployment, thereby eroding skills and alienating retrenched workers from the job market. The incidence of long-term unemployment has been rising since 2007. In recent years, the government has introduced a range of measures aimed at increasing labour market flexibility and improving incentives for labour market participation. Existing programmes, however, may be under-resourced for the needs of the large number of people who are losing their jobs, and the downturn will add to pressures on the low-skilled. The government has allocated substantial additional funding for active labour market policies in the Pre-Budget Report and in the Budget. Any further fiscal measures could fund an expansion of these programmes. However, these measures should be subject to careful ongoing evaluation to ensure that returns are sufficient. When the economy recovers, efforts to avoid entrenched long-term unemployment and low employment among some groups will be important. The recent success of the New Deal for Young People programme in activating long-term unemployed youth could be applied more broadly. The proportion of people on disability benefits remains high. The number of beneficiaries has fallen slightly in recent years, reflecting the Pathways to Work scheme and other reforms. The important next step is for the scheme to be expanded to the entire stock of disability benefits recipients as the government plans to do from 2010 onwards.

Source: Based on OECD (2010) *OECD Economic Outlook*, Vol. 2010/1, OECD Publishing

 Questions

Why do you think economic downturns can have long-lasting effects on the labour market?

What types of incentive can a government introduce to improve labour market participation?

Why is it essential to ensure that all measures are subject to 'careful ongoing evaluation'?

Why is it important to review benefit schemes such as disability benefits?

What do you think?

Does unemployment matter? Why?

Should reducing unemployment be a priority in the UK?

Case study Changing the welfare system

When the new coalition government was elected in the UK in 2010, it soon proposed a series of major welfare reforms to try to get more people back to work. The proposal was for all out-of-work benefits and tax credits to be scrapped and replaced with a single payment. The previous system, it was felt, with many different types of benefit, led to waste and also was open to abuse.

Ian Duncan Smith, who was responsible for the new proposals, said that 'ghettos' of worklessness had been created in Britain where generations were growing up without hope or aspiration. He said that the danger of providing benefits that were adequate in amount and indefinite in duration was that 'men settle down to them', and the benefit system had created pockets of worklessness in which 'idleness' had become institutionalized. He believes that it is a scandal that there are 5 million people on out-of-work benefits—nearly 1.5 million of them for nine out of the last ten years.

The aim was to remove disincentives in the tax system to finding work, making sure that claimants did not find themselves worse off when starting a job than on state support, which some say is often the case under current arrangements.

To achieve this, the government wanted to:

- combine elements of current income-related benefits and tax credit systems;

- bring the 50 or so jobless benefits into a single 'universal credit'; and

- supplement monthly household earnings through credit payments reflecting circumstances such as children, housing, and disability.

People who genuinely could not work would carry on receiving the same level of benefits, but for the rest, work would be made more 'attractive' than staying at home on benefits.

❓ Questions

- Explain how unemployment is measured in the UK.

- Using a diagram, show the effects of Duncan Smith's proposals on unemployment should they prove successful.

- What factors might influence the success of the new government proposals?

- Given that unemployment was nearly 8 per cent of the UK labour force in the recession, to what extent do you think these proposals would help reduce this figure?

Checklist

Now that you have read this chapter, try to answer the following questions.

☐ Can you explain the possible causes of unemployment?

☐ Can you outline the costs of unemployment?

☐ Can you examine ways of reducing unemployment?

Review questions

1   What is the difference between voluntary and involuntary unemployment?

2   Would increasing the aggregate demand reduce unemployment?

3   What supply-side policies can be used to reduce unemployment?

4   Why does the level of unemployment in an economy matter?

5   What would the opportunity cost be of trying to reduce unemployment?

Key learning points

- There are different ways of classifying unemployment, such as structural, seasonal, frictional, and cyclical, or voluntary and involuntary.
- Unemployment may be reduced through demand-side or supply-side policies.
- The appropriate methods to reduce unemployment depend on the cause.
- Unemployment imposes both private and social costs.

Learn more

To learn more about levels of unemployment in the UK and government measures to influence these, visit the Online Resource Centre.

 Visit our Online Resource Centre at http://www.oxfordtextbooks.co.uk/orc/gillespie_econ2e/ for test questions and further information on topics covered in this chapter.

» 27 Money and monetary policy

At the heart of an economy is money. We earn it, we save it, and we spend it! This chapter looks at the meaning of money and the functions that it performs. It examines the market for money and considers the consequences of an increase in the amount of money in the economy. It also examines monetary policy in the UK and the role of the Monetary Policy Committee.

LEARNING OBJECTIVES

By the end of this chapter, you should be able to:

✔ explain the key features of money;

✔ explain the factors influencing the demand and supply of money;

✔ outline ways of controlling the money supply.

■ Introduction

'Money makes the world go around' according to one song, but what exactly do we mean by 'money'? Money is something of which we usually want more. It is something for which we work, that we try to accumulate, and something by which we measure success. But what exactly does money do? The answer is that money performs a variety of functions, such as the following.

- **It is a medium of exchange** This means that it is something that the various parties involved in a transaction are willing to accept as payment. If we do not have money to buy products, then we have to exchanges goods and services; this is what happens in a barter economy. The problem with a barter system is that it relies on a double coincidence of wants—that is, you must find someone who wants what you have and who has something that you want—and this is not always easy to find.

- **It is a store of value** For it to be an effective medium of exchange, users of money must be confident that it will hold its value (they would obviously be reluctant to accept something that then became worthless). This, in turn, means that they are confident that others will accept this money in the future in return for products (otherwise it is not much use to them when they want to buy things later).

- **It is a unit of account** This means that money must be in a form whereby it can be used to measure the value of things—for example, the value of an item may be equal to £1, £2, or £10.

Economics in context   **When 2 pence is 3 pence**

A few years ago, the price of copper reached what was then an all-time high of $8,000 per tonne. This was due to major buying by commodity brokers and traders. Every 2 pence piece made before 1992 is 97 per cent copper—that is, it comprises 6.9 g of the metal. Approximately 145,000 coins would equal 1 tonne. The face value of these coins is just £2,900. However, given the level of copper prices at the time, this meant that they were worth around £4,400—that is, they could have been sold for a profit of £1,500. A 2 pence piece was therefore worth over 3 pence!

? Question

The value of the paper used in banknotes or the metals in coins is usually very low and nothing like the value of the money itself (except in the unusual case above). Why, then, are we willing to accept the face value of notes and coins?

In reality, there are different forms of money. For example, if you are asked how much money you have, then you may think of it in terms of the cash that you have in your pocket or the money in your bank account. What about any shares that you may have? What about other forms of savings? Which of these would you count? If you own property or other assets, such as a car, then are these also forms of money?

The answer is that it depends how you want to define 'money'. Some definitions of money are 'narrow'; these concentrate on cash or other items that can be quickly turned into cash (this means that they are 'liquid'). Other definitions of money are broader. This means that they include items that are less liquid (that is, less easy to turn quickly into cash), such as deposit accounts. The various definitions of money are all equally valid, but simply include different items; they highlight that actually defining what money is is not as simple as it may seem.

The narrowest definition of money is M0. This comprises notes and coins (in circulation and in banks' tills), plus the balances that banks hold at the Bank of England. However, notes and coins only represent a relatively small part of what most of us would include when we think about what 'money' we have. Money in a broader sense will include what is held in bank and building society accounts. The measure of money that includes these is called M4.

■ The Bank of England

The Bank of England was established in 1694. It is the UK's central bank and plays a critical role in determining how much money there is in the economy. The role of the Bank of England (and, indeed, any central bank) is to:

- be the banker to the government;

- manage government finances;

- be the banker to commercial banks, such as Lloyds TSB;

- hold gold and foreign-exchange reserves that can be used when trying to influence the exchange rate;

- control the issue of notes and coins; and

- promote and maintain monetary and financial stability to contribute to a healthy economy.

@ Web

For more information on the Bank of England, visit http://www.bankofengland.co.uk

■ Banks and financial institutions

The 1979 and 1987 Banking Acts defined the UK banking sector as consisting of a series of financial institutions the activities of which are supervised by the Bank of England. To be recognized as a bank, a financial institution must be granted a licence.

Financial institutions in the UK include the following.

- **Commercial (retail) banks** These banks, such as Barclays and HSBC, provide banking facilities for individuals as well as businesses. They provide facilities such as current accounts and loans.

- **Merchant banks** These specialize in receiving large deposits from, and lending to, businesses. They also help firms to raise finance.

- **Building societies** These are organizations that are owned by the people who save with them, as opposed to outside investors. However, many former building societies, such as Halifax and Abbey National, turned themselves into public companies owned by shareholders in the 1990s.

- **Finance houses** These organizations specialize in lending money to enable individuals to buy items, such as sofas and electrical goods.

- **Discount houses** These organizations specialize in the short-term lending of money to the government through the Bank of England and to local authorities. To do this, the discount houses obtain money from the banks by borrowing money on short notice that they then lend out.

The role of banks and financial institutions

Banks and other financial institutions exist to make a profit by investing and lending money. To do this, they need money in the first place, which they get via savings. To attract money, banks will offer interest. If you put money into a bank, then it will reward you by paying you interest on your savings. The amount of interest that it offers will depend on:

- for how long you are prepared to leave it in the bank (the longer you can tell the bank that the savings will be left with it, the longer it will have to earn profits with the savings, which should mean that it will pay you higher interest); and
- the amount that you put in the bank (the more money that it has to generate profits, the more that it can offer you).

If you are borrowing money from financial institutions, then the interest rate charged will depend on:

- how much you are borrowing;
- your track record (that is, whether you have a good credit rating; the better your rating, the lower the interest rate that banks can charge);
- for how long you want it; and
- what assets you have as security (collateral) (the lower the risk you are, the lower the interest rate that banks can charge).

There are therefore many different interest rates in an economy that depend on factors such as whether you are borrowing or saving. However, they will be linked to each other—for example, if one savings rate were significantly different from another, then savers would move their money to the institution with the higher rate if they could. Differences in interest rates are due to differences in factors such as the terms and conditions—for example, for how long you are borrowing the money and whether the interest rate is fixed or can fluctuate.

What do you think?

What are the circumstances required to get a low-cost loan?

Changes in the interest rate will affect households and firms in many ways. They will affect:

- the amount that you have to repay on any loans or credit card borrowing, or on any money that you have borrowed via a mortgage to buy a property;
- the cost of any new borrowing (if you go to the bank to borrow money and the interest rate has increased, then this may deter you from borrowing; this will then reduce your spending); and
- the costs to firms of borrowing money and determining whether it is profitable to invest. Higher interest rates usually lead to less investment.

So interest rates obviously have a big impact on the level of spending in the economy. High interest rates will tend to reduce borrowing and spending by firms and households, thereby reducing the aggregate demand. Less investment will also reduce economic growth. An understanding of how interest rates are determined is therefore important. The interest rate is the cost of money (that is, the amount that you pay to borrow it), and, in a free market, would be determined by the supply and demand of money.

Put into practice

High interest rates can reduce the aggregate demand. What others factors might reduce demand in the economy?

■ The market for money

The money market, like any other market, is made up of supply and demand. The interest rate is the price of money, which adjusts to equate the supply and demand of money.

The demand for money

There are various reasons why individuals and firms want to hold money—that is, factors that influence the demand for money. These motives include the following.

- **The transaction motive** People hold money because they need it to live their daily lives. To pay our bills, pay for the bus, and buy a drink, we need money—that is, we need money to finance our transactions. Similarly, firms need money to buy their supplies, pay their rent, and reward their staff.

    The amount of transactions demand will be determined by the following.

    - **Real income levels** With more real income, we are likely to undertake more transactions (buy more things) and therefore need more money for this.
    - **How often people are paid** The less frequently that people are paid, the more they hold on average. Imagine that you are paid £500 per week. When you are paid, you have £500; by the end of the week, you have spent it and have £0. On average, you will have held £250 (see Figure 27.1a). If instead you were paid £26,000 once each year (equal to $52 \times £500$) and spent this over the year, then the average holding during the year would be £13,000 (see Figure 27.1b). The overall annual earnings are the same, but when you are paid less regularly, you hold more on average.
    - **The rate of interest** With higher interest rates, households will try to reduce the amount of money that they need for transactions because of the higher returns from saving. Whilst this might have some effect, it is not likely to be much. For simplicity, we assume that the transactions demand motives are not affected by the interest rate.
- **The precautionary motive** This refers to the way in which people hold money 'just in case' something happens. For example, you may hold some money in case urgent repairs to your house are needed.

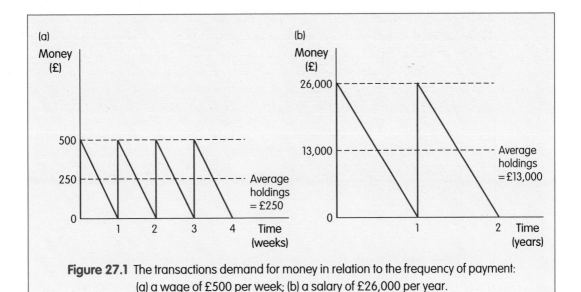

Figure 27.1 The transactions demand for money in relation to the frequency of payment: (a) a wage of £500 per week; (b) a salary of £26,000 per year.

Holding money for transactions and precautionary reasons is described as holding active balances. There is a positive reason why people hold money for these motives.

- **The speculative motive** This is where people hold money whilst waiting to invest it in other assets. If, for example, you are worried that the price of shares is going to fall off, then you might sell your shares and hold the proceeds in the form of more liquid assets for the short term. This level of money holdings is therefore determined by expectations. If you think that the values of some assets are going to fall in the future, then you may hold more money now. If, however, you think that the values of assets are low at the moment, then you might hold less money and invest in other assets instead. This is shown in Figure 27.2. Speculative holdings are called idle balances; you are holding money because you feel that you have to do so, due to what you expect to happen in other markets.

The relationship between interest rates and asset prices

The speculative demand for money is inversely related to the interest rate. This is due to the relationship between interest rates and asset prices. Imagine that you buy a government bond (an 'IOU') for £100 and the government agrees to pay £10 per year until it repays the loan in ten years. The £10 per year represents a 10 per cent return on the £100 spending. If you had paid £200 for this bond, then the return would have been 5 per cent—that is:

$$\frac{£10}{£200} \times 100 = 5\%$$

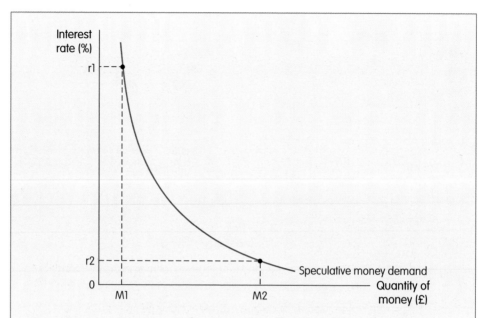

Figure 27.2 The speculative demand for money. For the quantity of money M1 and the interest rate r1, high returns are available on other less liquid assets (their prices are relatively low); firms and households will not want to hold much speculative money. For the quantity of money M2 and the interest rate r2, low returns are available on other assets (their prices are relatively high); firms and households are willing to hold high levels of money.

The higher price of the asset means that the rate of return is lower. The same sort of analysis can be used with other assets. Imagine, for example, that you are going to buy a house to rent out for a given amount per month. The more you pay to buy the house, the lower the rental income will be as a rate of return.

Asset price and interest rates (rates of return) are therefore inversely related. The more that you pay for an asset, the lower the rate of return, and vice versa. This therefore affects the speculative demand for money; when asset prices are perceived to be low (that is, interest rates are high), individuals would rather hold assets than money, believing that they will increase in value. When asset prices are high and interest rates are low, individuals are more likely to want to hold money, because they will fear that asset prices will fall in the future.

What do you think?

If you had £500,000 to save, into what would you put your money? What factors would influence your choice?

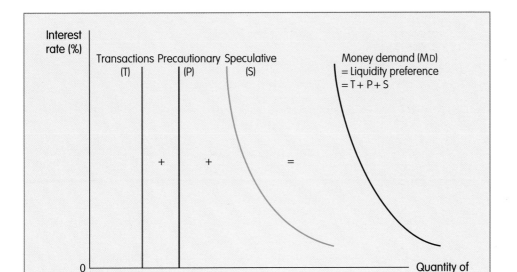

Figure 27.3 The demand for money: the liquidity preference schedule.

The overall demand for money made up of transactions, precautionary, and speculative motives is known as the liquidity preference schedule. This is illustrated in Figure 27.3.

The supply of money

The supply of money at any moment is taken as a given amount. The money supply is, therefore, shown as being completely inelastic relative to the interest rate. Changes in the interest rate are assumed to have no impact on the supply of money available at any moment (see Figure 27.4).

Equilibrium in the money market

Equilibrium in the money market is brought about by changes in interest rates. The interest rate is the price of money and it adjusts to equate the supply of, and demand for, money.

When analysing the money market, we must also consider other asset markets. At any moment in time, households and firms will want to hold a certain amount of money and a certain amount of other assets (such as shares or property). Their decisions about how much to hold of each depend on their desire for liquidity and the returns available in each market. The demand for money is also called liquidity preference; firms and households should hold money because it is liquid and/or because the returns available elsewhere are not attractive.

At any moment, there is a given amount of money available in the economy—that is, the money supply. Imagine that we are at equilibrium at r0 (see Figure 27.5). Households and firms are happy holding the amount of money available.

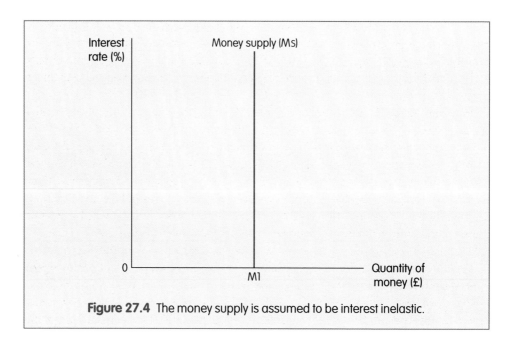

Figure 27.4 The money supply is assumed to be interest inelastic.

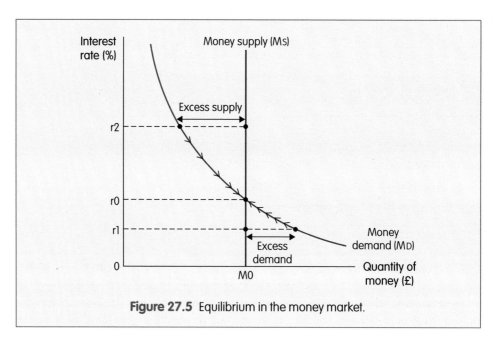

Figure 27.5 Equilibrium in the money market.

Now consider the situation at r1 in Figure 27.5. At r1, there is excess demand for money. At this low rate of return, there is more demand for liquid money than the amount that there actually is available. The return available on other assets is low (which means that their price is high), so households think that they might as well hold liquid money.

They will want to sell their other assets and hold liquid money. As they start selling their other assets, this drives their price down and their rate of return up. This process will continue until the price of assets is so low and the return on them so high that households have no further incentive to hold more money, and are content holding the amount of money M0.

Now consider the situation at r2 in Figure 27.5. At r2, there is excess supply of money. The rate of return on other assets is high, so households want to hold more of them. The excess supply of money means excess demand for other assets. This leads to more demand for other assets, thus bidding up their price. As their price increases (and therefore the return on them falls), this makes these other assets less attractive relative to money. With rising prices and falling returns, people become more willing to hold money, thereby reducing the excess supply. This process continues until equilibrium is reached at r0, and households and organizations are content to hold the amount of money M0.

As you can see, the money market and other asset markets are completely interrelated. An unwillingness to hold the amount of money available in the economy leads to excess demand in the other asset markets. This affects asset prices and returns until people are willing to hold the amount of money available. Similarly, excess demand for money means excess supply of other assets, which again leads to changes in asset prices and returns until equilibrium is restored.

Put into practice

Which of the following statements are true and which are false?

a. The precautionary demand for money is to purchase day-to-day items.

b. When the interest rate is high, demand for money is likely to be high.

c. The supply of money is assumed to be interest inelastic.

d. Excess demand for money is likely to lead to an increase in interest rates.

e. When the price of assets is high, the return on them falls.

f. Liquidity preference schedule is the supply of money.

The growth of the money supply: The money multiplier

When money is deposited in banks, the financial institutions would like to lend it all out or invest it all; in this way, they can earn profits by earning or charging interest. However, they know that the depositors may come and ask for some of it back at any moment. Therefore the banks have to hold some money in reserve. The amount held depends on how much they think is going to be asked for by depositors.

The money that is not kept back can be lent out. For example, it may be lent to individuals to go on holiday or to buy a new house. The money borrowed is therefore likely to be spent on goods and services. The people who receive this spending will deposit it in their banks. Once again, a proportion will be kept in reserve and the remainder will be lent out. Again, it is spent, and again a proportion will be kept back by the banks, and the remainder will be lent. This process continues and is known as the 'money multiplier'. It is equal to:

$$\frac{1}{\text{Reserve ratio}}$$

If, for example, the banks keep 10 per cent in reserve, then the money multiplier is:

$$\frac{1}{0.1} = 10$$

An initial deposit of £100 would therefore increase the total deposits and the money supply will be equal to £1,000.

The money supply may therefore grow if:

- more money is deposited in banks and lent out; and
- the banks keep a smaller proportion of the money deposited in reserve and lend out more at any stage.

The effect of an increase in the money supply on the economy

The effect of an increase in the money supply can be analysed in the following series of stages.

Stage 1: Lower interest rates

Imagine that the money market is initially at r0 (see Figure 27.6a). If there were then an increase in the money supply, this would lead to an excess supply of money at the original rate. Households and firms will want to invest this 'excess money' into other assets. This will lead to more assets being bought, making them more expensive and reducing the return on them. As this happens, these assets become less attractive to invest in (as their price has gone up) and so people become more willing to hold the additional money in the economy. This process continues until the price of the other assets is so high that people are now willing to hold all of the extra money. This happens when the interest rate is at r1 in Figure 27.6a.

Stage 2: Higher aggregate demand

The fall in the interest rate is likely to increase the aggregate demand (see Figures 27.6b and 27.6c). This is because the increase in the money supply affects each of the following.

- **Consumption** With lower interest rates, it is cheaper for households to borrow money and there is less incentive to save. This should lead to extra consumption, thereby increasing the aggregate demand.
- **Investment** With lower interest rates, there will be more projects that have a higher marginal efficiency of capital than the cost of borrowing. This should lead to an increase in investment (how much depends on how sensitive the demand for capital goods is to changes in the interest rate). This will also increase the aggregate demand in the economy.

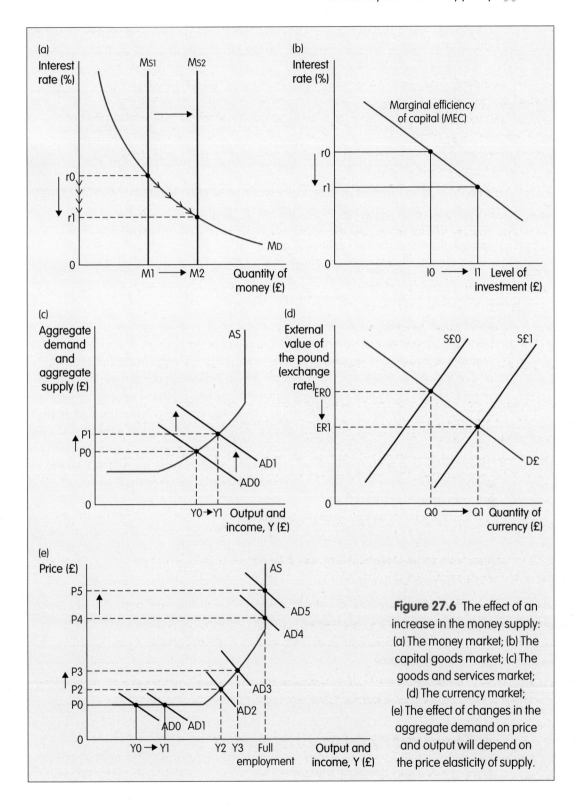

Figure 27.6 The effect of an increase in the money supply: (a) The money market; (b) The capital goods market; (c) The goods and services market; (d) The currency market; (e) The effect of changes in the aggregate demand on price and output will depend on the price elasticity of supply.

- **Exchange rates** Lower interest rates may lead to an outflow of money from the economy because investors will seek higher returns abroad. This is likely to reduce the external value of the currency.

Put into practice

In addition to interest rates, what are the influences on consumption and the influences on investment?

With more money in the economy, there will also be an increase in demand for foreign products and assets. This will lead to an increase in the supply of sterling in exchange for foreign currencies (see Figure 27.6d). Other things being unchanged, this will further decrease the external value of the pound.

The effect of a weaker currency should make UK exports cheaper abroad in foreign currency, thereby boosting demand for exports. This, in turn, boosts the aggregate demand.

For more on exchange rates, see Chapter 20.

Stage 3: Higher prices and output

The consequences of an increase in the money supply are likely to be an increase in the aggregate demand either via interest rates boosting consumption, investment, and exports, or the exchange rate effect. If the economy is well below its potential output, then this increase in the aggregate demand means that there is a high level of unused capacity and there are likely to be high levels of unemployment. An increase in demand would, in these circumstances, lead to more output, as shown in Figure 27.6e when the aggregate demand increases from AD0 to AD1. If the economy is at full employment, then this means that the aggregate supply is completely price inelastic. An increase in demand will lead to an increase in prices (that is, inflation), as shown in Figure 27.6e when the aggregate demand increases from AD4 to AD5.

An increase in the money supply may therefore:

- increase output (if the economy is below full employment);
- increase prices (if the economy is at full employment); or
- increase prices and output (if the economy is approaching full employment).

The effects of an increase in the money supply on prices and output can also be analysed using the quantity theory of money.

Put into practice

Outline the possible impact of a decrease in the money supply on the aggregate demand.

▪ The quantity theory of money

The quantity theory of money states that:

$$MV = PT$$

where:

- M is the quantity of money in the economy;
- V is the velocity of circulation—that is, this measures how often money moves around or is used in any given period;
- P is the average price level of goods and services; and
- T is the number of transactions—that is, the quantity of national output sold in a year.

The quantity PT is therefore equal to the money value of the national output sold in a year (basically, Price × Quantity).

The quantity MV represents the total spending on national output and must therefore equal PT because, unsurprisingly, total spending must equal the total amount spent!

For example, if the money supply is £100 billion and each pound is spent five times then the total spending is:

$$5 \times £100 \text{ billion} = £500 \text{ billion}$$

This means that the value of goods bought is £500 billion. If 25 billion goods were bought, then the average price level would be £20.

If the economy is at full employment, then the number of transactions in the economy cannot increase. If the velocity of circulation is also stable, then this means that an increase in the money supply leads to an increase in the price level—that is, more money in the economy leads to inflation. An increase in M leads to an increase in P.

For example, if the money supply were now £200 billion and each pound were still spent five times, then the total spending would be £1,000 billion. If the number of goods were still 25 billion, then this means that the price level would be £40. A doubling of the money supply has doubled the price level.

However, if the economy is below full employment, then this means that an increase in the money supply can lead to more output (that is, more transactions). In other words, an increase in M can lead to an increase in T. This means that the price level may not increase—that is, an increase in the money supply may not lead to inflation.

For example, MV could be £1,000 billion, but if the number of transactions doubles to 50 billion, then the average price level remains at £20.

Also, it is possible that the velocity of circulation may decrease. This could be because of lower interest rates, so there is less pressure to pass money on quickly (due to a lower opportunity cost). In this case, an increase in the money supply might lead to a decrease in the velocity of circulation. This means that there may not be any extra overall spending in the economy and therefore the price level may not increase.

■ Monetarists

Economists known as monetarists believe that V and T are relatively stable. They therefore think that an increase in the money supply will lead to an increase in the price level. In fact, they think that 'inflation is always and everywhere a monetary phenomenon in the sense that it is and can be produced only by a more rapid increase in the quantity of money than output' (Friedman, 1968)—that is, inflation is always due to growth in the money supply. Over time, the full employment level in an economy can increase due to, for example, developments in technology. This enables some growth in the number of transactions (T), so the money supply can grow in line with this without being inflationary. However, 'excessive money supply growth' will lead to more demand and higher prices.

The monetarists argued that the cause of inflation must ultimately be the money supply. Imagine that we have a situation in which

- quantity of money (M) is £100 billion;
- velocity of circulation (V) is 5 billion;
- overall spending (MV) is:

    $5 \times £100$ billion = £500 billion

- number of transactions (T) is 25 billion.

Therefore the average price level is £20.

Imagine that the price level now increases to £50, perhaps due to an increase in wages or imported components. If the money supply does not grow to accommodate this and the velocity does not change, then this means that the total spending is still:

    $5 \times £100$ billion = £500 billion

Because the price level is £50, the number of transactions must fall to 10 billion.

The higher prices without more money supply in the economy lead to fewer goods being bought and probably unemployment. This will put downward pressure on wages and prices, which will force the price back down to £20. Inflation has not persisted because the money supply was controlled.

However, if the money supply were allowed to expand, then the inflation could continue. For example, if the money supply were to grow to £250 billion, then MV would become:

    $5 \times £250$ billion = £1,250 billion

Also:

    $PT = £50 \times 25$ billion = £1,250 billion

A growth in the money supply has allowed prices to stay higher.

According to monetarist theory, the temptation for governments is to let the money supply grow if prices increase. Although this leads to higher inflation, it avoids a difficult period of higher unemployment that is necessary to bring prices down if the money supply is not expanded.

Clearly, the growth of the money supply and, in fact, controlling its growth are key elements of the monetarist approach.

According to the Bank of England:

> The amount of money in the economy and the level of prices are positively related in the long run. Without money, inflation could not exist. And, across many countries, persistently high rates of money growth have usually been associated with high inflation . . .
>
> . . . Although money and inflation are clearly linked over the longer term, the usefulness of money as an indicator of inflationary pressures in the short to medium term depends on there

being a predictable relationship between money and the value of spending. For example, suppose money grew at the same rate as the value of spending over time. Then money growth of 4.0%–4.5% per year would be consistent with annual growth in economic activity of 2%–2.5%—the historical average in the UK—plus inflation of 2.0% per year, in line with the inflation target.

In practice, however, the relationship between money and inflation has not been stable. Money growth has been influenced by many other factors, including financial innovations—such as the introduction of credit cards—changes in banking regulations, and developments in international capital markets. The effects of these changes have not always been easy to predict accurately. So rules of thumb like the one above have not usually been useful guides for policy.

Put into practice

Which of the following statements are true and which are false?

a. An increase in the money supply, other things unchanged, is likely to lead to a fall in the interest rate.

b. The monetarists assume that an increase in the money supply is deflationary.

c. A decrease in the demand for money is likely to lead to an increase in interest rates.

d. A decrease in the amount banks keep in reserve is likely to increase the money supply.

 Web

For more information on the Bank of England, visit http://www.bankofengland.co.uk

---

What do you think?

According to the Bank of England, do you think that monitoring or controlling the money supply would reduce inflation?

■ Factors that might limit the impact of an increase in the money supply on prices

The impact of an increase in the money supply on prices might be limited by the following factors.

- **The liquidity trap** At very low interest rates (which means very high asset prices), an increase in the money supply may not lead to a fall in interest rates (see Figure 27.7). Firms and households would simply absorb the extra money. The returns elsewhere are simply too low to appeal. The extra money is held with no impact on asset prices or interest rates; the demand for money is horizontal. The velocity of circulation falls as the money supply increases.

- The demand for money generally may not be very interest elastic, so any increase in the money supply might have a relatively small impact on interest rates (and therefore on the aggregate demand).

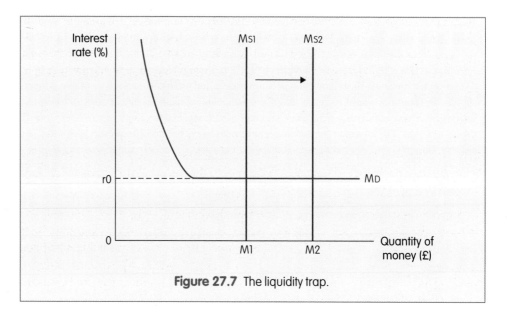

Figure 27.7 The liquidity trap.

- The impact of lower interest rates on consumption and demand may be limited. Investment in capital goods is very dependent on expectations, for example, so a fall in interest rates on its own may have a limited effect.
- The economy may be below full employment, in which case output increases and the number of transactions (T) rises.

In any of these cases, an increase in the money supply would not have a significant impact on prices and inflation.

Put into practice

Which of the following statements are true and which are false?

a. Lower interest rates should increase aggregate demand.

b. In the liquidity trap, an increase in the money supply does not affect interest rates.

c. An increase in the reserve ratio at banks should increase the money supply.

d. The quantity theory of money states that $MP = VT$.

Controlling the money supply

If an increase in the money supply does lead to inflation, then governments will want to try to control it to achieve their objective of stable prices if high inflation appears to be an issue. A central bank may attempt to reduce the money supply as follows.

- **Requesting that banks keep higher reserves and lend less out at any stage** The Bank of England, for example, can try to persuade other banks that this would be desirable for the economy. If the Bank of England can reduce the amount lent out at each stage by the banks, then this will slow the growth of the money supply.

- **Open market operations occur when a government buys or sells bonds** For example, to reduce the money supply, the government might sell bonds. To buy these bonds, households will use their money. This will usually be taken out of their banks. This reduces the amount that the banks have to lend out, thereby reducing the growth of the money supply.

Problems controlling the money supply

In the 1980s, UK governments tried to control the money supply in order to control inflation according to the monetarist view. However, there are often problems keeping the money supply under control, such as the following.

- **Knowing which definition of the money supply to control** Whichever definition you choose, you are likely to find that individuals and institutions find ways around these restrictions. For example, if you control the lending by banks, then you might find that building societies start lending more instead. According to Goodhart's Law, trying to control one particular indicator will simply lead to that indicator ceasing to be valid as banks find other ways of lending!

- **Disintermediation** If controls are put on bank lending, then banks may position themselves as financial advisers. For example, they may put a company that wants to borrow in contact with a business that wants to lend. For this, they charge a fee. They have, in effect, lent a business money, but not directly (which is why this is known as disintermediation), so it is difficult to regulate. Financial institutions make their money from lending, so whatever a government does to stop this will be resisted and ways will be found to avoid control (for example, organizing more lending via overseas banks).

Put into practice

a. If the money multiplier is 5, the reserve ratio is:
- 0.5 per cent.
- 5 per cent.
- 10 per cent.
- 20 per cent.

b. A central bank may increase the money supply:
- by increasing reserve requirements.
- by increasing Bank Rate.
- by means of an open-market purchase of government bonds.
- by reducing the government deficit.

c. A decrease in reserve requirements _____ the money multiplier and _____ the money supply. Which of the following best completes this statement?
- increases; increases
- increases; decreases
- decreases; decreases
- decreases; increases

▨ Monetary policy in the UK

After disappointing experiences trying to control the money supply in the 1980s, monetary policy in the UK in recent years has focused on controlling the interest rate set by the Bank of England (called Bank Rate) and using this to control the demand for money. Higher interest rates should reduce the quantity of money demanded; less will be borrowed from banks, thereby reducing the money supply (see Figure 27.8).

In May 1997, the Labour government gave the Bank of England's Monetary Policy Committee (MPC) the ability to set whatever interest rates it felt were necessary to achieve given inflation targets. This was made law with the Bank of England Act 1998. Price stability at present is defined by the government's inflation target of 2 per cent. By providing stable inflation rates, it is believed that this will encourage investment (for more on this, see Chapter 24). If inflation is more than 1 per cent above or below the 2 per cent target, the governor of the Bank of England must write to the chancellor of the exchequer to explain why.

Prior to the creation of the independent MPC, interest rates had been influenced by the government and were often used to achieve political, rather than economic, objectives. When an election was coming up, for example, the pressure was on to reduce the interest rate to make borrowing cheaper and therefore make the government more popular, even if it was not the right decision for the economy as a whole.

For much of the last decade, the MPC was trying to keep inflation down to achieve its target. This involved changing the interest rate to influence consumption, investment, and the exchange rate to achieve the desired levels of aggregate demand. If demand looked like it was going to be too high and pull up prices, the interest rate would be increased to dampen demand.

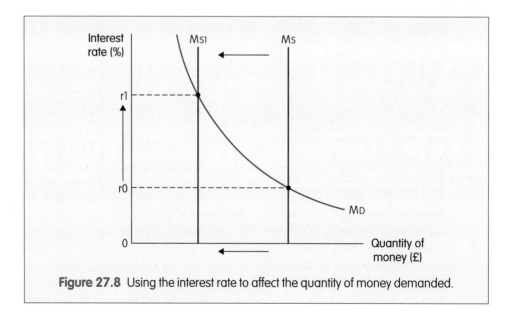

Figure 27.8 Using the interest rate to affect the quantity of money demanded.

Economics
in context　　India increases interest rates

In August 2010, the Reserve Bank of India (RBI) increased the rate at which it lends to banks to 5.75 per cent from 5.5 per cent. The aim was to reduce the high inflation in the country. Indian inflation had been in double figures for five months. Rising prices—particularly in food and fuel—had provoked public protests in India and become a major political issue. Food costs have been growing since last year, when the worst drought in 37 years hit farm output.

The RBI said in a statement that controlling inflation was more important than securing economic growth, which is forecast at 8.5 per cent for the coming year.

? Questions

Analyse the ways in which higher interest rates can lead to lower inflation.

Do you agree that controlling inflation is more important than securing economic growth?

When the recession hit, the problem was that demand fell dramatically and the MPC was worried about inflation being too low, not too high. In this situation, it lowered interest rates to encourage borrowing and spending. Despite lowering Bank Rate (the rate at which the Bank of England lends to other banks) to the lowest level for 300 years, demand remained too low and the MPC had to try to boost the money supply using quantitative easing.

Quantitative easing

On 5 March 2010, the MPC reduced Bank Rate to 0.5 per cent and undertook what is called quantitative easing. This meant that it began purchasing public and private sector assets, using central bank money. The purpose of this was to inject money into the economy to provide an additional stimulus to spending.

The conventional way for the MPC to conduct monetary policy is by setting Bank Rate. The introduction of asset purchases has shifted the focus of monetary policy, but the objectives have not changed. The aim of the MPC remains that of achieving inflation of 2 per cent (within a band of 1 per cent either side). Asset purchases provide an additional tool to help the MPC to meet those objectives.

The Bank of England is the sole supplier of central bank money in sterling. As well as banknotes, central bank money takes the form of reserve balances held by banks at the Bank of England. These balances are used to make payments between different banks. The Bank can create new money electronically by increasing the balance on a reserve account. So when the Bank purchases an asset from a bank as part of quantitative easing, it simply credits that bank's reserve account with the additional funds. This generates an expansion in the supply of central bank money. Commercial banks hold deposits for their customers, which can be used by households and companies to buy goods and services, or assets. These deposits form the bulk of 'broad money'. If the Bank of England purchases an asset from a non-bank company, it pays for the asset via the seller's bank. It credits the reserve account of the seller's bank with the funds and that bank credits the account of the seller with a deposit. The expansion of broad money is a key part of the transmission mechanism for quantitative easing.

Why use quantitative easing?

The reduction of Bank Rate to 0.5 per cent in 2009 in the UK should have encouraged borrowing and spending, and thereby boosted aggregate demand, and this should also have been supported by other factors, such as fiscal policy and a weak value of the currency (which should make exports relatively cheap and encourage export demand). Even so, the MPC felt that monetary policy needed to do even more (to be 'looser') in order to boost aggregate demand.

The decision to expand the money supply through large-scale asset purchases (or quantitative easing) shifted the focus of monetary policy towards the quantity of money, as well as the price of money. Asset purchases were intended to boost spending and so help to meet the inflation target.

However, there was considerable uncertainty about the strength and pace with which these effects would feed through. It depended in part on what sellers did with the money that they received in exchange for the assets that they sold to the Bank of England and the response of banks to the additional liquidity that they obtained.

Economics in context   ## Regulating the financial sector

The global recession of 2008–09 was linked to high levels of risk-taking by the banking sector. Given the property boom and growing economies, banks had been willing to lend with little collateral on the assumption that property would rise in value, and that individuals would earn more and be able to repay. This created a property bubble, which burst in 2007, leading to the collapse of several major banks and concerns over the stability of the banking system. The consequent tightening of lending (the credit crunch) then contributed to the recession as households and firms had to cut back due to a lack of finance. Not surprisingly, regulating the financial sector became a key issue in many economies.

In June 2010, the UK chancellor George Osborne announced that he would abolish the existing system of financial regulation and give the Bank of England the key role in regulating the UK financial sector. The Financial Services Authority (FSA) would 'cease to exist in its current form'.

Mr Osborne said that the new government wanted a system of regulation that 'learns the lessons of the greatest banking crisis in our lifetime'. He criticized the current tripartite system of regulation, which divided responsibility between the Bank of England, the FSA, and HM Treasury. 'No one was controlling levels of debt and when the crunch came, no one knew who was in charge,' he said. The changes meant that the FSA would be broken up, but the part that monitors financial institutions would operate as a subsidiary of the Bank of England. The government also created a powerful new Financial Policy Committee at the Bank of England.

BANK OF ENGLAND	FINANCIAL SERVICES AUTHORITY (FSA)	HM TREASURY
Risk-assesses banks	Regulates financial sector	Shares regulatory role with Bank of England and FSA under tripartite system
Provides intelligence to FSA and HM Treasury	Helps to fight financial crime	
NEW SYSTEM		
To take on most FSA functions to streamline decision-making	Effectively abolished	Remains regulator of last resort, but Bank of England takes day-to-day lead

Figure 27.9 Financial regulation: Who does what.

Gordon Brown, made chancellor when the Labour Party won the 1997 general election, created the FSA following criticism that the Bank of England had failed to regulate the UK's financial system sufficiently. But, in recent years, critics said that it was not clear who would be in charge in a crisis and that the tripartite financial authorities needed to communicate better with each other. The FSA was heavily criticized for not doing enough to prevent or limit the crisis in the financial markets.

? Questions

How might a government control the banking sector?

What problems might there be for a government trying to control the banking sector and restrict its lending?

@ Web

For more information on the Monetary Policy Committee, visit http://www.bankofengland.co.uk/monetarypolicy/overview.htm

Case study UK interest rates at 0.5 per cent

The Bank of England has voted to keep interest rates on hold at 0.5% amid concerns over the strength of the economic recovery.

The decision by the bank's Monetary Policy Committee (MPC) means rates will stay at their current record low for an 18th month. It suggests the committee does not see high inflation as a serious concern.

Inflation is still well above the bank's target rate of 2% on the Consumer Prices Index (CPI) measure. Last month CPI was at 3.2%, though it has been falling in recent months, and the bank expects inflation to fall to close to the 2% target this year.

The bank's programme of quantitative easing also remains on hold, but the option to pump more money into the economy remains open. Last year, £200 billion was injected into the economy by the bank in an effort to boost economic growth.

'Right decision'

Economists broadly welcomed the bank's decision, arguing that low interest rates were still needed to help the recovery in the economy, particularly with cuts in public sector spending expected to hit growth.

'While GDP growth in [the second quarter] was the strongest in four years, the data probably overstated the strength of economic activity,' said Nida Ali, economic adviser to the Ernst and Young Item Club. 'And with significant fiscal tightening ahead, growth is likely to slow significantly.'

Rising prices are not a major concern for the MPC: 'The tough deficit-reduction measures announced in the Budget, although necessary, will inevitably increase the threat of a UK economic setback.

'Given the precarious economic background, it is absolutely vital that the MPC maintains the current low level of interest rates until the second quarter of 2011 at the earliest.'

Losing momentum?

The concern over the economy comes despite the strong 1.1% rise in GDP reported in the second quarter of the year.

More recent economic data has added to concerns that the recovery may be faltering.

A recent purchasing managers' index report indicated that growth in the services sector had slowed to its lowest rate in more than a year in July.

The sluggish recovery is expected to limit individuals' spending power, preventing prices from rising further.

Source: http://www.bbc.co.uk/news/business-10880944

❓ Questions

- Why did the MPC decide to keep interest rates low?
- Explain why the UK government sets an inflation target.
- Explain what is meant by quantitative easing. What effect was it expected to have in the economy? Why was it regarded as necessary?
- Why was there little concern about inflation at the time?

Checklist

Now that you have read this chapter, try to answer the following questions.

☐ Can you explain the key features of money?

☐ Can you explain the factors influencing the demand for and supply of money?

☐ Do you understand the role of the Bank of England's Monetary Policy Committee?

☐ Can you outline ways of controlling the money supply?

Review questions

1 Is money the same as cash?

2 In a free market, what would determine the interest rate?

3 Does growth in the money supply lead to inflation?

4 What is the role of the Monetary Policy Committee?

5 Why do interest rates matter?

Key learning points

- Monetary policy uses the money supply and interest rates to control the economy.

- The motives for holding money include the transactions motive, the precautionary motive, and the speculative motive.

- The interest rate in the UK is determined by the Bank of England's Monetary Policy Committee; it is used to achieve an inflation target.

- The quantity theory of money states that $MV = PT$. If V and T are constant, then an increase in the money supply leads to an increase in the price level. This is known as a monetarist view of the causes of inflation.

- The interest rate affects borrowing, saving, the price of assets, and the exchange rate.

- Quantitative easing is intended to inject money into the economy to stimulate spending.

Reference

Friedman, M. (1968) 'The role of monetary policy', *American Economic Review*, 58(Mar): 1–17

Learn more

To learn more about the UK government's approach to monetary policy over the years, visit the Online Resource Centre.

 Visit our Online Resource Centre at http://www.oxfordtextbooks.co.uk/orc/gillespie_econ2e/ for test questions and further information on topics covered in this chapter.

Inflation

One common economic objective of government is to achieve stable prices. This involves controlling inflation. This chapter examines the causes and problems of inflation, and considers how inflation may be controlled.

LEARNING OBJECTIVES

By the end of this chapter, you should be able to:

✔ explain what is meant by inflation;

✔ outline the different causes of inflation;

✔ explain the costs of inflation;

✔ examine ways of reducing inflation;

✔ discuss the possible trade-off between inflation and unemployment.

■ Introduction

Inflation occurs when there is a sustained increase in the general price level over a given period. If annual inflation is 2 per cent, for example, this means that prices are generally 2 per cent higher than the year before.

Inflation measures the change in prices year on year—that is:

$$\text{Inflation} = \frac{(\text{Prices } t - \text{Prices } t\text{-}1) \times 100}{\text{Prices } t\text{-}1}$$

where:

- t is a particular moment in time; and
- t-1 is the year before.

In the UK, inflation is generally measured by the consumer prices index (CPI) and the retail prices index (RPI). These both compare the price of a typical basket of goods and services of a household with the price of the same basket the year before. They differ in the items included in the basket: for example, the RPI includes council tax, mortgage interest payments, buildings insurance, and house depreciation. This means that lower mortgage costs would reduce the RPI, but not affect the CPI.

Inflation reduces the purchasing power of a currency within its economy; it reduces its internal value. If prices are increasing in the UK, then £1 will not be able to buy as much as it did before the price increase. For example, if you were to have spent £1 on petrol in 1955, by 2008 you would have needed to spend £24.75 to have kept pace with inflation.

Economics in context | **Inflation basket**

The items in the typical basket of goods used to calculate the CPI are regularly reviewed to make sure that they match the current spending patterns. The ONS updates its 650-strong basket of goods and services annually, to better reflect public spending habits. It collects about 180,000 separate price quotations of these items in 150 areas of the UK. When the index first began, it included wild rabbits, candles, and corsets. In recent years, items such as salad cream and streaky bacon have been taken out, while herbal tea, mayonnaise, salmon fillets, and gym membership have been added in.

Changes to the basket used to measure inflation in 2010 included the introduction of lip gloss and electrical hair straighteners; these replaced lipstick and hair dryers as consumer buying habits changed. Blu-ray disc players, as well as computer games and accessories, also made their way into the basket, whereas disposable cameras and squash court hire have gone.

The 2010 basket also saw the entrance of small bottles of mineral water that reflect the 'on the go' drinks market. This has replaced the fizzy canned drink as consumers become more aware of a healthy diet. Greater interest in personal health and eating habits is also a factor in the introduction of cereal bars and allergy tablets. In the bathroom, liquid soap has replaced individual bars of toilet soap. Although the basket gives a snapshot of the UK's spending patterns, some items in the basket merit inclusion in their own right—such as petrol—whereas others are representative of an area of spending—such as spades, representing garden tools.

? Questions

What are the top ten items in your typical shopping basket each week?

To what extent do you think your basket of goods would be similar to a typical basket of goods? What does this mean about the value of the CPI as a measure of inflation for you?

@ Web

For more information on the CPI, visit the Office for National Statistics website at http://www.ons.gov.uk

You can calculate your own personal inflation index at http://www.statistics.gov.uk/PIC/index.html

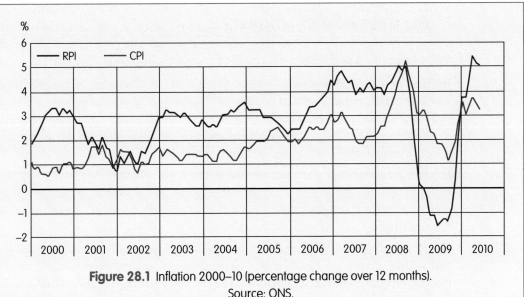

Figure 28.1 Inflation 2000–10 (percentage change over 12 months).
Source: ONS.

Economics in context

UK inflation

In December 2009, the CPI rose to 2.9 per cent, up from 1.9 per cent the month before. This was the biggest jump in the annual rate from one month to anther since records began. This increase in CPI mainly came about because of a number of unusual factors that had depressed prices a year earlier. These included a near-record fall in oil prices in December 2008, the VAT cut to 15 per cent, and retail discounting; once these were reversed, inflation jumped.

Source: ONS

 Questions

Are you necessarily worse off if inflation increases?

Who do you think is most likely to be affected?

What is inflation at the moment in your country?

Put into practice

Which of the following statements are true and which are false?

a. Inflation of 2 per cent means that the prices of all goods are increasing by 2 per cent.

b. Inflation increases the standard of living.

c. Inflation increases the cost of living.

d. If inflation falls from 3 per cent to 2 per cent, prices are falling.

e. If inflation is negative, prices are falling.

■ Why does inflation matter?

Inflation can cause a number of problems for an economy, such as the following.

- Inflation may damage business confidence because of fears about the future impact on costs. This may reduce levels of investment. Uncertainty about future inflation rates will make it difficult to estimate future profits and therefor may deter many projects, damaging economic growth. This is a key concern regarding inflation, because it can affect demand in the economy and its future growth.

- If prices are increasing, this creates costs for firms, because they may have to update their promotional material to reflect the higher prices. For example, this means reprinting brochures, updating price lists, and changing vending machines. These are called 'menu costs'.

- With higher rates of inflation, individuals and firms may have to search more to find the best returns on their savings. This will be necessary to preserve the real rate of return (that is, the return adjusted for inflation). The costs of searching around are called 'shoe leather costs'.

- Not all individuals will have the bargaining power to ensure that their own earnings rise at the same rate as prices are increasing. If their wages do not increase as much as prices, then, in real terms, they are worse off. Their real income has fallen. The ability of an employee to bargain for higher wages in line with inflation depends on the extent to which they are in demand and/or whether they are well represented by trade unions. Inflation may therefore redistribute real incomes. Some groups, such as pensioners, may find that their earnings keep pace with inflation; others may not. This means that inflation has redistributive effects.

- Internationally, if the prices of firms in the UK are increasing faster than those of their trading partners, then this may make the country's products uncompetitive compared with those of foreign firms. This may reduce the earnings from exports and increase the spending on imports. This will affect the balance of payments adversely. Domestically, the UK may also struggle to compete because imports will be relatively cheaper.

- Tax thresholds often do not increase in line with inflation. If employees gain a pay increase to match inflation, then they are not better off in real terms. However, with higher nominal pay, individuals may enter a higher tax band and therefore be worse off. This is called fiscal drag. Again, inflation is redistributing income.

The effects of inflation will depend partly on whether it is 'anticipated' or 'unanticipated' inflation. If you know that prices are going to rise and you have the bargaining power, then you can demand higher wages to compensate, for example. However, if you are locked into a 2 per cent pay increase and then inflation unexpectedly increases to 5 per cent, then you will be worse off in real terms. If inflation levels are regularly unanticipated, then this will lead to high levels of uncertainty in the economy, which may deter investment and affect spending, and impact saving decisions. The impact also depends on the rate of inflation; higher rates are more damaging than low rates.

What causes inflation?

The causes of inflation include the following.

- **Too much demand in the economy** This is shown by an outward shift of the aggregate demand curve. If demand is growing faster than supply, then this will pull prices up, causing demand-pull inflation. If firms cannot meet the demand, then they will increase their prices. Demand-pull inflation is characterized by shortages, low levels of stocks, long waiting lists, and queues. In this situation, firms will be eager to produce more as soon as they can. They may invest in extra capacity, but this can take time to come online. In the short term, supply is likely to be price inelastic because firms may not be able to recruit staff easily or produce more given the existing equipment. This means that an increase in demand will affect prices more than output. Inflation caused by an increase in demand is shown in Figure 28.2.

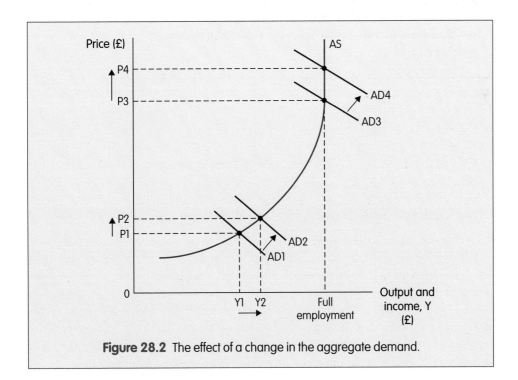

Figure 28.2 The effect of a change in the aggregate demand.

NOTE In this figure, an increase in demand simply leads to an increase in the price level; inflation measures the rate of growth of prices, so for inflation to be shown properly on this figure over time, aggregate demand would need to keep increasing.

- **Monetary inflation** According to monetarists, inflation occurs when there is too much money supply in the economy. With more money circulating, this leads to more demand in the economy, and then higher prices. This is a form of demand-pull inflation that is caused specifically by excess growth of the money supply.

- Cost-push inflation This type of inflation is caused by costs increasing—for example, this could be because of:
  - higher wages that are not related to productivity gains;
  - higher import prices—perhaps because the exchange rate has fallen, meaning more pounds are needed to buy the same goods as before (for more on this, see Chapter 30);
  - monopoly suppliers pushing up their prices; or
  - higher materials prices—for example, higher demand for oil might pull up its price, increasing energy costs; a supply shock in agricultural markets might increase food prices.

Faced with higher costs, firms increase their prices to customers to maintain profit margins. This shifts the aggregate supply curve to the left and causes cost-push inflation (see Figure 28.3). An inward shift of the aggregate supply will also lead to a fall in output and to firms operating under capacity. Again, to truly show inflation, aggregate supply would have to keep increasing so that prices are growing over time rather than only as a one-off increase. Much of the inflation in the last few years in the UK has been to supply-side shocks, such as increases in food prices or oil prices, caused by shortages that have pushed up the prices of a typical shopping basket.

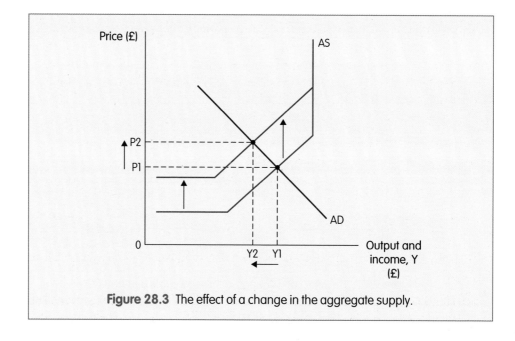

Figure 28.3 The effect of a change in the aggregate supply.

Put into practice

Which one(s) of the following might cause demand-pull inflation?

- An increase in export demand

- An increase in import spending

- An increase in savings

- A decrease in taxation rates

Economics in context   Hyperinflation

From 2006, Zimbabwe experienced hyperinflation; this means that it experienced extremely high rates of inflation. In 2006, for example, inflation reached 1,000 per cent. On average, goods were about 11 times as expensive in April 2006 as they were 12 months earlier. To respond to this massive increase in prices, the government introduced a 'bearer cheque' worth Z$50,000. This was 50 times the highest available banknote, but was actually worth only around half a US dollar (US$) and could only just buy a loaf of bread at the time. Hyperinflation continued for the next few years.

By 2008, the use of foreign currency as a common medium of exchange became increasingly popular, as fewer goods and services were being offered in local currency. The government actually licensed around 1,000 shops to sell goods in foreign currency.

On 12 January 2009, Zimbabwe introduced the Z$50 trillion note and announced plans for imminent issue of banknotes of Z$10 trillion, Z$20 trillion, Z$50 trillion, and Z$100 trillion. At the time it was announced, the Z$100 trillion note was worth around US$30.

On 29 January 2009, in an effort to counteract the runaway inflation, the acting finance minister announced that Zimbabweans were permitted to use other, more stable currencies (for example, the South African rand) to do business, alongside the Zimbabwe dollar. The following month, the government of Zimbabwe revalued its currency. One of these new Zimbabwean dollars is worth one trillion of the former dollars. This move took the number of decimal places removed during the period of hyperinflation to 25 (10^{25} is 10 'septillion'—thus, if no revaluation had taken place, Zimbabwe would now be issuing Z$10 septillion notes).

Questions

What problems do you think are caused by hyperinflation in an economy?

Do you think that changing the currency is likely to cure inflation?

■ Controlling inflation

To control inflation, there is a variety of methods that the government may use, such as the following.

- **Reducing the aggregate demand** To control demand-pull inflation, the government will want to reduce the level of the aggregate demand in the economy relative to supply.

This may be done using deflationary fiscal or restrictive monetary policies, such as reduced government expenditure, higher taxes, or higher interest rates.

- **Reducing costs** To control cost-push inflation, government would not want to reduce demand because this would lead to even less output in the economy (see Figure 28.4). In this situation, the government may do the following.

  - Government may introduce wage restraint in the public sector, where it can control wages. It may also introduce wage controls across the economy to prevent wages from increasing too fast. This is known as an incomes policy. However, incomes policies can lead to frustration on the part of employers, who want to offer more money to reward and attract good-quality employees. Employees may also be frustrated and look for better-paid jobs abroad.

  - Government may try to influence the exchange rate to make the external value of the pound stronger. This gives UK-based firms more purchasing power, making it cheaper to buy in supplies from abroad. However, it may affect exports adversely.

- **Setting inflation targets** By setting clear targets for inflation and giving the relevant organizations the authority to take actions to achieve these, a government can try to convince households and business people that such targets will be met. For example, the UK government, in 2004 onwards, had an inflation target of 2 per cent. Its success in achieving this target early on helped to convince individuals and groups that this was going to be the level of inflation in the future. As a result, wage claims and price

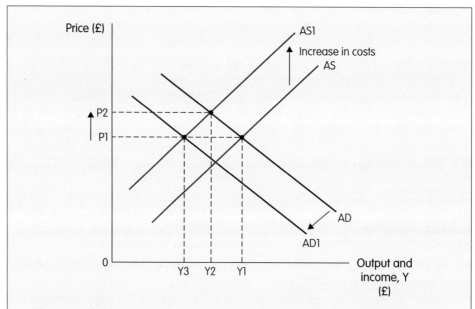

Figure 28.4 An increase in costs causes cost-push inflation. Prices increase from P1 to P2. If the government reduces aggregate demand to bring prices back down, the national income will fall to Y3.

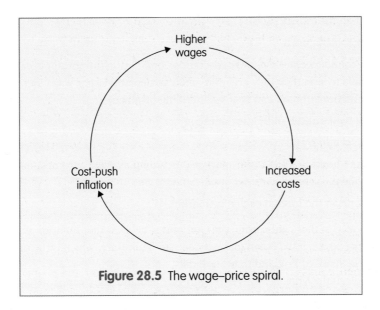

Figure 28.5 The wage–price spiral.

increases were linked to this level of expectations. If, on the other hand, people think that inflation is going to be very high, then they will demand high wages. This could cause higher prices due to cost-push inflation. This inflation could then stimulate higher wages, higher costs, and higher inflation again. This is called the 'wage–price spiral' (see Figure 28.5).

What do you think?

Do you think that the government should aim for an inflation rate of 0 per cent in the UK?

■ The Monetary Policy Committee in the UK

As we saw in the last chapter, in May 1997, the Labour government gave the Bank of England's Monetary Policy Committee (MPC) the ability to set whatever interest rates it felt were necessary to achieve given inflation targets. Price stability at present is defined by the government's inflation target of 2 per cent. If inflation is more than 1 per cent either side of this target, the governor of the Bank of England has to write a letter to the government's chancellor of the exchequer explaining why.

The MPC meets monthly to assess the possible level of inflation and to decide on what to do about the interest rate. The Committee is made up of nine members; some are from the Bank of England, but others are outsiders who provide a different perspective. The Committee considers indicators such as:

- the growth in the money supply;
- national income figures;
- consumer confidence surveys and expectations of inflation (important because if people expect prices to rise, then they are more likely to demand larger wage increases, and so expecting higher inflation can be a self-fulfilling prophecy);
- lending by banks and building societies;
- consumer spending and credit;
- trends in the housing and labour markets, including average earnings, unit costs, and unemployment figures;
- developments in the foreign exchange market.

If, having looked at these indicators, the Committee believes that inflation will be outside its target in the future, it may then make changes to Bank Rate, which is the rate of interest charged by the Bank of England to other banks.

For example, if the MPC believes that aggregate demand is growing too fast and pulling up prices, then it will decide to raise its interest rates.

The effect of an increase in interest rates by the Monetary Policy Committee

An increase in the interest rates charged by the Bank of England is likely to have the following effects.

- It will increase the rates charged by other banks. Most banks will need to borrow from other financial institutions at particular times. The Bank of England is known as the 'lender of last resort'. For example, a high level of withdrawals may leave a bank short of liquidity. The Bank of England may be called upon to lend money to other institutions. They will be influenced by the rate that the Bank of England charges, because they will want to charge their own customers more to ensure that they make a profit. If the Bank of England therefore announces that Bank Rate is increasing, then other financial institutions will usually follow to cover any increased costs that they might have if they need funds. Higher interest rates offered by financial institutions will encourage saving and reduce consumption spending. There will also be less demand for other assets (leading to lower prices) because of the high returns from saving. Lower asset prices will reduce individuals' wealth and dampen demand.
- It will send a clear signal that the Bank of England is prepared to take action to control inflation. This should lead to wage demands in line with the stated inflation target. This in itself should help to ensure that the target is hit, because it discourages inflationary wage claims.
- It will lead to more demand for the currency from overseas investors, who will want to buy sterling to save in UK banks to gain higher returns. This should increase the external

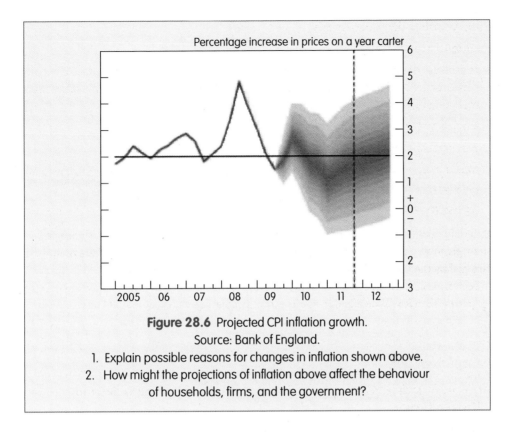

Figure 28.6 Projected CPI inflation growth.
Source: Bank of England.
1. Explain possible reasons for changes in inflation shown above.
2. How might the projections of inflation above affect the behaviour of households, firms, and the government?

value of the pound. This makes UK exports relatively expensive overseas, thereby reducing the aggregate demand. It also reduces import prices in pounds, thereby reducing cost pressure. Both of these help to reduce inflation. (For more on this, see Chapter 30.)

The effect of changes in the interest rate can be seen in Figure 28.6.

In recent years, the recession in the UK led to concerns about inflation being below the given target rather than above it. Levels of aggregate demand were low in the economy, leading to negative growth and high unemployment. In this situation, the MPC cut the interest rate to its lowest level ever (0.5 per cent) to stimulate demand in the economy. At times during 2009 and 2010, inflation still exceeded the inflation target, but this was seen to be due to supply shocks, such as higher oil, commodity prices, or VAT increases, rather than the underlying inflation rate. Low interest rates have been seen as necessary to maintain demand and prevent deflation.

What do you think?

Do you think that the MPC should cut the interest rate at the moment in the UK?

Economics in context **The Bank of England and interest rates**

The Bank of England lowered interest rates to 0.5 per cent in March 2010. This was the lowest that it had been since the Bank's creation 300 years before. Many economic forecasters believe that it will have to stay low for many years to come to counteract the governent's spending cuts.

According to a report by Professor Peter Spencer from the Ernst and Young Item Club:

A base rate of 0.5% will begin to look like the new normal. On the assumption that the government is able to implement the overall reduction of £40 billion set out in the Budget, we expect that UK growth will struggle to reach 1% this year but will gradually speed up in the following years to give the UK a high-quality recovery based on trade and investment.

According to the report, the CPI measure of inflation will stay above the Bank of England's 2 per cent target over the next 18 months, helped by high energy prices and increases in VAT. But inflation will then fall 'well below 2 per cent as these effects wear off, and spare capacity bears down on pricing decisions and wage bargaining'.

'To prevent CPI inflation moving below 1 per cent it will be necessary keep the Bank base rate low at 0.5 per cent for much longer than [others] . . . have anticipated,' the report said.

? Questions

What is meant by the CPI?

Why does the Bank of England have a 2 per cent inflation target?

Analyse the effects on the economy of a low interest rate.

Why is a low interest rate looking likely according to the item above?

Put into practice

Which one(s) of the following would be an appropriate response to reduce demand-pull inflation?

- Lower corporation tax rates
- Higher interest rates
- Increased government spending
- Higher income taxation rates

■ Deflation

Deflation occurs when prices in an economy are generally falling over a given period. It means that there is negative inflation in the economy. This may be due to the following reasons.

- Supply may be growing faster than demand. In certain markets, such as some consumer electronics markets, supply is increasing rapidly due to developments in technology. This causes deflation in these markets.

- Aggregate demand may be falling, perhaps because interest rates are too high, or because there is a lack of household and business confidence. Deflation is often associated with a recession in the economy. If deflation is caused by a lack of aggregate demand, this is unwelcome because it is likely to be associated with high unemployment.

Deflation may lead to the following.

- There may be lower profits for firms because of lower prices. This means that there are fewer funds for investment, which may delay the purchase of new machinery.

- There may be redundancies as firms try to rationalize their production and make it more efficient; managers will be pressurized to cut costs to maintain profit margins.

- Businesses may close because they may not be able to make profits if prices are falling.

What is particularly worrying is the possibility of a deflationary spiral. This could be due to:

- households and firms delaying buying decisions because prices are falling, creating even more downward pressure on prices; or

- negative real interest rates. If interest rates are cut to stimulate spending, but prices are falling, then it is still worth saving money because it is gaining in real terms. Even if interest rates were cut right back to 0 per cent, but prices were falling at 2 per cent, then by holding your money in a bank, in real terms you would be gaining 2 per cent (whereas if you were to hold an asset, it may fall in value). This may again lead to less spending and more downward pressure on prices as the economy shrinks. This is called a deflationary spiral.

Economics in context   Deflation in Japan

In June 2010, Japan's new government pledged to cut corporation tax from 40 per cent to nearer 25 per cent and beat deflation to achieve stable economic growth of 2 per cent a year. It said that it aimed to defeat deflation by April 2011, and Japan's central bank announced plans for up to 3 trillion yen (£22 billion; $33 billion) in loans to boost aggregate demand and to boost economic growth.

? Question
Why would the government in Japan be so keen to prevent deflation?

Put into practice

Using the aggregate demand and supply schedule, show the effect on the equilibrium price and output of a fall in the aggregate demand.

▣ Real interest rates versus nominal interest rates

When analysing the effects of interest rates on the economy, it is important also to consider the inflation rate. The rate that the Bank of England or high-street banks charge is the nominal rate. When this is adjusted for inflation this is the real interest rate.

Imagine the reward for saving is 5 per cent, for example, but prices are increasing by 5 per cent as well. This means, in real terms, the interest rate is zero. If you save your money, you will earn 5 per cent, but because prices have increased, you will not be able to buy more products.

The real interest rate can be calculated as:

Real interest rate = Nominal rate of interest − Inflation rate

For example, if the nominal rate of interest is 5 per cent and inflation is 5 per cent, this means the real rate of interest is:

$$5\% - 5\% = 0\%$$

The real interest rate is particularly interesting in times of deflation because leaving money earning interest will obviously be better than spending on or investing in items that are losing value. Even if the interest rate were 0 per cent, then given that prices are falling, this, in real terms, would be a positive rate of interest: leave your money in the bank and take it out six months later, and even if it has no nominal interest, you can buy more because prices are lower. This means that, when there is deflation, there is a real incentive to save even if nominal interest rates are low. This can further reduce demand and lead to more deflation (known as a deflationary spiral).

▣ The Phillips curve: Inflation and unemployment

The Phillips curve shows the relationship between the rate of inflation and the rate of unemployment in both the short run and the long run.

In the short run, there appears to be a trade-off between the rate of inflation and the rate of unemployment; the government can reduce unemployment below the natural rate at the expense of faster-growing prices.

Imagine that the economy is at full employment equilibrium at X (see Figure 28.7). Wages and prices are growing in line with each other at 3 per cent, and the rate of unemployment in the economy is at the natural rate. All unemployment is voluntary.

If the government then increases spending, this will create demand-pull inflation. Prices will grow faster than wages—for example, prices may grow at 4 per cent, whilst wages are still increasing at 3 per cent. This is because wages are often 'sticky' in the short term. Individuals will have agreed their wages for a given period (for example, for the next year) and will not be able to renegotiate them. Also, employees are often slow to realize that inflation has changed; they tend to focus on the prices of things that they buy regularly and do not appreciate the overall trend with inflation. This is called money illusion. With

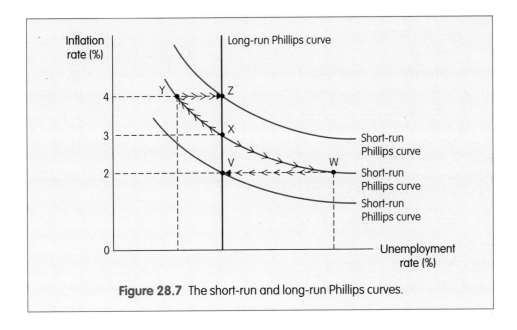

Figure 28.7 The short-run and long-run Phillips curves.

prices growing faster than wages, real wages actually fall. This makes it cheaper in real terms to employ people, which should lead to a fall in unemployment (the point Y in Figure 28.7).

Over time, however, employees will notice that their purchasing power has been reduced and will want to bargain for higher wages to compensate for the inflation. If they manage to match wage increases to the price increases, then, in real terms, wages and the economy will be back to where they started, except that prices and wages are now growing at a faster rate of 4 per cent, not 3 per cent (the point Z in Figure 28.7). Unemployment is at the natural rate again, but with higher inflation. In the long run, therefore, there has been no trade-off between inflation and unemployment.

Conversely, if the government brings down spending in the economy, then, with lower demand, inflation may be reduced and, in the short run, prices will be growing slower than wages. This is again because wages are slow to change due to contracts and because it takes time for employees to notice fully changes in inflation. If prices are growing slower than wages, then real wages have increased and so employees are more expensive to hire. This will lead to fewer people being employed and unemployment rising. Imagine that the labour market is in long-run equilibrium at X, with prices and wages growing at 3 per cent (see Figure 28.7). Then prices start to grow at 2 per cent, so real wages have increased. Employees are more expensive and unemployment increases; the economy moves to W. In the long run, however, because of higher levels of unemployment and because they realize that inflation has fallen, employees would be willing to accept lower pay increases; this would mean that real wages were back where they were originally. All that has changed is that prices and wages are now growing at the lower rate of 2 per cent. The economy moves to the point V. Once again, there is no trade-off between the rate of inflation and the rate of unemployment in the long run.

Put into practice

- If the rate of inflation is higher than the rate at which nominal wages are growing, then what is happening to real wages? Why?

- What might be the impact of this on the quantity demanded and the quantity supplied of labour?

What do you think?

To what extent do you think employees are aware of the rate of inflation?

The Phillips curve suggests the following.

- There is a possible trade-off between the rate of inflation and the rate of unemployment in the short run, provided that prices grow faster than wages. If the government intends to keep unemployment below the natural rate, then it will always need to keep prices growing at a faster rate than wages. Obviously, if the government adopts such tactics, then employees might soon realize this; therefore, to keep fooling people, the government would need to create ever-larger increases in inflation so that employees do not anticipate this.

- There is no long-run trade-off between the rate of inflation and the rate of unemployment. This suggests that efforts by the government to use demand-side policies to manipulate inflation and affect unemployment levels will not work. Attempts by the government to reduce unemployment below the natural rate will, in the long run, simply lead to more inflation. The implication is that a long-run policy by the government would be to focus on changing the natural rate of unemployment through supply-side policies (see Figure 28.8).

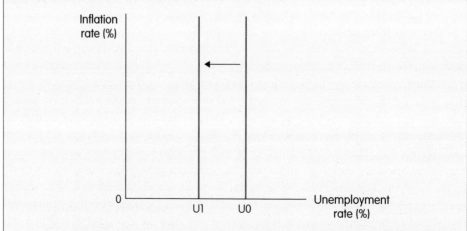

Figure 28.8 Supply-side policies may be used to reduce the natural rate of unemployment.

Case study A letter to the Chancellor

Letter to the Chancellor from the Governor of the Bank of England, 17 May 2010

Tomorrow the Office for National Statistics (ONS) will publish data showing that CPI inflation has risen from 1.1% in September 2009 to 3.7% in April. The MPC's assessment is that that rise is largely accounted for by three factors: first, the impact of higher oil prices, which on average in April were nearly 80% higher than at the beginning of 2009, pushing up on petrol price inflation; second, the restoration at the beginning of January of the standard rate of VAT to 17.5%, and third, the continuing effects on inflation of the sharp depreciation of sterling in 2007–08. The MPC judges that together these factors more than account for the deviation of CPI inflation from target, and that the temporary effects of these factors are masking the downward pressure on inflation from the substantial margin of spare capacity in the economy.

The change in VAT and higher petrol prices will continue to be reflected in the overall price level. But, unless they increase further, that should affect the twelve-month CPI measure of inflation for no more than a year. Moreover, the continuing impact of the past depreciation of sterling is still pushing up on consumer prices, but likewise the effects on inflation can be expected to wane over time. As this happens, the MPC expects that inflation will fall back. Nevertheless, inflation has been somewhat higher than expected over the past year, and the Committee is conscious that the pace and extent of the prospective fall in inflation are highly uncertain. It will monitor developments closely.

. . . The May projections also suggest that, absent further price level surprises, it is likely that inflation will fall back to target within a year. Thereafter . . . the MPC expects that the effects of the persistent margin of spare capacity in the economy—built up during the recession—will continue to pull down on inflation, probably bringing it below target for a period. But if the recovery continues as expected, that will gradually erode the slack in the economy, bringing inflation back to target.

. . . The low level of Bank Rate, together with the continued effects of money-financed asset purchases, are providing a significant boost to nominal spending which should continue for some time. That will help to keep inflation on track to meet the target in the medium term. But the MPC is very conscious that there are risks to inflation in both directions. On the downside, there is a risk that inflation will turn out to be weaker, perhaps because the influence of spare capacity in the economy could be more significant than assumed. On the upside, there is a risk that inflation may be raised by further commodity price increases or other price level surprises. And if the current period of above-target inflation causes inflation expectations to move up, that may lead to some persistence in the current high level of inflation.

The MPC will continue to set policy to keep inflation on track to meet the inflation target in the medium term, taking into account the balance of risks. We stand ready either to expand or reduce the extent of monetary stimulus as needed.

By keeping inflation close to the 2% target in the medium term, the Monetary Policy Committee will make its most effective contribution to economic performance in the United Kingdom. Price stability, as the remit to us states, is 'a precondition for . . . high and stable levels of growth and employment'.

And so, by keeping inflation low, we will thereby support growth and employment. The events of the past few years and the heightened degree of uncertainty have made clear that—now more than ever—the importance of a stable and transparent monetary policy framework is paramount.

? Questions

- Why did the governor of the Bank of England have to write the above letter to the chancellor?
- Why did inflation rise to 3.7 per cent in April 2010? What type of inflation is this?
- Why did the MPC not increase interest rates as a result of this higher inflation?
- Why is the MPC uncertain what will happen to inflation in the future?
- Why is 'a stable and transparent monetary policy framework' crucial for the economy?

Checklist

Now that you have read this chapter, try to answer the following questions.

☐ Can you explain what is meant by inflation?

☐ Can you outline the different causes of inflation?

☐ Can you explain the costs of inflation?

☐ Can you examine ways of reducing inflation?

☐ Are you able to discuss the possible trade-off between inflation and unemployment?

Review questions

1 Does inflation mean that all prices are increasing?

2 What are the causes of inflation?

3 What are the main costs of inflation?

4 Is it possible to control inflation?

5 Can the government reduce inflation and unemployment simultaneously?

Key learning points

- Inflation is usually measured by the consumer prices index (CPI) in the UK.
- The possible causes of inflation include demand-pull and cost-push.
- Stable inflation rates help to stimulate economic growth.

- The appropriate cures for inflation depend on the cause.
- The Phillips curve suggests that there is a trade-off between inflation and unemployment in the short run, but not in the long run.

Learn more

To learn more about rates of inflation in the UK over the years, visit the Online Resource Centre.

 Visit our Online Resource Centre at http://www.oxfordtextbooks.co.uk/orc/gillespie_econ2e/ for test question and further information on topics covered in this chapter.

»29 International trade, balance of payments, and protectionism

All countries engage in international trade, buying and selling from abroad, and this has a large impact on their economies. This chapter examines the reasons why international trade occurs and the benefits that can be gained from it. It then considers the reasons why protectionism exists and the effects of this on different stakeholder groups.

LEARNING OBJECTIVES

By the end of this chapter, you should be able to:

✔ explain the theory of international trade;

✔ explain the elements of the balance of payments;

✔ outline the key elements of the European Union (EU);

✔ examine the benefits of belonging to the EU;

✔ consider the issues involved in joining the euro;

✔ outline the possible elements of protectionism;

✔ analyse why governments might protect industries;

✔ examine the possible consequences of protectionism.

■ Introduction

Whenever you go shopping, you are likely to be buying goods from all over the world. Clothes produced in China, wine from France, oranges from Spain, ham from Italy—the shops are full of products imported into the UK. You are also likely to make use of foreign services on a regular basis: your phone enquiry may be directed via a call centre in India; your bank may be based in Hong Kong; and your energy provider may be from continental Europe. At the same time, UK firms are busy exporting a range of products, including music, films, and education. We now live in a global village, buying products from, and selling products to, countries all over the world, and in which travel and tourism into and out of the UK are routine. International trade therefore has a massive influence on the economies. This could be seen in the global recession in 2009 when recessions in one country triggered a fall in demand for products from trading partners, contributing to a recession in those partner countries as well.

Exports

The value of a country's exports measures the value of the goods and services that it sells abroad. In the case of goods, these may actually be transported abroad. In the case of services, they are more likely to have been consumed in the UK—for example, international students coming to study at a British university are UK exports. Exports are an injection into the economy and are an important element of the aggregate demand.

The level of exports from a country may depend on the following.

- **The quality of the goods and services produced relative to those of international competitors** This in turn will depend on a range of factors, such as the levels of investment in technology, the training of staff, and the investment in research and development. It will also depend on the level of competitiveness domestically; high levels of domestic competition may force domestic firms to improve the quality of their products, which will improve their ability to export.

- Protectionism Protectionism occurs if a government protects its own firms from foreign competition. The ways in which this may be done include placing taxes (called tariffs) on foreign products coming into the country or limiting the number of foreign products allowed in (a quota). In some cases, political disputes may lead to a complete ban (embargo) on products from a particular country, with the aim of putting pressure on the government there to change its policies. If other governments introduce protectionist measures, then this may reduce the export opportunities for UK firms.

- **Exchange rates** The exchange rate is the value of one currency in terms of another. If, for example, the pound sterling is expensive to buy in terms of US dollars, then, all other things being equal, this is likely to reduce the sales of UK products to the USA, because they will be relatively expensive. The exact impact of the price increase in dollars would depend on the price elasticity of demand for UK products. More generally, the relative price of one country's products compared to those of other countries will affect sales. The impact on sales will depend on the price elasticity of demand (see Chapter 30).

- **Customer preferences** The tastes and preferences of overseas buyers will obviously influence levels of demand for UK products.

- **Income levels abroad** If incomes are relatively high and growing abroad, then this may increase demand for UK products. With more disposable income, foreign buyers may buy more products in general, including UK products. The amount of UK goods purchased will be influenced by the other countries' marginal propensity to import

(MPM) in foreign countries. This highlights the importance of other economies to the UK. If countries abroad are in recession, then this will hit UK exports and may lead the UK into recession as well. Equally, if countries abroad are prospering, then this offers the UK export opportunities.

Put into practice

Which of the following statements are true and which are false?

a. Export spending is an injection into an economy.

b. An increase in export spending reduces aggregate demand.

c. If a currency is cheap, this is likely to increase exports.

d. Higher incomes domestically lead to an increase in exports.

▨ Imports

Imports are a withdrawal and reduce the level of the aggregate demand. The level of import spending into a country will also depend on factors such as the exchange rate, customer preferences, and the quality of products abroad. Import spending will also depend on the UK's MPM and the level of income in the UK. With more income, there will be more spending, and this will increase the spending on imports.

The difference between the amount earned by selling exports abroad and the amount spent on imports is measured by the balance of payments. The relationship between the balance of payments and national income levels is shown in Figure 29.1.

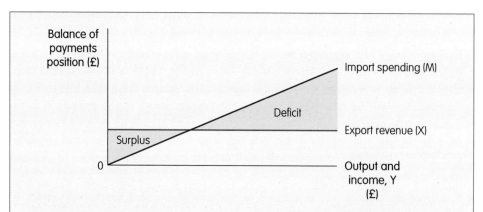

Figure 29.1 The balance of payments and national income. UK export revenue is not determined by UK national income; it is autonomous of UK income. Import spending does depend on UK income; with more income, spending on imports rises. This means that, all other things being unchanged, the balance of payments position would worsen as national income grows.

Economics in context

World trade

	Average 1997–2006	2009	2010	2011
World real gross domestic profit (GDP) growth (%)	3.7	−0.9	4.6	4.5
World real trade growth (%)	7.1	−11	10.6	8.4

Source: Based on OECD (2010) *OECD Economic Outlook*, Vol. 2010/1, OECD Publishing.

? Questions

How does the growth in world trade compare to the growth in world income? Why do think this might be?

Why do you think world trade shrank in 2009?

Put into practice

Which of the following statements are true and which are false?

a. Import spending is an injection into an economy.

b. An increase in import spending reduces aggregate demand.

c. If a currency is cheap, this is likely to make imports more expensive, all other things unchanged.

d. Higher incomes domestically lead to an increase in imports, all other things unchanged.

What do you think?

Some products are easier to trade than others. A car is easy to trade; a haircut is not. Can you think what determines how tradeable a product is?

■ Absolute and comparative advantage

In theory, an economy can be closed and not open to trade. This would mean that it would have to produce all of the products that it wanted by itself. In this case, production would be restricted by the resources of that one country. However, by engaging in trade, it is possible to benefit from the skills and resources of other countries.

Absolute advantage occurs when one country can produce a product using fewer resources than another—that is, it is more efficient. If one country has an absolute advantage in product X and another has an absolute advantage in product Y, then trade may clearly be beneficial, with each country specializing and trading with the other.

However, even if a country has absolute advantage in all products (for example, because it was more efficient at producing generally), then trade may still be possible, and indeed beneficial, due to differences in comparative advantage. This theory was developed by Ricardo (1817). For example, the USA may be more efficient than another country in all products and therefore would have an absolute advantage. However, this does not mean that trade cannot be beneficial between the USA and other countries. Although the USA is more efficient in all products, there will still be some product categories in which another country has a lower opportunity cost and therefore a comparative advantage.

Comparative advantage lies at the heart of international trade. Firms in a particular country or region have a comparative advantage in producing particular products if the opportunity cost of producing these products is less than in other regions. When producers in certain industries in one country sacrifice less than firms in other regions, then they are relatively efficient at producing these products. This means that they should be able to export them. At the same time, other areas will be more efficient at producing other products and therefore the first country can buy these in from abroad at a lower price than that for which it could make them itself.

The benefits of trade

Trade can enable more output in the world, as economies specialize in products where they have comparative advantage.

Consider two economies, X, and Y, in which resources are split equally between two products, A and B. In these economies, the outputs produced are as in Table 29.1, and so this two-country economy produces seven units of A and three units of B in total.

Table 29.1   The outputs of two products, A and B, produced by two countries, X and Y

	Product A (units)	Product B (units)
Country X	4	1
Country Y	3	2
Total	7	3

The opportunity costs show what is being sacrificed to produce one unit of A or one unit of B. In country X, for example, the country can produce four units of A or one unit of B, so the opportunity cost of one unit of A is $\frac{1}{4}$ unit of B and the opportunity cost of one unit of B is four units of A. The opportunity costs for countries X and Y are shown in Table 29.2.

Table 29.2   The opportunity costs of producing the products A and B in the two countries X and Y

	Opportunity costs of one unit of A	Opportunity costs of one unit of B
Country X	$\frac{1}{4}$ unit of B	4 units of A
Country Y	$\frac{2}{3}$ unit of B	$\frac{3}{2}$ units of A

From Table 29.2, we can see that country X has the lower opportunity cost in the production of A and therefore should specialize in this product. Meanwhile, country Y has the lower opportunity cost when it comes to producing product B and should specialize in this product. If, instead of splitting resources, these economies now put all of their resources into one product, then, all other things being equal, output in these products should double.

The output levels would now be as shown in Table 29.3. Compared to the original situation, world output has increased by one unit of A and one unit of B. Focusing on an industry in which there is a comparative advantage has led to more production of both products.

Table 29.3   The output levels for the products A and B in the two countries X and Y

	Product A (units)	Product B (units)
Country X	8	0
Country Y	0	4
Total	8	4

The model in the above example assumes constant returns to scale—that is, that by doubling the resources in an industry, the output doubles. In reality, there may be further gains because, by specializing in one product, the country's firms may be more productive due to economies of scale and output may more than double (that is, benefit from increasing returns to scale). This would further increase the benefits of specialization.

Put into practice

Consider two economies, X and Y, for which the outputs produced of products A and B are as shown below.

	Product A (units)	Product B (units)
Country X	6	2
Country Y	2	3
Total	8	5

- Calculate the opportunity cost of each product for each country.
- Identify which product each country would specialize in and the total output if all of the resources focus on this industry.
- What has happened to the world output of A and B as a result of specialization and trade?

What do you think?

The model above assumes that resources can move easily from one industry to another. Why might barriers to mobility exist?

Economics in context — Trade interdependence

China's growth at a time of global contraction was a major feature of the primary sector's recovery in New Zealand. In 2010, the New Zealand ministry of agriculture and forestry projected higher prices during the next four years for beef, lamb, wool, wine, kiwi fruit, and the forestry industry.

This is because China had dramatically increased its purchase of New Zealand agricultural and forestry products the year before, with primary product exports up 49 per cent to $2.19 billion.

'Most of our other trading partners have returned to growth as well, while the demand associated with growing incomes in key developing economies is ensuring conditions for food exporters have been buoyant,' said the ministry.

? Question

How does the above illustrate the benefits of international trade?

What do you think?

The World Trade Organization (WTO) believes that trade brings about peace. Why do you think this might be?

■ Terms of trade

In Table 29.2 above, each country ends up specializing in one product, so what is needed to enable them to consume both products is for them to engage in trade. For this to happen, it must be cheaper for a country to buy products from abroad than to produce them itself and it must achieve a profit from exporting the products in which it specializes.

If we consider country Y, then it is now specializing in producing product B. Each unit of B has an opportunity cost of $\frac{3}{2}$ units of A. Provided that it can sell its units of B for more than this, its firms will make a profit.

Meanwhile, in country X, one unit of B costs four units of A to produce; provided that its firms and households can buy units of B for less than this, it will be beneficial to trade.

For both countries to benefit from trade, one unit of B must sell for more than $\frac{3}{2}$ units of A, but less than four units of A—that is:

$\frac{3}{2}$ units of A < 1 unit of B < 4 units of A

The following are known as the terms of trade.

• Provided that one unit of B costs more than $\frac{3}{2}$ units of A, then country Y will be willing to export because it will make a profit from selling them.

- Provided that one unit of B costs less than four units of A, then country X will be willing to import because this is cheaper than it could produce this product itself.

For example, possible terms of trade that would prove mutually beneficial for both countries would be for one unit of B to cost the same as two units of A; exporters would then make a profit. Importers would benefit from buying from abroad, where the opportunity costs are lower than those of producing the product itself.

Put into practice

Calculate the possible terms of trade for the Put into practice example shown earlier, for which you calculated the opportunity cost of each product.

Trade is therefore based on the idea that a particular country is likely to be good at some things, but not at others. By engaging in trade, a country can benefit from the skills, abilities, and resources of others. Why do something yourself if you can buy it more cheaply from abroad? Free trade should benefit all of those involved.

However, there may be problems caused by specialization, such as the following, for example.

- Firms may suffer from decreasing returns to scale, in which case, the overall world outputs may not gain as much as suggested in Table 29.3.
- Countries may become overspecialized and reliant on a limited number of products. This makes them vulnerable to changes in that market or to political problems with other countries supplying key products.

The terms of trade index

The terms of trade index measures the prices of exports compared with the prices of imports. It is usually calculated as follows:

$$\text{Terms of trade index} = \frac{\text{Index of export prices}}{\text{Index of import prices}} \times 100$$

It shows how many exports can be bought relative to imports. For example, if the average price of exports is £200 and the average price of imports is £100, then one export buys two imports.

An increase in export prices relative to import prices is known as an improvement in the terms of trade. It means that if a product is sold abroad, then more imports can be bought in return than before. However, an improvement in the terms of trade does not necessarily mean that it is good for the economy (even though it sounds like it is); this is because if exports are more expensive relative to imports, then fewer may be sold. The balance of trade may worsen.

Put into practice

What are the likely effects of a fall in the terms of trade?

■ The balance of payments

The balance of payments is one of the UK's key economic statistics. It measures the economic transactions between UK residents and the rest of the world.

These economic transactions include:

• exports and imports of goods such as oil, agricultural products, other raw materials, machinery and transport equipment, computers, and clothing;

• exports and imports of services such as international transport, travel, and financial and business services;

• income flows such as dividends and interest earned by non-residents on investments in the UK, and by UK residents investing abroad;

• transfers, such as foreign aid and funds brought by migrants to the UK; and

• financial flows, such as investment in shares, debt, and loans.

A surplus on the balance of payments occurs if the inflows are greater than the outflows. A deficit occurs if the outflows are bigger than the inflows.

Economics in context **UK trade 2009**

UK trade in goods 2009	£m	UK trade in services 2009	£m
Food, beverage, and tobacco	−17,410	Insurance	6,042
Oil	−5,868	Financial	38,472
Finished manufactured goods	−54,273	Communications	683

? Question

The above are extracts from the UK balance of payments. What does it suggest about UK competitiveness in goods compared to services?

The balance of payments is made up of the following.

• **The current account** This comprises the following.
  • **Visible trade** This records the value of imports and exports of physical goods. The balance of trade measures the difference between the value of exported goods and the value of imported goods.
  • **Invisible trade** This records the value of imports and exports of services, and interest profits and dividends, into and out of the country.
• **The capital account** Ths records payments of flows associated with the disposal of assets, the transfer of funds by migrants, and the payment of grants by governments for overseas projects.

- **The financial account** This measures the flows resulting from changes in the holdings of shares, property, bank deposits, and loans. Whereas the current account measures the income flows such as dividends and interest, the financial account measures the actual purchase and sale of assets. The purchase of shares abroad would be an outflow on the financial account; when dividends are paid, this is an inflow on the current account.

The balance of payments also records intervention by the government, such as buying and selling of foreign currency reserves.

A balance of payments surplus means that a country's revenue from exports is greater than its spending on imports. This leads to extra demand in the economy because more money is coming in from abroad than is being spent on foreign products. A balance of payments deficit means that a country's export revenue is less than its import spending. This leads to less demand in the economy because less money is coming in from abroad than is being spent on foreign products.

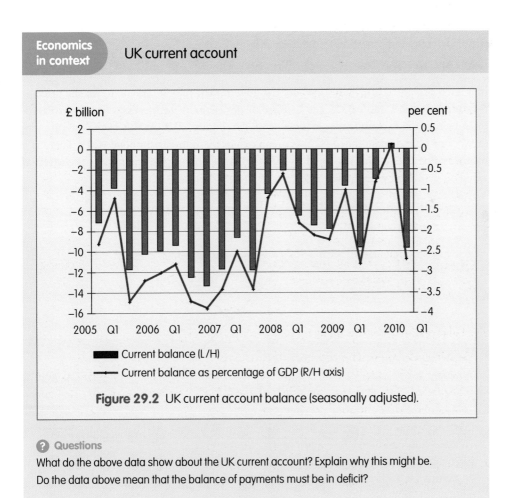

Economics in context

UK current account

Figure 29.2 UK current account balance (seasonally adjusted).

? Questions

What do the above data show about the UK current account? Explain why this might be.

Do the data above mean that the balance of payments must be in deficit?

▨ The balance of payments and exchange rates

Floating exchange rates

In a floating exchange rate system, the external value of the currency changes to equate the quantity of pounds supplied to change into foreign currency and the quantity of pounds demanded in exchange for foreign currency. This means that the number of pounds being given up is exactly equal to the number being bought, so overall the balance of payments equals zero. This does not mean that each element is in equilibrium, but overall the spending in pounds equals the income in pounds and the balance of payments 'balances'. Even so, equilibrium does not mean that there is no cause for concern. If, for example, there is a current account deficit, but surplus in the financial account, then this may be undesirable even if the overall balance of payments does balance. This is because, although in the short term it leads to a higher standard of living due to more consumption thanks to imports, this is being financed by capital inflows into the country. These represent purchases of UK assets by overseas organizations and will lead to dividends flowing out of the country in the future.

Fixed exchange rates

In a fixed exchange rate system, where the government may intervene to fix the price of the currency (see Chapter 30), the balance of payments is not necessarily equal to zero. Imagine that the exchange rate is fixed at ER1 in Figure 29.3. At this exchange rate, the number of pounds demanded (Q2) is greater than the number supplied (Q1). There is a balance of payments surplus equal to Q2 – Q1. In a floating exchange rate, the external value of the pound would rise.

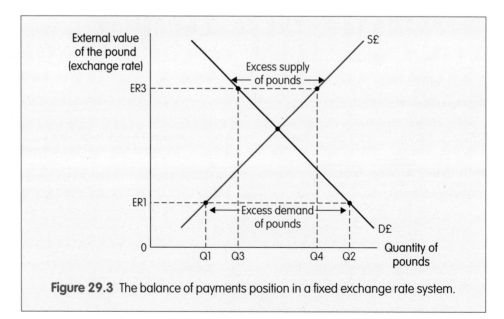

Figure 29.3 The balance of payments position in a fixed exchange rate system.

To keep it fixed at ER1, the government must sell pounds to meet the excess demand Q2 – Q1. It will sell pounds in return for foreign currency reserves. This is known as official financing. For example:

Balance of payments surplus = +£300 million

Official financing = –£300 million (selling pounds)

If the pound is fixed at ER3 (see Figure 29.3), then there is an excess supply of pounds equal to Q4 – Q3. The quantity supplied exceeds the quantity demanded and there is a balance of payments deficit. In this case, the government buys pounds equal to Q4 – Q3 to prevent the value from falling. To buy pounds, the government uses its foreign currency reserves. For example:

Balance of payments deficit = –£200 million

Official financing = +£200 million (buying pounds)

■ A current account deficit on the balance of payments

A current account deficit on the balance of payments means that the value of goods and services exported is less than the value of goods and services imported into a country. This may lead to a fall in the aggregate demand because money is leaking out of the economy (unless the increase in imports is actually caused by an increase in the aggregate demand in the first place). Domestic employment could fall as more imports are purchased.

If the pound does not fall to rectify the current account deficit, then this means that the capital and/or financial account must be in surplus to balance the balance of payments or there is official financing. This in turn may be due to the following reasons.

- **The central bank is buying currency, using foreign exchange reserves** This is possible in the short run, but in the long run the central bank will run out of foreign exchange reserves and so the value of the currency will have to change.

- **Hot money inflows** This represents speculative money placed by investors all over the world searching for a high return. It can be moved quickly out of one country into another. Banks may not be able to lend this money out because it may be withdrawn at any time. Alternatively, the hot money inflows may go into buying UK shares, thereby increasing share prices.

- **Foreign direct investment** This could create jobs in an economy and bring new technology. The investment may set up companies in the UK that then export and generate export earnings. The increased competition may also help to create greater efficiency domestically. However, the foreign investment may bring competition that destroys jobs domestically. Also, the profits earned in a country are often repatriated to the country of origin and do not remain in the domestic economy.

Economics in context

Current account balances in $ bn and as a percentage of GDP

| | % GDP | | | $ bn | | |
	2009	2010	2011	2009	2010	2011
USA	−2.9	−3.8	−4.0	−420	−560	−618
Japan	2.8	3.3	3.5	144	169	182
Euro area	−0.3	0.3	0.8	−38	32	101
China	6.1	2.8	3.4	297	154	212

Source: Based on OECD (2010) *OECD Economic Outlook*, Vol. 2010/1, OECD Publishing.

? Question

Compare and contrast the current account position of two of the countries or areas above.

Curing a current account deficit

To remove a current account deficit, a government may do the following.

- **Use demand-switching policies** This involves methods of protecting domestic firms from foreign competition, so that consumers switch to domestic firms. This should reduce the value of imports relative to exports. However, protectionism may not be possible (for example, within the European Union) or may lead to retaliation.

- **Use demand-reducing policies** This involves policies to reduce the total spending in the economy (for example, by increasing taxes). With less demand, there will be less spending on imports. However, these policies also lead to less spending on domestic products, which can slow the growth of the economy.

- **Use supply-side policies** These policies, such as training schemes and incentives to invest in research and development, should help domestic firms to become more competitive internationally and therefore to export more.

- **Allow the exchange rate to fall** There may be downward pressure on the currency anyway due to less demand for exports or the government can intervene to reduce the value of the currency (for example, by lowering interest rates, which reduces demand for the currency as the returns of saving in the currency are lower). If the currency depreciates, then this should make exports relatively cheaper in foreign currencies and imports relatively more expensive in pounds. This should encourage exports and reduce the volume of imports. However, the precise effect in terms of spending depends on the price elasticity of demand for imports and exports, and may need time to take effect. In the short term, for example, demand for exports may not respond very much (perhaps because contracts have already been signed with existing suppliers); also importers may have to pay the higher import prices because they cannot find alternative suppliers. This means that the current account deficit may worsen. Over time, when demand for exports and imports becomes more price-elastic, because customers can switch, the currect account should improve. The fact that the deficit may get worse before getting better is called the J-curve effect (because it dips before it rises). The improvement following a depreciation of the currency occurs when the price elasticity of demand for exports plus the price elasticity of demand for exports is > 1. This is known as the Marshall–Lerner condition (see Chapter 30).

Put into practice

Explain how the government might reduce demand in the economy.

What do you think?

Do you think that demand-switching policies or demand-reducing policies would be more politically acceptable?

Put into practice

Which of the following statements are true and which are false?

a. To reduce import spending, a government may try to reduce national income.

b. The balance of payments measures the value of all of the transactions within a country over a year.

c. A depreciation of the exchange rate should improve the current account position of a country in the medium term.

d. A depreciation of the exchange rate may lead to demand-pull inflation if there is substantial capacity in the economy.

■ Free trade

Free trade occurs when there are no barriers to trade. This means that products, money, and even people can move freely between one country and another. Free trade offers opportunities to businesses and consumers. Households and firms have a greater choice of goods and services because they can now buy from other countries, and are able to benefit from lower prices by importing from countries that have a comparative advantage.

This is why some countries join together to agree to remove barriers to trade between each other. However, there are different types of agreement, such as:

- In a free trade area, countries remove barriers such as tariffs and quotas on goods and services, but are free to determine their own trade policy with non-members.

- In a customs union, such as the European Union (EU), there is free trade between members and a common tariff on non-members.

Economics in context

East African Community (EAC)

The East African Community (EAC) is the regional intergovernmental organization of the Republics of Kenya and Uganda, the United Republic of Tanzania, the Republic of Rwanda, and the Republic of Burundi.

The vision of EAC is a prosperous, competitive, secure, stable, and politically united East Africa; the mission is to widen and deepen economic, political, social, and cultural integration in order to improve the quality of life of the people of East Africa through increased competitiveness, value-added production, trade, and investments.

The common market came into force on 1 July 2010, with free movement of labour being instituted between the five countries. The plan is also to do away with all internal barriers to trade, although it may take up to five years before this is completed.

Area (including water)	1.82 million km²
Population	126.6 million (2009)
GDP	$73 billion (2009)

? Question

Why would member countries want to join the EAC common market?

■ The European Union

The EU is a group of countries that have joined together to form a customs union. It was created with six members in 1957, but has grown in numbers ever since and has 27 members at the time of writing. The EU is now the largest single market in the world. There are over 450 million people in this market and its GDP is greater than that of the USA. The EU is the main exporter in the world and the second-biggest importer. The USA is the EU's most important trading partner, followed by China. The EU is also an important trading partner for less-developed countries, most of the exports of which enter the EU duty-free or at reduced rates of duty. This preferential access to the EU market is aimed at boosting the economic growth of poorer countries around the world.

Within the EU:

- standards have been agreed between member states so that if a product can be sold in one country, then it can also be sold in another member country—there do not have to be changes made to the product and no additional taxes can be placed on it; and

- member countries must stick to common agreed tariffs (taxes) placed on products from non-member countries.

The UK joined the EU in 1973 and, as one of the world's largest economies in the world, it is obviously a key member. Over half of the UK's trade is with other EU countries and the UK government estimates that over 3 million jobs are linked to exports to EU members. Around 100,000 Britons work in other EU countries and another 350,000 live in those countries.

Economics in context **The growth of the European Union**

At present, there are 27 members of the EU, with more eager to join. The history of their accession to the Union is as follows.

Year	Member
1958	Belgium, France, Germany, Italy, Luxembourg, the Netherlands
1973	Denmark, Ireland, UK
1981	Greece
1986	Portugal, Spain
1995	Austria, Finland, Sweden
2004	Cyprus, the Czech Republic, Estonia, Hungary, Latvia, Lithuania, Malta, Poland, Slovakia, Slovenia
2007	Bulgaria, Romania

? Questions

Do you know which countries now want to join the EU?

What do you think should determine whether they should be allowed to join or not?

The advantages to the UK of being within the EU are as follows.

- Being within the EU makes it easier for UK firms to access customers in other European markets. UK firms may therefore be able to sell more products. Given that standards are agreed across the Union, UK firms are not forced to change their product for each market to meet different regulations; this makes it possible to have longer production runs and possibly to gain from economies of scale.

- UK firms and households have easier access to products from other member countries. This may enable firms to find cheaper and better-quality supplies, and to have more choice. This can lead to better value for customers.

- There are lower costs due to the removal of technical and administrative barriers. Trade within the Union becomes easier, which should encourage investment.

- Greater competition within the EU stimulates competition and efficiency; UK firms can learn from their competitors and have to provide good value for customers to compete.

- The UK can benefit from the skills, expertise, and comparative advantage of other nations more easily.

Joining a customs union can lead to trade creation and trade diversion.

- **Trade creation** This occurs when firms and consumers can switch from higher-cost producers to lower-cost producers. With the removal of tariffs, UK firms could get supplies within the Union more cheaply than they could buy them before from anywhere in the world.

- **Trade diversion** This occurs when firms and households switch from a lower-cost producer outside the Union to a higher-cost producer within it. This can happen because of tariffs placed on non-Union members that raise the price of their products. It may now be cheaper to switch to firms within the EU, even though those outside were cheaper before the tariff.

Economics in context	Exports to other EU members as a percentage of each country's total exports (2005)	

Country	%
Slovakia (SK)	85.4
Czech Republic (CZ)	84.2
Portugal (PT)	79.8
Netherlands (NL)	79.2
Poland (PL)	77.2
Belgium (BE)	76.4
Hungary (HU)	76.3
Denmark (DK)	70.5
Austria (AT)	69.3
Slovenia (SI)	66.4
Germany (DE)	63.4
Sweden (SE)	58.4
United Kingdom (UK)	56.9
Finland (FI)	56.0
Malta (MT)	51.6

Source: Eurostat.

 Question

What do the above figures suggest about the success of the EU?

Put into practice

Would you accept any country that wants to join the EU? Why? Or why not?

European Union institutions

Being a member of the EU involves agreeing to European regulations and directives, and being accountable to European institutions.

The main institutions within the EU are as follows.

- **The European Commission** This consists of commissioners appointed by each member state; they propose new policies and administer existing policies.

- **The European Council of Ministers** This is made up of ministers from member countries. The Council receives proposals from the European Commission and can decide on all EU issues.

- **The European Parliament** Members of the European Parliament (MEPs) are elected within their own countries and represent them in Europe. The Parliament discusses proposals from the Commission.

Being a member of the EU also involves agreeing to common economic policies between member states, such as the following.

- **The Common Agricultural Policy (CAP)** This sets prices for food produced within the EU and places tariffs on imports (see the next section).

- **The EU's Monopoly and Restrictive Practices Policy** EU competition policy applies primarily to companies operating in more than one member state. Article 85 of the EC Treaty prohibits agreements between firms, such as overpricing, that adversely affect competition in trade between member states.

■ The World Trade Organization

The World Trade Organization (WTO) is an international body the purpose of which is to promote free trade by persuading countries to abolish import tariffs and other barriers. The WTO oversees the rules of international trade. It monitors free trade agreements, settles trade disputes between governments, and establishes trade negotiations. WTO decisions are absolute and so, when the USA and the European Union are disagreeing over products such as bananas or beef, the WTO decides.

The WTO was set up in 1995 and is based in Geneva. It replaced the General Agreement on Tariffs and Trade (GATT). WTO agreements cover goods and services, such as telecommunications and banking, as well as other issues, such as intellectual property rights. The membership of the WTO now stands at 149 countries. China joined in December 2001.

 Web

For more information on the WTO, visit http://www.wto.org

▨ Protectionism

Despite the apparent benefits of free trade, such as benefiting from comparative advantage and having access to more suppliers and markets, not all governments believe in it or believe that it is always appropriate. There are often instances in which governments try to restrict trade. This is known as protectionism. Protectionism occurs when governments try to protect their domestic firms from foreign competition. It prevents free trade and introduces barriers to trade.

The methods of protectionism include the following.

- **Tariffs** These are taxes placed on selected goods and services from overseas. The tax revenue raised from tariffs goes to the government that placed them on overseas products.

- **Quotas** These are limits placed on the number of products from a particular country. For example, a limit might be placed on the number of sales or the market share of new cars from a foreign country.

- **Legal restrictions** A country may impose certain regulations or standards on products from abroad to make it more difficult for them to be allowed in.

- **Voluntary export restraints (VERs)** These are agreements negotiated between governments to restrict exports.

- **Government intervention to keep its currency low in value** A government may sell its own currency on the foreign exchange markets to reduce its value and make its products more competitive abroad. (This is analysed more in Chapter 30.) The US government has accused the Chinese government in recent years of deliberately keeping its currency low in value to help to promote its exports.

Why do governments protect domestic firms?

Given the arguments for free trade, the idea of protectionism may seem odd. However, the reasons why a government may protect its domestic firms include:

- to retaliate against the protectionist measures of other governments;

- to protect industries that are regarded as strategically important—for example, a government may target certain defence industries or food producers, and protect these in case of times of emergency;

- to enable small and new firms to grow and benefit from the economies of scale and experience that might be needed to compete worldwide (known as the 'infant industry argument');

- to protect certain selected industries to keep jobs safe within them and to protect a way of life (for example, agriculture); and

- to protect jobs if a particular industry is struggling.

Economics in context   **Politics and trade**

In 2010, EU foreign ministers adopted tougher sanctions aimed at Iran's energy sector to try to end its nuclear programme. There are new restrictions on foreign trade, financial services, and the oil and gas sectors—essential elements of Iran's economy.

Officials said that the package was 'by some way the most far-reaching sanctions adopted by the EU against any country'. The EU is banning the export to Iran of key equipment and technology for refining, and for the exploration and production of natural gas.

? Question

Do you think that sanctions are likely to be an effective means of changing a government's policy?

Economics in context   **EU Airbus**

In 2010, the WTO ruled that the EU paid illegal subsidies to the aircraft giant Airbus. It took six years for the decision to be made.

According to the WTO judgment, European governments were found to have unfairly financed Airbus through risk-free loans, and research and infrastructure funding.

US trade representatives said: 'These subsidies have greatly harmed the USA, including causing Boeing to lose sales, and market share . . . [the] ruling helps level the competitive playing field with Airbus.'

But the WTO did not uphold all of the US complaints.

European support for Airbus was not found to have affected jobs or profits in the US aircraft industry, the report said, rejecting the US claim that state support had materially impacted the sector.

At the same time as the USA complained against Airbus, the EU has made a similar complaint over the USA's alleged support of its rival aircraft giant Boeing.

? Question

Why might governments want to protect their aircraft industries?

Economics in context   **Shoes**

In May 2010, a European Court rejected an appeal by a number of Hong Kong- and China-based shoemakers against import duties levied by the European Commission on shoes originating from China and Vietnam.

The EU General Court dismissed all five appeals lodged by the companies against a decision by the EU's executive arm to impose tariffs of up to 16.5 per cent on Chinese leather shoes and 10 per cent on those from Vietnam.

'The adoption of anti-dumping duties is not a penalty for earlier behaviour but a protective and preventive measure against unfair competition resulting from dumping practices,' the EU Court ruled.

The European Commission imposed the duties in 2006, following a complaint by European manufacturers, who argued that they were unable to compete with shoes dumped in the European market by low-cost producers in China and Vietnam.

The dispute has heightened trade tension between the 27-nation bloc and China, its second-biggest trading partner after the USA and its biggest source of imports.

EU ministers voted in December to extend the import duties for another 15 months, while Beijing launched a dispute at the WTO last month over the EU tariffs, saying that they were illegal.

 Question

Analyse the possible effects of having tariffs on Chinese and Vietnamese shoes.

What do you think?

Do you think that protecting a domestic industry is the right thing to do if it is struggling?

The appeal of protectionism

Protectionism is quite popular politically because a government is seen to be taking action to protect domestic firms. Domestic producers often organize themselves into effective lobbying groups to influence government policy and to try to bring about measures that will safeguard them from foreign competition. As comparative advantage changes over time, certain industries may be particularly affected and there may be high levels of unemployment in these industries as they struggle against worldwide competitors. Over time, individuals will be able to transfer to other industries or retrain, but in the short term, unemployment could be high. Governments—particularly if they are coming up to an election—may protect these industries to keep these people in work.

The stakeholder group that suffers most from protectionism is the consumer; consumers end up paying higher prices for goods and services that are being provided by inefficient domestic producers. However, consumers are from individual households and do not usually form pressure groups. They tend to have little effective representation in government; therefore they are less likely to influence government policy than the well-organized producers.

Bananas

The EU recently agreed a deal with Latin American countries and the USA to end the long-running 'banana wars' trade dispute.

The term 'banana wars' refers to a series of trade disputes between the EU, the USA, and several Latin American countries regarding access to Europe's banana market. The disputes surround EU tariffs on banana imports. The EU has many trade agreements with former colonies. Latin American banana producers who do not benefit from these agreements have been complaining about the unfairness of the EU tariffs ever since they were introduced. In 1996, Ecuador, Guatemala, Honduras, and Mexico, together with the USA, formally complained to the WTO about the tariffs.

Europe's banana market is the largest in the world. The EU imports around 5.5 million tonnes of bananas each year.

Since then, the WTO has repeatedly ruled that the EU tariffs are unfair, but little has changed thanks to continued discussions and arguments between the major parties. In the Geneva agreement on bananas, tariffs will be reduced on Latin American imported bananas.

? Question

Why might the EU impose tariffs on Latin American bananas?

■ The effect of tariffs

In Figure 29.4, the world price for the product is shown at a given level P1. Consumers in the country can buy as much as they want at this price on the world market. The result is that the quantity Q1 is demanded and bought. Of this, the domestic supply curve shows that, at this price, domestic firms can supply the quantity Q2. No more can be supplied domestically because, at this price, local suppliers cannot cover their costs at quantities beyond Q2. The quantity Q1 – Q2 is therefore imported from other countries. If the government now imposes a tariff on the product, then this will raise the price to P2. This means that domestic suppliers can now produce Q4. With the higher price, more local suppliers can cover their costs and afford to supply. With the higher price, the quantity demanded falls to Q3. This means that the quantity imported falls to Q3 – Q4.

The results of introducing the tariff are as follows.

- Consumers pay a higher price and buy less.

- The government earns a tax revenue, represented in Figure 29.4 by the area C. This is a transfer of money from customers to the government.

- Inefficient domestic producers who could not supply at the old price are able to produce at the higher price. The area B in Figure 29.4 represents the money paid to keep inefficient domestic producers in business.

- There is more producer surplus (equal to the area A in Figure 29.4) for local producers. This represents earnings over and above the price that they needed to supply.

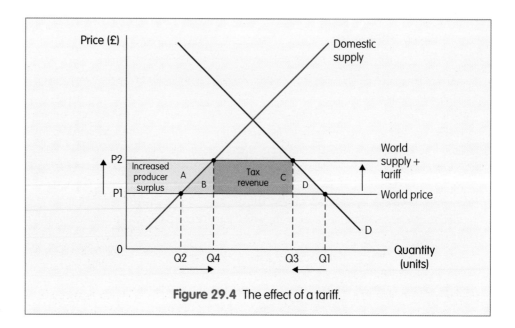

Figure 29.4 The effect of a tariff.

- The area D in Figure 29.4 represents a loss of consumer surplus; these units were consumed before the tariff, and this area shows consumers' utility over and above the price—that is, consumer surplus that is now lost.

What do you think?

Who wins and who loses from the introduction of a tariff?

The effects of quotas

In Figure 29.5, there is a limit of Q3 – Q4 on the number of products sold in the country. This quantity will be demanded only if the price is P2, which is above the world price. The producer surplus of domestic producers has now increased by area A. Domestic customers have fewer products at a higher price in comparison to the equilibrium price and output.

The effects of subsidies

One form of protectionism is to subsidize domestic producers. This is shown in Figure 29.6. The result is that more domestic producers can now supply the product. At the

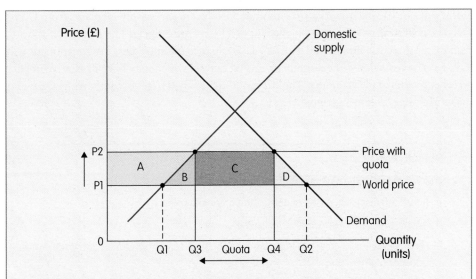

Figure 29.5 The effect of a quota. The imposition of a quota Q4 – Q3 on foreign goods increases the price of the product from P1 to P2. The area A represents the increased producer surplus for domestic producers. The area B represents the money paid to keep inefficient domestic producers in business, thus allowing inefficient domestic producers to supply. The area C represents the extra earnings for foreign producers. The area D represents the loss of consumer surplus due to the higher price.

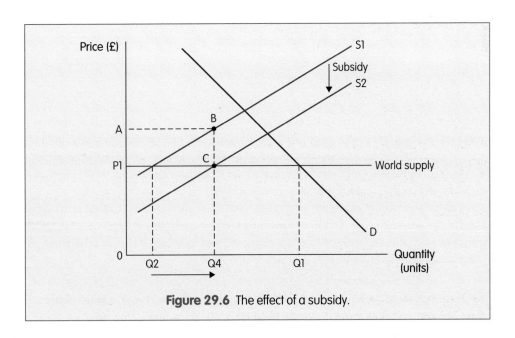

Figure 29.6 The effect of a subsidy.

world price of P1, the quantity that domestic producers can supply increases from Q2 to Q4. The government is enabling inefficient producers to compete. The amount of subsidy paid by the government is equal to ABCP1. To finance the subsidies, the government will have to raise revenue—for example, by raising taxes—which may have a negative impact on other sectors of the economy. The effect of the subsidy is to reduce imports by Q2 – Q4; the world price remains unchanged at P1.

Put into practice

Which of the following statements are true and which are false?

a. A tariff is a restriction on the quantity of imports into a country.

b. All countries in the world belong to the WTO.

c. Members of the EU have free trade amongst themselves, but agree their own trade policies against non-members.

d. In the EU, all member countries have the same taxation and government spending policies.

What do you think?

Should governments protect their domestic firms?
Assuming that governments should protect their firms, what do you think is the best way in which they might do this?

Case study Protecting the currency

The value of the Chinese yuan has been pegged to the dollar since 2008. US politicians have repeatedly threatened to impose trade sanctions on China if it continues to refuse to revalue its currency. Many US analysts argue that the yuan has been undervalued by as much as 40 per cent. This aids Chinese exports because the Chinese currency is cheap to buy and reduces US opportunities to export to China because the Chinese find US goods expensive as their currency is weak.

The USA believes that the Chinese government is intervening heavily in currency markets and artificially depressing the value of the yuan to make Chinese products more competitive. In response to this, the US government introduced a number of trade barriers against Chinese products, which then led to retaliation. Recent disputes between the two countries included the following.

- Poultry China introduced heavy taxes on US exports of chicken—one of the few US exports to China. US breeders, such as Tyson Foods Inc., sell chicken feet and wings, which are virtually worthless in the US market, to China, increasing their overall profits.

- **Tyres** The USA introduced a 35 per cent tax on Chinese tyres; China has taken this to the WTO to be removed.
- **Steel pipes** In 2009, the US Commerce Department introduced taxes on Chinese steel pipes of up to 99 per cent.

China argued that US protectionism threatened future trade. The annual level of Chinese exports to the USA approached $300 billion in 2009.

? Questions

- Who gains and who loses from a series of trade disputes such as those above?
- Was the USA right to retaliate to what it believes is unfair actions by the Chinese government?

Checklist

Now that you have read this chapter, try to answer the following questions.

- ☐ Can you explain the theory of international trade?
- ☐ Can you explain the elements of the balance of payments?
- ☐ Can you outline possible types of protectionism?
- ☐ Are you able to analyse why governments might protect industries?
- ☐ Are you able to examine the possible consequences of protectionism?
- ☐ Do you understand what the World Trade Organization is?
- ☐ Can you outline the key elements of the European Union (EU)?
- ☐ Can you examine the benefits of belonging to the EU?

Review questions

1 What is meant by free trade?
2 Is free trade a good thing?
3 Who benefits from tariffs?
4 Why do countries want to join the EU?
5 What is the World Trade Organization (WTO)?

Key learning points

- International trade is based on the principle of comparative advantage.
- International trade enables countries to benefit from more efficient production overseas; this can lead to more consumption and lower prices domestically.

- Protectionism can take several forms, such as tariffs, quotas, and legislation.
- Protectionism can encourage inefficiency, and lead to less consumption and higher prices for consumers.
- The European Union is a customs union.
- The Union offers opportunities and threats to member countries. It offers more customers to whom to sell, but also more competition.

Reference

Ricardo, D. (1817) *On the Principles of Political Economy and Taxation*, John Murray, London

Learn more

To learn more about the UK balance of payments over time, visit the Online Resource Centre.

 Visit our Online Resource Centre at http://www.oxfordtextbooks.co.uk/orc/gillespie_econ2e/ for test questions and further information on topics covered in this chapter.

Exchange rates

All economies are involved in international trade to some extent. The exchange rate is a key factor in determining the amount and value of trade between countries. This chapter examines the determinants of exchange rates and the effects of changes in exchange rates on an economy.

LEARNING OBJECTIVES

By the end of this chapter, you should be able to:

✔ explain the determinants of the external value of a currency;

✔ distinguish between a floating and a fixed exchange rate system;

✔ explain the possible impact of a change in the external value of a currency.

■ Introduction

If you have ever gone on holiday abroad, you will have had to change your pounds sterling into another currency. The amount of foreign currency that you received in return for your pound depends on the exchange rate. Sometimes, you might have felt that you received a lot of money in return for your pound; other times, you might have felt that the money you received did not go very far. The value of the exchange rate clearly matters to tourists and this is a very important sector of the UK economy. It also matters to any firm buying or selling products abroad. Given that the UK is a very open economy, which means that there is a high proportion of exports and imports, and that trade is very significant to the economy, changes in the exchange rate have a big impact on jobs, prices, and growth.

■ Exchange rate

An exchange rate measures the value of one currency in terms of another—for example, the value of one pound sterling in terms of US dollars or Japanese yen. It measures the external value of a currency. The external value of a currency is important because of its impact on trade, and its impact on export revenue and import spending.

■ What determines the external value of a currency?

If a government does not intervene in the currency market, then the value of the exchange rate is determined by the supply of, and demand for, this currency—that is, by market forces. This is known as a floating exchange rate system. Currency markets are often referred to as forex (foreign exchange) markets.

The demand for the UK currency will be influenced by the following.

- **Demand for UK goods and services from abroad** To buy UK products, overseas buyers will need pounds. Overseas buyers will have to give up their own currency and change it into pounds. If demand for UK products increases, then, all other things unchanged, the demand for pounds will increase as well.

- **Relative interest rates** If UK interest rates are higher than interest rates elsewhere in the world, then, all other things being unchanged, the demand for pounds will rise. Overseas investors will look to buy pounds to save in UK banks and earn higher returns. High UK interest rates will attract what is called 'hot money' flowing into the country.

- **Relative inflation rates** If UK goods and services are relatively expensive, then this is likely to reduce demand for the products and therefore for pounds. With less demand for the currency, it will fall in value, all other things being unchanged.

- **Expectations** If currency speculators believe that the pound will rise in value in the future, then they may buy now so that their investment will become worth more. This increase in demand will in itself increase the value of the currency, all other things being unchanged.

The demand for pounds will be downward-sloping. As the exchange rate increases, the price of UK goods and services will become greater in foreign currencies, all other things being unchanged. For example, at $1:£1, a £10 UK product is $10; at $2:£1, it is $20. This will lead to a fall in the quantity demanded of UK products and therefore a fall in the quantity demanded of pounds. The greater the price elasticity of demand for UK products abroad, the greater the fall in the quantity demanded of pounds (that is, the more price elastic the demand for pounds will be) following an increase in the exchange rate (see Figure 30.1).

Example

Imagine that a UK firm produces a product for £100 and sales abroad are ten units. Imagine that the exchange rate now rises from $1.5:£1 to $2:£1. The price of the product abroad rises from $150 to $200. Originally, the firm earned:

$$10 \times £100 = £1,000$$

If demand is price elastic, then demand falls to, say, two units. This means that earnings fall to:

$$2 \times £100 = £200$$

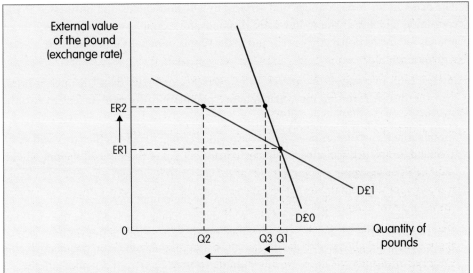

Figure 30.1 The demand for pounds sterling in the currency market. For the demand curve D£0, the demand for UK exports is price inelastic. For the demand curve D£1, the demand for UK exports is price elastic.

If demand is price inelastic, then sales may fall to nine units. The earnings are now:

$9 \times £100 = £900$

The more price elastic demand is for UK products abroad, the greater is the fall in the quantity of pounds demanded given an increase in the external value of the pound.

A change in the exchange rate leads to a movement along the demand curve for pounds. Changes in other factors, such as demand for UK products or UK interest rates, will shift the demand curve for pounds in the currency market.

Put into practice

a. Imagine that a UK firm produces a product for £200. What would the price in dollars be:
  - if the exchange rate is $1.5:£1?
  - if the exchange rate is $2:£1?

b. Suppose that the original level of sales was 500 units and then sales fell to 450 units.
  - Calculate the original and new value of sales in dollars.
  - Calculate the original and new value of sales in pounds.

The supply of UK currency to change into foreign currency will depend on the following.

- **The demand for foreign goods and services by UK households and businesses** If UK consumers and firms want to buy more US goods, for example, then they will sell more pounds to buy the dollars they need, and so the supply of pounds to the currency market will increase.

- **Interest rates overseas** If the interest rates overseas are higher than UK interest rates, then the British investors may change more pounds into foreign currencies to save abroad.

- **Speculation** If speculators believe that the pound is going to fall off, then they will want to sell now. This selling in itself is likely to lead to a fall in the value of the pound due to an increase in supply.

The supply of pounds is usually upward-sloping. As the pound increases in value, fewer pounds are needed to buy foreign products. If the exchange rate is $1:£1, then £100 is needed to buy a $100 product; if the exchange rate is $2:£1, only £50 is needed. With a high value of the pound, the price of foreign products falls in terms of pounds. This should increase the quantity demanded of foreign products. If demand for these products is price elastic, then there will be an increase in the overall spending on imports and therefore an increase in the supply of pounds. The increase in the value of the pound increases the quantity supplied and the supply curve is upward-sloping (see Figure 30.2).

If, however, the demand for imports is price inelastic, then a fall in price in pounds will lead to a relatively smaller increase in the quantity demanded. This will lead to a fall in the overall spending on imports. An increase in the value of the currency in this case leads to a fall in the supply of pounds. This means that the supply curve for pounds is downward-sloping (see Figure 30.2).

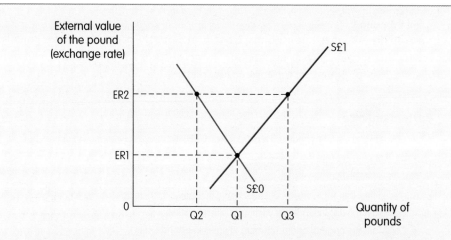

Figure 30.2 The supply of pounds sterling in the currency market. The supply curve S£0 represents the supply of pounds if the demand for imports is price inelastic. The supply curve S£1 represents the supply of pounds if the demand for imports is price elastic.

Example

Imagine that a US firm produces a product worth $300. A UK business imports ten of these. The exchange rate is $1.5:£1, so the US product costs:

$$\frac{\$300}{\$1.50} = £200$$

The UK firm spends:

$$10 \times £200 = £2,000$$

If the UK exchange rate now rises to $2:£1, then the US product now costs:

$$\frac{\$300}{\$2} = £150$$

Suppose that demand for the import is price inelastic and the firm now buys, say, 11 units. This means that it spends:

$$11 \times £150 = £1,650$$

Because the price is lower and the increase in quantity demanded is relatively low, the amount spent abroad (that is, the supply of pounds) falls. The supply of pounds falls as the exchange rate rises, as shown in Figure 30.3.

Suppose that demand for the import is price elastic and the firm now buys, say, 30 units. The firm spends:

$$30 \times £150 = £4,500$$

The increase in the quantity demanded is so great that, even with the lower price, there is more spending in pounds on foreign goods and so the supply of pounds rises, as shown in Figure 30.3.

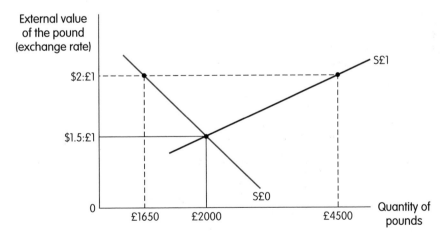

Figure 30.3 Upward-sloping and downward-sloping supply curves for a currency. The supply curve S£0 represents the supply of pounds if the demand for imports is price inelastic. The supply curve S£1 represents the supply of pounds if the demand for imports is price elastic.

Put into practice

The exchange rate appreciates from $1.5:£1 to $2:£1. The US price of a product is $300. A UK consumer buys 20 units initially and then, when the exchange rate changes, 40 units. What happens to the amount of pounds spent on this import?

Equilibrium in the currency market

In a floating exchange rate system, the value of the currency will change to bring about equilibrium automatically, so that the supply of the currency equals the demand for the currency. The exchange rate is the price mechanism that equates supply and demand in currency markets. There are, of course, many different markets for any currency (such as the pound against the yen, the US dollar, and the euro); in each market, the exchange rate will fluctuate to bring about equilibrium.

For example, if the value of the pound is at ER2 in Figure 30.4, then there is excess demand for the currency (equal to Q3 – Q2). This means that overseas buyers want to buy more pounds than others want to sell and convert into other currency. This will pull up the value of the pound. As the value (price) increases, the quantity demanded will fall, whilst the quantity supplied increases (assuming that the price elasticity of demand for imports is price elastic and the supply of currency is upward-sloping). This process will continue until equilibrium is reached at ER1. At this value, the supply of the currency equals the demand for the currency.

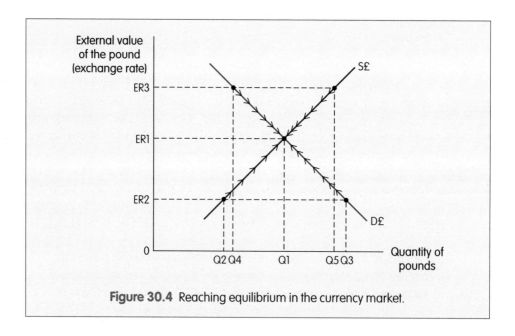

Figure 30.4 Reaching equilibrium in the currency market.

This means that the number of pounds demanded by overseas buyers equals the number of pounds sold. This is equilibrium in the currency market.

If the exchange rate is at ER3 in Figure 30.4, then there is excess supply of the currency (equal to Q5 – Q4). This means that the sellers want to change more pounds than buyers want to buy in exchange for foreign currency. This means that the value of the pound will fall. As it does so, the quantity demanded of this currency will increase and the quantity supplied will decrease until equilibrium is reached at ER1.

Given that there are so many different exchange rates showing the value of the pound against many different currencies, it is useful to be able to use one indicator that reflects the overall movement of the pound against these, taking account of their relative importance. If the UK trades a great deal with countries using the euro, then changes in the value of the pound against this currency are particularly important. The effective exchange rate is a weighted average of an exchange rate against its trade partners; this means that it takes account of the relative importance of different currencies depending on the relative amount of trade with these countries.

Put into practice

Which of the following statements are true and which are false?

a. Each country has one exchange rate.

b. An increase in domestic interest rates is likely to increase the value of the currency.

c. High domestic inflation is likely to increase the value of the currency.

d. A fall in the value of a currency makes its exports cheaper in foreign currencies, all other things being equal.

■ Appreciation and depreciation of the exchange rate

An appreciation of the exchange rate means that it has increased in value. It is more expensive in terms of other currencies. For example, if the value of £1 rises from $1.50 to $1.60, then this is an appreciation of the pound. This might be because of an increase in the demand for the currency or a fall in the supply (see Figure 30.5). If a currency has increased in value, then it is sometimes called a 'strong' currency.

A depreciation of the exchange rate means that it is less expensive in terms of other currencies. For example, the pound depreciates if its value falls from $1.50 to $1.40. This might be because of a fall in demand for the currency or an increase in the supply (see Figure 30.6). If a currency falls in value, then it is said to have become 'weaker'.

What do you think?

Do you think that a strong pound is better than a weak pound?

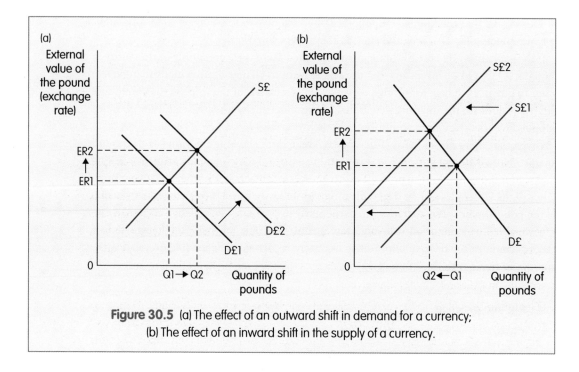

Figure 30.5 (a) The effect of an outward shift in demand for a currency; (b) The effect of an inward shift in the supply of a currency.

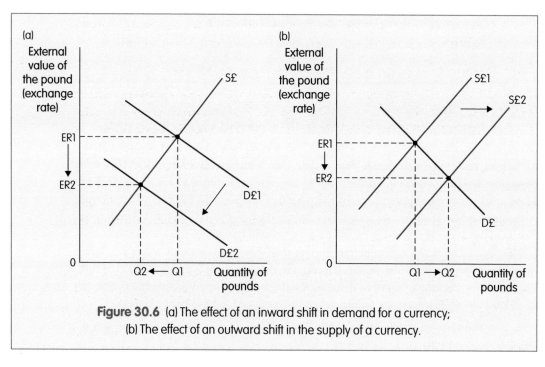

Figure 30.6 (a) The effect of an inward shift in demand for a currency; (b) The effect of an outward shift in the supply of a currency.

■ The advantages and disadvantages of a floating exchange rate system

A floating exchange rate system means that the exchange rate is determined purely by market forces and that governments do not intervene.

The advantages of a floating exchange rate system are as follows.

- The value of a currency will adjust to reflect changing market conditions. For example, if UK inflation were to increase faster than that of its trading partners, then, at the original exchange rate, its products would become more expensive abroad. This would be likely to lead to a fall in demand for UK goods and services, and therefore the demand for pounds. This in turn would reduce the value of the currency, which would:
  - make exports relatively cheaper, which would offset the higher inflation; and
  - make imports relatively expensive.

  The fall in the value of the currency should eventually restore equilibrium, so that the supply of, and demand for, the currency will be equal. This means that the balance of payments will balance (see Chapter 29); the number of pounds being supplied to the currency market will equal the demand for them.

- There are no costs of intervention. The government will not have to use its resources to buy and sell currency. This enables the government to focus on internal domestic economic issues.

The disadvantages of the floating exchange rate system are as follows.

- The value of the currency will change regularly (literally every minute), making it difficult for firms to plan ahead. UK exporters, for example, will not know at any moment what the actual price of their products will be to overseas buyers; UK importers will not know what they will have to pay to buy in foreign products. This makes planning difficult and will deter investment. It may lead to resources being invested in other countries.

- Given that the value of the currency can change all of the time as demand and supply conditions alter, this encourages speculation. By buying and selling currency in the belief that it will change, this leads to greater instability.

- In reality, the exchange rate may not be able to adjust to bring about equilibrium. For example, if the supply of pounds is downward-sloping, then the currency market may not settle in equilibrium. At ER1 in Figure 30.7, there is an excess supply of pounds. This leads to a fall in the value of the currency. In this case, the excess supply increases (for example, to ER2). Changes in the exchange rate in this situation move the market away from equilibrium.

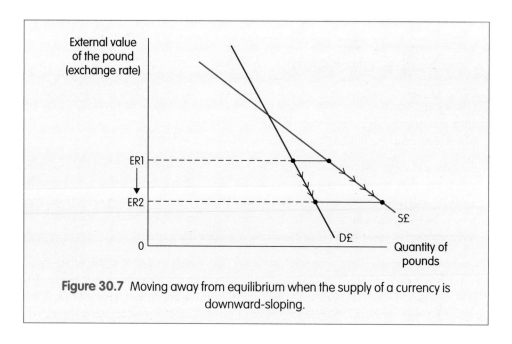

Figure 30.7 Moving away from equilibrium when the supply of a currency is downward-sloping.

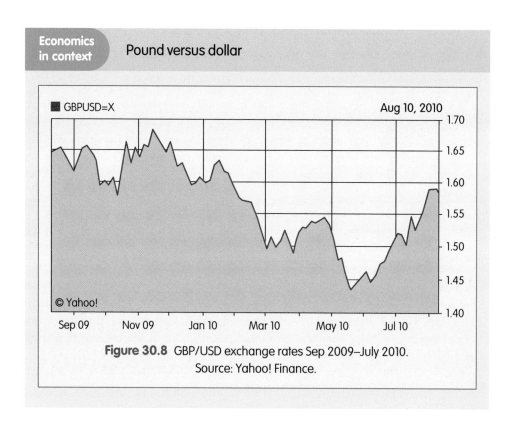

Figure 30.8 GBP/USD exchange rates Sep 2009–July 2010.
Source: Yahoo! Finance.

❓ **Questions**

Summarize the changes in the value of the pound against the dollar in Figure 30.8 above.

Use supply and demand analysis to explain possible reasons for the major changes in value.

What is the value of the pound against the dollar now? Has it appreciated or depreciated? Do you know why?

▩ A fixed exchange rate system

In a fixed exchange rate system, a government intervenes to maintain the value of a currency at a fixed value or within a given range.

A government can intervene in the currency market as follows.

- The government may buy or sell its currency. If it wants to increase the value of its currency abroad, then it can buy it in return for foreign currency that it holds. To decrease the value of its currency, it would sell it in return for foreign currency. This type of intervention involves transaction costs to monitor the possible currency movements and to exchange currency.
  - Suppose that equilibrium in the market is at ER1 in Figure 30.9. If this is below the rate that the government is trying to achieve, then it could increase demand for the currency by buying it in return for selling foreign reserves.

- Suppose that equilibrium is at ER1 in Figure 30.10. If this is above the rate at which the government would like it to be, then it can sell pounds in return for foreign currency.

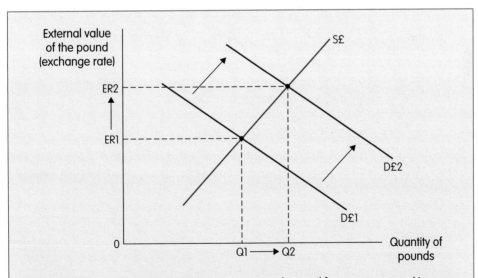

Figure 30.9 Government intervention to increase demand for a currency and increase its external value. The government buys pounds to increase demand, using foreign currency reserves.

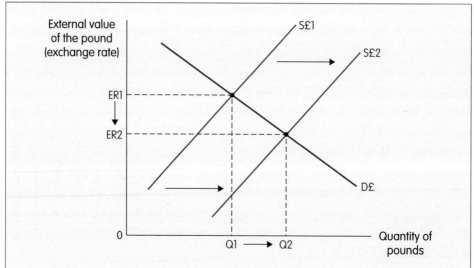

Figure 30.10 Government intervention to increase supply of a currency and reduce its external value. The government sells pounds in return for foreign currency.

- The government may change the interest rate. An increase in the UK interest rate is likely to attract investment (hot money) from overseas, which increases the demand for pounds; this should increase the external value of the currency, all other things being unchanged.

- The government may use reflationary or deflationary policies to affect the level of demand and spending in the UK. Deflationary policies, for example, would reduce aggregate demand spending. This would reduce spending on imports. With less spending on imports, there is less demand for foreign currency and therefore less need to change pounds. This reduces the supply of pounds.

Economics in context   Relaxing currency controls in Russia

In 2006, Russia lifted controls on its currency, the rouble, making it fully convertible with other currencies. Previously, there had been severe restrictions on the amount of currency that could be changed from roubles to other currencies and on the movement of money into Russia. The Russian government hoped that introducing convertibility would lead to a major inflow of foreign currency, but it also led to more roubles being converted. Prior to this change in policy, Russians wishing to transfer funds to a foreign bank account had to put a quarter of the sum in an account in the Russian Central Bank, and foreigners transferring money to Russia were required to deposit a 'collateral' amount as a security against speculative buying and selling of the currency. The rouble is now like the dollar and euro, and can be converted without any restrictions.

 Question

Why would the Russian government have wanted to restrict the amount of money entering and leaving the country?

Put into practice

Outline three ways in which a government might reduce the value of its currency.

The benefit of a fixed exchange rate system is that it provides stability for importers and exporters because they know at what rate they will be trading. However, decisions to intervene to affect the value of the currency have an opportunity cost and side effects that might disrupt other policies. For example, higher interest rates might increase the value of the pound, but will also have an impact on domestic savings and borrowings. High interest rates are likely to decrease domestic demand, and may cause slower economic growth and unemployment. The external value of the pound may be kept stable at the expense of UK jobs.

Also, as market conditions change, the fixed value of the currency may become too high or low. This will affect the competitiveness of a country's products abroad and a country's balance of payments position.

Put into practice

Which of the following statements are true and which are false?

a. An increase in demand for a currency is likely to lead to an appreciation of the currency in a floating exchange rate.

b. To increase the value of its currency, a government might sell its foreign currency reserves.

c. A decrease in supply of a currency to the currency markets is likely to decrease its value.

d. A floating exchange rate makes planning more difficult than a fixed exchange rate.

The exchange rate mechanism

The exchange rate mechanism (ERM) was a system in which member European countries fixed their exchange rates against each other. The aim was to stabilize exchange rates in Europe and thereby encourage trade. The currencies of member countries were given an upper and lower limit on either side of a given central rate within which their currencies could fluctuate. The UK joined the ERM at a rate of DM2.95 to £1 in October 1990.

The system collapsed on 16 September 1992, when countries could not keep their currencies within the set limits. On what became known as 'Black Wednesday', the British pound was forced to leave the system; it was then followed by the Italian lira. The UK government had fought against speculators who were selling pounds, believing that the fixed rate of the pound had been set too high. In a floating exchange rate system, this sale of pounds would drive the value of the pound down. However, because it was in the ERM, the UK government had to try to keep the value of the pound constant; it did this by buying billions of pounds with its foreign currency reserves and increasing domestic interest rates. In the end, the UK government recognized that it could not keep intervening like this (not least because of the impact of such high interest rates domestically) and left the ERM. Speculators such as George Soros made a fortune because they had been selling pounds; once the pound fell, they could buy them back much more cheaply.

■ The single European currency: The euro

The euro is a currency that has been adopted by a number of European Union (EU) members, which collectively are known as the eurozone. It was introduced on 1 January 1999, with the notes and coins being released at midnight on 31 December 2001, when national currencies started to be withdrawn from circulation. The transition period was needed to allow time to print the 13 billion banknotes and produce the 52 billion euro coins that went into circulation.

In 1997, the UK government set out five tests that would have to be met before the UK would join the euro. These were:

- that UK and European economies were converging, so that, for example, one interest rate would suit all countries;
- that the economies were flexible enough to cope if things were to go wrong;
- that joining the euro would encourage companies to invest in the UK;
- that joining the euro would be good for financial services; and
- that joining the euro would be good for jobs.

There is still debate over whether these criteria have been met and, at the time of writing, much of the pressure to join the eurozone has reduced in the UK. Economic problems of member countries, such as Greece, have highlighted the potential problems of a currency the value of which will reflect the position of economies that could be performing very differently. For example, concern over some economies might lead to a fall in the value of the euro, making imports very expensive for members with economies that are relatively still strong.

The advantages of being a member of the euro include the following.

- Firms and households do not need to change currency when visiting or trading with another euro country. This saves on transaction costs (for example, the fee paid to change currency), which should lead to lower prices for consumers.
- It becomes easier to plan ahead. If the exchange rate is constantly changing, then managers and households cannot be certain of the value of a pound; they will not know what they will get when they change their currency to go on holiday, or when they want to buy products from abroad. Equally, they will not know what the price of the products that they want to sell abroad will be in terms of the foreign currency. This can add further risk to any spending or investment decision, which may prevent the decision from being made. Within the eurozone, all other things being unchanged, the price is more predictable, which makes trading easier and less uncertain.
- It becomes easier to compare prices. This is known as 'price transparency'. If a firm is searching for possible supplies in several countries with different currencies, then managers will have to convert the prices into pounds and try to estimate possible changes in the future. It is simpler to operate and choose a supplier if the prices are all in the same currency.

- Competition between firms in the member countries will be greater because of price transparency. This may lead to greater efficiency, which should lead to a better use of resources and an outward shift of the aggregate supply.

- There may be less need to control inflation domestically. If the UK were to have higher inflation than other countries, then this would automatically affect its price competitiveness (it cannot be offset by a fall in the external value of the currency within the eurozone). This is likely to make it harder to export, which dampens demand and therefore brings inflation down again in line with other countries.

- It creates the possibility of internal economies of scale. With trade being easier due to prices being easier to predict, this could lead to higher outputs and internal economies of scale, thereby reducing unit costs.

The disadvantages of joining the euro include the following.

- **One-off changeover costs** Changing the currency from pounds to euros would inevitably incur costs, because brochures have to be rewritten, price lists updated, and vending machines changed to accept new coins.

- **One-off inflationary effects** These are likely to happen because, when changing prices, firms are likely to round up rather than down.

- **Emotional costs** Some people are attached to their national currency, and see this as a sign of independence and heritage. Changing to the euro is sometimes resisted on the basis of national pride rather than economics.

- **Loss of economic policy control** The value of the euro will be influenced by changes in the levels of interest rates within those member countries. Decisions about interest rates must therefore be made in terms of the 'right' rate of the euro for all countries involved. At any particular moment, what is right for the euro members as a whole may not be right for a particular member—for example, a weak euro may stimulate demand generally within the eurozone, but cause problems in an area in which there is already demand-pull inflation. By joining the euro, the UK government and people would have to accept that interest rate decisions would be less UK-focused and more eurozone-focused. Interest rates are set by the European Central Bank (ECB) and not the Bank of England. The ECB is the central bank for the euro. The ECB's main task is to maintain price stability in the eurozone; it would not focus specifically on the UK's economic position. The significant differences between relatively strong economies (such as Germany's) and economies such as those of Portugal, Ireland, Greece, and Spain have put real pressure on the euro in recent years.

Members of the eurozone in 2010

The eurozone members at the time of writing are: Austria; Belgium; Cyprus; Finland; France; Germany; Greece; Ireland; Italy; Luxembourg; Malta; the Netherlands; Portugal; Slovakia; Slovenia; and Spain.

 Question

Why might countries not want to join the euro?

Pound versus dollar

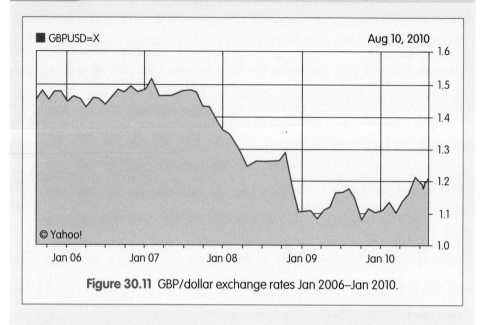

Figure 30.11 GBP/dollar exchange rates Jan 2006–Jan 2010.

? Questions

Use supply and demand analysis to explain possible reasons for the major changes in value of the pound against the dollar.

Discuss the possible effects of the fall in the value of the pound against the dollar over the period covered for UK businesses.

What is the value of the pound against the dollar now? Has it appreciated or depreciated recently? Do you know why?

Put into practice

Which of the following statements are true and which are false?

a. All members of the EU have the euro as their currency.

b. If the pound falls in value against the euro, the euro must rise in value against the pound.

c. Higher interest rates in eurozone countries are likely to lead to an increase in the value of the euro.

d. If the euro is weak, this makes goods from these countries expensive in foreign countries, all other things unchanged.

Economics in context ## The euro

Some British business leaders still argue that the UK should join the euro in the future.

Lord Simon, the chairman of BP, said that 'It is time to recognize the importance of a more integrated economic/political system in Europe.' Sir Nick Scheele, former chief operating officer of Ford, stated that, 'despite the debt problems in certain eurozone countries my belief that we should join the euro is based on the fact that 70 per cent of our trade is with euro-based economies'.

For many others, however, the government debt crisis in euro economies such as Greece and Spain in 2010 meant that the debate was over because the currency was too vulnerable to economic problems in member countries.

In 2001, the Labour government, re-elected for a second term, said that it would assess its five tests for euro entry within two years. This sparked a divisive debate, with high-profile campaigns both for and against entry. But in June 2003, the then chancellor Gordon Brown told MPs that the conditions for entry had not been met. In his first Budget in June 2010, the chancellor George Osborne confirmed that he had scrapped the Treasury's Euro Preparations Unit and redeployed its staff.

? Question

Do you think that the UK should join the euro in the near future or not?

Economics in context ## Estonia's bid to join euro

In 2010, EU finance ministers supported Estonia's bid to become the eurozone's 17th member on 1 January 2011. The small Baltic state had fixed its currency—the kroon—to the euro ever since the single currency's inception in 1999. However, for many years, Estonia was unable to fully join the euro, because its inflation rate was deemed too high. With the global recession, the country finally met the eurozone's inflation criterion.

Unlike many existing eurozone members, Estonia has stayed within the euro's criteria on budget deficits and total government debt for several years.

? Question

Analyse the potential benefits to Estonia of joining the eurozone.

The real exchange rate

When analysing the effect of exchange rate changes, it is important to consider what has happened to prices in the countries involved. If, for example, a currency were to fall in value, then, everything else unchanged, this would mean that a country's products were relatively cheaper in foreign currency. If, however, prices in this country were rising faster than in its trading partner, this would offset the effect of the falling exchange rate. If a currency halves in value, but prices double, then, in real terms, the exchange rate is the same. The real exchange rate therefore adjusts the nominal exchange rate for the relative prices in different countries.

For example, if there is a £100 UK product and the exchange rate is originally $2:£1, but falls by 50 per cent to $1:£1, then the product would sell for $100 rather than $200. The UK products are more competitive because of the fall in the currency. If, however, prices in the UK were to double, so that the product now costs £200, then this would mean that, even with the fall in the currency, it was selling for $200. Assuming that nothing has changed with the US prices, the product is exactly as competitive as it was originally.

The real exchange rate can be calculated as:

$$\text{Real exchange rate} = \frac{(\text{Nominal exchange rate} \times \text{UK prices})}{\text{Overseas prices}}$$

For example, imagine that the nominal exchange rate is $2:£1, but a pair of jeans sells for £10 in the UK, whilst jeans generally sell for $12 in the USA.

This means that the UK jeans would sell for $20 in the USA (given the nominal exchange rate), which is the top line of the equation:

$$\text{Real exchange rate} = \frac{(\$2 \times £10)}{\$12} = \frac{\$20}{\$12} = \$1.67$$

The real exchange rate is therefore $1.67:£1.

Put into practice

a. The nominal exchange rate is €1.5: £1. A product sells for £5 in the UK and typically sells for €4 in the eurozone. What is the real exchange rate?

b. What is the effect on the real exchange rate if:
- the price in the UK increases to £10?
- the price in the eurozone increases to €8?

▪ Purchasing power parity (PPP)

Purchasing power parity (PPP) is the exchange rate that gives one currency exactly the same purchasing power when converted into another—for example, £1,000 when converted into the other currency could purchase the same goods and services. If, for example, £1,000 of goods in the UK costs $1,700, then the exchange rate that would lead to PPP would be $1.7:£1. Thus we have:

$$\text{PPP exchange rate} = \frac{\text{Consumer price index in other country}}{\text{UK consumer price index}}$$

$$\text{PPP exchange rate} = \frac{\$1,700}{£1,000} = \$1.7:£1$$

To maintain PPP, the value of a currency must move to offset differences in inflation rates. If UK inflation is relatively high, then the pound will need to fall; £1,000 will buy less in the UK because of domestic inflation and, when converted into other currencies, it needs to buy less there as well.

Burger index

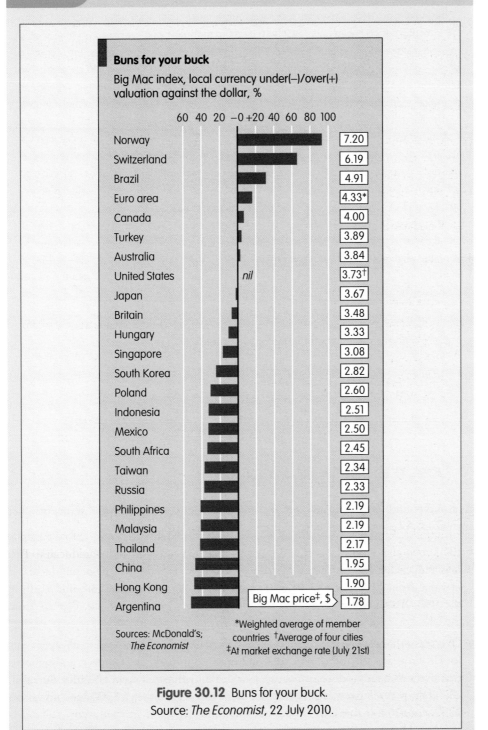

Buns for your buck

Big Mac index, local currency under(–)/over(+) valuation against the dollar, %

Country	Big Mac price‡, $
Norway	7.20
Switzerland	6.19
Brazil	4.91
Euro area	4.33*
Canada	4.00
Turkey	3.89
Australia	3.84
United States	3.73†
Japan	3.67
Britain	3.48
Hungary	3.33
Singapore	3.08
South Korea	2.82
Poland	2.60
Indonesia	2.51
Mexico	2.50
South Africa	2.45
Taiwan	2.34
Russia	2.33
Philippines	2.19
Malaysia	2.19
Thailand	2.17
China	1.95
Hong Kong	1.90
Argentina	1.78

*Weighted average of member countries †Average of four cities ‡At market exchange rate (July 21st)

Sources: McDonald's; The Economist

Figure 30.12 Buns for your buck.
Source: *The Economist*, 22 July 2010.

The Economist's exchange-rate scorecard, the Big Mac index, showed that in July 2010 currencies continued to be cheap in the developing world but overvalued in Europe.

The index is an attempt to gauge how far currencies are from their fair value. It is based on the theory of purchasing power parity (PPP), which argues that in the long run exchange rates should move to equalize the price of an identical basket of goods between two countries. *The Economist* basket consists of a single item, a Big Mac hamburger, produced in nearly 120 countries. *The Economist* then calculate the exchange rate that leaves burgers costing the same in America as elsewhere, and compares this with the current market exchange rate to decide if it is overvalued or undervalued.

Asia remains the cheapest place to enjoy a burger. China's recent decision to increase the 'flexibility' of the yuan has not made much difference yet. A Big Mac costs $1.95 in China at current exchange rates, against $3.73 in America. Our index suggests that a fair-value rate would be 3.54 yuan to the dollar, compared with the current rate of 6.78. In other words the yuan is undervalued by 48%.

Other Asian currencies such as the Thai baht and the South Korean won are also undervalued. The Brazilian real is one of the few emerging-market currencies that is trading well above its Big Mac benchmark. With interest rates high—the policy rate now stands at 10.75%—Brazil has attracted lots of attention from yield-hungry investors. Burgernomics suggests that the real is overvalued by 31%.

 Questions

What is meant by PPP?

Analyse the possible effects of the currency valuations relative to the Big Mac index shown above.

Why might the euro have been 'overvalued by 29 per cent'?

Does a strong pound matter?

A strong pound sterling means that the pound is relatively expensive in terms of other currencies. All other things being unchanged, this means the following.

- UK goods and services become relatively more expensive in other currencies. This may reduce demand for them and reduce UK export earnings. If the pound increases in value from £1:$1.5 to £1:$1.6, then a £100 good now costs $160, not $150, in the USA. This is likely to reduce the volume of, and earnings from, exports from the UK.

- Overseas products become relatively cheap in pounds. This may lead to cheaper costs for UK firms and therefore an increase in firms' profit margins. However, it also means that overseas final products are cheaper, which may threaten some UK sales domestically. If the pound increases in value from £1:$1 to £1:$1.5, then a $300 good now costs £200, not £300, in the UK.

The extent to which a strong pound has these effects depends on:

- how much the pound increases in value and for how long;
- the time period being considered (many prices are fixed for some periods, for example, until brochures are updated or contracts renegotiated); and
- how sensitive demands for imports and exports are to price (it may be that the quality of the products means that demand is not that sensitive).

▪ Effect of a falling pound: Depreciation, the J-curve effect, and the current account

If the pound depreciates, then, all other things being unchanged, UK products become cheaper abroad in terms of foreign currency, whilst imports become more expensive in pounds. The cheaper exports should lead to more sales and greater income for UK firms. The extent to which sales abroad increase depends on how price sensitive demand is for UK products abroad. If demand is price elastic, then the increase in sales is greater than the fall in export prices (in percentage terms) and spending on UK exports rises relatively significantly. If demand is price inelastic, then the increase in sales will be less than the increase in price (in percentage terms) and so the increase in the number of UK products sold will be relatively low; therefore the increase in UK export earnings in pounds will also be relatively low.

Meanwhile, the increase in the price of imports in pounds is likely to lead to a fall in the quantity demanded. If demand for imports is price elastic, then this will lead to a larger fall in sales than the increase in price (in percentage terms); this will lead to a fall in the total spending on imports. However, if demand is price inelastic, then this means that the fall in sales is less than the increase in price (in percentage terms); this leads to an increase in the total spending on imports.

The effect of a depreciation in the value of the currency on the current account of the balance of payments therefore depends a great deal on the price elasticity of demand for imports and exports.

In the short run

In the short run, UK importers and exporters may have negotiated and fixed prices with their trading partners. They may also find it difficult to find alternative suppliers abroad at short notice. The result is that demand for UK products abroad is likely to be price inelastic and demand for imports is also likely to be price inelastic. This means that the increase in export sales is relatively low, so export revenue does not increase much; at the same time, demand for imports is not sensitive to price, leading to more being spent overall on them given the higher price.

Overall, the current account of the balance of payments position is likely to worsen in the short term following a fall in the value of the pound, because demands for imports and exports are likely to be price inelastic.

Over time

Over time, following a fall in the value of the pound, buyers abroad are more likely to switch to the cheaper UK products, thus boosting UK exports. This should lead to an increase in export revenue. At the same time, UK firms may switch to UK suppliers rather than stick with relatively expensive foreign products. This leads to a fall in the total spending on imports. This means that, in the long run following a fall in the value of a currency, the balance of payments position should improve.

The current account of the balance of payments position will improve following a depreciation of the currency provided that the price elasticity of demand for exports plus the price elasticity of demand for imports is greater than one (> 1). This is known as the Marshall–Lerner condition.

The short-term deterioration of a country's balance of payments following a depreciation of the currency before an improvement in the long term is called the J-curve effect. This is because the current account of the balance of payments moves into deficit before rising into surplus. The J-curve effect is illustrated in Figure 30.12.

The very long run

In the very long run, the higher import prices may lead to cost-push inflation. This is because UK firms will be dependent to some extent on imported goods and services, and will try to pass on their higher costs to consumers. This will push up UK prices, thus offsetting the export benefits of a fall in the value of the currency. This may lead to the balance of payments position returning to its original position, but with higher domestic inflation. This suggests that a fall in the value of a currency may have only limited beneficial impact

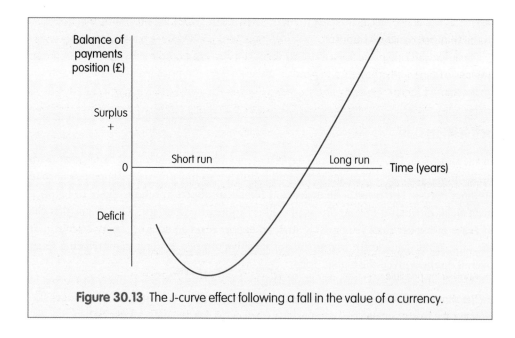

Figure 30.13 The J-curve effect following a fall in the value of a currency.

over time. This means that intervening to weaken the currency is not a very long-term solution by government to a problem on the current account of the balance of payments. Other problems with depreciating the currency include the following.

- **A crisis of confidence** If a government devalues the currency or allows it to depreciate, then this may trigger concerns that there are problems. This may lead to an outflow of capital on the capital account, causing a worsening of the current account of the balance of payments.

- **A lack of capacity** If the economy is near capacity, then a fall in the currency would boost the aggregate demand and lead to demand-pull inflation. In this case, it may be necessary for a government to create capacity in the economy before depreciating the currency.

Case study A fall in the value of the pound

In May 2010, the value of the pound fell sharply against other major currencies after news came out that the UK's trade deficit had widened.

- The pound fell nearly 1.2 per cent against the dollar at $1.4646 and by a cent against the euro.
- The value of UK imports exceeded exports by £3.7 billion ($5.5 billion) for the month before.
- UK exports increased by just 1 per cent, whereas imports rose by 5.2 per cent compared with the previous month.

The rise in imports was driven by a jump in imports of intermediate goods such as mechanical and electrical engineering components, as well as cars, chemicals, and oil. Although the falling pound suggested reduced confidence in the UK economy, it also helped exporters by making UK goods cheaper for foreign buyers. The pound fell against the euro to 1.1650, and was also down against the Japanese yen and a range of other foreign currencies.

The Bank of England governor said that the UK's economy should shift its weight towards exports, rather than relying on domestic consumption. Economic experts expressed concern over the rising trade deficit.

❓ Questions

- What determines the value of the pound in a floating exchange rate system?
- What is meant by a trade deficit?
- Explain why the value of the pound might fall after the announcement of a large trade deficit.
- Analyse the possible reasons why UK exports increased more than imports.
- Analyse the possible effects on the trade deficit now that the pound has fallen.
- The Bank of England governor said that the UK's economy should shift its weight towards exports, rather than relying on domestic consumption. How could it do this? Why is it desirable?

Checklist

Now that you have read this chapter, try to answer the following questions.

☐ Can you explain the determinants of the external value of a currency?

☐ Can you distinguish between a floating and a fixed exchange rate system?

☐ Can you explain the possible impact of a change in the external value of a currency?

Review questions

1 What is a floating exchange rate?

2 Explain the determinants of an exchange rate in a floating exchange rate system.

3 How can a government control the external value of its currency?

4 For what reasons might the value of a currency increase?

5 Does controlling the value of the currency conflict with other economic objectives?

Key learning points

• The value of a currency is determined by supply and demand in a floating exchange rate system.

• In a fixed exchange rate system, the government intervenes to keep the external value of a currency stable.

• If a currency depreciates, then the J-curve effect shows that the current account position on the balance of payments may get worse before getting better; the position will only improve if the Marshall–Lerner condition is met and the price elasticity of demand for exports plus the price elasticity of demand for imports is greater than one (> 1).

• The euro is a single currency used by members of the eurozone (most members of the European Union) that removes the problem and cost of converting currency.

Learn more

To learn more about the value of the pound over time and the impact on the UK economy, visit the Online Resource Centre.

 Visit our Online Resource Centre at http://www.oxfordtextbooks.co.uk/orc/gillespie_econ2e/ for test questions and further information on topics covered in this chapter.

Glossary of key terms

Abnormal profit (or supernormal profit) Abnormal profit occurs when the total revenue is greater than the total costs.

Accelerator The accelerator shows the relationships between the level of net investment and the rate of change of national income.

Adverse selection This occurs when individuals have inside information and use this to decide whether to accept or reject an offer.

Aggregate demand The aggregate demand is the total planned demand for final goods and services in an economy.

Aggregate supply Aggregate supply is the total quantity of goods and services that firms in an economy are willing and able to produce at each and every price, all other things being unchanged.

Allocative efficiency Allocative efficiency occurs when the price paid by the customer equals the social marginal cost of producing the good.

Ansoff matrix This shows the strategies open to business in terms of targeting new and existing markets with new and existing products.

Asymmetric information Asymmetric information occurs when there is a difference in the information available to buyers and sellers.

Average cost (also known as average total cost) The average cost is the cost per unit.

Average product The average product is the output per variable factor (such as the output per worker).

Balance of payments This measures the economic transactions between one country and the rest of the world.

Cartel A cartel occurs when there is an agreement between the firms in a market regarding the price and output to set.

Change in demand A change in demand refers to a shift in a demand curve, showing a change in the quantity demanded at each and every price.

Classical (real wage) unemployment Classical unemployment occurs when the real wage is maintained above equilibrium.

Community surplus The community surplus is the sum of the consumer surplus and the producer surplus.

Comparative advantage A country has a comparative advantage in the production of a product if it has a lower opportunity cost than other countries.

Conglomerate integration Conglomerate integration occurs when one firm joins with another organization in a different market.

Consumer prices index (CPI) This is a measure of inflation.

Consumer surplus The consumer surplus is the difference between the price charged for a product and the utility that consumers derive from it.

- Consumption Consumption shows the level of planned spending by households on final goods and services.

- Contestable market A contestable market is one that is relatively easy to enter.

- Cost–benefit analysis A cost–benefit analysis is an approach to investment decisions that takes into account social costs and benefits.

- Cost-push inflation Cost-push inflation occurs when higher costs force producers to put up their prices.

- Cross-price elasticity of demand The cross-price elasticity of demand measures the responsiveness of demand for one product in relation to changes in the price of another.

- Current account of the balance of payments The current account of the balance of payments measures the difference in the value between the exports from, and imports of goods and services to, a country.

- Cyclical unemployment Cyclical unemployment occurs when people are unemployed due to a lack of demand in the economy.

- Deflation This occurs when prices are falling. It means that there is negative inflation.

- Demand curve A demand curve shows the quantity demanded at each and every price, all other factors being unchanged.

- Demand for labour The demand for labour shows the quantity of labour demanded at each and every wage, all other factors being unchanged.

- Demand for money The demand for money shows the amount of money that people want to hold at each and every interest rate, all other things being unchanged.

- Demand-pull inflation Demand-pull inflation occurs when the aggregate demand is greater than the aggregate supply, thereby pulling up prices.

- Direct taxes These are taxes placed on households' incomes and firms' profits.

- Diseconomies of scale Diseconomies of scale (internal) occur when there are increases in the long-run average costs as the scale of production increases.

- Diversification Diversification occurs when a firm develops new products to offer in a new market.

- Divorce between ownership and control A divorce between ownership and control occurs when there is a difference between the people who own an organization and those who manage it day to day.

- Economic cycle The economic cycle shows the pattern of GDP growth in an economy over time.

- Economic growth Economic growth occurs when there is an increase in the real national income.

- Elasticity of demand for labour The elasticity of demand for labour measures the responsiveness of the demand for labour in relation to changes in wages, all other factors being unchanged.

- Equilibrium Equilibrium occurs when the quantity supplied equals the quantity demanded at the given price and there is no incentive for change.

- Euro The euro is a single currency adopted by most members of the European Union.

▨ **European Union (EU)** The European Union is a customs union. This means that there is free trade between member countries and common external tariffs against non-member countries.

▨ **Exchange rate** An exchange rate is the price of one currency in terms of another.

▨ **External economies and diseconomies of scale** External economies and diseconomies of scale occur when the long-run average costs of a firm change at every level of output.

▨ **Externality** An externality occurs when there is a difference between private and social costs and benefits.

▨ **Fiscal drag** Fiscal drag occurs when individuals pay more tax because their nominal incomes have increased, which has moved them into higher tax brackets, even if, in real terms, their incomes have not increased.

▨ **Fiscal policy** A fiscal policy uses government spending, taxation, and benefit rates to influence the economy.

▨ **Fixed costs** Fixed costs are costs that do not change with the amount of products produced.

▨ **Fixed exchange rate system** In a fixed exchange rate system, the government intervenes to maintain the external value of a currency.

▨ **Floating exchange rate system** In a floating exchange rate system, the external value of a currency is determined by the supply of, and demand for, it.

▨ **Free market** A free market allocates resources via the price mechanism, and market forces of supply and demand.

▨ **Frictional unemployment** Frictional unemployment occurs when people are between jobs.

▨ **Game theory** Game theory is an approach to oligopoly in which each firm's strategy depends on its expectations of how the others in the market will behave.

▨ **Gini coefficient** The Gini coefficient measures the extent of income inequality in an economy.

▨ **Gross domestic product (GDP)** The GDP measures the value of final goods and services produced in an economy.

▨ **Gross national product (GNP)** The GNP equals the gross domestic product plus the net property income from abroad.

▨ **Horizontal integration** Horizontal integration occurs when one firm joins with another at the same stage of the same production process.

▨ **Income elasticity of demand** The income elasticity of demand measures the responsiveness of the demand for a product in relation to changes in income.

▨ **Inflation** Inflation occurs when there is a persistent increase in the general price level.

▨ **Injection** An injection is spending into the economy in addition to consumption; injections increase the aggregate demand.

▨ **Interdependence** Interdependence occurs when the actions of one firm directly affect another.

▨ **Internal diseconomies of scale** Internal diseconomies of scale occur when there are increases in the long-run average costs as the scale of production increases.

▨ **Internal economies of scale** Internal economies of scale occur when there are reductions in the long-run average costs as the scale of production increases.

Involuntary unemployment Involuntary unemployment measures the number of people who are willing and able to work at the given real wage, but who are not in employment.

J-curve effect The J-curve effect shows how a depreciation of a currency can make the current account of the balance of payments worse in the short run before it improves.

Laffer curve The Laffer curve shows the relationship between the tax rate and the level of tax revenue.

Less-developed country A less-developed country is an economy with low income, and is usually associated with low life expectancy and low levels of literacy.

Liquidity preference Liquidity preference (the demand for money) shows the amount of money that people want to hold at each and every interest rate, all other things being unchanged.

Long run The long run is the period of time during which all of the factors of production are variable.

Marginal cost The marginal cost is the extra cost of producing an extra unit.

Marginal efficiency of capital (MEC) The MEC shows the expected rate of return on investment projects.

Marginal product The marginal product measures the extra output produced when another unit of a variable factor of production is added to the fixed factors of production.

Marginal propensity to consume The marginal propensity to consume measures the amount spent out of an extra pound by households.

Marginal propensity to consume domestically The marginal propensity to consume domestically measures the amount spent out of an extra pound by households within a domestic economy.

Marginal revenue Marginal revenue is the extra revenue earned by selling another unit.

Marginal revenue product of labour (MRPL) The marginal revenue product of labour measures the value of the output produced by employing an extra worker.

Market development Market development occurs when a firm offers its existing products to a new market.

Market share A market share is the sales of a firm or brand as a percentage of the total market sales.

Marketing mix The marketing mix is the combination of factors that influence a customer's decision to buy a product, such as the price, the product itself, the promotion, and the place.

Maximum price A maximum price occurs when a price is set by the government and firms cannot charge more than this.

Merger A merger occurs when two or more organizations join together to form one.

Minimum efficient scale (MES) The minimum efficient scale is the first level of output at which the long-run average costs are minimized.

Minimum price A minimum price occurs when a price is set by the government and firms cannot charge less than this.

Mixed economy A mixed economy is an economy that contains both private and public sectors within it.

- **Monetary Policy Committee (MPC)** The MPC is the body responsible for setting interest rates in the UK to achieve a given inflation target.

- **Monopolistic competition** Monopolistic competition is a market structure in which there are many firms, but each offers a differentiated product.

- **Monopoly** A monopoly is a firm that has seller power.

- **Monopoly power** Monopoly power occurs when one firm dominates a market.

- **Monopsony** A monopsony occurs when a buyer has power in a market (whereas a monopoly occurs when the seller has power).

- **Movement along a demand curve** A movement along a demand curve refers to a change in the quantity demanded that is caused by a change in the price, all other factors being unchanged.

- **Multiplier** The multiplier shows how an increase in the aggregate demand leads to a greater increase in national income.

- **Nationalization** Nationalization occurs when a government takes ownership of an organization.

- **Normal profit** Normal profit occurs when the total revenue equals the total costs.

- **Objective** An objective is a target (such as to increase profits by 20 per cent over five years).

- **Office of Fair Trading (OFT)** The OFT is a government regulator of competition policy.

- **Oligopoly** An oligopoly is a market structure in which a few firms dominate the market.

- **Opportunity cost** The opportunity cost (in the context of a production possibility frontier) is the amount of one product that has to be given up to produce more of another product.

- **Patent** A patent is a legal protection for an invention.

- **Perfect price discrimination** Perfect price discrimination occurs when a different price is charged for every single unit of the product.

- **Phillips curve** The Phillips curve shows the short-run and long-run relationships between inflation and unemployment.

- **Planned (or command) economy** A planned (or command) economy allocates resources via government orders.

- **Porter's five forces** These are the forces that determine the likely profitability in an industry—that is: buyer power; supplier power; entry threat; substitute threat; and rivalry.

- **Potential growth** The potential growth represents economic growth with resources fully employed—that is, it represents an increase in the economic capacity.

- **Price discrimination** Price discrimination occurs when different prices are charged to different customers for the same product.

- **Price elasticity of demand** The price elasticity of demand measures the responsiveness of the demand for a product in relation to changes in its price.

- **Price elasticity of supply** The price elasticity of supply measures the responsiveness of the supply for one product in relation to changes in its price.

- **Price war (or predatory pricing)** A price war (or predatory pricing) occurs when one firm undercuts others to gain control of the market.

- **Principal–agent problem** This occurs if the manager (the agent) is not the same as the owner (the principal), which can lead to differing objectives.

▦ **Privatization** Privatization occurs when there is a transfer of assets or services to the private sector.

▦ **Producer surplus** The producer surplus is the difference between the price paid to producers for products and the cost of producing the items.

▦ **Production possibility frontier (PPF)** A production possibility frontier shows the maximum combination of products that an economy can produce, given its resources.

▦ **Productive efficiency** Productive efficiency occurs when more of one product can only be produced if less of another product is produced. It also occurs when a firm produces at the minimum of the average cost curve—that is, at the lowest cost per unit possible.

▦ **Productivity** Productivity measures the level of output in relation to the inputs used (for example, labour productivity measures the output per worker).

▦ **Profit-maximizing condition** The profit-maximizing condition occurs when firms produce at the output at which the marginal revenue equals the marginal cost.

▦ **Progressive taxation system** In a progressive taxation system, the average rate of tax increases as people earn more money.

▦ **Protectionism** Protectionism occurs when a government protects its domestic firms against foreign competition.

▦ **Public sector net cash requirement (PSNCR)** The PSNCR measures the amount that the government has to borrow to finance its spending in a given year.

▦ **Public good** A public good is a product that is non-diminishable and non-excludable.

▦ **Purchasing power parity (PPP)** This is the exchange rate that gives one currency exactly the same purchasing power when converted into another.

▦ **Quantitative easing** This involves purchasing public and private sector assets using central bank money. The purpose is to inject money into the economy to provide an additional stimulus to spending.

▦ **Quantity theory of money** The quantity theory of money states that $MV = PT$, where M is the stock of money, V is the velocity of circulation, P is the everage price level, and T is the number of transactions.

▦ **Quota** A quota is a limit to the amount that a firm can produce.

▦ **Recession** A recession occurs when there are two or more successive quarters of negative economic growth.

▦ **Reflationary fiscal policy** An expansionist or reflationary fiscal policy attempts to increase the aggregate demand.

▦ **Regressive tax system** In a regressive tax system, the average rate of taxation falls as income increases.

▦ **Research and development (R&D)** R&D involves the use of science to develop new ways of producing, and to develop new products.

▦ **Resources** Resources are inputs, such as land, labour, and capital, that are used in the production process.

▦ **Second-best World** The Second-best World is one in which market failures and imperfections exist. In this situation, the existence of some market failures may cancel out others. The theory of second-best highlights that intervening in a market to correct one failure (such as removing the monopoly) may actually move the economy further away from the optimal allocation of resources.

- **Short run** The short run is the period of time during which at least one factor of production is fixed.
- **Shortage** A shortage occurs when the quantity demanded is greater than the quantity supplied at the given price.
- **Supply curve** A supply curve shows the quantity that producers are willing and able to produce at each and every price, all other factors being unchanged.
- **Surplus** A surplus occurs when the quantity supplied is greater than the quantity demanded at the given price.
- **Tariff** This is a tax placed on selected goods and services from overseas. The tax revenue raised from tariffs goes to the government that placed them on overseas products.
- **Terms of trade** The terms of trade measure the prices of exports from a country compared with the prices of imports into the country.
- **Total cost** The total cost equals the fixed costs plus the variable costs.
- **Total revenue** The total revenue is the value of sales (calculated as the price of a product multiplied by the quantity sold).
- **Trade unions** Trade unions represent employees and bargain with management to protect their interests.
- **Utility** The utility refers to the satisfaction that a consumer would receive from consuming a product.
- **Variable costs** Variable costs are costs that change with the amount produced.
- **Veblen good** A Veblen good is an ostentatious good of which people buy more when the price is high.
- **Vertical integration** Vertical integration occurs when one firm joins with another at a different stage of the same production process.
- **Voluntary unemployment** Voluntary unemployment occurs when people who are looking for work are not yet willing to accept work at the given real wage rate.
- **Withdrawal** A withdrawal is a leakage from the economy and it reduces the aggregate demand.
- **World Trade Organization (WTO)** This is an international body the purpose of which is to promote free trade by persuading countries to abolish import tariffs and other barriers.

Useful websites

The following lists some of the websites that contain useful economics information. Why not visit them and see what you can discover?

Adam Smith Institute 'The Adam Smith Institute is Britain's leading innovator of free market economic and social policies. Since 1977, it has played a key role in developing practical initiatives to inject choice and competition into public services, extend personal freedom, reduce taxes, prune back regulation and cut government waste.'

@ http://www.adamsmith.org

Bank of England The Bank of England is the UK's central bank. This website provides information on monetary policy, inflation, interest rates, the Monetary Policy Committee (MPC), and the role of the Bank of England.

@ http://www.bankofengland.co.uk

BBC The BBC website contains numerous news stories about business and economics. Visit either the main section:

@ http://www.bbc.co.uk

or go straight to the economics section:

@ http://news.bbc.co.uk/1/hi/business/economy

Biz-ed 'A website for students, and educators in business studies, economics, accounting, leisure, sport, and recreation, and travel and tourism.'

@ http://www.bized.ac.uk

Company Annual Reports Online (CAROL) 'CAROL is an online service offering direct links to the financial pages of listed companies in Europe and the USA. CAROL provides direct access to companies' balance sheets, profit-and-loss statements, financial highlights, etc.'

@ http://www.carolworld.com

CIA Factbook This website provides information and data on countries around the world.

@ https://www.cia.gov/cia/publications/factbook/index.html

Competition Commission 'The Competition Commission conducts inquiries into mergers, markets, and the regulation of the major regulated industries.' This site provides information on ongoing and previous inquiries.

@ http://www.competition-commission.org.uk

Confederation of British Industry (CBI) 'One of the UK's leading independent employers' organizations . . . The CBI's mission is to help create and sustain the conditions in which businesses in the United Kingdom can compete and prosper for the benefit of all.' This website has data and surveys produced by the CBI, and highlights the view of many businesses in relation to economic, social, and political issues.

@ http://www.cbi.org.uk

Department for Business, Innovation and Skills (BIS) There is information on the website about innovation, employment matters, regional economic development, business sectors, and the business environment.

@ http://www.bis.gov.uk

Department for International Development (DfID) This is the website of the UK government's Department for International Development. It contains information about current government policy on development issues.

@ http://www.dfid.gov.uk

Europa This is the official website of the European Union.

@ http://europa.eu

The *Guardian* This is the website for The *Guardian* newspaper, providing access to articles and surveys.

@ http://www.guardian.co.uk

HM Treasury The HM Treasury website provides information on the UK budget, enterprise and productivity, economic data, tax, work, and welfare.

@ http://www.hm-treasury.gov.uk

Institute for Fiscal Studies (IFS) 'IFS® is an independent research organization. We aim to promote effective economic and social policies through rigorous analysis of their impact on individuals, families, firms, and the public finances.'

@ http://www.ifs.org.uk

International Monetary Fund (IMF) 'The IMF is an organization of 184 countries, working to foster global monetary cooperation, secure financial stability, facilitate international trade, promote high employment and sustainable economic growth, and reduce poverty.'

@ http://www.imf.org

Office of Fair Trading (OFT) 'The OFT is responsible for making markets work well for consumers. We do this by promoting and protecting consumer interests throughout the UK whilst ensuring that businesses are fair and competitive.' This website has information on a range of issues, such as consumer rights and competition legislation.

@ http://www.oft.gov.uk

Office for National Statistics (ONS) This is a government website that contains information on 'Britain's economy, population, and society at national and local level. Summaries and detailed data releases are published free of charge'.

@ http://www.statistics.gov.uk

Organization for Economic Cooperation and Development (OECD) The Organization for Economic Cooperation and Development is an organization of 30 countries 'sharing a democratic government and the market economy'. Best known for its publications and its statistics, its work covers economic and social issues from macroeconomics to trade, education, development, and science and innovation.

@ http://www.oecd.org

The Times This website provides access to the articles of *The Times* and *The Sunday Times* newspapers.

@ http://www.timesonline.co.uk

Trade Union Congress (TUC) The TUC represents the major trade unions in the UK: 'With member unions representing over six and a half million working people, we campaign for a fair deal at work, and for social justice at home and abroad.' This website provides information on employee rights, trade union objectives and initiatives, and the trade union stance on many economic and political issues.

@ http://www.tuc.org

World Trade Organization (WTO) The World Trade Organization is 'the only global organization dealing with the rules of trade between organizations. At its heart are the WTO agreements, negotiated and signed by the bulk of the world's trading nations, and ratified in their parliaments'. This website provides essential information on the WTO, its role, and developments in international trade agreements.

@ http://www.wto.org

Index